glino's with June Mendoza

John Ryan

James Beetham

Putting the Eagle to bed

hands and knees and

by Rosemary Garland c.1950.

# Living with Eagles

# Living with Eagles

## Marcus Morris, Priest and Publisher

## Sally Morris and Jan Hallwood

### Foreword by Sir Tim Rice

The Lutterworth Press

Cambridge

For Marcus, Jess
and Simon

First published in 1998 by

The Lutterworth Press
P O Box 60
Cambridge
CB1 2NT
England

British Library Cataloguing in Publication Data:
A catalogue record is available from the British Library

Printed and bound in Great Britain by Bookcraft (Bath) Ltd.

# Contents

# List of Illustrations

# Foreword
## by Sir Tim Rice

It is almost impossible to exaggerate the importance of the *Eagle* comic to boys of my generation, i.e. those born in the forties. In April 1950, when I was just five years old, my father, Hugh, brought home the first issue of this mould-breaking publication. Hugh, then aged 32, had the foresight to spot that *Eagle* was no ordinary comic and made sure that the clumsy hands of his offspring never damaged any copy. He kept every issue in pristine condition and as a result I now have every one of the first fifteen years of *Eagle* in my study today. The influence of *Eagle* upon almost every British boy (and plenty of girls) growing up in the 1950s cannot be underestimated – it was truly a remarkable enterprise, a creation of genius, the genius being the Reverend Marcus Morris.

I still derive enormous pleasure from re-reading the adventures of Dan Dare, PC49, Harris Tweed and, indeed, of real life characters such as the back page stars St Paul and St Patrick. On more than one occasion those *Eagle*s have helped me in my story-telling efforts through musicals many years on. Readers of *Eagle* learned, sometimes without realising it, about the joys of science, art, humour and social conscience (the "Mug of the Month" was a brave concept, never as powerful when the selfless deeds of readers were honoured by the title "Silver Eagler of the Month".)

At last a biography of Marcus Morris. I met the great man once when my brother Jonathan and I interviewed him for Capital Radio in the early 1970s and I found it hard to believe that this apparently diffident man had been the fount of such a cultural impact, as significant in Britain as the Beatles' was to be a decade or so later. Marcus's mission was to educate through entertainment, at which he was phenomenally successful.

I had no idea that he was a churchman until *Eagle* had ceased to be an important part of my life – and *Eagle* only slipped from a crucial position in my day to day existence after Marcus left the editor's chair. Yet somehow *Eagle*, during the Morris years, made Christianity make sense within a turmoil of distractions – which I am glad to learn through this wonderful biography, often claimed Marcus's attention. He was the most modern of men and the most British of men in that no-one really knew, until now, what enabled him to capture the hearts and minds of a generation. He lived life to the full; he had his share of human frailities. Yet he always hoped that wisdom and morality would improve the lives of those who would inherit the religious and social order, and thus the establishment itself.

The thrill of winning a five-shilling postal order for having a letter published in *Eagle* in 1957 is matched by the honour of being asked to write a foreword for this biography. I now know that Marcus Morris had other eagles in his life besides the one that so profoundly affected mine – and also know that millions of other middle-aged Eaglers will be fascinated to discover how this extraordinary man served them all so well.

# Acknowledgements

We would like to thank everybody mentioned or quoted in the book, especially Ruari McLean, who at one stage was replying to almost daily letters. Also Steve for reading and correcting the manuscript umpteen times and putting up with Jan on all too frequent visits, and Kate for checking the proofs.

We interviewed, spoke on the phone or corresponded with over 300 people during our researches; not all are mentioned in the book but the information they gave us was invaluable and we thank them all very much. We would need a second book to mention everyone individually, but our special thanks go to:

Dean Close School and Marcus's contemporaries who remembered their schooldays. The Archivist and Bursar of Brasenose College, the Archivist of Wycliffe Hall, and Marcus's fellow undergraduates.

The present Rector, former curates and parishioners of Great Yarmouth. The RAF Archivist and former RAF colleagues. The former Rector of Weeley and Mr & Mrs Fred Weatherly and fellow parishioners who entertained us so well.

All our Southport friends and relations especially Mary Arden, Lionel & Peggy Lister, Joan Rylance; Ken & Nancy Duncan, Ursula Maddocks and the late Alan Joyce. The parishioners of St James's, Birkdale, without whom neither this book, nor *Eagle* itself, would have seen the light of day. Particular thanks to Kate Carr (Audrey Entwistle) for allowing us to quote from her diary. The many friends and members of the clergy who contributed to *The Anvil*; Southport College of Art and friends and relations of Frank Hampson and Harold Johns.

The ex-Hulton Press people who gave us fascinating insights into that remarkable company, and the many contributors to the children's papers; with special thanks to Dr James Hemming, Charles Chilton, Sir Bernard Audley, Derek Lord, Peter Cooper and Joan Porter, and members of the Hulton 20 Plus Group.

Adrian Perkins and the members of The Eagle Society, whose in-depth knowledge of *Eagle* and its contributors has been so helpful.

Marcus's former colleagues at The National Magazine Company and The Hearst Corporation, especially Terry Mansfield who has allowed us a free hand in conducting our researches and who has been very supportive all through our work on the book; also Brian Braithwaite and Joan Barrell for permission to quote from *The Business of Women's Magazines*.

Mary Pearce for the use of John's unpublished biography. The following for allowing us to quote from their books: Lord Cudlipp, *At Your Peril*; the late Sir Tom Hopkinson, *Of This Our Time*; Chad Varah CBE, *Before I Die Again* and Bernard Palmer, *Gadfly for God*.

Egmont Fleetway for allowing us to reproduce pages from *Eagle* and *Girl*. Peter Brookes and Times Newspapers for permission to reproduce *Dan Blair*.

Sir Tim Rice for writing the foreword and Chad Varah for all his help and for suggesting the book in the first place.

Particular thanks go to the artists who have provided drawings to illustrate this book – for no payment, but in remembrance of times past: Martin Aitchison, James Beetham, Jack Daniel, Rosemary Garland, Michael Gibson, David Langdon, June Mendoza, Joan Porter, John Ryan and Bill Todd.

# Chapter One

October 1949. A slim, fair-haired young man in an ill-fitting suit and down-at-heel shoes walked doggedly down Fleet Street with a dummy magazine under his arm. He had been trudging the streets of London for months, searching for a publisher. Since May he and several artists had been working on the dummy – a strip cartoon paper for boys. It was beautifully drawn, much of it in colour, the contents exciting. Some publishers had been enthusiastic, some sympathetic, some bewildered, some patronising; but all had turned it down. 'Not suitable', 'We have no paper', 'It wouldn't sell', 'It would be too expensive to produce'.

The young man was on the verge of bankruptcy and probable de-frocking for, although he wasn't wearing a dog-collar, he was a Church of England vicar. He had produced a parish magazine which was being read all over the world, but it didn't pay its way; its costs and the wages of the artists came out of his stipend of £800 a year; he owed his bankers and his printers £3,000. His parishioners in Southport, Lancashire, and his beautiful actress wife and three young daughters felt somewhat neglected but they supported him loyally. He was tired and despondent but never gave up hope. The thought of his debts, and his belief in his brain-child, drove him on.

The Reverend Marcus Morris turned off Fleet Street into Shoe Lane and walked into the offices of Hulton Press. . . .

John Marcus Harston Morris was born on 25 April 1915 – the day the Allied forces landed at Gallipoli. It was a Sunday, which should have made the baby 'bonny and blithe and good and gay'. His arrival was not recorded in *The Times* of the following day; the news was all of the war: 'British Grip on Hill 60' 'Italian Adriatic Ambitions' 'The Breach in the Line' 'New German Onslaught' 'The Attack North of Ypres'. Rupert Brooke had died four days earlier and Mr Asquith was having trouble with the miners.

In the following November Marcus's grandfather, the Reverend David Morris, died aged eighty-one. David was the eldest son of a building contractor in Newport, Monmouthshire, who had fallen on hard times. There was no money to spare for his son's education but David was clever and determined; he taught himself Latin and Greek and matriculated at London University. In 1858 he married a young schoolteacher, Mary Anne Lawler, daughter of an Irishman from County Kerry who was at that time groom and coachman to a Yorkshire landowner. David worked as a classical schoolmaster in Leeds and Liverpool until he was ordained (and wrote a history of England for schools). In 1864 he was appointed Chaplain at the newly built Walton Gaol, Liverpool, where he remained for thirty-two years. David and Mary Anne's ninth child (of eleven, two of whom died in infancy); Walter Edmund Harston, was born in the gaol in 1872. (All David's children were given the name Harston after the rather mawkish friendship Mary

*Happy family – Teddy, Mary, David and Marcus, 1928*

Anne had formed with John Euclid Harston and his wife when David was a curate at Everton. His Morris descendants unto the third generation have been burdened with that name.)

Walter (known to his grandchildren as Gramp) wrote of his youth in the Chaplain's House: 'We soon got used to living at the gaol gates. Well do I remember the first execution at Walton in 1887, the ghastly tolling of the bell at five minutes to eight, the hoisting of the black flag at five minutes past and the nailing of the death notice on the outside of the great gate for morbid people to go and stare at. It was my father's first experience of an execution and it completely staggered him, almost to the point of a nervous breakdown, – particu-larly as it was a woman, Elizabeth Berry, who had murdered her daughter.

Walter remembered seeing Florence Maybrick whose sensational trial, in 1889, for poisoning her husband James ended in conviction and a death sentence, commuted at the last minute to fifteen years in prison.

After his retirement David told a local newspaper that he had had Mrs Maybrick under his care for the whole of the six months she was in Walton Gaol but, 'Mrs Maybrick is now a free subject and, therefore, it would be unwise and undutiful on my part to make any reference to the subject. All I need say on this matter is that I always found Mrs Maybrick well disposed and highly intelligent.'

David never expanded on this, even to his family. On his deathbed, a nurse employed to look after him said, 'You won't remember me, Mr Morris, but I have seen you before – at the trial of Mrs Maybrick. I nursed James Maybrick in his last illness. I suppose you and I are the only people who know the real truth about that affair.' Did they know not only whether Florence was innocent but also that her husband was Jack the Ripper, as has recently been claimed?

In 1891 Walter went up to Trinity College, Cambridge, on a 'sub-sizarship' (a poor student's grant) and a Bishop Jacobson's Memorial Scholarship, to read Classics. 'I met Gresford Jones, one day to be Bishop of Warrington, who was a great rowing man. When he asked me if I'd been in a boat before I was able to reply that I had been over to the Isle of Man several times. In spite of this, he agreed to coach me and I rowed stroke in the bump races the next term.'

After graduating in 1894 Walter spent four years teaching before following his father into the Church. He was ordained Deacon in Chester Cathedral and went for his first curacy to St George's Church, Stockport, where he met Edith Neild, whom he married in 1906. Fifteen months later their first child, Edith Mary Harston Morris, was born, 'destined to be a source of much comfort to her ageing parents'.

His next appointment, to Emmanuel, Preston, was opposed by a large section of the congregation who wanted their existing curate to be vicar. Walter's induction service was enlivened by a walk-out of fifty parishioners and the new vicar had to be escorted back to the vicarage by four burly policemen. Emmanuel was 'a purely working-class parish of 14,000 people – nearly all mill workers, weavers, spinners, tenters and so on. The knocker-up started at 4.30 a.m. and at 5.30 a.m. we heard the clogs going to the mills.'

It was in Preston that John Marcus Harston made his appearance, followed in December 1916 by Walter Edward Harston, known to the family as Teddy. That year their father suffered a nervous breakdown as a result of the constant hassle with his parishioners and in 1917 he was offered a country living at Balderstone, a rural idyll at the feet of the Pennines. But having recovered from his breakdown the life was too quiet: 'We were very happy at Balderstone. The people were most friendly and responsive, but I felt all the time that I ought not, at the age of 46, to be settling down to what almost resembled retirement. So when at the end of 1918 I was offered the living of All Saints, Southport, I decided to accept.' He was Vicar of All Saints for thirty-eight years.

In 1934 Walter was appointed Rural Dean of North Meols and, in 1938, a Canon Residentiary of Liverpool. He was presented to the Queen three times, a fact of which he was very proud: 'I was the more pleased because she stopped and spoke, asking about my work and the Cathedral. She is the kindest and most gracious of women and, to my mind, the most beautiful.'

The vicarage in Rawlinson Road, near Hesketh Park, was large and Victorian and smelt of books and pipe tobacco. Walter and Edith's fourth child, Peter David Harston, was born there in 1923. David was a bonny child and, like the rest of his family, he took his religion seriously. When, at the age of four, he was informed that Mrs Melling, the curate's mother, a large woman, had died, been buried and gone to heaven, he told Edith that evening that he wasn't going to say his prayers. Asked why not, he replied that 'God will be too busy unpacking Mrs Melling'.

A year later David died at the vicarage after an emergency appendix operation performed on the kitchen table by a drunken doctor. Walter was devastated; Edith was stoic in public, but Mary had to run the household for many months afterwards. Marcus seldom talked about the tragedy, but he must have been aware of the effect on his father. He said in later years that the worst possible thing he could imagine happening would be the loss of his son.

Walter was a kind and loving father. He had an impish sense of humour, was a wonderful storyteller and was renowned as one of the finest preachers in the north of England. There was no playing to the gallery. Looking down at a huge congregation one Sunday just before the start of World War Two, he said from his pulpit: 'I suppose you think I should be pleased to see the church full like this? I'm not. Half of you have come through fear and you won't enter a church again. I want people here who mean it.'

Walter would regale (and terrify) his grandchildren at Sunday lunch with riddles and nonsense poems like 'The Jabberwocky', 'You Are Old, Father William' and 'A Sausage To Its Mother Said', having first ascertained that they had been listening to the sermon by asking what it was about. His letters to his children and grandchildren were full of wit and wisdom. Marcus described him as 'an old-fashioned evangelical, having been brought up in the low church tradition as were most of the clergy of his generation in the north. But he was a broadminded evangelical and if he didn't approve of ritual or ceremony himself, he was perfectly content that others should indulge. He drew the line at really high church people: these roused in him an almost atavistic evangelical disapproval.'

Walter once had to attend a very high church communion service in his role as Rural Dean, and didn't know how to put on all the vestments: 'I stood there and they dressed me up.' He thought candlesticks were positively popish, although he did get a new altar at All Saints to replace what he called the not very superior kitchen table.

Marcus recalled, 'My up-bringing was comparatively broadminded. From quite a young age my father allowed me to have parties which went on rather late. In my university days, bottles of various kinds were often brought in; my friends used to leave them at the vicarage gate for collection when the party began. Of course things were done in moderation and I think my father, as a cleric and as a man, was very sensible to have encouraged rational ideas about the use and abuse, the dangers and proper pleasure, of alcohol.

'I often brought friends home after nights out, for coffee and bacon and eggs. My father was very tolerant and understanding and I am grateful to him.'

Marcus doesn't mention his mother's reaction to this dissipation. Edith was more strict and narrow minded than her husband and could have done with a sense of humour. She was, however, a wonderful organiser and ran the parish and the huge rambling vicarage, to say nothing of the Mothers' Union, with great efficiency. Her grandchildren remember her as bossy and interfering; they always had to be on their best behaviour in her presence. Walks with her in Hesketh Park were very sedate and accompanied by strictures on deportment. But she could be kind in her own way, she loved jelly babies and allowed clockwork trains to be set up under the dining room table. Marcus kept a rabbit, and snakes which regularly escaped into neighbours' gardens. The house and garden were always open to friends and parishioners for fêtes, tennis parties and advice.

Walter retired reluctantly at the age of eighty-four, declaring that he would now have time to make a proper study of the Bible. He was greatly loved and honoured by his parishioners, having ministered to them with affection, firmness and humour. He had also achieved his ambition of altering the interior of All Saints, so that 'it is now a very beautiful church, to vie with any of its kind in Southport or elsewhere'. He would have been shattered to know that it was burnt to the ground in 1977, the result, it is thought, of arson – or divine retribution: the new incumbent had had the audacity to dedicate candlesticks to Walter, who would by then have had some authority in heavenly circles. Their beautiful vicarage has been demolished by purely earthly means and replaced by a ghastly block of flats.

Walter and Edith are still fondly remembered in the parish. An imaginative new church has been consecrated in the converted parish hall which has some wonderful modern stained-glass windows. Their grandchildren donated a set of brass collection plates to the church in their memory in 1993.

The Canon and his wife hated retirement. After a few years in a small flat on The Promenade in Southport, where Gramp would sit on a bench and chat to passers-by, they moved to Weston-super-Mare to be near their daughter. Edith died in 1962; Walter moved to Chard with Mary and her husband and died there six years later.

Mary was a bright girl, one of the gay young things of Southport society. She matriculated and was offered a place at London University. Unfortunately, family finances wouldn't stretch to three children at university so, in the manner of the Victorians, that honour was reserved for the boys (one of whom didn't make it). She worked as secretary for the Diocese of Liverpool and in 1933 married her father's curate, Eric Vallance Cook. Walter wrote, 'The wedding was a memorable occasion; the parish hall was well filled and the wedding presents and felicitations were bounteous.' Eric became Curate in Charge of St Stephen, Hightown, in Southport, before going as Vicar to Padgate, Warrington. He was later appointed Vicar of St Martin, Worle, near Weston-super-Mare and finally to St Mary, Chard.

The Vallance Cooks had a long and happy marriage which produced three daughters: Rowena, Marcus's god-daughter, Sheila and Erica. Eric was a kindly, funny man who enjoyed smoking a pipe and drinking and playing the piano. He died of cancer in 1969; Mary developed Parkinson's Disease and her health was not improved by looking after her aged and sometimes cantankerous father. She survived Eric by twelve years.

From an early age there was rivalry between Marcus and Teddy. There was a sense of competition, of Teddy desperately trying to catch up with a brother only eighteen months older. Letters written by him to Marcus at school contain more than an edge of spitefulness, even though Teddy was the spoiled one of the family after David's death. Walter wrote to Marcus at school: 'Teddy is better than he was and will be glad to have you to play golf with him: he says however that he is not going to caddy for you. . . .'

'Tedward [sic] has just gone to bed: he does his prep in my study, after which I see no more of my blotting paper, rulers etc. He confronts me with fresh problems every night: tonight he had to explain the working of a gas engine. Both of us were stuck: fortunately I remembered the book *How it Works*. Victory! Tedward is looking better: he is still a bad starter in the Pudding Class, but well off the mark on to the Meat. Love and kisses, your loving Daddy.'

A neighbour, Phyllis Tomlinson, who was a parishioner at All Saints for over eighty years, remembered them both as unprepossessing, very serious small boys, running a bran tub at a sale of work with rigid discipline: 'No one was allowed to dip until their money had been handed over.'

The brothers' early schooling was at Sandringham School in Southport, run by Esmond Corelli, a descendant of the composer Arcangelo Corelli. Walter was Chaplain to the school, where he would preach, teach and invigilate at exams.

Marcus wrote of Sandringham: 'My prep school was what one would have to call slightly off-beat. Esmond Corelli was no conventional pedagogue. He took the aesthetic approach and was more interested in modern experimental ideas and a different type of educational theory than in instilling the three Rs. He was very interested in diet, vegetarianism and so on. Discipline and general procedure were unimportant to him. His methods certainly promoted my interest in literature. One of my clearest recollections is of his readings on Sunday nights when I was a boarder – Rider Haggard and Jerome K. Jerome's *Three Men in a Boat*. This was probably very good for my imagination – but I didn't get the kind of grounding in Classics I really needed and suffered from this afterwards. But I can't claim that I had any clear-cut plan, at the age of five, to become a great scholar.'

In the summer of 1928 Marcus sat the Common Entrance exam for Marlborough College (where sons of clergy get reduced fees) whence his friend Gerald Taylor wrote to commiserate when he failed. Edith also wrote: 'My dearest Marcus, I am sorry dear boy that you were not lucky this time. Never mind, better luck next time. You must not be downhearted about it, you did your best and that is the chief thing. There are other schools just as lovely as Marlborough. . . . Dear love to you and Teddy, your loving Mummy.'

Walter wrote: 'Dear old chap, Don't worry over the Marlborough disappointment. *On peut reculer pour miex sauter.* You were the youngest boy in and it was your first stiff exam – you did your best. . . . Probably you will try at Haileybury in November – it is quite as good a school as Marlborough. Start now, and while you are working – WORK. I want you to begin Greek at once. Dear love to you.'

But in January 1929, at the age of thirteen, Marcus was sent to Dean Close Memorial School in Cheltenham, where Walter became a school governor soon afterwards. He often went down there to preach and would take Marcus and his friends out to tea.

Contemporaries remember a slight, shy boy with a squint and glasses, although one declared that he was very much more socially aware than most of them – 'a model of suave sophistication'.

Marcus wrote: 'This choice of public school indicates my father's level of churchmanship and the general background of my life: in those days, Dean Close was an extremely evangelical Church of England school. It was founded in memory of Dean Close, a big figure in the evangelical revival of the last century, with the object of counteracting, in some measure, the doctrines of the Oxford [Anglo-Catholic] Movement of Newman, Pusey and Keble. Despite that, it wasn't in my time a particularly pious school, nor did many of its students go into the Church, perhaps because the chapel services were notably drab and dull. I took the school's religious interpretation for granted, of course, because I wasn't then aware that there was any other.

'On the whole I liked school and did quite well there, though it has to be said that its academic standards weren't particularly high and it was then in financial difficulties. In common with most boys I disliked the discipline and formalities. I objected very much to the long Sunday walk round the countryside in dark suit and stiff collar, with prefects checking at various points to see that one didn't dodge the beastly thing. I remember I didn't mind them half so much when I was a prefect.'

Walter wrote in June 1929, 'I do congratulate you upon being made a *Scholar* of Dean Close. It is a proud position to hold. Of course if the money grant had been increased it would have been all the better, but . . . as long as you did your best, I don't mind. Mr Bolton [the headmaster] said that you did some very good work in the exam.

'Now you want to have your eye on a scholarship to Cambridge. . . . I think you have a good chance of one – IF you concentrate on whatever you are doing, I don't think these things are got by mere swotting, but by giving one's whole mind to whatever subject is before one. . . . Tedward is looking better, but he looks very tired sometimes, especially when he has a dirty face, which is often. . . . Heaps of love from us all, Your loving Father.'

Walter's elder sister, Lucy Carpenter, a formidable woman who bullied her brother and her husband, wrote to Marcus in November: 'You seem to have a very busy time at school with so many different kinds of occupation. No long dull hours like we of our generation had. . . . We always knew that our father was poor and that life was difficult for him. As far as you are concerned you too know already that your parents' lives are "difficult", because so much more has to be done with their income. It is a very *great* pride to me and to them, to feel you are really doing well at school. Keeping the "Morris end up" – like your clever grandfather. . . . We spent the night at the Vicarage but it was very cold and rainy so I did not see your rabbit. The rest of the pets were in very good condition. . . . I am glad father spoke so well at your College; you would feel quite important to be "the preacher's son" [or very embarrassed!]. Teddie looked quite robust and has I think at "long last" begun to grow. Very much love to you Marcus, and I hope you will win lots of prizes.'

Marcus became captain of cross-country running, obtained his athletics and hockey colours and was head of his house, a prefect and second head of school by the time he left. He played football and the cello, was a sergeant in the Officer Training Corps, a member of the Music Club and the Photographic Society, was secretary of the Literary Society and the History Club and edited the school magazine, *The Decanian*. He also acted in plays produced by his housemaster C. A. P. 'Amby' Tuckwell; a review of *Twelfth Night* in *The Decanian* of July 1931 reported that 'J. M. H. Morris showed taste and talent in the charming part of Viola'. His Banquo in an open-air *Macbeth* caused much amusement when the ghost backed rather noisily into a tree. Stanley Hoare, one of the housemasters, recalled that Marcus was 'a slightly above average scholar'. He achieved five credits in School Certificate at the age of fifteen but, to his intense irritation, failed his Higher two years later 'by a very narrow margin'. It will surprise no one who knew Marcus that it was the mathematics paper on which he failed.

He was developing a decidedly philosophical bent. 'I loved talking and arguing. I was always challenging the orthodox and exploring the philosophical arguments for and against the established order of things. I am told that I was, on the whole, purposefully rebellious, with a marked capacity for indignation which showed itself quite early in life. Quite possibly I had, or was given, what one must loosely call "a complex" about the very bad squint I had, which was not cured until I had an operation at the age of sixteen. I can't honestly say that I was made to feel so very awful about this defect, but I certainly felt that I was never sufficiently appreciated. I wasn't anybody's favourite, or highly approved, pupil – at either prep or public school. But as I didn't lie on my back and drum my heels on the floor, or gnash my teeth and bite the pillow at nights, I can't take the deep psychological approach too seriously in my own case.'

An essay called *Counterblast* began thus: 'Laziness is an inherent quality of man. It is, by no means, a vice. A man without a streak of laziness or, to speak euphemistically, love of liesure [*sic*], is a man who is insufferably boring. . . .

'The chief thing that wireless has done for the world is to pander to men's laziness. It has given them opportunities of liesure [*sic* again] . . . broadcasting's main advantage is educational. It has made every individual from bank clerk to bishop, a man of the world. Before wireless was invented many of us did not even know the meaning of "Fat Stock", and depressions over Ireland were mysteries never to be solved except by Greenwich officials. Now, however, they are household words to all of us and none of us would have any interest left in life if we felt that our further outlook was anything but unsettled.'

He got an Alpha Plus for that one.

On *The strangeness of luxury*: 'Luxury is a Will o' the Wisp; it is elusive, like eels. It is a taunting demon flitting before one's eyes always just out of reach and almost impossible to catch. When, perhaps, one has managed to catch it by the tail so to speak – eels have tails even if Will o' the Wisps don't –

*Captain of the cross-country running team (second from right) 1934*

it changes its form like a mirage in a desert. For it is an essential of the meaning of the word Luxury that it is always unattainable in a permanent form. If it becomes an accomplished fact, it is no longer a luxury but a commonplace.

'To certain people a bath is a luxury, a rarity only indulged in on special occasions . . . but others are more fortunate; they have the privilege of at least one a week. . . . One of the chief incitements to get rich quick, is not that I may have cars or a magnificent house or an unceasing supply of food, but that I may have baths – not through any desire to be cleaner than I am at present but that I may soak in the sheer luxury of it.'

His English master said that 'the essay as a whole is a pleasure to read' and gave him Alpha Plus again. Hardly revolutionary philosophy though.

In March 1930 Walter wrote, 'how bitterly disappointed I am that I cannot be present at your confirmation. I have had a bad attack of flu. You know that I shall be thinking about you tomorrow and praying for you. It amounts to this – making up your mind – definitely – that you will be on the side of God and his Christ and never ashamed of it. This does not mean a lot of "pi" talk and cant, but just living it, quietly and steadily. So many young fellows today seem to give up all religion as soon as the school days are over and just live to have a good time. Well – I am just hoping and praying for better things from you and Teddy. You can have the good time just the same, without leaving God out of life . . . Love and kisses Your loving Daddy.'

When he was sixteen Marcus wrote a letter to his sister Mary, who was taking part in a diocesan conference in Liverpool on *The Church And Youth*: 'Instead of squabbling about ridiculous points of ritual or discussing uselessly deep theology, neither of which are any good to the world, let the authorities in the Church turn their attention to something useful for a change and see to it that the young people of today grow up into men and women who are really worthy of their country, their king and their God.'

He commented later, 'Looking at the letter now, twenty-odd years on, I can see that I was rebelling not against the principles on which I had been brought up but against the failure, as I saw it, on the part of people in authority to apply those principles and give them new meaning in a modern context. My sister quoted my letter at the conference: it became the subject of much discussion and was also quoted in the *Daily Express* in an article headlined "A Schoolboy on Religion". I don't pretend that this schoolboy protest was the beginning of a great personal mission, or that it had any shattering effect on the world. It does show, however, that I was already at variance with my superiors. The fact that I nevertheless pursued my studies shows equally clearly that my religious convictions were definite and sincere.'

They must have been, for when he was seventeen he made the decision to enter the Church. Phyllis Tomlinson was convinced that parental pressure was brought to bear, especially by Edith, but his father had written, 'Don't worry about it: if God wants you to be a Priest, He will open the way for you. Leave the matter in His hands.'

His mother wrote, 'Don't bother your head about sermons, that will come soon enough.'

Walter was still trying to be impartial: 'My darling Marcus, We have all been thinking much about you this week, and I know how difficult a problem you have before you. We are praying that you may be guided right. In your thinking out of the matter I suggest that you make this the chief thought: 1) What does God want me to do with my life? 2) What am I most fitted for? Have I got those gifts which would be of use in the Ministry – sympathy, influence, capacity for speaking or preaching, organising power, leadership, persuasiveness, a good speaking voice, a certain amount of music? Personally I think you have some of these things. 3) The Ministry is not only a vocation, it is also a profession. Consider it from a business point of view. 4) Don't form your ideas of clerical work from the conventional view of the man in the street, or even from the work here. There are all sorts of parsons – schoolmasters, secretaries, parochial clergy etc. 5) Put clean out of your head the idea that, if you decide to take orders, you have to become "a boy apart" – a member of a special class, rather looked askance at. The fact that I was going to take orders made no difference to me at Cambridge. My friends there were going into all sorts of jobs – but we all lived the same life and had a rollicking good time.

'This letter looks to me as though I were trying to persuade you to decide "yes". I am not. After all, it is your life and it is yours to decide, and may God help you to make the right decision, whatever it is. Our dear love to you, Your very loving Daddy.'

A week later, Marcus heard again from Walter: 'I was very pleased to read your letter. I think that you have done the right thing and I believe that you have been guided to do it. When I last wrote I tried not to say anything that might seem like persuasion – one way or the other. But now that you have decided I feel more free to write. I doubt if ever the Church of Christ more needed the best men – spiritually and mentally. There have been many others trying to crowd into it, not quite of the best kind either in influence or personality. You – with all your opportunities and with your natural gifts and scholarship – ought to go far. If you get a scholarship for Queens, a First in the Tripos and your Rowing Blue, you would certainly finish as a Bishop, and as a very old man, if I am spared, I should have to call you "My Lord" (though I rather fancy I should be disrespectful enough to call you "Marky" even if you had gaiters on, as I should call Teddy "Thankless Child" even if he were at Lambeth).'

Teddy had joined Marcus at Dean Close in 1930 and was nicknamed Brutus. He is remembered as 'an ordinary boy with not much distinction, but no trouble'. His school reports follow the usual lines of 'could do better'.

Edith wrote to Marcus, 'I am sorry you are still feeling lonely. I wish dear you could have more in common with Teddy, after all he is only 18 months younger than you and it is a pity there is not more brotherly friendship between you. He is young I know for his years, but he would be so proud and happy if you talked to him sometimes on "things that matter" and treated him a little more as a "chum". This should not be so difficult now you have a study. He is always very loyal and proud of your achievements, all younger brothers are apt to be cheeky at times especially if treated very much as the small boy.'

Walter hoped that Teddy, would also decide to enter the Church, but Teddy had neither the aptitude nor the vocation. After leaving school he worked for sixteen months in Martin's Bank in Liverpool, getting more and more frustrated and unhappy. In 1937 he went to Ceylon (now Sri Lanka) and trained as a planter. The Vogan Tea Company reported that he 'will make a keen and good planter. He has picked up Tamil very well. . . . He has also had slight experience in the rubber replanted fields, and shows commendable keenness and quickness in picking up his work.'

Meanwhile, Marcus was having doubts about his vocation. In February 1933 Walter wrote from the Spa Hotel, Bath, where he and Edith were taking the waters: 'Do not *worry* over the matters we were discussing. It all boils down to this – that at 18 (prox) you must settle down, and show yourself qualified for responsibility. Don't go in at the deep end every time you can't get just what you want at the moment you want it. That is childish: it also makes you irritable. And don't get into the habit of looking at things from your own point of view. A thing is not right just because you think it is right, any more than a thing is right because I think it is right. I think you often make yourself unhappy unnecessarily, just because you have a very strong sense of rightness and of justice, which in itself is an excellent thing. Further than all this – I guess that you are finding what we call Religion a little difficult just now. *Pour moi* – I am continually doing so. Our spiritual faculties are liable to the same limitations as our mental and physical ones. We can't *always* be at the top of our form. . . . My rule is to hang on to what I have got. The old fervour will come back again. . . . Keep on with your prayers, and my idea of prayer would be simply to tell God all about it – quite frankly. "I find it hard to pray, even to believe, a church service does not mean what it did, and the Bible is not interesting me: help me to get right again." '

A wise old bird, was Gramp.

Having failed his Higher Certificate, a year later Marcus failed to get an Open Scholarship to Jesus College, Cambridge. But in 1934 he won the Colquitt Exhibition to Brasenose College, Oxford, a scholarship worth around £50, for men destined for the Church. Walter had written to the college principal explaining his circumstances: 'My income here is about £800 a year. . . . For the last five years I have had two boys at Dean Close which has cost me nearly £300 a year . . . and my savings are now nearly exhausted. . . . For Marcus I have a promise (and for Teddy I probably shall have) of £50 a year from the Diocese of Liverpool. Marcus is nearly up to Scholarship form, Teddy is not . . . unless Marcus gets a scholarship I shall be unable to send either of the boys to any of our major universities. . . . The immediate future of both boys seems to depend very largely on Marcus's success in the next few months.'

Although Marcus got his scholarship, it doesn't seem to have made him any happier. Edith wrote in May that year, 'I am sorry you have been feeling so miserable dear, try to be interested in your last term at school. It is a pity we do not get more chances of a talk in the hols, I feel I am always shut out of your confidences, I wish you would try and talk more openly to me it would make things easier for us both and would help to make me more understanding. We all have our difficulties, nobody goes through life without them. As for the future being blank – I cannot think of any boy at the moment whose future is more full of promise than yours. . . . You *must* remember dear that you can only do your little bit, and that the work of putting the world right is not on your shoulders alone.'

Walter took the same bracing tone: 'I hope you are fighting that inferiority complex. . . . It seems to me that Teddy is the one who might more reasonably feel disappointed. He got no prize, but he takes things more equably than you. I think that when you get to Oxford you will find things very different, and discover all sorts of new interests.'

Marcus may have been small and pale when he arrived at Dean Close, but by the time he left he was a tall, slim, fairly good-looking lad and his eyes no longer squinted, they roved. The vicar's son developed quite a reputation in Southport and anxious mothers warned their daughters to beware of his wandering hands. There were rumours of girlfriends fighting for their honour in taxis.

Before he left school he, Teddy and Gerald Taylor went on a White Star Line scholars' cruise to Madeira, Tangier and Gibraltar. The organisers assured parents that services would be held every Sunday and on Good Friday. Marcus was impressed by the SS *Doric*, especially the jazz band. He felt slightly

*'decidedly smarmy'*

queasy at first, but soon got used to the rolling. He was 'much annoyed at rumoured regulations [unspecified]. Disregarded them.' 'Much indignation at list of rules. Tempers ruffled. Decided to resist them.' 'Dancing. Stiff at first as knew no women. Better outlook later.' 'Summoned up courage to ask Hilda Moss & friend to deck tennis. Then to iced lemonade. Dancing. Not too good – inferiority complex.' 'Dance. Not too bad. Saw Tully. Row. Challenged to fight. Nothing doing.' 'Dancing. Viennese girl. Super. Drinks. Doctor barged in. So I to bed.' 'Talked to Malvern girls . . . talked again to Malvern girls . . . very hot.' Thereafter he was too busy – or too hot – to keep a diary.

Kenneth Duncan's first sight of Marcus was of the future parson careering down Lord Street, Southport, on a brakeless bicycle with Gerald Taylor on the cross-bar, and falling off in an attempt to avoid a policeman.

On one occasion, Ken held the jackets while Marcus and another young blade fought over two sisters in the gents of the Prince of Wales Hotel. The fight ended when Marcus managed to hit his opponent and make his nose bleed. Ken said, 'Marcus so enjoyed life. We always wondered why he'd gone into the Church. I remember collecting him in the car to go to a dance; he was sitting on the vicarage steps, six bottles of beer on one side, six bottles of beer on the other. He was a bit out of the ordinary, terribly suave with rather long hair. Not that he was effeminate; it was attractive to girls. He wasn't good looking, he just had something. He had a way of making a woman feel important, he preferred talking to women rather than men and he could dance better than anyone else. He always looked as though he'd been scrubbed, very clean-shaven. He took a lot of interest in his looks, but I wouldn't say he was vain. We were all a bit jealous.'

He sounds decidedly smarmy.

The other two candidates for the Colquitt Exhibition that was to take him to Oxford were John Evans and Eric Wall, who became respectively Canon and Bishop. Marcus claimed later that, as the exam was uninvigilated, they told each other the answers; Eric Wall maintained that, though they were none of them great theologians, Marcus probably knew his Bible better than they did!

# Chapter Two

Marcus matriculated at Brasenose on 13 October 1934. In those days, the last few years before the war, Oxford was a place of gracious living, dinners, cocktail parties, bridge, good conversation. This was the last generation to experience the unhurried elegance and austere luxury of a civilisation soon to be destroyed. Summer evenings on the Cherwell, Oxford bags and floating dresses; dinner in Hall was served on priceless College silver, which could be hired by students for parties in their rooms as long as there were ladies or clergymen present to deter riotous behaviour. Students were discouraged from associating with locals and were barred from city pubs. Huntin', shootin' and fishin' were rife; if you had the money you spent more time socialising than at lectures and tutorials. To quote one contemporary: 'One spent a lot of time with people who were at Eton with one and who knew each other well before one arrived at Oxford. As far as I remember one spent most of one's time away from Oxford at race meetings or going shooting and up to London for theatres, dances etcetera.'

There were reading parties in Cornwall for those who could read, days of serious confabulation and evenings in country pubs with the companionship of like-minded students and tutors. There were dinners with the Principal, William Teulon Swann Stallybrass (who had changed his name from Sonnerschein in 1917, and was known as 'Sonners'), starting at 7 p.m., where 'you found yourself having revealed a great deal about yourself by 2 a.m.'. They were years of maximum freedom and minimum responsibility in a magical setting. It was a generation that looked back on the fine summer before the world changed.

Marcus's contemporaries at Brasenose included Jack Profumo and Prince George Galitzine. Marghanita Laski and John Freeman edited *Cherwell*, the University student newspaper, Edward Heath was President of the Oxford Union, Harold Wilson was at Jesus, Reginald Maudling at Merton, Dennis Healey at Balliol, Brian Johnston at New College.

Marcus (who was called John or Johnny at Oxford) wrote: 'I was a very average sort of undergraduate. I was neither introvert nor extrovert. I had very little money but made myself as much social life as possible among my own circle of friends.'

This circle included Lester Moller, later Sir Lester, a Rhodes Scholar from New Zealand who became a High Court judge, Harry Hopkins, another New Zealander (also later knighted), Eric Wall and John Evans, Roy Davey and Bill Toulmin, George Joseph, George Galitzine and Prince Alex Obolensky. They would all meet for bridge and half pints of beer in the buttery down Staircase 12. Long sunny afternoons were spent on the punt that Marcus, John and Eric shared, very often in company with nurses from the Radcliffe Infirmary.

Marcus said: 'I didn't work as hard as I should have done; nor did I take sufficient advantage of the social and political side of the university. I regret to say that I never once opened my mouth in anger in the Union. I played some hockey and was secretary of the College Hockey Club, an office which was of no importance and passed almost unnoticed in a college which was then jam-packed with Blues of all brands. It was a tough, hearty college and I was a little on the outside. The Brasenose dons of those days really did like a good muscular extrovert.'

In fact he played hockey for the Oxford University Occasionals and Brasenose Cuppers, so he must have been a fairly good player but 'in no danger of getting a Blue' as John Evans put it.

Marcus joined the Brasenose Players and played a small part in *Libel*, which was reviewed in *Cherwell*: 'Junior Counsel were adequately represented by Mr John Morris and Mr Kenneth Carrdus.'

He was on the committee of the Pater Society in which members gave a paper and then sat around for coffee and discussion. Marcus spoke on *Free Love*; a contemporary, Ken Bayley, recollected, 'It was a pre-war, straight-laced, middle-class society, full of inhibitions and he was saying "Gold is where you find it, enjoy the pleasure that God has given us". Terribly relaxed. We all went away saying "You know, we seem to have missed out somewhere" '.

Roy Davey recalled Marcus's nervousness before he gave that paper: 'He was on absolute tenterhooks, scared stiff at the responsibility rather than the writing. It created an impression of profound wisdom and thought-fulness emerging from clouds of cigarette smoke.'

Others remember Marcus as a rather flashy dresser, suave, with a slight Lancashire accent and a sophisticated air, always smoking, sometimes with a holder – a touch of the Noel Cowards. He gave the impression of liking the good life and was in danger of living above his means.

John Evans said, 'That charm hid almost any faults he might have had.

*... sunny afternoons on the Isis in the shared punt ... Marcus and his father, 1937*

He was a person who had very firm and fixed ideas but if there was any possibility of a confrontation building up he would retire, he wouldn't let it build up. He used to shut up like a clam if he disapproved of anything, or something was getting his goat. He wouldn't say "I think you're talking rubbish". I never saw him lose his temper.'

Marcus always said that he made the intellectual decision when at Oxford never to get drunk; in later life his alcohol consumption was legendary. John Freeman told us, 'I never saw him paralytic drunk, but I remember a party in Wellington Square when, I suppose in response to a bet, he wee-ed from the balcony. There was something a bit flashy about him, he liked cutting a dash. When I heard he'd gone into the Church I thought it a remarkable conversion. I always remained slightly surprised about his life.'

Marcus was renowned as a dancer with a wonderful sense of rhythm, but few of his college friends knew that he gave displays at the Randolph Hotel to earn money to support his lifestyle.

It was one of his dancing partners with whom he fell deeply in love in the summer of 1937. When she married someone else Marcus was heartbroken and wandered the streets at night, contemplating suicide – but his lost love wore the silk stockings he had given her at her wedding.

Another girlfriend wrote him a stinging letter which can have done nothing for his self esteem.

From Margot, Bayswater: 'There is no thread between us strong enough to stand the strain of a criticism from me of you – Besides it would not do you any good, a) because you would put it down to my "abysmal ignorance of that complicated and highly valuable psychological machine which" – as you artistically put it (and rather unforgivably I thought as it wasn't followed by any exclamation marks) – "makes up you". b) because you already think far too much about John Morris. You see everything through the faulty focus of John Morris . . . try to find a little of what is really right and matters in life and in people. You would realise that knowledge from books has to be applied. . . . What is the "strain and stress" of Oxford? There are kids . . . growing up to eight hours a day at a factory who can feel joy – laugh inside and feel it as you never have. . . . If you'd only learn to see the good in other people. . . . Learn to laugh. . . . '

During the long vacation of 1935, Marcus went to Germany and Austria with Eric Wall and Bill Toulmin in the latter's mother's Austin 7. Eric Wall remembered, 'I was driving the car when we crashed. We'd had a marvellous day, driven a heck of a long way and I said it was time to stop. But they both said we should carry on to Wurzburg and that it was my turn to drive. It was entirely their fault – they both went to sleep of course. I turned the car gently over going round a corner, fast asleep. I remembered to wake up and turn off the ignition. We had a marvellous day in Wurzburg swimming in the river while the car was being mended. We saw lots of Brown Shirts around. It was rather sad. We knew it was happening. All my generation knew it was happening, no question about it.'

For the two months of the Long Vacation of 1937 Marcus went on a canoe trip down the Danube with Brian Whitlow, a friend from Southport up at St Edmund Hall, who later became Dean of Christchurch Cathedral, Victoria, British Columbia. This was to be Brian and Marcus's last summer of freedom, the last long vacation before they both went to theological college and ordination. They bought a collapsible canvas canoe with a wooden frame – not very sturdy – and practised on the Isis during the summer term.

Before they went, Walter wrote Marcus an admonitory letter: 'It seems to me that you must have been letting other people drive the car during its stay in Oxford: it is only bent in THREE of its wings: the fourth is in fairly good condition. I suppose the repairs will cost me £1 or 30/- at Whitesides, but that doesn't matter.' There followed long and detailed instructions on the use of his camera and fatherly advice: 'Don't go near any fortifications with your camera, or you will get run in. I hope you have a good time and weather like this: beware of strangers, however affable and remember the "female of the species is more deadly than the male".'

Brian described 'cooking meals on a primus stove and camping on the banks of the Danube. We canoed naked most of the time and got very brown. We had natty gents' suiting with us in the front of the canoe and when we got to Budapest and Vienna, where we stayed a week each, we got out our suitcase and dressed up and gave the girls a treat. There was a lot of evidence of Nazism – offensively so.'

The pair wrote an article about their experiences which was published in the *Southport Visiter* [*sic*]: 'Nazi symbols can be seen side by side with the traditional figures of local saints and even the crucifixes in wayside shrines are occasionally draped with Nazi flags. . . . Landlords waxed fierce in broken English to our very broken German on the political situation, revealing a

*'We canoed naked' some-where on the Danube*

fervid nationalism, a hatred of France and a distrust of English "dilly-dallying"....
There seems to be mutual antipathy between the peoples of South-Eastern
Europe, and in Vienna we were warned that we should meet with high-handed
treatment from Czecho-Slovakian officials . . . these individuals became
increasingly resplendent as we progressed eastward. But we found such
panoply far less irritating than the childish pompousness of Nazi militarism.

'At the Yugoslavian frontier we were searched for the first time . . . to
see if we were importing matches, in which there is a state monopoly. At
Constanta we offered our collapsible Primus stove for sale to the loafers on
the quay . . . after half an hour of polyglot bargaining, managed to get quite
a good price. When trying to run the boat up onto the beach one night, an
extra large breaker carried us against a rock. A hole was pierced in the
canvas and the canoe filled with water. We are waiting for a boat to Istanbul,
from where we shall return home through the Mediterranean.'

Brian Whitlow said, 'John lent me the money to buy an engagement ring
for my fiancée, a nurse at the Radcliffe Infirmary. I had no money at all and
he was the man I turned to – though he didn't have much either. I also went
to him for help with tying my white bow tie for a May Ball.'

In 1937 Marcus was given a grant of £35 from the Hulme Poor Students
Fund and in 1938 received a further grant of £50 from the Poor Students
Aid Fund. In his letter of thanks, he said, 'I have been in pretty deep financial difficulties but now, with what I hope to get from other sources, I
think I shall have sufficient to pay for my last year here.' In fact, the debts
he incurred at Oxford were not finally discharged for nearly ten years.

Marcus wrote later, 'I went to Oxford with the intention of being ordained
and although, after a time, I went through the usual phase of being doubtful
about the whole idea of ordination, I did come to the conclusion that the
Christian philosophy made a great deal of plain sense. I enjoyed reading
Greats, mainly because of its philosophical emphasis (my best subject was
metaphysics, which quite fascinated me). My first contact with the philosophers,
so far at least as my faith was concerned, was more than a little disturbing
and it shook me out of many of the ideas which I had absorbed from the
background of my up-bringing; but its final effect was to strengthen my
belief in the sense that I took a more intellectual and, therefore, I think a
more effective view of the things in which I believed. Unhappily, such
studies were not going to make it any easier for me to fit into the pious
atmosphere of Wycliffe Hall Theological College, my ultimate destination.

'The main influence on me at Brasenose was my philosophy tutor, K. J.
Spalding. He was, I thought, like a saint, and was probably a mystic – the
quality he had was an intangible thing, difficult to identify or describe, yet
most powerfully there. He was an enlightened person, charming and quite
delightful and I used to get great pleasure and profit from my tutorials with
him. Collingwood also impressed me considerably, although he was regarded by most orthodox philosophers at that time as more of a brilliantly
entertaining lecturer than a really sound thinker.'

Jimmy McKie, a philosophy don, wrote to Marcus, 'You will have seen that you got a second in Greats, but I imagine you will like to have your marks, so here they are. I'm glad that you managed to score a decent Logic mark, in spite of the distractions which (I suspect) hindered you from making as full use as you needed to make of some of your earlier vacations. I think that's about your real level you know. As things were, some of the weaker papers were rather patchy – a fact with which the final marks deal perhaps rather kindly. None the less the result, though one could hardly call it a strong second, is quite creditable, considering you didn't start with the advantage of being a "star" classics man.'

Many friends were surprised, like John Freeman, that Marcus entered the priesthood. Eric Wall thought 'he was one of those who might decide not to be ordained. He was partly committed by going in for the Colquitt, but Marcus was the most likely of the three of us to break away. How respectable the other two became. I don't think Marcus was a natural for a parish ministry. I suspect his literary exploits in their own right became predominant. I suspect in a sense they were a way out.'

Marcus entered Wycliffe Hall, Oxford in January 1938. He hated it from the start. 'My translation to Wycliffe Theological College landed me in an atmosphere of almost catastrophic change. Perhaps things were rendered almost impossibly difficult by my three years at Brasenose – so different a place – and by the way my recent experience and background cut me off or, at least, set me apart from my fellow students. Wycliffe Hall was situated just north of the centre of Oxford and consisted of a collection of utterly dreary Victorian buildings, somehow admirably suited to the institution's spiritual mood. The students were, by and large, studious if not obviously intelligent. In any case, no great demand was made of their intellects, as the majority were merely studying for general ordination examination, which was not much more difficult than school certificate.'

Some of those fellow students remember Marcus being very worldly-wise and man-about-town. It is probable that his way of life did not endear him to the college authorities, especially as he was often late in paying his dues and even borrowed money from the secretary so that he could take his fiancée out – he repaid it the following week. There were rumours that he sometimes climbed clandestinely into college at rather late hours.

The college authority Marcus disliked most was the Principal. He described Ralph 'Puffy' Taylor, later to become Bishop of Sodor and Man, as 'a pale, uxorious, fleshy man who considered that it was wrong to drink, dance, smoke or go to the theatre.' (Bishop John Taylor, his son, refutes this.)

'What terrified me more than anything else at Wycliffe were Mr Taylor's Sunday evening prayer meetings. I believe in prayer, very strongly, and in its efficacy, but these Sunday occasions might have destroyed a weaker belief. We knelt in the orthodox evangelical position, elbows on very low chairs, in a circle round the room, with bottoms pointing towards the centre. Mr Taylor led. He prayed for practically everything there was and moved all over the world as he did so: a kind of Cook's Tour in prayer. A large dog used to come into the room about half way through, sniffing all over the place with that disconcerting universality of interest which only a really big dog commands. I have never since been able to treat that form and posture of prayer with much seriousness.

'Ralph Taylor made no attempt to conceal the fact that he thoroughly disapproved of me and others like René Tassell, Arthur Morton and Angus MacIntyre and we were promptly dubbed the *anamoi*, Greek for "the law-less ones". I'm quite prepared to admit that I didn't do anything to help myself here, but the Principal seemed unnecessarily fussy about the odd undergraduate escapade.

'I felt very rebellious – a kind of Angry Young Theologian – about the way Christianity was often explained and expounded in the official language of the Church. There was a total failure to communicate what Christianity is about; a failure to display it as something in which any rational, intellectual, intelligent man could believe without feeling that he had done his mind an injustice.

'I was an obvious target for the Oxford Group, who very quickly decided that they should try and do something with me. One of the chaplains at Wycliffe, Alan Thornhill, invited me to go with him to one of those lavish conferences which they hold in Interlaaken. I had never been to Switzerland and my finances would not have allowed me to go on my own.

'I did my best to co-operate and be polite – I owed that at least to my host. I listened carefully while not very dirty linen was washed in public. Most of the proceedings I thought quite fatuous. I came to the conclusion that there was nothing in the Group for me and I even doubted there was anything in it of real value for anybody else. However, I could certainly approve the Group's choice of venue.'

Marcus was, perhaps, being rather unfair to Wycliffe Hall and its Principal. As John Taylor said, 'It was unfortunate that Liverpool sent him to Wycliffe. Marcus was strongly rebellious, he would have felt the odd man out, starved of the freedom to talk and experience aesthetically. He too quickly threw up barriers. He decided to dislike the place – people were judging him, he judged back in self-defence. His slightly anti-establishment stance was a source of health and vitality within a setting that was inevitably prone to adopt conventional attitudes. He stood for personal freedom and integrity and a slightly debonair approach to things spiritual which concealed a depth of personal conviction.'

René Tassell also thought that Marcus over-reacted. 'I don't think Puffy Taylor was as narrow as Marcus said. The Sunday prayers, known as a Puffy Blind – or Bottoms Up, as Marcus called them – weren't compul-sory; Chapel at 7.30 a.m. was – after that you could do as you pleased. I don't remember Wycliffe Hall as being particularly oppressive.'

One incident at Wycliffe in the spring of 1938, which had a profound effect on everyone there, was the arrest of John Philips, an advanced student of theology, on his way back from church one Sunday. He had murdered a pantry boy and put the body on the roof. Marcus was convinced that 'the murder had a sexual element and there had probably been a number of covert meetings before the fatal one. The student was a schizophrenic and therefore difficult to help; but one couldn't avoid feeling that he would have been assisted by a different atmosphere at Wycliffe, where too much was said about the evils of the flesh.'

The students had to account for their movements; Marcus and Angus MacIntyre had to admit that, although supposed to be at a lecture, they were in fact in the Lamb and Flag in St Giles – a splendid alibi.

The official line was that the murder had nothing to do with sex, and Angus, who had been at school with the murderer, agreed; nevertheless, Arthur Morton thought that there was an unhealthy repression at Wycliffe. 'After the murder we were given a quick lecture on sex, but it was so badly done, we were all struck dumb.'

About halfway through his time at Wycliffe, Marcus became so despondent that he went to see the Principal of Westcott House, Cambridge, where John Collins was Vice-Principal. B.K. Cunningham was an understanding listener and offered Marcus a place at Westcott, but 'relieved of my immediate frustration by a sympathetic hearing, I decided that having gone so far at Wycliffe I might just as well stick it out to the end.'

Angus MacIntyre shared a room with Marcus at Wycliffe; they had to be careful not to breathe too heavily in chapel after their periodic visits to the Lamb and Flag. Angus edited the Wycliffe Hall magazine briefly: 'I remember discussing with Marcus how to pep it up. He approved of controversial articles. This was the first indication I had of his interest in journalism. He could be infuriating, but he could never be boring. He could appear arrogant or intolerant, he didn't suffer fools gladly, but he could be very kind and generous to people who didn't threaten him. I always found him easy to get on with, a person who could take having his leg pulled. He and I did *The Times* crossword puzzle before morning chapel, when we should have been meditating. He was always well-dressed, owed a lot to tailors, insisted on having engraved headed notepaper. He tended to splash out on taxis rather than wait for the bus. He spent a lot of money but he didn't spend it all on himself. He was very generous – would pay for meals – thought nothing of giving boxes of a hundred cigarettes as presents.

'The teaching at Wycliffe which we thought to be positively harmful was the kind of Billy Grahamish emphasis on personal salvation, put across in a nauseatingly unctuous fashion. Marcus and I were thrown together by the fact that we were both fish out of water. Neither of us fitted into the conservative evangelical atmosphere of the place and were the leaders of the rebels. We weren't happy there or proud to have been there. It may well be asked: what the hell were we doing there? The somewhat shameful answer is: money. There were no student grants from the government in those days. You had to have either a scholarship or parents who could pay your fees, or sometimes a vocational grant on condition that you became a teacher. Both Marcus and I had scholarships, but these were not enough. You could get a grant on condition that you became a parson, but it had to be either a high church or a low church one – the money was distributed by party trusts. I wanted to go to Westcott House, as Marcus did, but was told that the money would stop if I did. So if we wanted to be ordained, it was Wycliffe Hall or nothing.'

The Northern Evangelical Ordination Council laid out strict conditions to the awarding of grants and students were required to furnish a certificate of residence and of good conduct each term! Marcus was under no contractual obligation to repay the grant, but the Council hoped 'that some real recognition of the help given to its grantees will always be willingly made, so that to others may be extended help such as they have themselves received.'

Marcus was vivaed (interviewed) for a First Class Honours Degree and liked to think that he would have got one if he'd worked a little harder; but he didn't do the work and had to be content with his Second.

His tutor wrote, 'You got a very good Second, one of the soundest. As you see, you only managed one Alpha but you didn't fall anywhere. . . . I HAD read the paper you were most grumbly about. I marked it Beta Plus.

'You usually did one really good question in each paper . . . but there were not often enough good ones to get a final Alpha. . . . I think you may be well satisfied, I am certainly. I hope too that this will give you a little more self-confidence and that the practical work of a parish will give you something of a rest from your present worries. I have enjoyed working with you.'

Angus MacIntyre commiserated, 'When my friends get a Second I generally pat them on the back, shower congratulations and wonder how on earth they managed it. But knowing that you deserved, even if you didn't expect, a First, I feel that sympathy is more appropriate. Hard luck, sir.'

One reason for his failure to get a First may have been a beautiful London model called Rita Foyle whom he had met in Oxford in June 1938. At Christmas that year he took her home to All Saints Vicarage to meet his parents and two weeks later they announced their engagement. Walter was enchanted; Edith put a brave face on it, but Rita's mother was none too keen on her daughter marrying a penniless student. Edith wrote in typical vein: 'I am sure your engagement will make a big difference to you in every way. You will have the feeling of responsibility – as you say – a sense of stability and I am glad to hear you are getting down straight away to the two chief things – work and economy. . . . Canon Twitchett says it is only fair to the person who has "sponsored" you that you should be ordained as soon as possible and begin to earn something. You will have something to pay back, but don't let that worry you *now*, get on with your work and don't let anything interfere with it. . . . Dad hasn't got over the shock of the telephone bill which came yesterday. I knew what it would be. I enclose a statement of some of your calls – the bill for this *quarter* is over £7. . . . I don't think Rita would wish a register office marriage if you can now

*The tall and elegant Rita Foyle, between Aunt Lucy and Edith at All Saints' Vicarage*

definitely fix a time for your marriage. She will want three months, I'm sure, to get her things ready and get her mother used to the idea. When all is said and done if she cannot be true and loyal for that short time there isn't much hope for the future. . . . Give my love to Rita and see what she thinks about asking her mother up at Easter. It might make Mrs F more amenable and reconciled to the marriage.'

It was a period of turmoil for Marcus and for others about to be ordained. The war had been regarded as inevitable for months. Fellow student John Halsey said, 'All of us, I think, found it difficult to decide what to do – whether to go and enlist or to continue to ordination. But having virtually completed the course most of us went forward to ordination. The early months of the war presented no immediate threat and confirmed us to follow that route.'

Marcus was beset with doubts about his ordination but, as Angus said, less about whether he was worthy to join the Church than whether the Church was worth joining. Angus wrote from his first parish in Leeds to reassure him: 'It is natural that you should doubt your vocation now and good that you should be honest enough to say so. . . . If your retreat and ordination service are anything like mine were, I am sure they will set at rest any lingering doubts you may have about the business. If I may say so, I think your vocation is worth far more than most people's, my own included, because you have had the courage to think the whole thing out and to refuse to be blind to difficulties and doubts about it. And if two years at Wickers have failed to shake your convictions I don't see what else can.'

War was declared on 3 September. Three weeks later, Marcus was ordained deacon in Liverpool Cathedral by Bishop Albert David.

# Chapter Three

'The Suffragan Bishop of Liverpool said: "Morris, I don't think you're really a Christian at all."

'In case I hadn't heard he repeated: "Morris, I don't think you're a Christian at all." Then he developed the theme a little by adding, "Are you quite sure you are right to be ordained? . . . Quite sure? It's not too late to draw back, even now, you know. . . ."

'No doubt he meant well, according to his lights; but I remember that I was for a moment violently, though wordlessly, angry. The Bishop of Warrington was tall, gaunt, gaitered, with greyish white hair and a long, pale English puritanical face which, at the same time, was curiously plump. We had met half an hour before; and yet he seemed certain that I wasn't a Christian. I can't remember what I said, though I would have liked to have said a great deal. I might have said to him that my father was a parson, that I had been born in the diocese, that as a child I had been dandled on the knee of a real Bishop of Liverpool, Bishop Chavasse, predecessor of the David who, I hoped, was to ordain me in Liverpool Cathedral the next day.

'But the argument would have been a feeble one. If such a background could make Christians, we would have a lot more Christians.

'Bishop Gresford Jones and I were walking round his garden on the evening of Saturday, 23 September 1939. His house was large and pleasant, a typical house in a Liverpool suburb. The garden was fairly big and served well enough for pacing round and having a rather one-sided theological discussion. Because it was wartime, ordinands in the Diocese of Liverpool, as in most dioceses, had not gone into the long retreat which in other years would have preceded their ordination, but instead were allotted to various clerics for a short time – in my case, mercifully, just half a day and a night. (I found out later that I had not drawn the Bishop out of a hat – I was deliberately allocated to him so that we could have that encouraging conversation.) This cleric shared the grim evangelical outlook of my former Principal, Ralph Taylor. Their brand of Christianity consisted of a series of negative precepts: thou shalt not smoke or drink or dance or in any way enjoy thyself. They had an emotional and sometimes sentimental piousness which was far too personal, a rigidly literal view of the Bible and a failure to recognise the element of community which is one of the vital elements in the Church. They were subjective, not objective: they tended to be smug, "pi" and afraid of life.

'The Suffragan, from his point of view, was right. If being a Christian meant following their code then I certainly wasn't one and no amount of walking round the rectory garden would turn me into one.

'Further pacing along the path revealed the fact that the Suffragan had received a letter from Ralph Taylor. "I have heard from your Principal, Morris, he's rather worried about you too." I never saw the letter and I was never told what was in it. Even now I would be very interested to know.' Marcus never did know, as the diocesan records were destroyed during the war.

'After a dull dinner with no wine (the Bishop confused abstinence and temperance) I was glad to be sent upstairs for reflection and a succession of much longed-for cigarettes. The theological discussion continued later in the Bishop's study – to little effect. Finally, as a last resort, the Suffragan suggested we should pray together that I might be guided to do what he thought right. We got down on our knees on the thin carpeted floor, elbows on seats of chairs, bottoms pointing inwards to the centre of the room. We didn't get the guidance the Suffragan wanted so at ten o'clock we went upstairs to bed.

'I lay and smoked in the darkness and remember thinking before I went to sleep that if the Suffragan and the Principal were right in their faith then I most certainly should not, and would not want to be, ordained.

'But I did not think they were right. I was quite sure in my own mind about my vocation and eventually succeeded in convincing my host, in terms as firm as an ordinand may prudently use to a Bishop.

'The ordination service was held at Liverpool Cathedral. The ceremony was plain and simple. The Suffragan preached a sermon on temperance, not the most relevant subject for the Ordering of Deacons. [Unless, of course, the main thrust of Ralph Taylor's letter concerned Marcus's drinking habits!]

'The line of Deacons was presented before the Bishop seated on his throne; the Archdeacon told him that he considered we were apt and meet for our learning and Godly conversation, to exercise our ministry duly to the honour of God and the edifying of His Church. The Lord Bishop of Liverpool and the other Bishops present laid their hands on our heads.

'My father was present in the Canons' Stall in the Sanctuary. Somewhere behind me in the great building were my mother and sister.'

After the ceremony Walter took the family to lunch at the Bear's Paw in the city centre, a solid restaurant with heavy Victorian appointments where you could be sure, even in September 1939, of an excellent meal.

'It was a happy family party and I could see that my father, though he never showed his feelings easily, was pleased that I had been ordained to the ministry in which he had spent his already long and distinguished life. My mother's pleasure was rather more apparent. I told them about my session with the Suffragan. My father said irreverently that the Bishop had been a silly ass.'

Later, the Canon wrote indignantly to the Bishop of Liverpool, receiving a reply which was a model of episcopal tact and subtlety; Albert David was sure that his Suffragan had been carried away by his enthusiasm and that when Marcus got to know him better he would find him a very nice man. Marcus never did get to know him better and remained convinced that whatever Gresford Jones was enthusiastic about it was not Marcus.

'When I left the Bear's Paw I didn't have far to go to my first parish. It was at Roby on the outskirts of Liverpool where, some six or seven hours after ordination, I preached my first sermon. The text was "Light is sown for the righteous".'

Roby until the 1930s had been a small country village with a Manor House, a Lord of the Manor and Victorian church surrounded by fields. The fields had recently been built over with lines of semi-detached houses with small gardens, to accommodate the increasing population of Liverpool city centre. Today it is a pleasant suburb and the church has an active and thriving community.

As junior curate at St Bartholomew's, Marcus found it all rather depressing. His vicar, C.R. Jarvis, was a blunt man in early middle age, of low-church convictions, who greeted him warmly. He placed great faith in the effectiveness of parish visiting, but Marcus quickly formed the view that it was a waste of time and energy. Every afternoon he would cycle up and down the long rows of houses feeling like a brush salesman. People were suspicious and thought there must be a catch. They would stand around, embarrassed, making small talk. The only people who really enjoyed his visits were already keen church goers and in no need of conversion. Marcus found it deadening work and came to the conclusion that it did nobody any good, least of all himself.

'I felt I was simply not wanted and was regarded as a ruddy nuisance. Only in households which had suffered a bereavement would I be welcome and feel I was achieving something of value.'

Marcus did not blame the parishioners for their apathy: 'To many, I was an unfamiliar and not particularly agreeable phenomenon. I don't suppose I was a very impressive figure either, tired from an afternoon's cycling. Churchgoers who knew who I was frequently gave me cups of tea – I found more than four cups hard to absorb – on other days, of course, when I was hot and dusty, I was offered none. The parish presented a problem which I am sure is typical. The majority of people felt that the Church was irrelevant to their problems and activities.

'I came face to face with the problems that beset the Church, although I was not very certain about many of the answers. Of one thing I was convinced: in some way or another the Church had to discover methods of reaching people with more clarity and simplicity and a sharper impact, otherwise the drift away was likely to accelerate.'

Not all his time was spent visiting, which even Jarvis admitted 'is exceptionally difficult in this parish of mushroom growth'. Marcus was put in charge of the Junior Sunday School of some 150 children, ran a branch of the parish's 'Life Boy Team' and organised a club for sixteen to twenty-five year olds. He learnt about the taking of services (firmly crossing out the prayer 'From fornication and drunkenness, at home or in the field, and from all the deceits of the world, the flesh and the devil, Good Lord deliver us' from the special wartime litany) and began to appreciate the problems and difficulties of preaching. At first he was too stiff and stylised and his sermons were too long and dull.

'Gradually I came to see that ten to fifteen minutes was long enough and I should make one point only and deal with it vividly and entertainingly. I have always felt that a sermon needs careful preparation. I used to write it all out and learn it by heart; I had the script in front of me when I preached, but developed a technique of not appearing to rely on it. A preacher must give the impression of speaking spontaneously to his congregation.'

By the time Marcus left Roby, Jarvis was able to say, 'His preaching is scholarly and both the material and the delivery are good, and I believe that in time he will become a very good preacher. He invites criticism and profits by it, which I think is rather rare.'

Marcus was living in digs in Pilch Lane East, one of Roby's long streets, on a salary of £250 p.a. which didn't leave much over for a social life. The monotony was enlivened by the appearance of Rita at weekends, by nights out with Angus MacIntyre in Leeds and Liverpool, and occasional binges with his brother-in-law Eric Cook. He and his father played golf for the Diocese of Liverpool, both receiving three strokes in a match against the Diocese of Chester.

After nine months as deacon Marcus was ordained priest in Liverpool Cathedral. Even before his ordination as a deacon Marcus had approached the Bishop of Liverpool for permission to marry Rita; but ordinands in the diocese had to agree to take a curacy for two years and give an undertaking not to get married in that time. The Bishop was naturally unwilling to make an exception for Marcus: 'There are two or three others in the same position, and it grieves me to refuse you all, but this is a time when first things must come first. Marriage means heavy responsibilities which would be almost certain to interfere with the main work of a priest. We must be content, like a great many other people, to wait for what we want for ourselves until better times come.'

Marcus was not content and continued, against the advice of his father and his vicar, to press for permission to marry. Mr Jarvis said, 'He has never let the subject drop . . . this pre-occupation with private affairs has affected his work increasingly.' Bishop David was sympathetic and, after talking at length to Walter, he agreed that they could marry – if they moved to another diocese.

Marcus set out to find another curacy, armed with testimonials from Bishop and Vicar. He turned down the offer of a job as assistant priest of St George's, Hanover Square, but was regarded as too young for a post in Wimbledon. An interview in Cheltenham was unsuccessful (not enough experience), but in Great Yarmouth, with the largest parish church in England, the rector, Canon Aitken, offered him a job.

Marcus and Rita agreed to meet at Euston Station and journey together to Great Yarmouth to go flat-hunting. Marcus travelled down from Liverpool and waited, drinking tea and smoking, watching the soldiers of wartime London come and go. After several hours Rita arrived, tall and beautiful, only to tell him that she had transferred her affections to a naval officer and that their engagement was at an end. Marcus was flabbergasted; they talked and talked, 'though I realised it was quite useless. No woman can be argued back into loving a man she has ceased to love.'

This devastating change of heart made all Marcus's and Walter's efforts, and the Bishop's understanding help, pointless. He might just as well have stayed at Roby. But he was committed to Great Yarmouth, so he crossed London to Liverpool Street Station and took the train to Norfolk alone. 'We parted good enough friends. I saw her once or twice afterwards. It was no consolation that she didn't marry him. She joined the Wrens and soon married another naval officer.'

Great Yarmouth was utterly different from Roby, a difference epitomised by the two parish churches: in Roby, small and prim; in Yarmouth, a vast grey-stoned Gothic edifice, founded in 1101, clothed in the dignity of an age before the Reformation. (St Nicholas' Church was badly damaged in an air raid in June 1942, was restored in the 1950s and is still beautiful, though now a trifle run-down.) The community was old and well-established, even a little in-bred.

The vicar, too, was very different. Canon Aubrey Aitken had a grand manner and gave the impression of being stand-offish and difficult to approach and his parishioners resented it. However, Marcus liked him and they got on well enough in spite of Aitken's initial patronising manner.

Marcus was the junior chaplain of four (one was a Church Army captain) and they looked after three smaller churches as well as the great parish church. His stipend was £280 a year and, having moved out of digs into a flat in Wellesley Road, he found it necessary to augment his income. He earned £2 a week as tutor to the two sons of Lieutenant Colonel and Mrs Spencer at Mantly, whither he travelled by motorcycle to coach the boys for their common entrance in all subjects except French. When the elder boy passed his entrance to Pangbourne. Marcus decided he was tired of it and handed over the younger to his fellow curate, A.W. Alexander.

Initially Marcus's duties lay mainly at St Nicholas where he came under the sharp eye of the Canon who started by criticising Marcus's sermons, telling him his voice lacked variation and needed development. So Marcus took lessons in voice production from a Miss Neave who worked on him with some success and he would rehearse his sermons with Victor Wynburne, another of the curates.

Yarmouth was a mixed parish: as well as the many well-to-do solid citizens there were areas of slum property which Marcus had never experienced before. Even at that early stage of the war the town was being evacuated. Yarmouth was one of the nearest towns to German-occupied Holland and the noise of German bombers hummed and throbbed above streets where the shutters were up and houses empty. The Promenade was deserted, with barbed wire along the sea front and beaches mined. The docks stood empty and forlorn.

Yet there was always more than enough to do for the four curates. Marcus started a Youth Club with between sixty and eighty members which met three times a week at St Paul's Clergy House. He acted as secretary and disciplinarian, the only one of the curates who would (and could) exercise any authority over the youngsters. It was a successful club, with regular dances, plays, talks and a Christmas party – he is still remembered with affection by former members.

His preaching seemed to appeal to the younger section of the congregation (one talk was entitled 'Why I am a bloody parson') and although he said that he wasn't conscious of any special talent or interest in dealing with young people, he started a children's church in St Andrew's with about twenty girls and a dozen boys. The services were exclusively for children and they took the leading part, reading the lessons, taking the collection and doing all the singing. It didn't last long, due in part to St Andrew's being in a 'poor' area with little Sunday School tradition, and in part to an increase in the evacuation of children when serious bombing began at the start of 1941. One of the curates' duties was firewatching on the roof of St Nicholas – and more than once helping to dowse flames which threatened the church.

Marcus was assigned to the hospital as chaplain and saw a good deal of the results of German activity. It was his first real experience of hospital visiting and a gruesome and harrowing one, the majority of patients being sailors from bombed ships, and wounded airmen, terribly burned. He took services in the hospital and, inevitably, the number of funerals in the town soon outnumbered weddings and baptisms.

It was at this time that he first tried to get his views on the Church into print. He wrote an article, intended for the *Yarmouth Mercury*, and sent it to the Canon for approval. Aitken was in hospital recovering from an operation and indicated that it would be prudent not to publish it since it would doubtless cause controversy. Marcus thought that controversy was just what the Church needed, but had to accept the Canon's ruling.

The article was entitled *Christian Hypocrisy*: 'Does Christianity make any difference at all to the behaviour of the world today? Europe is given over to the struggles of three mighty modern nations at war and no-one imagines that there is anything very Christian about that. . . .

'How much difference does Christianity make to the way nations and governments and town councils and business firms behave? Does it affect our attitude to this war? Will it affect the terms of peace? . . .

'It seems that the majority of people if they are Christians at all confine their Christianity to their private lives and take great care that it does not interfere in politics or business or social affairs. . . .

'We see that the underlying motive of big business is profit-making and more profit-making at the expense both of employee and competitor. Unscrupulousness, dishonesty and vested interest are taken for granted even by professing Christians as being a normal part of business methods. . . .

'Both in home and foreign affairs we expect [our politicians] to act from motives of expediency and self-interest. We have only to remind ourselves of our treatment of Germany since the last war and our scornful treatment of Abyssinia at the time of the Italian invasion and then think of our present flattering and patronising attitude towards her. There are many now who call themselves Christians who are filled with hatred of the German people and who, when peace is made, will scream hysterically for revenge and retribution. Yet there is apathy and indifference towards our own most urgent problems – slums, poverty, disease and the like.

'We must have Christianity on a large scale not just private Christianity. As Christians it is our national and social sins that we must remember first of all.'

Marcus wrote later, 'The views which I expressed in the rejected article were a development of those which had been growing in my mind since Oxford days. I felt that the Church was not getting its message over to the general public. I was very critical of church-going people: I found them smug, self-satisfied, inhibited; concerned only with attending church on Sundays, and totally uninterested in and incapable of acting as apostles, of spreading the Faith to those with whom they came into daily contact. The practice of Christianity seemed to me conventional and impotent. The man in the street had precious little use for the Church and I didn't blame him. How many parsons had been heard to express concern for people's jobs and pay, housing problems, bombing?'

Marcus had a long correspondence on the subject with his father, who wrote, 'When you say "The Church has failed" what do you mean by the Church? People so often speak as though the Bishops or the Clergy or both were the Church. If one of my laymen were to say to me "The Church has failed" I should answer "Have you? I *am* sorry to hear it." If you mean that organised Christianity has not succeeded in converting the masses, I should agree. It has not; it never did, and I doubt if it ever will. . . . I am actively in agreement with you about the deplorable state of religion in this country. It is simply a Pagan country influenced subconsciously by certain vague ideas of Christian ethics.'

In January 1941 the Revd Kenneth Budd wrote a letter to the *Church of England Newspaper*: 'The younger generation . . . are bitterly disappointed at the failure of the Churches to speak the word of life to a world in the shadow of death. We need at once to call together those of the younger clergy and laity who are alive to the seriousness of the situation and are anxious to grapple with it.'

Marcus wrote to Mr Budd at Holy Trinity Vicarage, Upper Tooting: 'Large-scale, national Christianity has failed both by failing to exercise authority in matters of State and by not giving to the average man a pattern of goodness relevant to present-day conditions.

'I feel strongly that the fault does lie with the Bishops and the older generation of clergy. My own experience as a very young curate is that I am firmly sat on when I venture to suggest that things are not quite as they should be and am told that I shall grow out of it. So I feel quite hopeless about doing anything useful about it at present. But I know several of my contemporaries who feel as I do and possibly if only we could get together we might have some small effect.'

Mr Budd replied that he had had several letters in the same vein and that he would keep them all in the hope of arranging a conference of like-minded churchmen. 'Meanwhile, keep a good heart; the day of the rebels will surely come!'

On 15 April 1941, Edith wrote to Marcus from Southport: 'Very many thanks for the lovely chocolates. They are *very* scarce here and so were quite a treat. We took them to the Little Theatre tonight – we saw *Marigold* a very delightful period play. It was very well done. Can you get cigarettes? There were *none* to be bought in Southport yesterday. The siren has just gone and we have just heard two big bangs which sounded like bombs. We also had an alert at noon today – most unusual in the daytime.'

The following day Marcus received a telegram: 'BOMBED ALL SAFE CAN YOU COME – MOTHER.' German bombers attacking Liverpool had ditched their bombs over Southport. One landed in Rawlinson Road, killing a doctor and his wife living nearby, and blowing Walter and Edith into a glass cabinet.

Marcus got permission to leave Yarmouth and caught the train for London, where he was held up by a heavy raid. He arrived home safe but anxious and found his mother rather shaken but calm and his father's injuries not too serious. Walter sat in bed in the Infirmary looking rather distinguished and grumbling in his usual manner – definitely a sign that he was on the road to recovery. Edith had discharged herself because the authorities had had the effrontery to write her age on a board outside her room.

His mind relieved of worry, Marcus decided to enjoy the break. On Friday, 18 April, an old friend, Joe Crossley, who worked on the *Southport Guardian*, took him to the Little Theatre, normally the home of an amateur theatre group, which the (professional) Sheffield Repertory Company had taken over for the duration of the war. The leading lady of the company and star of *Marigold* (she was also playing Cathy in *Wuthering Heights*) was Jessica Dunning, a beautiful, talented young actress from Sale, just south of Manchester. She had made a great hit in Southport and had many devoted admirers, but she had the reputation of being rather unapproachable, a little disillusioned with men and desirous only of being left in peace to concentrate on the theatre.

After the show Joe took Marcus round to the flat in Lord Street which Jessica shared with actresses Lally Bowers and Joan Knowles and, as Jessica put it years later, 'the bells rang'. She confided rather poetically to her diary: 'The door opened and my love walked in. Tall he was and fair and open like the wind blowing over green fields. The room was shining light like the sun up and the air in it filled with a singing. The party people moved about in it like two-dimensional cardboard figures but we were real, the only two that were. The others knew it too for their talk faded away to a murmur like bees, and for all they were between us the things we said were clearly heard and freely understood.'

The next day, Saturday, Marcus delivered a very proper note to the flat inviting Jessica for a drink on the Sunday, ending, 'I'm afraid I haven't got a car as the garage fell on it. But no doubt there are places within walking distance.' Later that evening, having had a drink with Joe which gave him a bit of Dutch courage, he took a hasty note round to the stage door, written on the back of a page of meat coupons: 'Can you come out after the show for a drink and/or some food?' The note was returned with an addition: 'I *am* so sorry, we've got people coming to supper. I would have loved to, especially as I see you have plenty of coupons! But I'll see you tomorrow. Thank you.'

The following day, after preaching his first sermon at his father's church, Marcus took Jess to the Royal Hotel and the Cheshire Lines. On Monday he went to see her in *The First Mrs Fraser* and after the show they went to the Hole in the Wall for a meal. On Tuesday Marcus heard Jessica read her lines at the flat. They met for lunch on Wednesday and, in the evening, after the performance of *They Walk Alone*, they had a drink together at the Houghton Arms just round the corner from the theatre. At closing time they went for a walk on The Promenade: Marcus asked Jess to marry him and she said yes.

The next day the bath in the flat in Lord Street was full of red roses – Lally and Joan were not amused. Marcus bought an engagement ring and his friends Geoffrey and Raymond Ball (who owned the flat in Lord Street) insisted on throwing an engagement party at the Royal Hotel with Lally, Joan and Cyril and Twin Luckham, also members of the theatre company. Marcus went round to the Infirmary with a half bottle of champagne and told his father that he was engaged to the most famous and best-loved actress in town. Walter was a little taken aback, but enjoyed the champagne.

On 27 April, Marcus preached his second sermon at All Saints with his fiancée in the congregation. The following week, on 2 May, with Jess playing in *The World of Light*, and Walter out of hospital, Marcus went reluctantly back to work. The train journey to London and Yarmouth passed uneventfully: '*It went almost too quickly – I could have sat for hours more just dreaming. I've been thinking of you all the day long, as I sat gazing out of the carriage windows, remembering the perfection of the last ten days – the greatest days of my life. You've become part of me and you've given me tremendous new strength, my darling.*'

Jessica was the youngest of three children born to Hamlet and Alice Dunning. Her father (christened Hamlet instead of Hamnet by a hard-of-hearing vicar), who had been a salesman for Clark's shoes, died in January 1940, aged fifty-nine. The eldest child, James Forsyth, was a very talented musician and light comedian and could have made a name for himself on the stage – but show business was not a respectable profession for middle-class men in Cheshire and Jim went into shoes. The area around Sale was a hotbed of amateur dramatics and Jim, sister Ruth and their friends would rehearse at home while the young be-tunicked and bespectacled Jessie, a pupil at Sale Grammar School, sat in a corner and studied – always very quiet and self-contained and imperturbable. She was occasionally dragged in to play small parts in their shows.

Jess was the brainy one of the family but caught the acting bug at Manchester University where she joined the Stage Society. Gradually her history studies under A.J.P. Taylor took second place: 'In Sean O'Casey's *Within the Gates* chief honours go to Jessie Dunning for an extraordinarily good performance in the leading part of a woman of the streets. It is the first time that this play has been performed by amateurs, and the first performance in this country outside London.' Her father was not best pleased at this development. His elder daughter was already away, having taken over the lead from Wendy Hiller in *Love on the Dole* at the Garrick Theatre in London. But Jess was allowed to have her way and she left university without getting her degree. She began her career in 1936 in *Once a Gentleman* with the part of 'a girl of attractive appearance and personality who plays the piano' at the Manchester Repertory Theatre at Rusholme. She progressed to Leading Juvenile in plays such as *Lady Precious Stream*, *The Constant Nymph* and *Little Women*. From the *Manchester and Salford Woman Citizen*, August 1937: 'The most generally interesting feature of the whole season has undoubtedly been the gradual development of Miss Jessica Dunning. It was apparent from her very first appearance (as a student) that here was an actress worth watching. She is rapidly fulfilling that promise.'

Following encouragement from Sybil Thorndike, Jess went to the Bournemouth Repertory Company early in 1939 and thence to the Playhouse Theatre in London, home to Nancy Price's People's National Theatre, whose aim was to 'present the best without commercial consideration'.

From 1938 to 1940 Jess also worked on a dozen *Children's Hour* programmes for the BBC, the start of a life-long friendship with Nan Macdonald, organiser of Northern Children's Hour. By February 1940 she was wowing them in *Short Story* by Robert Morley at the Little Theatre, Southport.

Jessica wrote of herself: 'My brother was ten years and my sister six years older than I. Being born with a nice sense of my own importance it was only natural that the difference in age should have a great effect on me. My sister naturally had a great influence, conscious and unconscious. I think I was always conscious that my innate mental powers were greater than hers and the greater development of six extra years irked me, and also her naturally-adopted air of superiority. Natural because if I wanted to know anything she was the obvious person to ask and to be a giver of information puts one above the interrogator. One of my earliest memories is of my sister and I bathing together. I happened to notice her nipples and so I pointed to my own small nipples and said "What're these for?" The burst of outraged refinement and virtue that followed sent me scrambling out of the bath in terrified hysterics which brought my mother up to comfort me, *but* – I had asked what was to me a simple open question and in reply I had received a mental lashing, always with me the most effective punishment for wrong doing. It was one of the things which for many years stopped me asking the questions I wanted to ask; although I was quite sure in my own mind that she was wrong and that there was nothing "unrefined" about my body, that was the beginning of the idea of shame in my mind, the beginning of that secretiveness and mental swerving away from physical things that could only be worked out twenty-odd years later in such a drastic and wearying manner' – a reference to an unhappy love affair and an unwanted pregnancy which was dealt with by her efficient and loving brother Jim, who arranged and paid for a termination.

It wasn't until Jess met the young curate from Southport that her mental and emotional barriers fell and she was able to become the vital, physical being that was her natural self.

Marcus should, of course, have told his vicar of his intention to get married – but Aitken was conveniently still in hospital, so Marcus postponed what would be a painful interview. Instead he set about making the flat in Wellesley Road a little more comfortable. He dusted and swept – and didn't sweep the dust under the carpet. He bought some fabric to make curtains before realising that he had no idea how to go about it. The shop girl in Palmers, who happened to be a member of his Youth Club, took pity on him and offered to make the curtains up; as she refused payment for this service Marcus bought the biggest box of chocolates he could find and presented them to her, rather shyly, at the next Youth Club dance.

The next five days passed with a profusion of letters criss-crossing the country and hours spent trying to reach each other by telephone (two to three hour waits were not uncommon, and much of the time operators were accepting only calls 'of national importance').

2 May: *'More people are leaving every day and more still sleeping out in the country. This place will be bleaker than ever and my work even more futile. But it doesn't matter much now. It's a proof of your effect on me that you can shed even round Yarmouth, a roseate aura.'* 'You are still here my darling, in me and about me; but I do miss the little things quite dreadfully: your sniff, and your fascinating cigarette-shop smile, and having your arms round me. . . . I'm in a bit of a quandary. I feel that Mother and Father Morris would like me to take communion. Which I haven't done for years, it being one of the things of the truth of which I have been least convinced. If and when I am convinced, I should like to take it with you for the first time.'

3 May: *'My sweet, please don't go to Communion yet awhile. Just tell my people that you are waiting to go with me – they will understand. . . . I've been quite incapable of concentrating on a sermon. So I'm going to give them an old one. . . . I managed to get through to the parents. They tell me they are having tea with you tomorrow – how grand. I hope they won't be as terrified as I was the first time.'*

4 May: 'Dearest love, I baked them a cake, but the oven wasn't hot enough and it was sad. They were very noble – ate some of it. Last night I had quite decided to pack my bags and leap over to Yarmouth. . . . If you think we can manage if I get three months without pay, with the definite promise of my job back at the end of it, get a special licence and I'll come over. . . . This job of mine here is only really important to my career in that it gives me a living. And you my love are of more importance to me at this moment than fifty careers.'

5 May: *'My darling one – I hope you managed to avoid any trouble last*

*night. The raids seem to have been fairly widespread over the NW. . . . I have just returned from taking a funeral – rather a grisly one. Yesterday, I baptized four infants, including one bastard. Cor! We do see life. . . . I have heard from the RAF this morning and there seems a good chance of my getting a chaplaincy as soon as I'm free. . . . Several people have noticed a far-away look in my eyes, when I'm trying to carry on a conversation.'*

6 May: *'Thank you for the wire. It was a great relief to know that you are alright. . . . I've just come back from a Rotarians lunch. I'm not a member but I've been several times and met all the local capitalists. It's really very nice being a capitalist, I should imagine.'*

7 May: 'Mrs Rigby has let me have 80 cigarettes since last Saturday – more than I've had in a fortnight before. Really we shall have to stop smoking so much soon or we shall be a couple of crocks the rest of our lives. And we've got too many wonderful things to do. . . . Look dear love, don't overdo the economy business as far as not having somebody to clean for you. . . . I don't suppose they'd have the decency to put us both in the same debtor's prison. . . . My darling it's so incredibly stupendously wonderful that you are there to understand. It's like layers and layers of flannel petticoats taken off my mind. . . . I find myself spinning along at least six inches above the ground which, while a little disconcerting to others, is a very pleasant means of progression.'

The same day, after managing to get through on the telephone at last, Marcus's letter was eleven pages long: *'If you decided to take 2–3 months off work, you should come here and we'll get married immediately, but my parents would be very disappointed at our being married so quickly and away from Southport; they've done so much for me that I feel I owe them something. . . .*

*'Next week I might manage to get home for two days. We could then be married at All Saints by licence and come back here the next day. . . . It would solve the question of a big or small wedding – we could be married very quietly with just relatives. . . .*

*'I'm afraid there is no chance of my getting away from here for any length of time. If I were just to leave now, I should not get the Bishop's approval to the chaplaincy and I should be without a job. . . . one is bound by one's reputation and standing with the authorities and, if I really got across them, they might turn nasty. I don't want that to happen now – I want to do well for your sake. . . . I only wish I had more money . . . I'm trying to sell various things.'*

They managed to talk on the phone at length the following day.

8 May: *'My darling one, I've been wandering about in a daze all day – a glorious daze – first because of the possibility of our being together in five days time – really together so that nothing can separate us; and secondly because I've had four superb, wonderful, breath-taking letters from you today. . . . Oh my darling one, I adore you with everything that is in me – so that it almost hurts. . . . As regards the cash, we certainly ought to be*

*Jessica Dunning marries the Canon's eligible son. With Lally Bowers, Rowena Cook, Geoffrey Ball and Mother Dunning*

*able to live on my income – the other two married clergy here get the same. . . . I feel terribly guilty about even suggesting marriage when I'm in debt. . . . And darling, if you'll come, I promise I'll bring you an early cup of tea and light the fires and cook the breakfast and help with the washing up. You can hardly refuse now. . . . You have lifted me from commonplace mediocrity to a new vision, so that with you, I know we can conquer life and can never despair. . . . My dear darling – I want you here so much – to talk to you and know your mind and learn from you and with you to explore and find out things together.'*

At noon on Tuesday, 13 May 1941 Marcus and Jess were married by Walter and Eric Cook at All Saints' Church. Marcus's pious hopes of a quiet wedding did not materialise. Every pew was packed. The wedding created a sensation in Southport: the local lasses were very indignant that the most widely sought-after actress in town had whipped off with the

Canon's eligible son. The press had a field day; even the *Daily Mirror* turned up, but the photograph they published dismayed many of Jess's relatives – Marcus's fair, slicked-back hair gave the impression that he was bald. The wedding was written up for the *Southport Journal* by a young reporter, Jodi Hyland, who lived in the parish of St James, Birkdale (a suburb of Southport) and who had typed Marcus's almost illegible Oxford theses while she was at secretarial school.

Marcus's best man was Geoffrey Ball, who died two years later during a tonsillectomy. He was unofficially engaged to Jess's chief bridesmaid, Lally Bowers, who remained a close friend of Marcus and Jess. Eight-year-old Rowena Cook was also a bridesmaid. Jim, by then in the RNVR, dashed up from HMS *Wildflower* stationed at Sheerness to give the bride away and Mother Dunning's sisters arrived from London and Chepstow. Jess's sister Ruth was married to the actor Jack Allen, at that time a captain in the Royal Ulster Rifles and stationed in Ballymena, Northern Ireland. Ruth and Jack received a telegram informing them of the marriage and Jack didn't meet his new brother-in-law until the end of the war. Teddy was in Ceylon and received his mother's cable three days after the wedding.

The newly-weds had to fight their way through the crowds of well-wishers outside the church and the reception in the Scarisbrook Hotel (paid for by Mother Dunning) was as spectacular as wartime restrictions allowed – 26 lunches at 7/6*d*, 15 bottles of wine – total £23.17*s*.6*d*. Mindful of the bishop and the vicar, their honeymoon was one night at the Royal Hotel in Kirkby Lonsdale in the Lake District (at a cost of £2.4*s*.9*d*).

On 15 May the most junior curate in the parish arrived back in Great Yarmouth with his bride and created another sensation. The Canon was still in hospital so Marcus prudently decided to confront him when he returned. When eventually he did see him, Aitken was justifiably annoyed that Marcus hadn't told him of his intentions, but accepted the situation and made Jess welcome. Mr Alexander's wife was not so forbearing and disapproved strongly of Jess – but the two curates' wives didn't have to endure each other for long.

# Chapter Four

In spite of German planes overhead, bombs falling in and around the town, bad news on the fall of Crete, rationing, and the marked disapprobation of Mrs Alexander, Great Yarmouth became a place of joy and beauty as Marcus and Jess talked and learned and explored and found things out together.

They went rowing and swam naked in the Norfolk Broads. They saw Douglas Byng (an acquaintance of Jess's who had been at their wedding) at the Theatre Royal in Norwich and lunched with him at the Royal Hotel. They attended a dance at RAF Coltishall, where Angus MacIntyre was now a chaplain: 'Jess changed in the WAAF and looked very lovely in plain black with a red rose at the neck.'

Marcus was very keen to become a chaplain in the armed forces and started fighting his way through the bureaucracy. On 12 June he had his medical and interview for the RAF.

Canon Aitken wrote a glowing reference: 'Mr Morris is keen on his work and is specially interested in work among the young. He has always been most ready to tackle any jobs given him and has shown initiative and enthusiasm. The matter of his sermons is always interesting and his delivery of them will improve with experience. I confidently expect that a career of real usefulness lies before him and he takes with him my warmest good wishes.'

At the beginning of July Mr and Mrs Morris left Great Yarmouth and returned to Southport, Jess to take up her job in Geoffrey Ost's Sheffield Rep and Marcus to await his call-up papers.

On 28 July, Jessica opened in the lead in *Sixteen*.

'The play ran smoothly for a Monday and was well received except for a few misplaced laughs. Jessica received an ovation on her entrance and made a speech at the end – and all through the week. She played a tricky part extremely well – a restrained and sympathetic performance. She lives the part and I myself regarded her as Sixteen, and not just as my wife.'

*They swam naked in the Norfolk Broads . . .*

*Wedded bliss, Gt.*
*Yarmouth, June 1941*

On the 31st, Marcus received notification from the RAF that he was posted to Bircham Newton, not far from Great Yarmouth. *'Just typical of officialdom to post me as far away as possible, when there are so many stations near.'* He was granted a commission for the duration of hostilities with the relative rank of Squadron Leader, Chaplain's Branch, RAFVR, with effect from 5 August 1941.

4 August: 'Dear love, I'm going to miss you. You've given me so much strength though, so I think I shall be able to keep up, and I have got you within me growing. You'll be busy with new people and new experiences so don't give yourself too much time to think too much of missing me.... And you look quite frighteningly impressive in uniform. I do hope the journey isn't going to be too bad. Take good care of yourself, change your shoes if they get wet.'

Telegram to Jessica Morris, Southport, 5 August: *'Practically there darling.'*

Telegram to Revd Morris, RAF Station Bircham Newton, Kings Lynn, 6 August: 'In case letter not arrived, Good Morning Darling.'

6 August: *'I got some food on the train – there's one thing about this uniform, it earns one much more attention and respect. I ate the sandwiches later on. Somehow it gave me rather a thrill to know you had packed them – there seemed a loving wifely touch lingering around them. ... There seems practically nothing to do here. One just wanders about picking up*

*what knowledge one can . . . no one would be any the wiser if I weren't here at all. I can't decide whether this job is going to be futile or not. . . . I doubt if religion cuts any ice with people here – at least the officers – I haven't come across the men yet.'*

7 August: *'The officers are not interested in religion except when drunk. . . . This job needs to be taken with a fairly light heart as one would, I imagine, become bitter and disillusioned. . . . I'm really going to try to get into the discipline of prayer and some devotional reading every morning.'*

8 August: *'Last evening after dinner I went into the NAAFI and wandered about talking with the men at various tables. Apparently it was rather an unusual thing to do. One man told me that I was the first padre they had seen there and they seemed very pleased and welcoming and talked very freely and easily. It wasn't as difficult as I expected and I felt really exhilarated and cheered afterwards. Felt I was beginning to get down to things a bit. It's really amazing that none of the other chaplains have ever been in. It's supposed to be our main job – gaining contact with the men. And to me it's much the most interesting part.'*

10 August: *'At first sight, the Senior Chaplain seems very pleasant. On Monday he is going to instruct us in the strange routines of an RAF station. So perhaps he's going to train me a bit more than I thought. He doesn't spend much time on the station – and no time at all with the "other ranks". We had a service (voluntary) this morning in the NAAFI – no move or push or energy and he gave a very feeble wandering talk. There were about 50 men there (out of 4,000) and no officers. It's all so uninspired. I felt somehow that I could put a good deal more into it and that my kind of address would interest them more. And yet I get horrible doubts that after all I may be quite wrong, inexperienced and just youthfully enthusiastic. I'm trying with your support to get a firm faith in myself – and it is only you that can give it to me.*

*'I've just found your parcel and your letter. My dear darling, thank you so much. And the cigs are terribly welcome. We can get very few. But please don't go without yourself my dear – let's share things as always. I'll soon be back, angel, and you have a precious charge to care for for me. We have so much that others never have. . . . Last night I played bridge in the mess – I won 2/9d at 1s a 100 (don't tell the parents, they might disapprove).'*

10 August: 'I feel more certain than ever that you're going to make a tremendous thing of this job. You may make yourself not very popular with people like the Chaplain but the men themselves are what counts. . . .'

On the 12th Marcus learned that there was to be a general shift around of padres within the RAF and he would be posted to Cosford, a training station of some 8,000 men, nine miles from Wolverhampton. He managed to sneak three days' leave before the move.

17 August: *'It was hell leaving you. But the thought of those 2–3 days is so warming and exhilarating that the memory of them goes with me all the time and bears me up. . . . On the journey, I picked up an excellent Penguin* The Quest for Corvo *– a biography of one Baron Corvo (alias Fr Rolfe)*

*who wrote among other things, an amazing novel called* Hadrian the Seventh. *Have you come across him? It sounds well worth looking into.'* [Thirty years later, Jess got to know it very well.]

On 19 August he wrote from Cosford: *'I think this place is going to be alright from what I've seen of it so far. My boss – one Bryan – seems a very good lad. They seem to have everything – the church is very good – really properly equipped with Hammond organ and pulpit and all. There is also a magnificent gymnasium and swimming pool, cinema and concert hall with properly equipped stage – they have an Ensa show every Monday.'*

Much of Marcus's time was spent trying to find somewhere outside the station where they could be together: he looked at digs, flats, cottages, caravans, rooms – all of which seemed to be outside the Morris pocket. Jessica had been advised to give up work by October at the latest. She wrote: 'I think we ought not to mind about doing without a few mod con if we get something for about 10/- a week. It'd probably mean coping with oil-lamps and stoves and things like that, and even bathing in a hip-bath, but it'd be worth it, and might be quite fun for a bit, and might mean that we could afford to have a little woman, which otherwise we couldn't. Anyway, you might try, angel.'

23 August: *'It's cold and pouring with rain and there's nothing to do and no one to see. . . . I so often get the feeling that I'm just a nobody after all with no personality and nothing to make me get on with people or win any appreciation. And then I realise that you are there all the time and that you love me and it makes me feel proud and confident again. . . . The money business is certainly hellishly hard but I personally would sooner starve to be with you than bloat without you – if you see what I mean. . . . I have you in my heart and mind every moment and it's nice to know that, next to bananas and cream, I come a close second in your thoughts.'*

On 27 August, Marcus suddenly appeared in Southport – apparently without leave. 'Dearest Love, it wasn't a dream, it was a real and wonderful happening. Oh darling, you just saved my life coming then. . . . I hope you weren't too rushed this morning sweet, and that nobody noticed you weren't about.'

28 August: *'My dear dear darling wife, In some ways these snatched moments are so cruel – wonderful and happy at the time – but it's so awful to have to leave you again. Everything is alright here. . . . No-one is any the wiser.*

*'You do give me strength and comfort you know – though I may not show it at the time. . . . It's so silly of me to get these fits of depression. I know there is no real cause of it – that there is no concrete fact I could point to as illustrating that I am a complete flop. On the face of it, I get on quite well. It's just that inside me I have the feeling that all my hopes and aims are futile, and that I just haven't got what it takes. . . . It's very weak of me – but I seem to need concrete proof and encouragement – perhaps that's just vanity. But it's a relic of the past – and it's only come on more now – because you have given me higher aims and hopes than I ever had. I expect more from myself now and so I'm more easily disappointed in myself.*

*'I'm afraid darling, I'm not turning out to be all that you thought I*

*was. . . . It tears at my heart to see you cry. I can't cry – but my heart is aching for you. . . . You are more precious to me than life – you are my life and more. Take care of yourself and my child – our child. God bless you, my darling one. You have a strong firm faith – stronger than mine – faith to inspire us both.'*

29 August: 'There hasn't been any post to-day – I think they're giving us a post-less day, like meat-less and milk-less. . . . I went and registered yesterday at the Women's Labour Exchange in Portland Street. Several rather dazed young women, registering people, they'd been at it all day and without a break, poor souls. Took down my particulars. Asked "Any children?" so I said "not yet"; so she said "Expecting? I must put that down. When?" "March" "Next year?" I don't know if she thought it was delayed action till the year after, or what. So there it is on record. I do wish you were here, it's fun firewatching with you, but not otherwise.'

31 August: *'I've just got in from taking the service in the hospital chapel. I gave a 10 min talk on Faith – religion being a faith not a code of morals. They seemed to listen – in fact, I think I heard a pin drop. Anyway, I'm more than ever convinced that you don't just have to give people little stories with a moral or bright and breezy talks. I think if you talk naturally about a subject which is important, and give them a few new ideas – that's what they want. At least, I hope so. . . .*

*'My god – the laziness and the opportunities missed. There is so much to be done but I don't get the chance to do it. I just don't see what the use is of more than one man here in our job. This hanging about, doing office-boy's work, is getting me down.'* Most of his time was spent sorting and delivering registered mail to hospital patients. Cosford was a vast place with a constantly changing population which meant that no airmen were there long enough for the padres to get to know them and their problems – which, in Marcus's opinion, made a chaplain's life pointless and frustrating. He was kept going by (almost) daily letters and rather too frequent telephone calls which contributed to an escalating mess bill. Having little to do apart from the mail, a daily service, occasional confirmation classes, and trying to keep his mind off the separation from Jess, he joined in the activities of the officers' mess with more gusto than might have been expected.

He quite enjoyed the company of the permanent staff, the instructors, medics and administration officers. He drank in the mess with the other officers, played inter-station hockey, golf, squash, bridge and was instructed in the mysteries of shove ha'penny and snooker.

It wasn't long before he was in trouble. 'My fame as a player of shove ha'penny and imperfect bridge had spread widely. Someone wrote to the Bishop of Lichfield in whose diocese we were and complained about me. Shove ha'penny and bridge were apparently sinful occupations for a chaplain. The Bishop wrote to the Senior Chaplain to demand an explanation of this dastardly conduct and I was asked to explain myself. I wrote to the Bishop, indicating that I was not quite clear in what respect bridge and shove ha'penny were specially sinful, and the little storm blew over.

'This incident revealed again the problem of the double standard applied to parsons. All sorts of people seem to enjoy denouncing them behind their backs for behaving like ordinary mortals. What on earth these people expect a parson to be I have never quite found out. I suppose one should try to see this as the failure of religion to make its position clear.'

By 2 September Marcus was complaining: *'I'm bored, bored, bored.'*

4 September: *'The Rector of Wolverhampton has asked me to preach for him on Sunday evening! It's rather a privilege. I feel pretty thrilled. What shall I give 'em – tell me, my darling – "What is Man" "Our sufficiency is of God" or what. I wish you were here to help me and inspire. I shall be very nervous. But at least it's something interesting to look forward to after the dullness of this place.'*

24 September: *'There's such a lot of pettiness and childishness about the place. One or two of the old fossils object to anyone young and young padres in particular. Bryan is so damn casual – but it does seem one has to sit down under a lot of things in this racket. It's hard to get used to and damned undignified. I'm taking the Parade Service on Sunday – and I'm a bit frightened now.'*

30 September: *'I'm afraid I didn't put the sermon across as well as I might on Sunday, I was frightened of the microphone so couldn't let myself go or send my scintillating personality floating across so powerfully as usual.'*

Early in October Jess left the repertory company for the last time (her husband making a flying visit to Southport to attend her last night party). Marcus took seven days' leave and they spent an idyllic belated honeymoon at Lake Vyrnwy in the Cambrian Mountains. Back at Cosford they moved

*Marcus and Jess*

into a flat in Albrighton owned by a friend of the Senior Chaplain, 'two very small rooms upstairs with the use of a posh bathroom and a kitchen and pantry below'. Marcus was, of course, much happier with his lot when he could go home to Jessica, but he was still bored and frustrated. Towards the end of the year he started what he called a 'C of E Club' for discussions, brains trusts and debates and 'to inculcate a sense of fellowship. High ideals – much too high probably. But worth trying.'

At the beginning of February 1942 Marcus and Jess decided that, since Marcus was expecting (and hoping for) another posting in the near future, it would be sensible for Jess to return to her parents-in-law to await the birth of their child. Marcus accompanied Jess up north and left her with Edith and Walter, returning to the lonely bachelor life at the camp.

On the 24th Janet Victoria Harston Morris made her appearance at the Christiana Hartley Maternity Hospital in Southport. Mother Dunning joined the family party at the vicarage and Marcus, unable to get away for more than twenty-four hours, again resorted to long letters.

1 March: '*So you are getting along pretty well are you and giving the stuff to the troops regularly. I wish I could be in Janet's place for a bit and have you put your arms around me. . . . My darling, I don't want to worry you, but I'm in rather a fix financially. I've paid off rather too much on bills this month and after paying off my mess bill (only £3!) I shall have 14/- to last me the whole of March. Once I'm through March I shall be almost clear of current bills and quite clear in another month or so. But I'm worried because I promised to send you at least £5 this month. . . . I'm not much good to you, my darling, I'm afraid. I am trying though and perhaps someday I may be a bit more worthy of you. Forgive me again, will you my dear.*'

4 March:' I'm sorry about the money, love, but don't worry – something'll turn up – we'll manage, never you fear. . . . Janet's a gem – definitely an acquisition to the family – family habits too, eats like a horse, sleeps all day and wakes up at night. She's a pretty handsome piece too – Mummy says she's exactly like you although she's so dark.'

Jess was in hospital for two weeks under a regimen that would astound modern mothers: 'Wake at 5, cup of tea, feed infant, wash & brush up, bed made, breakfast 7.30, pause until elevenses at 10, feed infant. That takes until about 10.45 after which I try and get a little exercise – consisting of lying first on my right side for 10 minutes, then on my tummy then my left side. Then either letters or blanket bath then lunch then sleep, then feed infant at 2, then visitors, tea at 3.45, wash & brush up, feed infant at 6, visitors 6.30, supper 7, finish visitors 8.30. After which your time is more or less your own, apart from a wash & brush up at 9.30 until you feed the babe at eleven.'

Marcus got forty-eight hours leave to help Jess and Janet move to the vicarage and on his return to Wolverhampton learned that he was posted, with immediate effect, to Oxfordshire (much to the relief of his mother, who had feared his being sent abroad; Teddy was with the RAF in Ceylon).

Letters show that, although Marcus thought he had not been getting anywhere at Cosford, he certainly did good in some quarters and was remembered with much more affection than was his Senior Chaplain, with whom Marcus was on terms of some acrimony.

'I shall never be able to thank you enough for the wonderful way in which you helped me at Cosford. I was really fed up during my first few days but after meeting you my life began anew and at the time of my posting overseas it was to me, a second home.'

'You helped me through a very bad bit of road and I am very gratified. God bless you and help you in your very difficult job.'

'I have thoroughly enjoyed the activities of the Club, and I wish it every success in the future. I also wish you every good wish in the future – and may some, at least, of our common hopes be realised. I hope that there will be some similar activities where I am posted. Please accept my thanks for all you have done for us at Cosford and for the interest you have taken.'

'Your going has been a definite loss to the Station. After all, the impression seems to be that you were a person of colour, and did amount to something. There is at least one person with whom contact with you resulted in a definite benefit. If I were you I should forget all about Bryan. After all, he never amounted to very much and would have made quite a passable compère on most seaside piers during the summer.' This last from Frank Pritchard, an officer at Cosford who remained a friend for many years.

The new posting, RAF Benson, near Wallingford, was a photographic reconnaissance unit. The station had been brick-built in the 1930s and was very comfortable. There were three chaplains, Anglican, Roman Catholic and Non-Conformist; the Station Commander had no use for any of them and made no bones about it. Initially, however, Marcus was full of hope and enthusiasm:

*The doting parents*

15 March: '*This place is going to be pretty good. I'm the only C of E Chaplain here, and Comforts and Welfare Officer as well – so perhaps there'll be enough to do. . . . There's quite a lot of cleaning up to do and plenty of opportunity for starting things. . . . We got a trip into Oxford yesterday and had tea. It gave me acute nostalgia to see it all again. . . . Rex Harrison is stationed here, we had quite a chat yesterday. He seems very pleasant. They are getting up a concert soon – with big pots from round about – Ivor Novello etc.*'

17 March: '*You know, coming to a new place isn't too easy. One feels a little uncouth and raw. But now whenever I feel a bit distrait or uncomfortable and nervous, I just to have to think of my wife and I feel alright again immediately. . . . I have an elderly Waaf clerk to do odd jobs for me so I'm beginning to feel like a city businessman.*'

He certainly had more to do than at Cosford. 26 March: '*Can you please forgive me? It is such ages since I wrote to you. I have been so very busy. I go down to the office every morning soon after nine and am there till nearly one. Then in the afternoon, sick visiting, seeing prisoners in the guardroom, going to the Satellite Station and/or more office till six or seven. Then in the evening I'm either doing sermons or going round to various do's which I'm expected to put in an appearance at. Last night there was the fortnightly Ensa show – and very good. Tonight the Waafs are having a dance and I promised to look in. Tomorrow morning, I have to go into Oxford to see solicitors on behalf of an airman. Then back for the afternoon's office and choir practice in the evening and more sermon.*'

By the end of April Squadron Leader The Reverend and Mrs Morris, and Miss Morris, had settled in at Turner's Court, near Benson, a training school for backward boys, where Ivy Morgan took them in. 'They just arrived on the doorstep; people did in the war. I lent them cutlery and sheets and put them up in a gardener's cottage in the grounds for a while, then they moved to a nice little wooden cottage in the middle of Oakley Wood.' Ivy was a good friend to Marcus and Jess and stood as godmother to their second child. Marcus helped out at Turner's Court and acted as chaplain there, which he found of rather more value than his RAF chaplaincy. The indifference of his superiors and fellow officers soon began to irk.

He found he could not communicate with the pilots, who flew Mosquitos solo from Benson. He visited the squadron huts, thinking that religion might help them in their dangerous work, but they had no use for him. And 'the non-flying personnel, basking with unpleasant and unjustifiable conceit in the fighting man's glory, displayed an almost complete lack of discipline and leadership. Very few officers turned up at church parade, the CO only once, when he read the lesson on Easter Day. I can't imagine the CO in the Navy or Army giving such a bad example.

'I am not in favour of compulsory church parades, but I seemed to have the worst of both worlds. I always suspected that the small congregation had been detailed off to attend.'

In spite of the Commanding Officer's antagonism, Marcus organised a series of lectures at Benson. The scheme worked well and aroused a goodly amount of interest, but suffered a setback when one of the lecturers, a well-known titled gentleman, arrived at the Station drunk. 'I will not readily forget that evening. I was quickly aware that the distinguished and famous lecturer had been to a lively and lavish party. He recaptured its atmosphere in the Mess bar until dinner, when he became rather aggressive and kept referring to the CO as "You silly little man". The CO behaved with considerable restraint and politeness, but the strain was beginning to tell.

'The lecture hall was packed out. The lecturer rolled around the stage; muttered and gabbled incoherently; read the same page of his notes several times and found it equally uninteresting each time. In the end I couldn't stand it any longer. I sneaked out as quietly and inconspicuously as I could, and paced up and down outside until it was over. The Station Commander stuck it out – showing the superiority of service over clerical discipline.'

Fortunately for Marcus his other celebrities remained sober. When John Masefield came, 'the hall was packed and the poet, white-haired, shaggy-maned, mounted the platform and read some of his poems in a quiet voice. The audience was silent and spellbound – rows and rows of Air Force men and women, absolutely still, absolutely fascinated.'

The lecture by Sir Richard Acland, MP, founder of The Commonwealth Party, was not so uncontroversial. Marcus wrote to him: 'I am told that politics are barred in the services. I don't quite know what that means and it seems very ridiculous. I don't think it really affects these talks. I imagine Social Reconstruction can be discussed without fear of mutiny.

'I am quite prepared to carry the can; in fact I should enjoy it on an issue such as private ownership. I have already been accused to the CO of being a Bolshevic, which term apparently includes anyone who is concerned with the welfare of the airmen. He also questioned me about my intentions in arranging this series of talks and all I could do was assure him that I wasn't trying to start a revolution in the RAF. To my mind the whole purpose of these talks would be lost if they were restricted in any way.'

The charge of Bolshevism might well have arisen from Marcus's having invited the Russian Ambassador to speak at the Station (he declined due to pressure of work). Other prospective speakers who turned down invitations for one reason or another included George Bernard Shaw (advancing years); Emlyn Williams (rehearsing new production); A.P. Herbert (away on duty with the RNAP); Sir William Beveridge (too busy but ask again later); J.B. Priestley (urgent work on hand); Leslie Howard (going to the USA for the opening of *The First of The Few*) and Professor C.E.M. Joad (Ministry of Information decides his speaking programme).

Lord Elton made time between his parliamentary duties to speak on 'Background for a new social order', a subject which so underwhelmed the personnel at Benson that Group Captain Busse felt obliged to apologise to the noble lord for the small audience. Elton replied that 'All speakers know that the attendance at meetings, in war or peace, is always unpredictable!'

Marcus wrote at length to Lady Ravensdale about a memo she had sent him concerning religion in the forces and assured her that she would not get shouted down if she gave a talk at Benson. 'I am sure you would be right to emphasise the spiritual and moral issues involved. I always feel that the reception of these matters depends on the way they are introduced and presented and they will be more impressed when it does not come from the Chaplain who is paid to say these things!'

Marcus fell foul of the powers-that-be by agreeing expenses with his lecturers without due authority. He put in a request for petrol coupons to the Regional Committee of Education for HM Forces, so that he could pick up his speakers from the railway station, but didn't wait for the go-ahead, which annoyed the Committee's secretary: 'You know already, I am sure, of the very strict regulations drawn up by the Air Ministry under which all lecturers under Regional Committee schemes are to be in possession of Certificates of Employment, stamped by the Provost-Marshal's Department of the RAF. I was a little uneasy, therefore, about accepting responsibility on behalf of my Committee for the definite arrangements which you appear to have made. . . . It would not be proper for us to issue petrol coupons for the journeys named.'

The matter was referred to the RAF's Chaplain-in-Chief's Chaplain and somehow the petrol coupons were found.

By the time the 'Red' Dean of Canterbury came to give his talk, Marcus had had enough of the petty bureaucracy and the indifference he found at the Station. 3 April: 'I feel compelled to write to you suggesting the cancellation of the visit which you so kindly agreed to pay to this Station. . . . The talks so far have been excellent but the attendances have been bad and the general response, official and otherwise has been negligible. In view of this I no longer feel justified in asking important speakers to come here when I know that their time is fully occupied with more important things. And I cannot feel that this Station deserves the privilege of hearing them.' But Dr Hewlett Johnson gave his talk and later wrote to Marcus, 'I have the happiest recollections of my time at Benson. I thought the numbers were splendid considering the difficulties, and more than worth while. I talked until after midnight in the Mess, practically never sat down from half past eight until twelve o'clock.'

Letters in the same vein to Dorothy L. Sayers and the Archbishop of Canterbury, with whom tentative arrangements had been made, were more successful in putting the speakers off.

Marcus asked his superiors at the Air Ministry to move him to a station with a more sympathetic CO; they thought it prudent to ignore the request and he continued his lonely battle. 'Perhaps the biggest disadvantage of all was that I held the rank of Squadron Leader and wore a Squadron Leader's uniform. That, I thought, was quite ridiculous. Chaplains should have no rank at all; then at least they would have been able to start without one of their most serious hindrances.

'In the end I found that I was just a welfare officer, with an occasional religious function. I handed out woolly mufflers and socks and scarves and weeded out those who genuinely needed compassionate leave. I do not criticise welfare officers, they perform an admirable and necessary function. But I was not a welfare officer, I was a chaplain, with mainly religious responsibilities.

'I'm prepared to admit that I was probably a bad chaplain.'

Not everybody thought so. WAAF Joan Parr: 'I should like to thank you very much for your kindness to me while at Benson. It does make such a difference to one to have a padre who is interested as to whether one goes to church or stays away. . . . I really enjoyed cleaning the chapel!'

Corporal Douglas Belston: 'May I sincerely thank you for all the opportunities you gave me to receive the sacraments and for worship and also for the assistance you gave me in my plans to take Holy Orders. Best wishes for the film services, dramatic and play-reading society and all your other enterprises at Benson. . . . I can most certainly assure you that there are many who really appreciate your help even if they are slow in expressing that fact.'

Marcus again: 'I wasn't alone in my predicament. John Collins, later to become Canon of St Paul's Cathedral, was an RAF chaplain and felt very much the same as I did. He had to fight quite hard for his rights although he was a much older man than I and his reputation carried a good deal of weight.'

Marcus complained that the Chaplain's Department failed to support their chaplains; that chaplains who fought for recognition of the importance of their spiritual work were liable to be posted 'for the sake of peace and quiet'. Chaplains were at the mercy of the CO, whose indifference or hostility could mean that religion played no real part in the life of a station. 'It is almost impossible to break through the barrier to get to the men.'

After a great deal of thought and indecision and advice from various quarters, Marcus decided that he had to get out of the RAF and started looking about for other jobs.

Dean Dwelly of Liverpool told him, 'You would be well advised to get experience as a teacher. Not for long. T [Temple, Archbishop of Canterbury] himself was not long a schoolmaster. . . . I have no hesitation in agreeing you leave chaplaincy for experience in a school.'

Kenneth Budd, with whom Marcus had corresponded in Yarmouth with a view to revolutionising the Church and who was now also an RAF chaplain, wrote: 'You would be well advised to take up different work which offers you the scope you need. I don't think that one is "running away" because one's fitness is for a sphere of work different from one's present job. You may have been unlucky in your station, but the whole business of chaplains' work in the RAF is unsatisfactory and I could write a considerable amount about my own experience and what I think of those who are responsible for our dept. All clergy ought to have a spell as chaplains so that they could see for themselves what we are up against. Go for a job for which you are more suited and in which your particular gifts would find the scope they ought to have.'

Messrs Gabbitas, Thring & Co, the educational employment agency in London, put Marcus in touch with a number of schools and colleges. Stallybrass of Brasenose, whom Jess and Marcus visited frequently during their time at Benson, wrote to the Oxford University Appointments Committee in March 1943, 'Morris is a thoughtful man, who had some religious difficulties before he got ordained. He feels that he is wasting his time in the RAF, and gets no chance of doing the more important work on the spiritual side. I have told him that I think there might be some criticism which it would not be very easy to answer if a man of his age at the present time wished to resign from the Service in order to take up a school chaplaincy. . . . He is anxious to read more widely in his own field, and would be much above the average in any teaching work that he might take. I think he ought to be quite effective with boys as a chaplain and that his wife would be a help rather than a hindrance. I think the only thing that would make me hesitate if I had the appointment would be my fear that he is by nature rather unsettled. . . . I myself think that he would do much better to take a living. . . .'

While Marcus was debating whether or not to take up a post at Cranleigh School, 'Sonners' mentioned that there was a living in Essex in the gift of the College which had fallen vacant; Marcus could have it if he wished. Marcus did wish. On 2 April 1943, Stallybrass wrote formally, 'I am happy to inform you that the College has unanimously decided to present you to the living of Weeley. I hope that you and Mrs Morris will be very happy there.' The Bishop of Chelmsford gave the depressing news that 'the income of Weeley is depleted to £300 p.a.'. At the beginning of the nineteenth century it had been worth £600.

Marcus wrote to Dwelly, 'I looked first for a school job as you suggested but there seemed to be nothing suitable and I thought that if I went to a school at all it ought to be a really good one. And then the offer of Weeley came out of the blue. . . . It will give me the independence and responsibility and security that I want so much now.'

On 20 April, Marcus sent a letter of resignation to the CO at Benson and wrote more fully to the Chaplain-in-Chief of the Royal Air Force: 'I have tried for nearly two years to adapt myself to the life and work of a chaplain but it has now become quite clear to me that I shall never be able to do this. I am convinced that I am totally unsuited for this type of work and have no sense of vocation for it. As a result, I have become increasingly unhappy in my work until now I feel that I can endure the strain no longer and that to continue would only be harmful.

'I am very sorry from every point of view that this should be so as I very much hoped when I joined up that I should be able to do useful work. . . . I have been offered a Benefice in Essex which offers just the kind of work for which I feel I am most suited and I am sure that I could exercise a much more effective ministry there. In these circumstances, I shall be most grateful if you will accept my resignation.'

On 26 May he received a reply from the Secretary at the Air Ministry: 'I am commanded by the Air Council to convey approval of your application to resign your commission in the Royal Air Force Volunteer Reserve on the understanding that you refund two-thirds of the outfit grant which was issued to you when you were commissioned. . . . I am to take this opportunity of bringing to your notice the provisions of the Official Secrets Acts, 1911 and 1920, which make it an offence for any person who has held office under His Majesty to disclose any matter or information which he has obtained or to which he has had access in the course of holding that office. This covers disclosure in any form, whether orally or in writing or by publication in the press or in book form.'

Why was Marcus allowed to resign his commission in the middle of hostilities? There can have been very few people who were happy about their situation during the war. Indeed, the Bishop of Liverpool commented, 'I wonder a little how you can have secured your release, for the RAF are very short of chaplains as it is.'

Did the RAF object to his 'Bolshevism', to his rabble rousing sermons, to his habit of consorting with the 'other ranks'; or did he make a pass at the CO's wife? He had signed on for the duration. Why was he not posted to another station, or overseas? (Other married padres – for instance, Angus MacIntyre and Brian Whitlow, not to mention his brother-in-law, Eric Cook, who was posted to Norway towards the end of the war – went overseas.)

When Ruari McLean (about whom more later) was writing his autobiography, he included – verbatim – what Marcus had told him about his RAF days: 'Marcus was told "Oh no, you won't have anything to do with the airmen, you're an officer" and Marcus said he was expected to play strip poker with the officers and was not allowed to talk to the Erks. That was what he told me – so he resigned – but when I put that more or less word for word in my chapter on Marcus, he made me modify it and tone it down.'

The Venerable Brian Lucas, the present Chaplain-in-Chief of the RAF, wrote to us: 'A member of my management team has investigated the matter. After so many years it is impossible to ascertain the precise reasons behind [Marcus's] resignation. Certainly there is no indication in the records held here that his resignation was prompted by anything other than [his] view that he was not the right type of priest to be a military chaplain. There is not the slightest suggestion that he was asked to resign and I cannot believe that the Chaplain-in-Chief of the day would have viewed his sermon of 24 January 1943 [at Benson] as grounds for dismissal/resignation.

'It is often the case that we discover our rightful sphere of ministry by the experience of mistakes and disappointments. . . . It is likely that he moved on to a new sphere of ministry simply because of a realisation that the RAF was not the right place for him.

'Such changes of direction happen today. No doubt they always have and always will.' Even during a war?

The sermon referred to by Brian Lucas may not have been resigning material, but it can hardly have been popular with the high-ups, either within the Service or the Church. Marcus said: 'The masses of ordinary working people are beginning to look for a far larger part in the running of the country. They are struggling for power and the right to govern themselves. The time is past when people are willing to be governed by the so-called upper classes – the professional politicians and old-school-tie rulers. . . . The life of the ordinary working man is full of troubles and worries which, he feels, the church and the parsons don't experience.

'It is the greatest tragedy of our times that the ordinary person . . . is no longer willing to look to the Church for leadership in his struggle for betterment and security. I think it is that which is responsible for the decline of religion today, far more than any doubts about the truth of the Christian faith . . . the Church of England . . . must leave its secure position in the old order and voluntarily cross over to the other side and throw in her lot with those whom Christ declared that he came to seek and save. . . .

'It is certainly the duty of the Christian Gospel to see that every man gets good housing, good education, social equality and security – that's why the church *must* interfere in politics. . . . The Church must make drastic changes to prove that she is concerned with the well-being of the masses of mankind and she must stop just telling men to be good and not to break the ten commandments. . . . And on the other side, men will have to realise that their brave new world can only be solidly founded if they remember that central teaching of Christ – that man is *more* than a material being and life *more* than economic prosperity.'

One of the first letters Marcus received in his new parish was from the Warden of Turner's Court boys' home at Wallingford: 'The Committee last week resolved "that they place on record their appreciation of the services rendered to the colony by Sq Leader the Rev JM Morris during the nine months in which he assisted, as Honorary Chaplain, and his contribution to the religious life of the colony" and I was requested to convey their thanks to you which I do most cordially.'

A little later, A.G. Leslie Smith, Marcus's successor at Benson, wrote, 'I am afraid I am beginning to feel much the same as you did; the situation here hasn't improved at all, in fact I think it has got worse. . . . The new CO seems less interested in our side of things than his predecessor. I feel very disappointed and discouraged, I am quite sure I did far more good in a parish: I regret now I ever came into the Service. What I want to know is, what are the chances of getting out? I don't want to stay in, wasting my time on so many secular jobs when so many parishes are understaffed and where one can really do the work for which one was ordained. I believe there are others who have got out beside yourself, so I know it is not impossible, although I was told by the Senior Chaplain that no one could be released till after the war!'

# Chapter Five

At the end of May 1943 Marcus, Jess and Janet arrived in the small Essex village of Weeley, between Colchester and Clacton. Saint Andrew's Church was set on top of one of the few hills in the area, surrounded by fields and some way from the village. The huge rectory, a good mile from the church, was old and beautiful, rambling and primitive; it had five stables and was surrounded by a lovely garden, wild and overgrown but full of potential. There were great oak trees in the grounds and seven acres of glebe.

There was no power in the rectory and to begin with they used candles and oil lamps; water had to be pumped by hand into the cistern. Soon after they arrived Jess's Aunt Nell came up trumps with the offer of furniture for the house, bare save for beds and the piano. The following year the Patrons of Brasenose agreed to a loan from Queen Anne's Bounty for the installation of electricity.

The previous incumbent, Mr Alfred William Moore Weatherly (brother of the lyricist Frederick, who formed a partnership with Michael, brother of James Maybrick, and wrote 'Danny Boy' and 'Roses of Picardy'), had been there for many years and was an old man when he retired. He was most anxious that Marcus and Jess should enjoy their new living and feel at home in Weeley. In a long correspondence he described the kitchen oven as 'in good condition and careful firelighting may lengthen its life for some time. The Ideal Boiler with its cylinder is a good asset. . . . The anthracite stove in the study will be a great advantage in the winter.'

Marcus's institution took place on 29 May. The Bishop of Colchester wrote, 'It was a great pleasure to me to come and institute you and I was sorry I could not stay to the tea. The large gathering of clergy and people must have been a great encouragement to you. I was very glad your father was able to be present. May all your and Jessica's wishes be fulfilled in November.'

Jess was expecting again. Marcus wrote, 'As my family was about to be enlarged and I was very short of money, I decided I had to make full use of the garden and glebe land. Although I'd never worked with my hands before, I became a market gardener.

'The villagers thought I was mad. I had help from a seventy-year-old farm worker, Bill Martin, who irritated me with his slow and steady pace – but I soon realised that, when I gave up exhausted from hacking and digging, he was still going strong. I wore breeches, boots, a sweater and gloves and attacked the land with billhook and saw, and found I had a fine garden with walnut trees, peaches, apples, pears and plums.

'I laid down an asparagus bed, double-trenching two spits deep with the spade, manuring and setting the plants. But we were gone before it matured and never enjoyed the fruits of my back-breaking toil. [Marcus was to be retired and living in the west country before he was able to enjoy his own home-grown asparagus.]

'We kept a goat, but I found the milking of it excessively fiddly and replaced it with a cow called Flossy. She was a patient, peaceable, friendly animal, a cross between a Guernsey and a Red Poll. She needed to be understanding and tolerant. Sometimes I forgot to milk her until 10 o'clock at night, when I would go down with a torch or candles and milk pail. She never seemed to hold it against me, apart from the odd reproachful look. She tended to swish her tail rather a lot and I used to tie it to her leg with a handkerchief.

'Unhappily, like all cows, Flossy didn't give milk all year round. When she went dry my farmer friends advised me it was time to take her to the bull. I was surprised and a little touched to find that Flossy must have been the most reluctant cow the bull had ever seen. She was extraordinarily coy. I don't know whether living in ecclesiastical surroundings had had any effect on her.

'We also kept ducks and geese, which I penned in very carefully and fed very generously with Christmas in mind. It was very disillusioning to go out one morning and find that the fox had taken every one. The pig was more satisfactory and showed some return for the food and care I lavished on him. When he was ready the local butcher came round and slaughtered him with a long knife. The pig had time to give one shrill, human-sounding shriek, which made the killing sound like murder. The pork, however, was very welcome; so too was the ham which I cured myself.' They also kept a sow, which had at least one farrow.

'I became the very model of a domesticated parson. I designed a fireplace for the dining room, using a great oak beam given to me by Mr Weeley, the eccentric and irascible lord of the manor. One of the local farmers told me that the magnificent copper boiler in the huge boiler house simply cried out to be brewed in. He gave me the recipe and we produced some magnificent home-brew. If I had known it was illegal I wouldn't have done it; but I was happily ignorant and happily not found out. I don't think I have ever drunk a beer which tasted as good. When Jess's brother Jim, who was stationed at Harwich, brought over a party of sailors and Wrens to give a concert in the village hall after the fête, we entertained them with this beer in the rectory afterwards.

'We tidied up the glebe and planted potatoes. I did the ploughing myself; the farmers lent me a plough and tractor and turned up to give advice as I worked. When the time came I harrowed between ridges and used a spinner to lift the crop. Some of my female parishioners – not the ones I saw most often in church – picked up the potatoes. I tried to grow cucumbers but the weather was too dry, the ground became parched and not one seed came up. I had a certain amount of success with lettuces which we sent up by lorry to London. It always amazed me that when they were bought from me they were a penny-ha'penny and when they were sold half a day later the price had gone up to 1/3d. I still do not understand.'

He tried to grow mushrooms in the cellar in carefully tended buckets of manure. When nothing happened he threw the lot on the compost heap, where the mushrooms immediately flourished.

'I made some money cutting down trees to sell as logs, not realising that I needed permission. I got my knuckles rapped but didn't have to repay the money. I was young and very fit and the outdoor life agreed with me. '

Walter wrote with tips for growing broad beans and tomatoes. He hoped that Marcus was keeping separate accounts for his garden produce and sent £5 to help pay for the cow. 'You need to give a lot of thought to this farming business. You can *not* go on, going to bed at one and getting up at 6.30 – and I am rather disturbed at your idea of doing still more. . . . You cannot possibly have time for much serious reading, to prepare yourself for a bigger job. BNC have some really important livings. . . .

'I hope you are getting over your worry complex. . . . We should like whatever you can get us for Christmas in the way of birds: send them in *boxes*, if you can, so that their nature is not too obvious to the railway thieves.'

The domesticated parson appears to have kept his parents well supplied with chickens, ducks, geese and eggs, sent up to Southport by train. Marcus started a youth club and its members were roped in to help with the house and garden; they were very shocked to hear the parson swear at them when they knocked over his cabbage plants or trod on his lettuces.

Meanwhile a pregnant Jess was coping with a young child in the vast, cold rectory with occasional help from people in the village. There were also those who disapproved of the rector's beautiful young wife.

'I produced the children in charades and plays.' Jess said. 'Did Shakespeare of course, poor little beasts. The mother of Bottom was one of my fiercest enemies. On the morning of the production she said that her son was not going to play Bottom, so I did.'

They held a fête in the rectory garden in August which was a great success. The children of Weeley presented two short plays. A space ride was rigged up between two of the huge oaks. There were horse and pony rides, bowling for the pig, sports and games, vegetable and wild flower competitions, a Fancy Dress Parade. It ended with a concert and dancing in the village hall and raised £149.10s.5½d. Mr Weatherly wrote, 'Thank you so much for your letter and its account of the fine result of your fête. I hope it will start a fresh era of annual fêtes. . . . I think with great happiness of your warm reception. . . . Mrs Weatherly came back very happy in having formed a friendship with you which for both of us will be an abiding possession.'

But Marcus found that village life was riven with strife and petty jealousies. Not everybody approved of the dashing young parson going to dances and drinking in the Black Boy where, as he said, 'the sinners gather – if the congregation won't come to me, I must go to them.' Rumours of immoral goings-on circulated; Marcus was suspected of having affairs. No change then, from the sixteenth century, when the curate was accused of misbehaviour with a married woman.

In June he was given a bicycle to ease his journeyings around the parish. Annie Fisher wrote: 'When my husband brought the bicycle to Church on

*Weeley Rectory*

Sunday evening for your inspection he was acting on my suggestion as I remarked that you looked tired on Sunday afternoon and I was sorry you had so much walking to do. . . . Last night it was suggested to him that he was combining with Mr Syrett to dispose of an inferior machine. . . . I lived very pleasantly with everyone until I started helping at the Sunday School when a little unpleasantness arose. . . . although [my husband] has no office in the Church and we are socially unimportant he will always be ready to help the Church in any way he can.'

Walter sympathised: 'Your experience with certain parishioners is common everywhere. As long as you give them no real handle, ignore it. The fête and your church life shows that you have some good friends.' He advised Marcus not to worry about his parish; he should do more visiting, he should not restrict his social club to church members and should think twice about starting a parish magazine.

A parishioner wrote, 'Your acute depression rather concerns me.' There followed a long lecture on the parson's lot and the jealousy of an un-named parishioner who was trying to undermine Marcus's good work. 'The vast majority of the people are all for you. Even you must be convinced by now . . . you will go from strength to strength in your great work here.'

Joan Weeley, the squire's daughter-in-law, remembers Marcus and Jess as 'an extremely nice couple, we were all very fond of them. He was a wonderful rector, one of the best we've ever had. I think he visited everybody, he was always out and about. Being wartime there were lots of things going on in the village. The Red Cross had a dance every week. He was always down there. I remember him dancing, he was very good at it. He was good at listening and advice and very kind with it. He made his sermons very interesting too, one didn't mind going to church when he was rector.'

Parishioner Beth Blowers remembers some of the sermons even now:

'There was an Easter sermon called "The Empty Tomb" – he made it into a detective story. It was very impressive to somebody in the early teens.'

Among Marcus's papers was a manuscript of a detective story called 'The Case of the Missing Body' dating, we believe, from the early 1950s, hand-written by Marcus. It began: 'I was feeling pretty cheerful as I walked briskly along High Street. It's not every day that a budding private detective gets summoned by the city's leading man. Usually it's the same old routine – petty thefts, domestic troubles – and occasionally a nice juicy murder thrown in.

'This looked like being something good. The High Priest's message had sounded urgent. Maybe, I thought, I'm on to a really interesting job for once.

'So I was pretty pleased with life as I approached the house, in spite of the gossiping crowds in the street that you had to push out of the way to get past. I never did like these big Festivals that pack the city like a tin of sardines. [Tins in AD 32?!] And this time it was worse than usual – there was some excitement about that kept people talking and chatting so that you could hardly get along.

'I was shown straight into the High Priest's room. He was evidently in a hurry.

' "There's not much time to spare, Captain Caleb. This matter has got to be settled at once – before it gets out of hand.

' "Here's a problem that will test your wits. I think we might call it 'The Case of the Missing Body.' You've heard about the carpenter from Nazareth who claimed to be the Messiah, I take it?"

' "I've heard rumours, Your Grace."

' "Well, he's disappeared. At least, his body has. And you've got to find it. He was executed last Friday – Pilate was a bit awkward, but we managed to frighten him by threatening to complain to the Emperor if he let the fellow go. He was properly buried – and now we can't find him anywhere. The grave's empty."

' "Why should that worry you, Your Grace? What's so valuable about his body?"

' "Valuable nothing! Haven't you heard, man? His friends are saying he's come back to life again."

' "It sounds like a lot of nonsense to me."

' "Of course it's nonsense. But you know what these peasants are like. These men have stirred up enough people already with their talk. They're getting dangerous. We've got to *prove* it's nonsense."

' "That's not going to be easy, is it?"

' "Only by producing the body – that's why I've sent for you." '

There is nothing to show that this 2,500-word story was ever published, but it seems likely that it was inspired by that Easter Sunday sermon in Essex.

It isn't only Marcus's sermons that are remembered today. Parishioner Betty Betts was very grateful for his help when her father died. 'Marcus took my mother to the hospital in London where my father wasn't expected to last the night, and phoned me to come quickly from Cornwall. He arranged everything and conducted the funeral. Everyone came away elated.'

Fred Weatherly, son of Marcus's predecessor, was away fighting when his father died in October 1943. 'My mother used to mention Marcus and seemed very fond of him. She was so delighted when he took the funeral. She was always grateful for that.'

Marcus started an arts and literary society and held debates, Weeley Street against Weeley Heath. Ignoring Walter's advice, he revamped the parish magazine and talked about starting a religious paper for children.

Six months after the family's arrival in Weeley, 'I shall always remember one meeting of the Parochial Church Council which was held on a dark November evening in 1943 in the rectory dining room. Upstairs in one of the bedrooms, Jess was about to give birth to our second child by the light of oil lamps and candles, attended by the district nurse and the local doctor who, though genial and quite competent, was often not completely sober. There was a very companionable smell of alcohol on his breath. At about midnight came the usual cry which signals a new arrival – a girl we called Kate.' – Jenifer Kate Harston Morris, to give her her full name.

'The growth of the family increased my financial responsibility and I had taken a job in a factory. I wasn't so much a worker-priest as a priest who became a worker to make ends meet. I used to get up before dawn and catch the 7 o'clock bus for Colchester. When I got to the factory I put on overalls, got a large spanner and took my place on the factory floor. I unscrewed bolts. I spent the whole day unscrewing bolts. When I had un-screwed them someone else screwed them up again. I never discovered what the end product was. It gave me some idea of the kind of soulless labour carried out by great numbers of people of whom the Church ought to have the care. I earned between £4.10s and £5.10s a week. My workmates were friendly but showed remarkably little interest in me and my priesthood. At 5.30 in the evening we knocked off and I caught the bus home. I then did my best to clean the oil off my face and hands and changed into clerical clothes and went about my parish work. At some stage I had to remember to milk the patient Flossy.'

The parish was divided about the desirability of their rector covering his hands in oil. 'Those who thought I was mad were confirmed in their opin-ion. Friends approved; others were doubtful or suspicious or highly criti-cal. In the end they decided that a priest-cum-factory-worker was too much and they subscribed the extra money to enable me to support my family and I resigned from my repetitive job.'

The PCC held an emergency meeting two weeks before Kate was born, to discuss their parson's dire financial straits; they were worried that 'the strain of the additional work with its consequent travelling would ultimately prove detrimental to your general health and ... it would be extremely difficult for you to carry out to the full your functions as Rector. ... As the living had depreciated considerably owing to the passing of the Tithe Redemption Act ... a sub-committee should be formed ... to explore the possibilities of the augmentation of the stipend from outside sources.'

Meanwhile they made him a gift of £125 with which to buy a car, the first Marcus had ever owned.

One of the churchwardens, Stanley Sarson, and his wife Mary, were two of Marcus's staunchest supporters and kept in touch for many years; Mary was godmother to the third Morris child. By May 1945, Stanley had lent Marcus £300, free of interest and on flexible repayment terms, although perhaps not intended to be quite as flexible as things turned out. It wasn't until February 1950 that Marcus arranged to pay a small amount each month by banker's order. Other loans were also repaid in those more affluent days. Mr Blowers had asked to be repaid 'When you are a Bishop'. Marcus had the knack of attracting – and keeping – some very good, if long-suffering, friends, in spite of being a hopeless correspondent.

Even his mother and brother complained. Edith: 'We *hope* you are well and flourishing, though we hear nothing at all of you. . . . We should be glad of an *occasional* letter, we have had two from you and one from Jess since we left you in February. . . . Of course we have spoken to you, but these long distance calls are not very satisfactory and are most expensive! Six shillings for about six mins – and we are asked not to make them unless it is absolutely necessary.'

The factory job was not the only one that Marcus took to make ends meet; from January 1944 he also taught Divinity at Hockerill Church of England Training College for Women Teachers at Bishop's Stortford for two guineas a week. In May he was gently upbraided for marking papers in the Archbishop's Examination in Religious Knowledge too severely.

Thanks to the gift of the car, Marcus was able to get about the parish and to his teaching job with more ease. The family of four appears to have been taken to the hearts of much of the parish, but the gossiping continued. In September 1944 Marcus preached a thundering sermon at St Andrew's which seems to show that it was getting to him. Talking about things that spoil community life, he said, 'What, for instance, about endless, futile, dangerous, interminable gossip? There's a dirty habit if you like.

'There are certain people who have nothing better to do than to talk about other people – often spitefully, pettily and maliciously.

'It is commonly said, "Oh, you always get gossip in a village". Well, so much the worse for our villages. If you came to a village where everyone slept with their neighbour's wife, would you be content if someone said, "Oh you always get it in a place this size"? I think you'd say, "Well, let's have a lot less of it". I believe gossip is the most pernicious and underhand, anti-Christian and anti-social immorality that anyone can indulge in.'

He went on to the problem of youth: 'Speaking as a young man myself, I'm a little frightened by all this modern pampering and petting and fussing of young adolescents. Everything, it seems, must be done for the young people. They can do no wrong.

'Well, let the government make a fool of itself over its youth policy. . . . I don't think I'm very narrow minded and I'm as fond of children as anyone, but when I find parents afraid to restrain their offspring and children doing as a matter of course things for which I – and probably you – would have been beaten – then I feel everything's not quite right with the younger generation. He put the problem down to their not receiving a Christian education.

It looks as though the rumours and the rectory got too much for Jess; she wrote a farewell note on a sticky wartime economy label: 'I've left your presents on the bed – except the Carroll which you have apparently taken back. You can send my things. I'll let you know where. I hope you and the children get on better. I think you will. I shall love you to the end of my days and after. Your late wife.'

His mother wrote to Marcus in February 1945, 'I don't like to think of you being all alone at the Rectory with the two children. I thought the Roger Weeleys were staying while Jess was away. . . . '

Edith was under the impression that Jess had been ill and had gone away to convalesce. In later years, Jess often threatened to leave and got as far as packing her bags – only to find, as often as not, that there was no petrol in her car. On this occasion, she wasn't away for long; by the middle of the month Jess and the two girls were at Turner's Court: 'Weeley got more and more difficult. I went and stayed with Ivy and Marcus went up to Southport. When he came back we had a new parish.'

Stallybrass wrote, 'I am very glad that you enjoyed your time [at Weeley] and very sorry that you should be leaving, though I congratulate you on the important job which you have got.'

The parishioners may have been 'troublesome rumour-mongers' but they missed him when he left. One wrote 'I often think about you. Our Friday tea-parties were good fun. . . . It was grand hearing Jess on the wireless . . . we were both excited about it.' Stanley Sarson wrote in December, 'I'm going to miss our Christmas Party this year.' The rest of the letter was full of local news.

Alf and Ella Ellis wrote from The Forge, Weeley Heath, 'We do wish you were still in Weeley, it is so very different now. . . . Alf and I will never listen or believe anything that people say about you or Mrs Morris because we know it to be all lies and spite.' 'Thank you for your good wishes of this morning. I was so disappointed I could have cried as there was no letter from you Rector since June and I feel hurt. We both think the world of you all and always shall.' 'How I should love to see you all again. Weeley is not the same without you. . . . I went to church Christmas morning, it was a cold service no hymns.'

Bill Martin of Amperswick Farm kept the Morris family supplied with chickens, geese and rabbits at Christmas and even the odd piece of butter, and wrote with news of Weeley. 'We only had the children's party this year, no grown-ups' party. The people were very disappointed. I wished you were here. I still go to church, but very few people go.' Mrs Everett: '. . . please don't forget that if you ever want me I will come.'

Kate's godfather Raymond Pearson wrote, 'Both Sarson and I felt that the party concerned endeavoured to use you for a particular reason, possibly to cover up faults on his side. . . . Do you remember the night of Kate's christening? What fireworks. . . . Your successor is not very popular and often I hear people say they wish you had never left. I really smile at that, because it so happens that it comes from quarters where you were not appreciated whilst you were here.'

Marcus's reply was non-committal: 'The food here is not what it was at Weeley. Janet still regards Weeley Rectory as her home and still assumes that we shall be going back there one day. It is really rather pathetic.'

Jan was very upset that Flossy couldn't go with them.

# Chapter Six

Birkdale was a prosperous suburb of Southport – of which town Mr Oglethorpe in J.B. Priestley's *Good Companions* said, 'I once went for a day to Southport to see t'sea, but I nivver saw it, not a drop. It were a take-in, that.' The sea at Southport is certainly elusive – the wide flat beach is backed by large dunes covered in coarse grass as sharp as a knife.

Rich Victorian manufacturers from Liverpool had built grand houses with spacious gardens in Birkdale and before the war it was reputed to be the richest parish in England. It is said that there were seven millionaires living within a quarter of a mile of the church.

The Parish of St James had for many years been presided over by an ancient cleric, Canon Lancelot, who had retired there in 1917 through ill health, at the age of fifty-three, and surprised everyone by living another twenty-seven years. When he died in December 1944 the trustees decided that a younger man was needed to rejuvenate the stultified parish. In January 1945 the Secretary of the Parochial Church Council was asked to write to the Bishop and say that it was desirable that the new vicar should be young, married and appeal to the younger generation.

Marcus Morris was an obvious candidate. Walter always swore that he did nothing to influence the trustees, but the Morrises had known one of them, Canon Blakeney, Rector of St Cuthbert's, Southport, for many years.

Canon Blakeney told Marcus, 'All your qualifications as far as I can see meet the wishes of the PCC. The living is financially a good one to a man who puts life and energy into his work, is tactful in dealing with people and a helpful and thoughtful preacher and who is definitely a broad-minded evangelical and has a wife who will take a lead in the life of the parish. . . . The house is a very good one and not too large and there is a small garden. There are two other men being considered but I brought your name before the Committee.'

Walter simply advised, 'The time to go into details will be when you have been offered the job. . . . The attractions to you probably are 1) The position. 2) The money. The highest consideration is "Where can I best do my work and serve God?" Don't worry – if you pray . . . you will be led aright. . . . I don't believe that St James is an "only chance" not to be missed. With your degree you ought to have many chances in the days to come. The Churchmanship at St James is definitely evangelical, and if anyone went there and tried to make changes too soon, the people (and the income) would just "go". . . .'

Edith wrote, 'We have not heard anything about St J except last week Canon B told Dad he heard from you and you would be considered along with the other two. We don't know who they are and Dad has not enquired anything about it, so that if it should be offered to you it cannot be said he had anything to do with it.'

At the end of February Marcus had lunch with Canon Blakeney and the other trustees, who included Alderman Charlton, fifty-ninth mayor of

Southport. They appeared to like him. Marcus promised not to introduce popish practices to Birkdale and was offered the living.

Dean Dwelly of Liverpool dashed off a quick note to Jess in his barely legible hand: 'My dear, This is just a line to say how glad I am that you and your Marcus are coming to Birkdale – you will both enjoy putting young life into it.'

Eric Cook congratulated the parish on its good fortune by writing to the vicar-elect, 'I have every confidence that your work will be full of success, and that you will find happiness in Southport once again. . . . It will be great to have you near us when we settle down again, and between us all we should be able to keep the diocese agog. No wonder the Bishop of Warrington [Gresford Jones] has asked to be relieved of his duties!

'Mary has sent me a copy of the [Southport] *Visiter*, detailing all your past accomplishments. I had no idea you were such a brainy bird, and am more convinced than ever that you will end up as my Archdeacon. . . . I should like to have added further details of your career such as your search for human contact in such fruitful spheres as the Ritz, the Berkeley and the Dorchester. . . . I can see Jess becoming nostalgic for the Little again. . . . She will lend that oomph so lacking in the circle of our clergy wives. . . .'

Inevitably some people thought it was a bit of a fiddle and that Walter had used his influence but Gerrard Clough, a parishioner over the years of both All Saints and St James, says, 'Canon Morris didn't push it; the one who encouraged and persuaded Marcus was Blakeney.'

The Victorian vicarage in Lulworth Road was large by modern standards but smaller and more manageable than the rectory at Weeley; so too was the garden and there was no glebe. It must have been a great relief to Jess after the primitive life in Essex, though she may have felt uneasy about living so close to her mother-in-law who, she said, bullied Marcus (and everybody else!).

The Institution of the Revd J.M.H. Morris by the Lord Bishop of Liverpool to the Living of St James and his Induction by the Archdeacon of Liverpool took place on Friday, 1 June, in the red sandstone church which was built in 1856 to serve a population of 625.

By 1945 the population had risen to 3,000 but St James had a very small congregation of old ladies and, despite being surrounded by wealth, the church and church hall were very run down. Marcus forgot about market gardening (though he kept chickens in the back garden) and got down to the real job of being a parson.

His first task was to clean up the parish Memorial Hall. It had been rarely used; Canon Lancelot had not approved of frivolous activities, apart from the occasional supper, and it was full of dusty old books of sermons and theological dissertations. The books were sold in aid of church funds and Marcus went down on his hands and knees and scrubbed and polished the floor. The walls were painted and a stage (of sorts) installed.

Then, as at Yarmouth, Cosford, Benson and Weeley, the activities started.

In his first issue of the parish magazine, Marcus expressed his gratitude for the family's welcome in the parish and for 'the generous financial help that has been given us through the Easter offering towards the renovations at the Vicarage and the cost of removal. . . . I naturally have many hopes and plans which I shall put before you as time goes on. . . . Our common faith is expressed and the foundation laid of a sound and vital parish life, first of all, by uniting regularly in public worship.

'But the Church ought to be the centre of parish life in a wider sense. . . . It should be possible for us to meet on many occasions for social activities of varied kinds.'

Parishioner Audrey Entwistle was then aged fourteen. She remembers the morning in 1945 when her elder sister, Phyllis, rushed into their house round the corner from the church, bright-eyed with excitement, crying, 'Guess who's going to be our new vicar! Jessica Dunning's husband!'

Audrey kept a detailed and very personal diary of the next few years describing her highly charged relationship with Jessica Dunning and her husband. She wrote of their first meeting: 'That first close-up impression of him stamped on my mind a feeling of awe. By no stretch of the imagination could he be called good-looking, but there was a merry twinkle in his clear blue eyes and the occasional smile, playing at the corners of his mouth, had a fascinating charm of its own, which made him look positively attractive.' Audrey was in love!

Audrey's father, Edward, had been a member of the PCC since 1940; most of the Entwistle family attended Marcus and Jess's first At Home in July and Audrey was an enthusiastic helper at the first garden party, in August, which became an annual event.

'Gosh, he looked warm! Mr Morris was busy with a dibber, boring holes in the well-kept lawn to take the posts for the cocoanut [sic] shy. Perspiration was streaming down his flushed face, long strands of fair hair dangling in his eyes, dog collar and black front cast aside and striped blue shirt open at the neck.

' "I don't think we shall be troubled with wind tomorrow," remarked Mr Dennis Watson, whereupon the Vicar, sans dog collar, sans black front, and sans dignity replied, "That rather depends upon what we have for dinner." '

The following morning, Marcus was up at six o'clock. 'It was a magnificent success and I think everyone agreed that even if we had had the ordering of the weather in our own hands we could not have managed it better. The vicar had effected a quick change during the dinner hour and now looked immaculate in dog collar, black front and dark grey suit with a red-speckled yellow carnation in his button-hole and his fair hair, so recently tousled with exertion, was brushed sleek and shiny, so that in some lights it seemed to form a sort of halo round his fine shapely head.'

The event, duly recorded in the PCC minutes, raised £187.17s.9d (over £3,500 in today's terms).

Of course they weren't always so lucky with the weather. In 1946 the garden party had to be opened in the Memorial Hall by Sir William Clave Lees, Bart.; it was attended by the Mayor and Mayoress and made a profit of £320. The 1948 fête was interrupted by the worst storm on record and Winterdine School tower was struck by lightning. Lulworth Road became a river and everything had to be hurriedly moved into the hall – even so they made £350. In 1949 (light drizzle, sunny spells) a concert party, the St James' Follies, was an added attraction, performing, when it wasn't raining, on an improvised stage in the vicarage garden.

The garden party was an encouraging start to Marcus's plans to enliven the parish. He told his parishioners, 'Pleasure is God-given and we present a false as well as a repelling view of Christianity if we allow that fact to be obscured.' He quoted Saint Thomas Aquinas to lend strength to his argument, that people who never do anything amusing are 'clownish boors'. 'Unfortunately the spontaneous enjoyment, which is the really valuable element in pleasure, is lacking from so many of our modern mechanised commercialised amusements.

'Christianity has to be lived in society. . . . That is why social life around the church is so important. We must meet not merely in the church porch. Dances, a game of cards, a "party", may be just as appropriate a part of church life as a meeting or discussion group. . . . We need once and for all to rid ourselves of that false antithesis between spiritual and material, sacred and secular, body and soul, which is a legacy from a perverted puritanism.

'With this in mind and in response to many requests, we are proposing to start an organisation for social activities during this winter. It will cater for all ages and all tastes and we hope that you will enjoy membership of it. That one finds pleasure in it will indeed be the only justification for taking part in it.'

Thus was born the St James' Society, with all its offshoots: literary, musical, dramatic, photographic, terpsichorean.

Jess reported on the inaugural meeting in November: 'The Hall was packed to capacity to hear Sir Paul Dukes, KBE, with his Worship the Mayor very kindly acting as Chairman. Sir Paul gave an extremely interesting and entertaining talk on European affairs. But I think that to the Committee the main interest of the evening came at the end when, after the ladies had given us delicious refreshments, we found that the idea was in full working order, as the St James' Society, with a large initial membership.'

Jess also reported on the first dance and the first children's party. Audrey Entwistle was one of 160 guests: 'What a party it was! Mr and Mrs Morris had left no stone unturned to give the children of the parish the best night they had had for a long while. The very littlest parishioners, including Janet and Kate, had started at three o'clock and were now having their tea. As soon as they had finished, we had ours – tea to drink, sandwiches, pineapple cream and hordes of cakes – after which we were told to arrange the chairs in rows in front of the stage, where we were entertained by a conjurer, a ventriloquist and a man who called himself Uncle George.

'After that good old Caspar organised team games for us which was followed by dancing. To cool down Caspar suggested that we should sit down on the floor and sing carols. After the carols we all stood up and sang "Jerusalem". The grand climax came when we all joined hands for "Auld Lang Syne." We had three cheers for Mr and Mrs Morris. Holy Mackerel how we cheered!'

There was another Christmas party at the Memorial Hall for Society members, ' . . . something for everyone, and young, not so young and the young again joined in the games, competitions and dancing.' Audrey went along to help in the kitchen. 'Caspar is the most magnificent dancer I have ever seen and looked magnificent in evening dress.'

Audrey's designation of Marcus as 'Caspar' sprang from the St James' Society's first nativity play, *He That Should Come* by Dorothy L. Sayers. Audrey went to see it twice. 'Especially to be congratulated was Mr Morris who, at just a day's notice, learned and played the long part of Caspar, the second Wise Man. "Good old Caspar" I exclaimed as soon as I heard of this phenomenal piece of memory work.' Fifty years on, Audrey can still hear Marcus's voice reciting the principal monologue, 'Will he come, will he speak at last, the ultimate wisdom, the unalterable truth, above and beyond appearance?'

One of the most tireless workers in the Society was Margaret 'Dargie' Corelli, then living in Birkdale with her husband Esmond, who had retired from his school and did a little private tutoring. Dargie was adept at getting people to join things.

By February 1946 the Society had 218 members. They held debates and brains trusts, hot pot suppers, talks, dances, bridge evenings ('partnership bridge as it seems more in line with the purpose of our society'), recitals, literary and dramatic society meetings. Of course, after the Shrove Tuesday dance, activities took 'a form more appropriate to Lent' – study evenings in the vicarage, which Dargie described: 'Marcus was awfully good, you could hear a pin drop. It was a greatness of depth that just belonged to him. After Canon Lancelot it was a real wakening up of the whole parish and the material was there to be used. They were awfully glad to have an outlet for the things they liked doing. They found they could act and sing who didn't realise that they could, everybody from children upwards. You knew that you had something to contribute and it put you on your mettle. We did things rather well. Marcus wouldn't let us do anything else would he? He trusted people to do a job then went off and forgot about it and when he came back you'd jolly well done it. I know I benefited very much.'

Joan Rylance had met Marcus before the war a few times, in Southport and Oxford. When she moved with her husband to Birkdale in 1947, 'I met Margaret Corelli in the village and she said "We're having a meeting of the St James' Society tonight, I'd like you to come, you'd enjoy it." Marcus was there and said "Good gracious, they've got you working quickly." I was hooked from that night. I was there practically every day. I had a bicycle and wore a rut in the road. It was like one big family. Societies met at the church practically every night. People weren't doing much entertaining

*The opening of the St James' Society, Jess and Marcus with Alderman and Mrs Charlton and Sir Paul Dukes (right)*

because they hadn't the rations. So we all went to St James. I don't think it could happen now. It was a very special time.'

In June 1946, Marcus consulted the PCC about 'his desire to get in touch with the younger members of the parish and he suggested that he would invite them all to an At Home at the Vicarage.'

Audrey Entwistle was there. 'In the evening went to the preliminary meeting of youth of St James. Five boys and four girls. We had refreshments and Caspar did most of the talking and asked us if we had any ideas. We hadn't any.'

Luckily Marcus had. He went to see the daughter and son-in-law of Alderman Charlton, Peggy and Lionel Lister, and dragooned them into going to church. Lionel was a local celebrity, having captained Lancashire at cricket from 1936 to 1939 and played amateur soccer for England three times. 'Marcus came to see us – we didn't go to church, didn't even know him. He said "If you come to church people might follow." And they did. We were staunch churchgoers by the time he'd finished with us. Then he asked me to open the youth club. I said yes and before I knew it I was running it – typical of Marcus, that, very persuasive he was.'

From the beginning of 1947 the Junior Club held monthly parish breakfasts, which were eventually extended to include the whole parish. Everybody paid a shilling. These were no bread-and-marmalade affairs; Dargie got hold of two ship's frying pans and cooked eggs, bacon and sausages for eighty people. She was rather coy about how she managed it so soon after the war. 'I wrote to Mr Perrins, the Town Clerk, and said I had a starving Youth Club to feed and could we have extra chocolate and cheese. We got extra butter too, he was very nice. I don't think we had a ration book.'

Joan and Jessie Firth, whose father was a renowned forensic scientist, lived opposite the vicarage and remember a great deal of to-ing and fro-ing. 'You never needed to go further than the church to have something to do on winter evenings.'

Shirley Heath was a Junior Club member who thought the vicar very sophisticated. When a crate of beer appeared backstage some older parishioners were horrified, 'but not Marcus or Lionel. We were very fortunate having two gorgeous men at the helm.

'When I joined the youth club we were asked if we'd been confirmed. I hadn't, so I joined everybody else and went to confirmation classes in the vicarage. They were lovely.' Marcus encouraged children as young as ten to attend the classes. 'I enjoyed going to church at that time, it was a great highlight in my life.' St James began to attract non-conformists and many young people who had never been to church.

Marcus started children's services and Sunday schools. Audrey Entwistle: 'A service where the children choose their own hymns and lessons and different children read the lesson was a decidedly good move. Usually he gives a short address, but there is a suggestion box in the porch and every few weeks he answers questions.'

A young parishioner wrote from college, 'I am missing St James more than I can say. . . . There is not the feeling of fellowship that there is at St James . . . we had a play reading of *Murder in the Cathedral*. . . . It was simply dreadful. . . . I could only bear a little of it and went away.'

Other people's amateur dramatics obviously fell short of the high standards of St James: Jess had made quite an impact on the parish. She was beautiful and fashionable; wore make-up, seldom wore a hat in church, smoked, drank gin and had been known to open the front door of the vicarage wearing only a bikini. But her charm and hard work soon won round even the most disapproving old ladies. Dargie said, 'Organising sewing parties and mothers' meetings was not her line, but she was so sweet and she did it all so beautifully and she always looked lovely.'

When the dramatic society, the St James' Players, was formed, Jess was naturally the leading light, acting, producing, making costumes and scenery. They performed plays and play-readings in the church and the Memorial Hall, including a reading of Dorothy L. Sayers's *The Man Born to be King* performed in Holy Week, and three performances of John Masefield's *The Coming of Christ* with music by Gustav Holst. There were three weeks of rehearsals for this difficult play, the first they put on in the church itself. It earned a glowing review in the parish magazine.

For that production, Jess made columns from corrugated cardboard and chain mail from string painted with aluminium paint. Marcus was in it too, playing The Power, wearing a wig made from a brass pan-scrubber, another of Jess's ideas.

Phyllis Entwistle was ecstatic. She wrote to Jess, 'I loved it – the singing – the colour – the wonderful shadows and lighting – the amazing and aweful effect of back views – the stillness with long speeches and no movement to distract – but for me the climax came – glorious and terrible at the end of your speech:

> Now God Himself is Man and all the banded Night
> Will perish and the Kingdom will unclose.
> O Man, praise God, praise him, you host of Heaven.

'I literally trembled at the knees and my heart was racing.'

Jess also produced the Coventry Nativity Play and *The Salutation and The Nativity*, one of the Chester cycle of mediaeval religious plays. But most productions were not religious – they put on *The Monkey's Paw*, *His Sainted Grandmother*, *Rosalind in Arden*, *A Quiet Weekend*. . . .

Alan Joyce was a Bevin Boy (young men conscripted to work in the mines) during the war. 'A day or two after I finished in the pits in 1947, Esmond Corelli was giving a talk on British Drama. I sat next to Margaret. She said they were having a concert and I said can I join in? Marcus wasn't in many plays, he didn't have time. Jess featured more as far as the parish was concerned. She didn't do parish visiting, neither did Marcus, who cared? It was alive. She'd a gorgeous sense of humour and beautiful blue eyes – magnetic. We had good audiences, I can't remember anything being a failure. Life was never the same for me after they left.'

*Tableaux Vivants* were staged in the Memorial Hall. Kate 'looked quite bewitching' in *The First and Second Sermons*, Jan was a small boy in *The Village Pedlar* with Peggy Lister and Jessica portrayed *Whistler's Mother*. Dargie said, 'She made up half her face, nobody sees the other half in the picture.' Esmond Corelli gave 'an instructive and amusing running commentary on the paintings'.

The literary section of the Society gave fancy dress banquets; guests brought their own silverware and table decorations. In January 1947 the 'banquet' consisted of hot pot and beetroot, apple tart and coffee – well, rationing was still in force.

The parish magazine reported that 'Ten famous guests of the past, real and fictitious, attended the Banquet – Dr Johnson, Mr Micawber, Uriah

*'The Coming of Christ' – St James' Church, 1948. Marcus (top centre) as The Power, complete with pan scrubber wig, with Jess (left) and Esmond Corelli (centre).*

Heep, Mrs Malaprop, Mr Chadband, Sherlock Holmes, Mr Pickwick, Priscilla, Portia and Alfred Lord Tennyson. They proposed toasts "in character" and made skilful use of this opportunity for wit and parody.'

Audrey reported that 'Canon Morris was screamingly funny as Mr Micawber', who proposed a toast to England and Empire. Marcus toasted Absent Friends – in rhyming couplets:

Comrades, leave me here a little, give me just a little time
To digest my hot pot supper and compose my little rhyme.
No – my merry comrade calls me, sounding like a bugle horn
To bring forth these foolish verses as a target for your scorn.
Through the place and all around it, when the nightly shadows fall
Here we meet and here we gambol, gathering in St James's Hall.
Eagerly comes a hungry people, supper-seeking young and old,
Friends from many a Birkdale mansion recking not of dark or cold.
Friends from lesser places also, districts somewhat down at heel
Hesketh Park* and saintly dwellings, gladly welcome to your meal.
But tonight we think of others, as becomes a perfect host
Who tonight are not amongst us; and to them I make my toast.
Some at home on easy carpet before their lonely fire content
Some upon a bed of sickness, colds and chills and coughs present.
Some in other towns are living, scattered through our English shires
Bolton, Manchester and Salford, salty-skied with furnace fires.
We regret they are not with us, gathering round this friendly board
But we hope that they will prosper safely under fortune's ward.
So my friends a toast I bid you as this friendly banquet ends
To all throughout the world I give you – absent friends.

(In later years the family would compete to write the wittiest words to calypsos and limericks – Marcus always won.)

A local newspaper reported that 'my bored complacency was shattered, for something startlingly new was being unfolded. '

Dargie Corelli wore her mother's wedding dress for an Edwardian Evening: 'The English drawing room of the days of Good King Teddy was there in all its glory of plush, whatnots and aspidistras.' An Elizabethan evening was 'a magnificent example of the imagination and skill that we have come to expect from these active members of the Society. Mr and Mrs Esmond Corelli had gone to great trouble to present a delightfully representative selection of Elizabethan songs.'

St James was developing quite a reputation for the quality of its music. Early in 1946 the honorary organist, who had offered his services for a fortnight at the beginning of the war, resigned and Marcus persuaded Wilfred Clayton, ARCO and LRAM, to become organist and choirmaster at St James. Marcus explained in the parish magazine that although he knew nothing about music himself he knew of its importance in enhancing church services. In fact, he often sang the Liturgy; Audrey described his 'super intonation, I never heard the like before or since'.

* The area of Southport where Walter lived.

Wilfred Clayton was a Royal Academy of Music accompanist, a brilliant pianist and organist. Some members of the PCC thought that the salary of £15 a year that Mr Clayton asked was too high; the vicar suggested a garden party to pay this extortionate fee and the council finally agreed. Though there were those who thought Clayton arrogant and a better accompanist than choirmaster, he transformed the choir into one of the best in the area. In September 1949 they won the Church Choirs section of the Southport Music Festival.

On Palm Sunday 1949 Clayton and the choir gave probably the first presentation in an English church of 'The Passion of the Lord according to St Matthew' by Heinrich Schutz and repeated it in St John's Church, Ainsdale, another suburb of Southport.

Marcus's ignorance of music didn't prevent his starting a musical society. He spoke a few words at its opening and left the rest to the Corellis and Wilfred Clayton. They gave concerts and recitals, in which Jess and Dargie sang duets, and formed the St James' Singers. Prominent musicians including Leon Goossens, Lionel Tertis and Kathleen Ferrier (who hailed from nearby Blackburn) were invited to give recitals in the church.

The parish magazine reported: 'Those who heard Kathleen Ferrier sing in St James shared in a musical experience long to be remembered and were the first Southport audience to hear her in person.' Leon Goossens' recital was described in a reader's letter as 'A performance of such exquisite beauty, such an unfolding of another world away from the drab, the dreary, the cheap, the garish, as to be unforgettable. The Church used to be the source of education for the people and I thought on leaving St James that here, perhaps, that is not forgotten.'

Marcus wrote, 'There was a time when it was taken for granted that all great art was sacred because it is God's creation and exists for His glory. There could be no more obviously right place for holding such a recital than in church.'

St James also gave birth to what was probably one of the earliest film clubs in the country. In 1949, when the Junior Club finished for the summer, member Ashby Ball suggested that they make a film.

'Someone's father had a cine camera; the film was called "The St James' Junior Jumble", a fictional thing built round the youth club – most of the members were in it. We filmed excerpts of one-act plays, with no sound, and went on and on from there.

'We were shown a higher technical standard by a photography student at Manchester and we became more professional. Someone from the Liverpool Blood Transfusion Service asked us to make a local recruitment film in colour. It was a great opportunity. We decided to form the St James' Film Society, separate from the Junior Club and we went on to make films for Southport Corporation.

'We're now the Southport Cine and Video Club. We still have friendly relations with St James, though only one of our members goes to church there. The vicar is our President.'

Marcus later said, 'The St James' Society did very useful work in taking up and developing a large range of activities in the parish and made them a centre of life in the church, giving it a new vigour and enthusiasm. People began to think of themselves as belonging to a parish which was a lively reality. They felt there was more to the life of a parish than just attending one service a week.'

Jess returned to professional acting at Southport's Little Theatre and she also contacted her friend Nan Macdonald at the BBC in Manchester. Doreen Slack, actress sister of Raymond, Geoffrey and Brian Ball, was also involved in *Children's Hour* and they often travelled together. Marcus would go to collect them sometimes; Doreen said, 'Whereas I wanted to go home, Marcus always wanted to go to the Midland Hotel for a drink.' Some parishioners were a bit shocked at first at the idea of their vicar's wife acting professionally but, apart from anything else, the Morrises needed the money. Jess had had to sell her engagement ring and her sainted Aunt Nell helped out by paying off some of the debts – some of which went back to Oxford days.

Marcus was almost financially illiterate. We found uncompleted tax returns (and where they were filled in the sums were wrong), polite letters from Inspectors of Taxes, frantic letters to accountants begging their help in sorting things out. The District Bank pleaded for 'a payment to credit before issuing further cheques'.

In July 1946 the Finance Committee of the PCC (Vicar not present) 'unanimously approved an increase should be made to him since the present total of about £600 appeared inadequate in view of the enormous energy which the Vicar was putting into his work for the benefit of St James and in view of the high cost of living and the large amount of secretarial work which was necessary. . . .

'Mr Mallinson asked if there would be any check on the expenses incurred.' At the next meeting the Vicar promised to present an expense account.

In September that year he was able to pay off a long-standing account with Blackwell's Bookshop in Oxford and immediately ordered more books: Fielding, Chaucer, Smollett, Trollope, Fanny Burney – books ranging from *Incarnation of Son of God* (4/6), through *Brideshead Revisited* (10/6) to *The Flopsy Bunnies* (3/-) with the odd Agatha Christie thrown in.

He spent large amounts on taxis to get about the parish, with a monthly account, rarely paid on time, with a local garage. In 1947, thanks to one of his wealthier parishioners, Marcus bought a car, a Ford 8. His income was augmented by writing articles and book reviews for *The Record*, edited by the Revd Clifford Rhodes, and he wrote to several friends in journalism for help and advice on how to earn extra money.

As Peggy Lister said, 'He really didn't have a penny to live on. Olga Watts lent him money but I know Marcus paid her back. I remember lending him £5; I didn't see it again and we weren't made of money either.'

In spite of that the friendship flourished. Lionel reckons he knew more about Marcus and Jess being hard up than anybody. 'They were short of nearly everything, food and drink and cigarettes.'

Further strain was put on the Morris finances in July 1946, with the birth of a third daughter, Sarah Jessica Ruth Harston, known to all as Sally (and to her paternal grandmother as Miss Personality after she won that title in an eponymous competition).

Sally's baptism, by Canon Morris, was reported in the November magazine: 'Her behaviour was exemplary throughout the proceedings.' Marcus asked Alderman Charlton to be godfather; he replied, 'Of course I shall be delighted. . . . In addition my association with her will always be a very happy reminder of your kindness to me as my Chaplain during my year as Mayor. . . . I hope between us Sally will grow up to be a credit to us all!!'

The vicarage was always a hive of activity. There was a constant stream of visitors to be entertained: actors, bishops, visiting preachers, uncles, aunts and parishioners. But not on Saturday afternoons. Saturday afternoons were sacrosanct. Nothing was allowed to disturb the peace. Sally may have tumbled downstairs, Jan may have fallen over the banisters, Kate may have cut her knees *again*; any screaming had to be out of earshot of the study: Daddy was writing his sermon.

Peggy says, 'I used to come round and look after the children. Dear Mrs Hunt was the daily. What they would have done without her I don't know. Jess was not frightfully domesticated.'

Jan remembers answering a knock on the door to a well-dressed woman who asked if she could use the lavatory. Jan showed her upstairs and was given half a crown for her pains. Jan later explained to a furious Jess that she hadn't wanted to let the woman use the downstairs cloakroom, it was too smelly.

Bill Todd, like the Listers, became a life-long friend of the Morris family. 'There was always chaos. I got very fond of the children which wasn't difficult to do, and the dog, which never had a name, nobody had time to give her a name.' The dog was in fact called Puppy, a springer spaniel, upon which was lavished a lot of love and neglect. She had a litter of variegated puppies every year and eventually died of exhaustion. Bill Todd said, 'I put the kids to bed and made up stories,' which they remember to this day, about a badger and a wise old owl who did *The Times* crossword every morning. Bill Todd is still known to the Morrises as Bill Badger.

'I loved them a lot. Marcus was completely skint, terrified that the brokers' van would arrive any minute. I was earning money, so I supplied the gin. He always aspired to good living even when he had no money.

'I think the children were neglected, but not deliberately.' They never felt neglected. 'Everything was neglected because there was so much going on. It wasn't unloving. Marcus was desperate to survive. He was as thin as a pipe cleaner, he had pills to keep him awake, pills to put him to sleep. He was living off his nerves, on the edge of collapse.'

Sally aged two and a half came across the Dexedrine and took one; Marcus was alarmingly careless about leaving pills lying about. The toddler was awake for twenty-four hours. She refused to keep still and kept jumping off Jess's lap, insisting that 'I must go and write my serming'.

Bill Todd continued, 'Marcus and Jess were not easy to be fond of, they were both very defensive, very private. At times I thought they were going apart because of the frenetic activity which they each had to express. They neglected each other as well as the children.'

There was a succession of Nannies and Nurseys and Nurses. Audrey Entwistle went round to the vicarage whenever she could, mainly in the hope of seeing Marcus, but she also adored the children and would play with them or take them for walks.

'We took them on the swings in the park. Kate livened up as they apparently hadn't been there for some time. Nanny told us how when you got to know the vicar how easy he was to get on with. She said she could discuss things with him which she could never discuss with her own father.'

'Got Janet and Kate ready for their beds. When they were in their birthday suits Caspar came in and picked them up, nakedness and all. Kate objected to being kissed, she informed him that he was a naughty girl.'

'Took the children home and Mum put elastic in Kate's pants.'

'Mrs Morris returns from the maternity home. There in a blue crib is SALLY. Caspar heard my indrawn breath and, grinning proudly, beckoned me in. Caspar was still grinning, children chattering. . . . Nursey tells of a gypsy woman who told Mrs M that her next would be a boy.'

Marcus and Audrey had many an earnest talk. 'We launched on an interesting chat during which he studied his foot as he waggled it round in the air, a common habit of his. He said he didn't think that school days were the happiest time of one's life but he thought they were as happy as any other time.'

Audrey asked Marcus to explain the facts of life. 'A lot of boys and girls get physical desires which they must learn to control.'

They talked about contraceptives and love and sex: 'It's a God given instinct, just like appetite. Sex isn't a thing to be frightened of.'

And masturbation: 'I don't believe it is wicked at all. It is certainly lower than our highest ideals, but then we are constantly falling short of those in every way. It helps a lot to pray about it.'

Sunday 8 September: 'Phyl goes to Liverpool with vicarage key. Morrises are away so vicarage is left unlocked. I go to Matins – most boring sermon for three years. Policeman comes to door. Would I go and sit in the vicarage till a key could be procured. Another superb young constable chases hens from kitchen for me. Start writing letter on C's notepaper but C's pen rotten. Hunt through bookshelves. Just found excellent book on *Sex, the Moral Adventure*, when mater arrives with key.'

25 November: 'Party. Dance Sir Roger de Coverley with Caspar. Fear again I love him more than God, but it's a different kind of love – wouldn't want to dance with God. I love C for the pure delight of being his devoted slave.'

Just before Christmas 1947, Audrey moved in to the vicarage to help look after the children and became, in Peggy Lister's words, 'a common drudge' – but a willing one – and for the next few months was at the vicarage nearly every day after school.

25 January: 'C said something about no specific creed being taught at school. J's come home an ardent Hindu and refusing to eat bacon.'

Friday 26 March: 'Hot Cross Buns for brekker over which C and K had discussion about Good Friday. "Don't you remember what I told you about Jesus being killed?" "Killed, why?" "There were a lot of bad men about in those days that just wanted to." K, incredulously, "Killed the Lord, did they?" C, gently, "Yes." "Oh wasn't that a cruel thing to do." C, almost as if he'd been hurt and Jesus was a personal friend of his, "Yes, it was very cruel indeed." K, sympathetically, as if to make the hurt better, "But he rose again." C, smiling seriously, "Oh yes, he rose again." It was a moving little scene.'

Sunday 28 March: 'Easter Day. C says only 317 at service this year, 321 last year, how long will it take him to empty church. Calculate it will take 79 years.'

In the middle of April, while Jess was in hospital having her appendix out and her mother-in-law was staying at the vicarage, Audrey, nominally in charge of the children, had a nervous breakdown, mainly due to the constant interference of Mrs Canon Morris, 'the silly old bat'. Peggy Lister talked her out of suicide and Audrey went home to her parents and wept 'tears of hate and frustration at this damnable woman who came and interfered at my vicarage, my territory, my children. Tears of loss and grief. Mum and Dad would never let me go to the vicarage again.'

There were no more diaries; the crush on the vicar was over. Audrey returned to school, continued on to college and became a very successful analytical psychologist – and a great friend to those three small children she looked after so lovingly.

One of the earliest and most pressing tasks in Marcus's ministry at Birkdale was to raise money for repairs to the church. In August 1945 he appealed for £5,000; the fund officially closed in March 1946 with a total of £4,600.

Work on the church started. The very bad copy of the *Last Supper* was replaced by a carved oak reredos; an altar, altar rails and, later, choir stalls, were donated. The lighting was renewed, a recorded peal of bells put in – part of the War Memorial to the seventeen parishioners (including Marcus's friend Gerald Taylor) who had given their lives. A side chapel and a children's corner were added. Parishioners donated candlesticks, altar frontals and a silver cross and vases in memory of Canon Lancelot. Audrey's parents gave a silver altar desk in thank-offering for the safekeeping of their six children through the war.

The Bishop came for the Dedication Service in March 1948 and Marcus brought in an orchestra for the first time. Disgruntled murmurings started about High Church Practices.

Marcus wrote in the parish magazine: 'It was said to me only the other day that there are not many parishes that would have accepted in so friendly a way so many changes in so short a time. Partly in order to reciprocate this attitude and partly to reassure any who might at one time have felt that I was trying to make St James "high church", I want to say that so far as I personally am concerned there is only one further addition to our church furnishings that I am anxious to have . . . a Processional Cross. . . . It may be that there is some parishioner who would like to consider presenting [one].'

Alderman Charlton coughed up and the cross was designed by E.P. Lancaster, brother of the artist Percy Lancaster.

Edward Entwistle was one of those who did not like these high-church fripperies and he protested strongly. When Marcus started using wafers instead of bread at Communion services it was too much and Mr Entwistle resigned from the PCC. He called Marcus a 'man of Satan' and referred to his daughters and Mrs Corelli as 'the vicar's lap dogs' but did not prevent Phyllis becoming Marcus's Sacristan. Phyllis was in charge of vessels and vestments until she left to go to college, when she handed over to Peggy Lister.

Phyllis was always ready to do anything for him, even washing and ironing. 'He was very keen on my getting to college, he encouraged me, helped me find my vocation. He told me "If you want to be a deaconess you want to do the job properly, it's no good messing about" – so I didn't mess about.'

Marcus persuaded the PCC to grant Phyllis £50 a year for two years to help pay for her course of preparation.

At college, she requested his help and prayers because 'I have so much more faith in your prayers than in my own. I always feel you are the one person to whom I need offer no explanations and no excuses for my actions unless I want to.'

Years later Deaconess Entwistle wrote, 'I have never ceased to be grateful for your ministry at St James, Marcus. . . . Often when I am reading this so-called new theology I think "That's only what Marcus was thinking twenty years ago". It seems to have shattered some people – but I was well prepared by the tornado that swept St James all those years ago. "It isn't adding years to life," you said once Marcus, "but adding life to years, that counts." And I'm sure it's true.'

Twenty years after that she congratulated Marcus on his OBE: 'I have learnt a lot since you first asked me "Will you be my Sacristan?" and I had never heard of the word!! I owe a lot to you in very many ways – you were the first person who ever really gave me any confidence – you just didn't take no for an answer! Bless you – I hope all goes well and that you are not still burning too many midnight oils!'

Phyllis was not the only one he encouraged. Other parishioners became lay readers and Bill Todd, now Rector of Hatfield, Hertfordshire and, over the years, a regular television 'God slot' broadcaster, was adamant that if it hadn't been for Marcus, he would never have become a priest.

'I was friendly with a girl who used to go to church and thought Marcus was the cat's pyjamas. I didn't go, it was the one part of life I hadn't shared with her. One wet Sunday morning she took me to St James. Marcus was holding forth. He was very good, an excellent sermon. Even to a non-believer he was very good. On the way out he said, "I don't know you." I said, "No you don't, I don't come to church, don't believe in it." He said, "Perhaps we could have a talk."

'That one service triggered it, then weeks and months of debate. I went to confirmation classes, Thursday night arguments and discussions. In the end the old boy convinced me that he had a more reasonable attitude to life than anyone else. I was confirmed by Charles Claxton, then Bishop of Warrington, and Marcus and I became friends.

'It was Marcus's priesthood that led me to be a priest – no question. He didn't talk me into it, but he taught me an understanding of Christianity that I could accept. I've always had a great love for him. He dragged me, a card-carrying atheist, into the Christian way of life and, to my astonishment, into the priesthood.

'He was light years ahead of his time. The things he said in those days would be reasonably commonplace today. If he'd given me the theology of the '40s I'd have said "up yours". He pushed his faith into reality. Underneath he wrestled, I can see that tortured face now. He was too untrusting of himself. He pushed and criticised himself, trying to reconcile his lifestyle with his faith. I can't bear him being criticised, because he battled on all those fronts. He was a one-off, he totally changed my life.'

Many of his parishioners found Marcus a kind and sympathetic pastor. He conducted the funerals of Elspeth Lewis's father and sister.

'Both funerals were from the house. The coffin was brought up to the door and my mother went out, she didn't want anybody with her. She said she was suddenly aware of someone behind her. It was Marcus, he'd slipped very quietly out, not saying or doing anything, just standing there. He knew not to interfere in what was a poignant moment; she never forgot that.

'I nearly joined the Methodist Church but the minister there couldn't answer what I was asking and Marcus could, so I was confirmed at twenty-three. He made things clear for me; the other was waffle.'

Dawn Lunt had reservations. 'I wouldn't say he enthused me at confirmation classes. I always felt as a child that he was a hard man, not a terribly religious man. I didn't think he was a terribly caring man either.'

Roy and Pat Ainsco were married by Marcus in 1949 but, 'he said you can't be married in church unless you're christened. So he christened me and we had a super party at the Belle Vue Hotel. That's a good thing about having a christening party when you're twenty-six.' Pat said; 'He gave us a pep talk before the wedding. He said, be careful, make an appointment with your doctor. No mention of religion. He poured me a very large gin and tonic and I sat there looking as though I knew it all. It didn't do any good because we had a baby nine months later. At the altar I noticed that Marcus was wearing check trousers under his surplice, I thought he might have put dark trousers on.

'When he came to the parish it was like a breath of fresh air. The old people didn't approve of small children running about the church. I remember Marcus saying "I want you to bring the family and the children to church and it doesn't matter if they make a noise. Don't worry if they're crying, we'll talk over them." It was the first time I'd heard anybody say that.'

In 1946, Peggy Taylor, widow of Gerald, was married by Marcus to John Wood, an old flame of Jess's. After the wedding Peggy wrote, 'My most sincere thanks . . . for the beautiful way in which you conducted the service – it was all so moving and the quiet way in which you talked to just "us" made a very deep impression.'

Marcus introduced public baptisms during Matins (he said he had pinched the order of service from Mervyn Stockwood [Vicar of St Matthew's, Bristol; later Bishop of Southwark]) but parents who wanted private ceremonies were still free to have them.

Mollie Martin was one who did. 'When we thought it was time to get my daughter christened, Marcus and Jess were away somewhere in Wales. So we telegraphed him and suggested a date and he sent back word, yes, delighted, so that was all right. We turned up at the church and sat there for about quarter of an hour and nobody came. So my husband went to the vicarage and banged and called and rattled the door for about ten minutes. Jessica appeared, looking a bit sheepish, and it turned out that he'd forgotten all about it and they were in bed. I can remember to this day, Jessica coming from the vestry all the way down to the baptistry at the other end of the church with a jug of supposedly holy water and one of the children hanging on to her skirt. A memorable christening was that.'

In August 1948 the girls went to stay with Mary and Eric and their cousins at Padgate while Marcus and Jess went to Amsterdam for the first Assembly of the World Council of Churches. Marcus commented, 'One of the most striking features of the Amsterdam Assembly . . . was the radicalism of the majority of delegates. . . . Capitalism and Communism were alike exposed as fake in their understanding of the purpose of life and the value of the human person.'

An appeal was launched by Christian Reconstruction In Germany. St James adopted the parish of Neuenkirchen and sent twelve packing cases of clothes, books and food, which could ill be spared from meagre rations. The Pastor of Neuenkirchen sent a letter of heartfelt thanks: 'That the Christian spirit of love makes such bridges from heart to heart let us hope will be a way out of the darkness and misery of our days.'

By 1948 the parish had a deficit of nearly £700, partly due to the increased Parochial Quota to the Diocese. 'Mr Morris was not surprised at the deficit, the result of three years' work to expand the church's activities in the parish. Special functions were needed to balance the accounts. Mr Morris suggested a two or three day bazaar.'

The Palace Hotel, then one of the largest hotels on the north-west coast, since demolished, lent their ballroom. Working parties were formed to organise stalls – the vicarage party appealed for household goods (the Misses Morris issued a special invitation to younger members to come and bring their mothers).

At 10.30 a.m. on Thursday, 25 November the ambitious fête was opened by Lady Paton and went on for three days. As Alan Joyce said, 'it set the whole town by the ears'. Alderman Charlton held an auction, there were stalls and side shows, a tombola, whist drive and chicken lunch at 4/6d for more than 200 people. Miss Marie Philpott and Her Orchestra played light music, there was a Fashion Parade of Rare and Lovely Furs by the Russian Fur Stores of Lord Street while over 300 afternoon teas were served. There was a children's fancy dress competition; the Vicar's daughters went as Rose Red, Snow White and Little Boy Blue, who won the consolation prize for youngest competitor. Lionel and Peggy Lister's son Jeremy won a prize for the most original costume, dressed as the Vicar. The days ended with Hot Pot Supper and dancing to Billy Bevin and his orchestra.

It was a resounding success and raised over £1,100 net, an incredible amount for those days. They repeated the event the following year, but only managed to raise £700.

Marcus wrote later, 'I tried to keep the parish fully informed about my problems and hopes. I made the annual meeting of the PCC as well attended as possible, presenting a formal report and carefully prepared accounts – parishes and churches need money if they are to keep going.

'In St James I learnt to deal with the numberless problems which the life of a big parish presents. I gained experience in many directions, not least in my preaching, in which I altered my technique completely. I used to have my whole sermon written out word for word and though I didn't actually read from the script, it was there in front of me in the pulpit. I found it increasingly unsatisfactory and no longer had time for it. I lost spontaneity without the advantages of formal adherence to a prepared text, which can be very impressive. It was Esmond Corelli who persuaded me to use extensive notes and I am sure I achieved a closer contact with the congregation. The more practice I had, the more I became convinced that sermons should be short, clearly expressed and confined to one theme which should be dealt with in a lively fashion.

'I preached once on the radio, when the BBC North Regional Home Service broadcast Morning Service from St James on 17 July 1949. I was pleased, of course, as would be any priest who has the opportunity to speak to such a vast congregation.'

He was taking no chances with that sermon – it was all typed out and underlined and timed to the minute. He was a good preacher, according to many parishioners, more intellectual in his approach than his down-to-earth but formidable father, with a tendency to quote from poets and philosophers.

John Cotterell remembered vividly the only time he heard Marcus preach, 'in a fairly staid church with a very staid vicar, he had the courage to get up in the pulpit and start with this couplet:

"There was a young man who said damn, It appears to me that I am / A creature that moves in pre-definitive grooves, I'm not even a bus, I'm a tram."

'As a youngster he appealed to me because he tried to bring Christian thinking into touch with everyday life.'

In addition to his vicarly duties, Marcus was also Chairman of the Southport Council of Social Service and gave lectures and talks. Local parsons wanted him for their debates. The Minister of the Congregational Church, Ainsdale, asked him to take part in a brains trust in September 1947. Marcus accepted and ended his letter 'I am going away for a holiday on Monday, I never looked forward to a holiday more.' Many parishioners thought that he worked too hard. After he left the parish Peggy Lister wrote to Marcus and Jess to say that the new vicar was out playing golf with her father, was due to play cricket the following day and 'spent all last weekend watching the Walker Cup. So I think Marcus should have got out a bit more!'

Marcus: 'Those five years in Birkdale were energetic and full. They taught me a lot about the day to day job of being a priest. I was still quite young and energetic and gave myself fully to the job.

'At the same time, a major interest in my life was the attempt to get the Christian message through to people by means of lively and adult publications.'

# Chapter Seven

The St James' parish magazine under Canon Lancelot had been a four-page leaflet called *The Parish Messenger*, which listed church services and local events. It was printed on cheap coarse paper and was delivered to every house in the parish.

Marcus wanted something better and just a month after his induction produced his first *St James' Magazine*, 'quite a good little effort, decently printed with a stiff cover, and eight pages', with a subscription of six shillings a year. There was an editorial, a short account of the induction, a brief section entitled The Church Year, a page and a half of random comments, some notes on local history, seven short paragraphs on church music by C. Sharp, a letter about the liberation of Norway by Eric Cook and two not very funny jokes. Deaths and marriages were recorded; the number of communicants in June was 148. The back cover carried an advertisement for Cannell's millinery shop in Lord Street and the information that the magazine was printed by the *Southport Guardian*.

It wasn't much, but it was a start.

In his editorial Marcus wrote, 'A parish magazine should be a magazine *by* as well as *for* the parish. In the pulpit the parson is inviolable. A parish magazine can restore the balance and give an opportunity for that discussion and debate which alone can vitalize our religious faith and invigorate our Christian life.

'I ask for your co-operation in this new venture that it may be a united effort expressive of a rich parochial life. I shall be most grateful for articles on any subject, and for parish notes and comments, for information about fellow parishioners – especially those in the Forces – and for contributions to the correspondence columns. Space is, of course, limited by the regulations of the Paper Control, but we shall include as many features as possible.'

Some parishioners thought that it was very high-fallutin', but the following month Marcus reported that 'I have received many kind and encouraging letters, commending our new magazine.'

His editorials ranged far and wide, from the Church's part in the reconstruction of Germany, to the atom bomb: 'It is we and America who bear the responsibility for all time of introducing this destructive power into the world. . . . We need before all else to understand the enormity of our offence before God and the depth of inhumanity in which we have become involved', and Sunday Observance: 'The Lord's Day Observance Society . . . are not Church people at all – they are a mixed bag of strange sects and only a tiny minority of Churchpeople support them. . . . The Christian Sunday is not the Jewish Sabbath and was not meant to imitate it. . . . '

He bemoaned the loss of 'God-centred principles of justice' and the increase in undemocratic ecclesiastical bureaucracy: 'It is still regrettable that the Church in a frantic effort to keep up with the times, can only trot excitedly after the procession of modern secular trends like a small boy running alongside a military parade. Certain Church authorities need to be reminded that they are the fellow-workers and not the masters of the parochial clergy. It is a scandal that reforms [of the Church] agreed by both clergy and laity should be at the mercy of a House of Commons which includes a considerable proportion of Jews, pagans and heretics.

The 'indiscriminate' administration of Baptism came under fire: 'To many parents it appears simply as something that has to be "done" to a child, like vaccination. . . . It is high time that the clergy everywhere took a firm stand against this prostitution of the Christian Sacraments.'

The December '45 issue included four 'Scraps '– 'a contribution from Mr C.S. Lewis', possibly the result of Marcus's glowing review of *That Hideous Strength*, Lewis's latest novel, in the previous issue: 'Here is imaginative power, wit and wisdom in abundance . . . a novel which fascinates, shocks, convinces – and warns.' (In 1964 Walter Hooper, compiling a Bibliography of C.S. Lewis, had a long correspondence with Marcus about the 'Scraps' and thanked him for inspiring 'these pieces of Lewisiana'.)

By January 1946 there were two children's pages, compiled by Phyllis and Audrey Entwistle, with a nursery rhyme quiz, a short story and advice on collecting. The magazine ran to sixteen pages.

In June Marcus thanked his readers for their welcome in his first year as their vicar: 'We have to look beyond the horizon of the Parish. . . . The Church can only survive if the Christian laity see that they have as large a part to play as have the clergy in the conversion of England. . . . We have to make use of all the modern methods of evangelism that are available . . . we are preparing for the time when we can use the magazine to present the claims of Christ to the apathetic and the "outsider".'

By November the magazine's circulation had doubled. It had twenty pages and carried advertisements from the Palace Hotel, Gibsons Household Furnishing and Horticultural Ironmongery, J.S. Sherwood High Class Confectioners and Caterers, Kay and Folbey Photographic Suppliers and Aldridges Music Shop.

Jodi Hyland, whose mother was a parishioner and a long-standing family friend, was now working in London on *Woman's Own*. On visits back home she would join Marcus in the study at the vicarage and over a couple of glasses of whisky give him advice on livening up the layout.

In December 1946 the *St James' Magazine* appeared under a new name, *The Anvil*, 'A New Magazine for Southport People'. Marcus's editorial explained, 'The new title is not original but it does express better than most, the aims of this magazine. The truth of Christianity has to be hammered out by hard work and thought into a shape which means something to the modern world. . . . Men complain that they cannot understand how God could become man and still remain God. Why should they expect to? There is no such thing as a "simple religion which the plain man can easily understand". There is no religion without mystery. Religion is about God.'

The new front cover was designed and drawn by Edward Lancaster.

'The symbolism of a typical Birkdale skyline and the Cross poised over it between sea and sky points us to a church which is a living part of the community.'

That month began a series of interviews with leading citizens and the Reverend (later Bishop) Eric Wild wrote on Christian Socialism. He was a frequent visitor to St James, preaching or talking at Society or Junior Club meetings. Marcus had written to him at St George's Church, Wigan, asking him for an article on an industrial parish: 'I want it to be as provocative and stimulating as possible.'

In fact, he agreed with Dr C.E.M. Joad's remark, which he put as a tailpiece to the 'Anvil Commentary': 'The secret of successful journalism consists in making people so angry that they will write half your paper for you.'

A member of the St James' Society, who described himself as a confirmed agnostic, wrote querying his involvement with the Society when 'I don't honestly feel that I could go to Church or enter into Church life'. Marcus replied, 'If you mean what you say about appreciating what you have found among us – though we have, as you say, no monopoly of virtue – why not respond by seeing whether there may not be more in it than you think. . . . '

Vernon Noble wrote that, although he called himself a Christian, 'I do not attend church because I cannot find God there.' The Editor responded, 'May I suggest that the first practical step in your circumstances is actually to join yourself on to the Christian Society – and be prepared to stomach all the irritations and distractions . . . and maybe God will find you instead?'

Politics loomed large. When a Labour Party discussion group decided that 'Christianity is dying out and Socialism will develop into a broadly based religion and replace Christianity', Marcus commented, 'Fortunately the majority of Socialists do not share the delusions of these pompous pagans.'

At the end of the summer of 1947, the Trades Union Congress conference, 'the most momentous in the history of the TUC', was held in Southport. Marcus issued a challenge to a Christian Trade Unionist, preferably a member of the Church of England 'so that I shan't get into trouble with my Bishop', to speak in the pulpit of St James and present the case for Trade Unionism.

Andrew Naesmith, OBE, member of the General Council and Secretary of the Amalgamated Weavers' Association, took up the challenge. 'An Accrington man who knows much about the early history of the TU movement, especially in Lancashire, Mr Naesmith spoke to a full congregation on Christianity and Socialism. We were glad to welcome him and his fellow-members from the General Council, other Trade Unionists and the fraternal delegates from USA and Canada who were in the congregation.'

Alderman Charlton, as an *Anvil* interviewee, said that 'the clergy should keep clear of politics and confine themselves to Church affairs', to which Marcus replied: 'In all England how many social services are there which do *not* owe their existence to the Churches? The Church has always led the way – in education, in the building of hospitals, in care for children and old people whom the state neglected. . . . The Church certainly ought not to ally itself with any political party. But if it is not concerned with the problems with which the politicians endeavour to cope, it might as well pack up.'

There must have been some lively discussions between Marcus and Ernest Charlton!

There were articles and news snippets from all over Lancashire. A reader wrote that 'Your very interesting magazine is read and discussed by several of us as far away as Devonshire. We enjoy its frank articles and wide outlook.' A mother said that her twelve-year-old daughter had replied to the question 'What is an anvil?' in a general knowledge quiz, that it was a 'missionary magazine'.

Esmond Corelli wrote regular book reviews, the roles now reversed; the former schoolmaster was being nagged by his erstwhile pupil for his 'homework'. There was an article by Dorothy L. Sayers on 'Christian Morality', reprinted by permission from *Unpopular Opinions*. The landlord of the Bold Hotel thought that parsons should go into pubs more often, although 'the annual returns for the United Kingdom showed Southport to be the fourth most sober town in the country'. There was a short story competition which was judged by the author Laurence Meynell, whom Marcus had met when he came to Southport to speak to the National Book League.

But *The Anvil* was by no means paying its way. At the beginning of 1947, the Parochial Church Council discussed the deficit; they had not so far given any financial support to the magazine and none was asked for, but they offered to lend money to defray outstanding costs. They would not be responsible for any further accounts apart from the usual annual payment of £25 towards the parish magazine.

A Spring Fair was held, which produced £262. 'This has since been increased by some generous donations. . . . The Editor wishes to express his delight and gratitude to all who helped in any way. . . . The result will enable us to persevere in our efforts to set *The Anvil* firmly on its feet as a church magazine for the people of Southport and (who knows?) beyond.'

With this in mind, Marcus sent copies to The Most Reverend His Grace the Lord Archbishop of Canterbury, hoping for a commendation. A lackey wrote back somewhat pompously from Lambeth Palace: 'His Grace is not able to issue commendations in respect to individual publications like this. I am sure you will realise if he were to begin it would be impossible for him to stop.' A week later the chaplain wrote guardedly, 'Since I last wrote to you the Archbishop has had an opportunity of glancing through the two copies of the *Anvil* you sent him, and he read them with considerable interest.'

Irritated, Marcus wrote to fellow clergyman Cedric Frank, 'I am getting very much more co-operation in selling *The Anvil* from the Nonconformists than from most of my Anglican brethren. As *The Anvil* will not survive at all unless it spreads widely throughout Southport, I am prepared to be as accommodating as possible to the Nonconformists, though I shan't go so far as to sell my soul. . . . We are blind and obscurantist in persisting in a hard and rigid attitude to the Nonconformists. I think it is a case of either

get together or sink. . . . The prime and vital necessity for the Church today is for unity.'

The Bishop of Liverpool was more enthusiastic than his superior: 'As usual I am very greatly impressed with its production; the articles are good, very readable and well set out. This magazine should make a much wider appeal than to the parish of St James. Go on with the good work.' The *Church Times* eulogised, 'None has a more completely professional stamp than *The Anvil*. Everything about it – typography, make-up and editorial presentation – is first class.' Mervyn Stockwood said, 'It is, I think, an admirable production; in fact the best I have seen so far,' and Canon Blakeney reckoned 'it is worthy of becoming a Southport Church Magazine'.

Marcus's ambitions were wider. He wrote later, 'We decided to take from the strictly parish character of the publication by producing an inset which would deal exclusively with the life at St James and would only go to my parishioners; for the rest, the magazine would be a Christian one, a kind of religious *Lilliput*, circulating we hoped through the whole of Lancashire.

'I approached some wholesalers myself and wrote to others. I also approached the clergy, explaining what we had in mind and asking for their co-operation in selling the magazine in their parishes. I had enough success to enable me to say to my busy and enthusiastic helpers that we had reached stage two and turned *Anvil* into a genuinely Lancashire magazine.'

*The Anvil* was no longer 'the new magazine for

*The changing face of* The Anvil, *1945-1950*

Southport people', it was 'A magazine produced by St James' Church, Birkdale'; there was no parish news, no 'In and Around St James', no local personalities. The Editor and Publisher was no longer Rev J.M.H. Morris; he was Marcus Morris. The following month, *Anvil* was 'a magazine for Lancashire'. Contributors included David, former Bishop of Liverpool and Lieutenant-Colonel Roger Fleetwood-Hesketh, the High Sheriff of the Duchy of Lancaster. Irene Hyland-Jones, Jodi's mother, described the Klu Klux Klan from personal experience of Florida in the 1920s; 'Onlooker' condemned the 'Gutter Journalism' surrounding the Clements murder case and Lieut-Col Eric Arden, Registrar of the Diocese of Liverpool, and Walter's cousin, wrote about Divorce and Re-Marriage.

Marcus thanked his parishioners for their good will and support. 'I should like to say how grateful I am for your backing. . . . It is no small comfort to know that this wider circulation will, we hope, ease our financial burden.'

It didn't. Marcus sent copies of the magazine to the *Daily Express* and to local newspapers throughout Lancashire, asking for publicity and advertising space. He wrote to the proprietor of Kemsley Newspapers in Manchester to enlist her support. Lady Kemsley's assistant replied that 'A copy of your very interesting magazine has already reached this office and was noticed at some length in the *Manchester Evening Chronicle* . . . we shall be glad to give subsequent numbers such mention as space permits.'

The Assistant Editor of the *West Lancashire Evening Gazette* wrote, 'What I like about the publication is the atmosphere of virility and realism which pervades it. The lay-out, too, is bright and imaginative without being "eccentric".' The British Council of Churches offered to display *The Anvil* on their book stall and the Archdeacon of MacKay, North Queensland, Australia, read about it in the *Church Times* and begged a copy. Marcus sent three with his compliments and the Archdeacon wrote back, 'I am afraid what you do is far and away beyond us. . . . The *Church Times* put me completely astray by calling your work a "parish paper".'

Line drawings by E.P. Lancaster and Jill Charlotte, who hailed from Southport but were in partnership in London, punctuated 'The Wasteland', an article by C.E.M. Joad (with acknowledgements to the *New Statesman*). Marcus had written to Edward Lancaster, 'We are limited by the type available at our printers, and the choice is really between Plantain and Gill, both of which I am now using. We wonder whether you would be willing to do some drawings similar to those which appear in the *New Westminster Review*.'

E.P.L. also designed Marcus's letterhead and thought the *New Westminster Review* 'lacks the interest and punch I find in the *Anvil* sub-titles. . . . Most certainly would I be willing to do line drawings. . . . PS Yes! I have done cartoons!' Marcus asked Lancaster for samples: 'I should rather like to put in a series after the style of the *Daily Express* "Pocket Cartoon". I want to be really pungent and witty. . . . I don't want them to be a take-off of the Church or clergy because that's too easy, but rather to hit out at the general materialism, ignorance and imbecility of our age.'

But 'I wasn't quite happy about the first drawing. I rather feel that the idea is too conventional and "churchy". I should have liked something more modern and up-to-date. I am afraid I don't quite know what to suggest in its place.'

Marcus knew what he wanted, though he couldn't describe it exactly.

He was always ready to help and encourage other editors of parish and ruri-decanal magazines. John Blair-Fish wrote from Surrey asking for comments and suggestions for his own parish magazine; he became a regular contributor and later an associate editor of *Anvil*.

Marcus told him, 'I myself have to do all the lay-out, typography etc in complete detail, giving the printer a lay-out sheet for every page. You might get assistance from a professional journalist . . . but I know of one magazine which has come unstuck because the journalist could not appreciate what the vicar was trying to put across.'

Phyl Entwistle wrote to Marcus from a summer school in Keswick. 'One of the four gentlemen came to sit beside me. In a minute he turned and said "Which parish do you come from?" When I told him he laughed softly and said "Aha! Marcus Morris – *The Anvil*".

' "Who sets it?" he asked. I said I thought you did with the collaboration of the [Southport] *Guardian*. He said "Of course, the set is marvellous isn't it – it's so beautifully spaced and *interesting*. It makes so much difference having all these little insets and pictures. How *does* he make it pay?" (Indeed – How?!!)'

The financial situation was fast deteriorating. That autumn, the Anvil Business Management Committee was formed and an appeal went out to the men of the parish (the 'women-folk' had made their special effort for *Anvil* with their Spring Fair) to attend a meeting to discuss ways of helping out. Readers were asked to become *Anvil* Founder Patrons and send cheques for five guineas, or any other amount. One committee member very generously promised £50.

Marcus tried another way of raising money: Auctioneers Valuers and Estate Agents Ball and Percival (Raymond, Geoffrey and Brian's family firm) did a valuation of furniture and effects at the vicarage (total value £400) with a view to selling some of it. Whatever else may have gone, the 'Oak Grandfather Clock with white dial (not working) value £1' was not sold, nor was the 'Pianoforte in Walnut Case by R Gors & Kallman (£42.10s)' – still loved and in use today – nor the 'Mahogany dining table with extra leaves, on turned legs (£5.5s)'. Maybe they sold the most valuable item, the 'Self-coloured Axminster carpet on green ground 4 x 7 yds, £50'.

Circulation of *The Anvil* reached 2,500, which was the limit allowed by paper restrictions, but it wasn't enough to make the magazine pay for itself. Marcus was desperate to expand. 'I could see no reason why we should stop at Lancashire; why should it not be read in every county in England? Without much hesitation we set that as our next target. My ideas were ambitious, but we had faith and hope.

'We prepared a brochure and sent out three mailing shots to clergy all over the country and I watched our finances weaken, with great anxiety. Even by that time I was seriously in the red. My bank manager was a kindly, sympathetic man, but I could see that there would be limits to his patience and understanding.

'The response I got from my mailing shots was disappointing. I can't say that I found my fellow clergy very helpful. They were narrow, suspicious and parish-bound and looked on me with the greatest circumspection.'

He wrote to everyone he could think of including London publishing companies and half a dozen bishops. Viscount Hambledon agreed to see him. He corresponded with Lord Inman, Chairman of Charing Cross Hospital, who had rescued the *Church of England Newspaper*, hoping that he might be able to take over *The Anvil* – but the paper shortage (or Marcus's presentation of the figures) changed his lordship's mind.

The Managing Editor of the Whitethorn Press, publishers of *Cheshire Life*, was sympathetic but eventually said no. The Student Christian Movement Press suggested the Society for Promoting Christian Knowledge. SPCK had no paper; they said they were sorry because 'we should like to see the SPCK being able to make constructive use of the ability shown in your excellent publication.' The Religious Book Editor of Lutterworth Press (Prop: United Society for Christian Literature) was sympathetic and offered constructive criticism but no hope.

Meanwhile, a special commission of the Church Assembly, under the chairmanship of Bishop Chavasse of Rochester, had produced a best-selling report in which it was pointed out that the Church had great need of modern methods of communication such as newspapers and magazines. 'Monthly periodicals are called for, which would interest and challenge the casual reader who purchased them at a railway bookstall. Every means at the Church's disposal must be fully used to explain and proclaim the faith and to spread news of events in the life of the Church.' It seemed reasonable to Marcus that the Chairman might consider giving him some help in his attempts to do just that.

To the Bishop of Rochester, 19 December 1947: 'In view of your great interest in Church publicity, I thought perhaps you might be willing to help me in a new kind of Church journalism in which I am engaged. . . . I am now threatened with having to close down. My only hope, I think, is to get it taken up by some publishing firm. . . . I hope you may perhaps think that those with influence and authority might feel it worthwhile to take the matter up. . . . I am determined to do everything I can to avoid having to cease publication because I firmly believe in the value and usefulness of this kind of work.'

The Bishop wrote back three days later, 'I do not see what I can do to help you in the continued publication of *The Anvil*, seeing that it is a Lancashire magazine.' It was this kind of parochialism that caused Marcus to tear his hair out in despair and contributed to his eventual disillusionment with the Church.

In correspondence with Alex Vidler, Canon of St George's Chapel, Windsor, Marcus wrote, 'I have no licence for paper. I simply approached the Paper Control for permission to use extra paper and eventually got as far as an Under-

Secretary to the Board of Trade, but he indicated that it was quite hopeless unless I was able to get really influential backing. I approached the Archbishop of York about this, but he was not willing to create a precedent by supporting an application on behalf of *The Anvil*. I have now written to Sir Stafford Cripps direct, and have a letter to say he is looking into it.'

In January 1948 Marcus requested an interview with the President of the Board of Trade, the Rt. Hon. Harold Wilson. Archdeacon Twitchett of Liverpool had been busy on his behalf and elicited a reply from Kenneth de Courcy, Wilson's secretary: 'If Mr Morris is using the maximum amount of his paper allocation now, I am afraid it would be very difficult to discover the right means [of expanding the circulation]. . . . I am a little disturbed by the editorial. The editor says that there are signs that the crisis is beginning to break already, indeed the article is headed "Turn of the Tide?". It is not easy to make the British public understand that the problem facing the country is not so much one of production . . . as of selling British goods to countries able to buy them with hard currency. At present there is no sign of improvement of any kind in this respect. . . . Were it not for the fact that we still have some gold which we are selling monthly for the purchase of goods vitally necessary to the community, we should already be faced with a physical catastrophe of the first magnitude . . . our resources are fast dwindling.

'Then I see the editor is also rather optimistic about Anglo-Russian relations . . . the relations are worse rather than better. . . . I wonder whether you would feel disposed to pass this friendly and private word of warning from me to the editor of *The Anvil*.'

Marcus's appointment with Harold Wilson in Liverpool was cancelled; there was no assistance from the Board of Trade and Mr de Courcy's 'friendly warning' put no constraints on future editorials, in which 'crucial problems' were discussed, including 'our crazy economic policy'. 'We need a faith which can arouse as great a religious fervour, and as unswerving a devotion, as the most rabid communist can find in his religion.' Christians were fervent, Communists, rabid! 'The imbecilities of American policy are added to daily. The economists, the scientists, the human idealists . . . are floundering in their own inanities . . . many town councillors are unfitted to represent a flock of sheep.'

On a lighter note was the introduction of the rather grandly titled Anvil Survey and Research Bureau, a somewhat haphazard poll conducted by friends in local parishes and believed by the editor to be the first undertaken by a small magazine. It concluded that only three people in ten disapproved of gambling.

*The Anvil* (in the person of Jess) interviewed Dame Sybil Thorndike in her dressing room at the Duchess Theatre in London. Marcus himself interviewed John Mills, 'England's most popular film star', and Learie Constantine, who lived locally.

In February 1948, a new name was added to the list of illustrators of *The Anvil*. Marcus had been on the lookout for an artist to help improve and enliven the magazine; his friend Joe Crossley, who worked on the *Southport Guardian* and had introduced Marcus to Jess, now made his second huge impact on Marcus's life by suggesting he approach a young artist just finishing at Southport College of Art.

Frank Hampson was born in Audenshaw, Manchester, on 21 December 1918, son of Police Constable Robert Hampson and his wife Elsie. The family (including brother Eric and sister Margaret) moved to Southport in 1919, just a year after the Morris family arrived from Balderstone.

Frank went to King George V Grammar School and started his artistic career at the age of thirteen, when he entered an art competition in *Meccano Magazine*, which resulted in a commission to produce comic illustrations. As a teenager he was a fan of the American strip cartoon artists Hal Foster, Milton Caniff and Alex Raymond, who drew the detective 'Rip Kirby'. When Frank left school he found that his first job, delivering telegrams for the Post Office, left him plenty of time to practise illustration. Robert Hampson, determined to encourage his son's artistic talent, arranged for him to attend life classes at the local art school on his days off. In 1935 Frank graduated to serving behind the counter and his Post Office colleagues became the subject of clever caricatures, which soon found their way into the GPO's official magazine.

In 1938 Frank enrolled full time at the Victoria College of Arts and Science in Southport where Harold Johns, son of a local headmaster, was a fellow student. A year later, having gained his National Diploma of Design (Intermediate), Frank was drafted into the Royal Army Service Corps, while Harold went into the Royal Armoured Corps. Frank survived the beaches of Dunkirk and after a couple of years on convoys was accepted for officer training and passed out as a lieutenant. He wanted to transfer to the RAF so that he could fulfil his ambition to fly, but the army hung on to him and he landed at Normandy and fought through to the Low Countries.

After the war Frank returned home to Southport and to Dorothy, whom he had married in 1944. His brother, a merchant seaman, had been lost at sea and his father had retired from the police force with the rank of Detective Inspector.

Frank and Harold Johns, both aged twenty-six, enrolled for a three year course at the Southport School of Arts and Crafts. Three months later Dorothy Hampson became pregnant and Frank realised he would have to augment his college grant when she left her job at a bank. He and Harold set up a commercial art business, experimenting with silk screen printing. With the birth of his son, Peter, in July 1947, it was inevitable that work began to take precedence over his studies.

One of Frank's freelance jobs was for Southport Council – a publicity poster of the town which was full of detail and brilliantly drawn. By 1948 he was only too happy to earn money working for Marcus, and sent in detailed accounts, his charges ranging from '2 illustrations @ 10/6' to a 'Two page border, lettered title & subheadings @ £1.15.0'.

He designed the leaflet for *Anvil*'s special appeal and, in April, redesigned the magazine's cover, showing a typically English street scene from above, with an anvil and hammer under the title and his signature at bottom right. Marcus wrote, 'Our new cover has been designed by Mr Frank Hampson, and we hope you will agree that he has done a fine piece of work, which illustrates exactly what *The Anvil* stands for. Our growing number of readers in all parts of the country will be able to find in it something that brings it home to them.'

By that summer Frank had ousted Edward Lancaster, except for EPL's heading for the editorial. In August Frank's bill came to £24.14*s*.0*d* – a lot of drawings. His illustrations were more lively, snappy and humorous than Lancaster's and he also did excellent more serious line drawings. In September there appeared in Anvil possibly his first published drawings of space ships, illustrating a short story about extra-terrestrials.

By the Spring of 1947 Marcus had begun to consider the advantages of co-operation with other parish magazines. In May he wrote to Eric Loveday, Vicar of St Martin-in-the-Fields, London: 'I shall be very pleased to come to London at any time to have a talk with you and other editors. I had already written to Mervyn Stockwood and George Reindorp [then Vicar of St Stephen, Rochester Row, London and co-editor of *New Westminster Review*, later Bishop of Guildford] suggesting that we might form a coalition to syndicate articles by well-known writers, but so far we haven't got

anywhere with the idea. I certainly think there is room for collaboration between those of us who are trying to do this kind of work.'

George Reindorp declined to join a coalition but was eager to help and advise. He and Marcus arranged to meet under the clock at the Victoria Street entrance to the Army and Navy Stores in London. Mr Reindorp would be wearing a clerical collar and a broken nose.

It was through his attempts to extend the reach of *The Anvil* that Marcus made one of his most firm and long-lasting friendships. 'Chad Varah was one of the people I met as I went round the clergy trying to make *Anvil* a Lancashire paper. Even he, to begin with, was sus-

*Possibly Frank Hampson's first published drawings of spaceships, from* The Anvil, *September 1948.*

picious. He was an extremely intelligent, highly strung, dynamic person, pin-faced, pin-bodied and giving the impression of great nervousness. Later I was to find he was both tortuous and complicated. He became, and remained, one of my closest friends.

'He was then the rector of Holy Trinity, Blackburn and editor of the Blackburn diocesan magazine, *The Crosier*, and very interested in the problems of Christian journalism. He also had a reputation, not entirely unjustified, as a wild man of the Church and a believer in the most direct action.

'I soon found that he was as keen as I was to do something effective about the whole question of Christian publicity, in particular the use of the printed word and when he suggested calling a conference to consider the whole question at Whalley Abbey, a lovely old place used for retreats and conferences, I supported him as strongly as I could. It was at this conference that our friendship really began.'

The Conference of Editors of Diocesan Publications and Periodicals at Whalley Abbey ran from 13 to 15 April 1948. It was opened by the Bishop of Blackburn and attended by twenty-two clergymen from all over the country.

After three sessions covering 'The Function of Diocesan Periodicals', 'Ways and Means' and a review of thirty diocesan publications (and one parish magazine), the delegates turned their attention to the formation of an association to commission and syndicate articles. A society called 'Interim' was inaugurated with the Revd E.C. Varah as Secretary. 'Pooling of experience and of outstanding articles is the object, rather than centralisation or the destruction of diocesan individuality.'

Marcus found the same parochialism among the diocesan editors at Whalley Abbey as he had among the clergy he had previously contacted, but at least he and Chad had made a start towards their ultimate goal, a Society for Christian Publicity.

Chad wrote later, 'The first author to whom I wrote was C.S. Lewis. He replied courteously that he was too busy to write something specially for us, but was so much in favour of syndication by a Society for Christian Publicity that he had dug out a piece he had written some time before but had never had printed and would be glad to give Interim the First British Serial Rights for the ten guineas I had offered. The piece was called "Where the Shoe Pinches", but with his permission I changed the title to "The Trouble with X. . .".'

Members of Interim were also offered translations from foreign publications, photographs and 'fillers'. Articles that had already appeared in *The Anvil* were syndicated, including the Sybil Thorndike interview.

Much of the work for Interim was done in St James' Vicarage. The dining room was entirely given over to the work of Christian journalism. The large Victorian mahogany dining table (which Marcus sold twenty years later, to the chagrin of his outraged offspring) was covered with piles of *Anvil* and subscription forms and envelopes. There were three typewriters and three secretaries and as many voluntary workers as would fit into the room, including Audrey Entwistle and other members of the youth club.

In his study the Editor wrote and edited and thought about the future. He was alone with *The Anvil*'s financial problems which became more and more pressing. To help alleviate these, Chad wrote articles for nothing under various pen names. 'The Secret of Soviet Strategy' appeared under the pseudonym Xenia Varyagh, who was described as 'an expert on modern Russia and the theory and practice of Soviet Communism'. Under his own name he wrote 'Should the United Nations Unite?' and then moved on to the subject to which he has devoted a large part of his ministry, sexual counselling, with an article called 'Unholy Wedlock', a conversation between a parson and a young couple about to be married.

Marcus's editorial took up the theme: 'The parson may explain that the spiritual and physical sides of marriage are equally important and inextricably interconnected. The fact is that most people find them incompatible and keep them separate. . . .

'Unfortunately the ignorance of many is equalled only by their squeamishness. By regarding sexual enjoyment as something quite apart from "being a Christian", they not only throw God's gift back at Him or fail to use it fully; they also fail to make their marriage a true marriage. Promiscuity is not the only cause of today's marriage failures.'

Six months after the formation of Interim, sixteen clergy and lay people gathered at St Ermin's Hotel, Westminster for the inaugural meeting of the Society for Christian Publicity. Kenneth Grubb (who chaired the meeting), Revd Stephan Hopkinson, John Blair-Fish and the Revd Selwyn Gummer were amongst those who joined Marcus and Chad. George Goyder, Revd Eric Wild and Revd Shaun Herron were among the twenty-five who sent apologies and fifteen more expressed interest, including the Revds John Collins, Joseph McCulloch, Joost de Blank (later Archbishop of Cape Town), George Reindorp and Cecil Rhodes.

Marcus gave the opening speech: 'The purpose of this meeting is to consider the inauguration of a new Church Society to produce one or more popular Christian magazines and periodicals aimed specifically at the average non-churchman and those on the fringe of the Church. . . .

'A small group of us has been producing *The Anvil* as a deliberate attempt to get across to the outsider.

'Our first suggestion is that this Society should be formed to take over the publishing of *The Anvil*. It is losing about £16 a month – which means that only another thousand subscribers would make it pay. There is as a result a deficit – but I should like to make it quite clear that if there is any question of this being an obstacle to our plans I will personally be responsible for it, so as to hand over *The Anvil* free of encumbrances. . . .

'There are other types of periodical needed for the Church – weekly reviews, a picture magazine, a strip-cartoon magazine for children. . . . '

The Resolution was passed, that the first charge on the Society for Christian Publicity would be to put *The Anvil* on a satisfactory basis and to extend its circulation.

Although four bishops promised their support, the two subsequent meetings were less well attended than the first and the editor of *The Anvil* reported that the deficit had risen to £24 a month with £450 owed to printers. He was paying almost all expenses out of his own pocket. More resolutions were passed but nothing happened. There was no fourth meeting.

From November 1948 *The Anvil* claimed on the back cover to be published by the Society for Christian Publicity. Marcus, now with associate editors Chad, John Blair-Fish and Keith Chivers, wrote: 'Some people are scared of the word "publicity" as if it were something vulgar and beneath the Church. Of course, to publicise simply means "to make public", and if it isn't the job of *all* Christians to make public the Gospel of Christ, then we will eat our four editorial hats.

'Now that we have the support of leading clergy and laity from bishops to MPs we hope for great things for the SCP and *The Anvil* in 1949.'

But, as Marcus wrote later, 'Taking over *Anvil* was never more than a formality and the whole responsibility, financial, administrative and editorial remained on my shoulders. The Society never provided anything substantial in the way of financial help which was becoming more and more urgent.'

Early in 1949 Frank Hampson wrote to Marcus: 'I feel the cover is too "static". . . . My idea is to have a standard frame all the time with a vacant central panel or area. In this space could be printed each month an illustration from that particular issue with a challenging headline. There is usually one illustration at least each month which could be used and I suppose the same block could be employed. We could also get a really modern feel into the standard frame. Do you think I've got anything here? I do feel that the same cover all the time is a handicap whereas a little figure like, for instance, the bishop in Canon Bezzant's swearing article or the civil servant in David Gunston's, might catch the eye. . . . If I'm just being fatuous forgive me for wasting so much ink.'

Marcus didn't consider the idea fatuous; in February he wrote in the editorial, 'The garb in which *Anvil* appears this month is, we admit, unusual for a parish magazine. But then *The Anvil is* unusual. And we see no reason why it should not *look* as cheerful as what it stands for. Since trying to be a Christian is one of the most interesting, amusing and stimulating experiences anyone could want, it's a pity that it should often be camouflaged in dull respectability.'

The cover is indeed colourful and no longer features an anvil. Frank's cartoon portrays a perplexed band leader and some sweating brass players (an illustration for a short story) with the legend *The ORIGINAL Christian Magazine*. Over the next year *Anvil*'s cover displayed more varied hues and humorous – and political – situations. Frank's design for the editorial heading showed the scale of *Anvil*'s interests: half a globe, a plane, a pylon, a factory, a car and a newspaper all jumbled up over the words *Under The Hammer*.

The Revd Dewi Morgan became a regular contributor, starting with an article on Christmas carols.

Dewi wrote to us, 'As far as I am concerned, Marcus Morris was preeminently the man who gave wings to a very old and tired cliché: "He changed my life. . . ".

'My hand-writing was atrocious, definitely a mighty drawback in parish work. I had to do something about it, like saving up for a typewriter. . . . I must look for an honest way of earning money. Freelance journalism perhaps?

'A trickle of unsolicited manuscripts began to leave my study. Some of them did not return but were replaced by an editor's cheque. I was exultant. I got my typewriter for my parish work and I would leave journalism to the journalist.

'Then came the day when a fellow-priest from Lancashire came to see his aged parents who lived in my parish. He knew someone called Marcus Morris, of whom I had never heard. "If you are going to do more journalism," he said, "keep an eye on him. His parish magazine publishes the sort of writing which helps the man in the street to become informed. . . . I am sure he would like to see your work." Before I went to bed I had spent another three-halfpenny stamp and my manuscript was on its way to Marcus Morris.

'Marcus accepted my verbal outburst and wrote asking me to do a series of profiles of outstanding Christians who were doing unusual jobs in unusual circumstances.

'I promptly phoned him and told him I knew nobody in the category he wanted. His reply was to reel off a list of names I had vaguely heard of. . . . Among them were several people who worked with missionary societies overseas. "Usually," said Marcus, "the societies have a lot of fascinating information about their staff but they have no-one to write it up in the way I want it. Will you do this for the sake of the Church and its mission?" "Very well," I said, "IF the missionary societies will supply the raw material I will write it up." . . .

'The Society for the Propagation of the Gospel promptly promised to send regular material, most of which appeared in *Anvil*. Subsequently other organisations sent me material and what Marcus Morris had begun was soon to become an acceptable routine in the secular as well as the religious press. As a result I shortly became Press and Education Secretary of the Society that first sent me material and from there moved on to working with media people for twenty-four years as Rector of St Bride's, Fleet Street.

'I have always been grateful to Marcus for so expanding my life and my vision.

'For over thirty years Marcus and I met frequently on both Church and media occasions. When I became Rector of St Bride's, he was already one of the Honorary Chaplains.'

Advertising in the magazine now extended beyond the boundaries of Southport – advertisers included Scourine 'a product of Paton Calvert & Co Ltd', Hartley's 'The greatest name in jam-making', Alexander Clark Silverware of London, Beecham's Pills and the Society for Christian Publicity – the latter drawn by Frank Hampson, depicting a copy of *Anvil* on a ski-lift 'Getting across to the man in the street'. Cannell's, Outfitters of Lord Street, Southport still loyally occupied the back cover.

Marcus's editorials during 1949 included diatribes against fox and stag

*Possibly Frank Hampson's first professional strip cartoon*

hunting, communism, racial discrimination in South Africa and support for Artificial Insemination by Donor. Frank provided increasing numbers of illustrations (twenty in the March issue) and in the April issue, possibly his first professional strip cartoon, to illustrate a 'Commentary' castigating strip cartoons: it showed an artist labelled FH fleeing from a flying anvil.

By May *The Anvil* was no longer published by the Society for Christian Publicity and the *Southport Guardian* was no longer the printer, having handed over that dubious privilege to John Sherratt & Son of Altrincham, Manchester. Whether Sherratt knew about the large sums owing to the *Guardian* is anybody's guess.

In the spring of 1949 Chad Varah moved from Blackburn to the church of St John with St Paul at Clapham Junction, London and handed over the Honorary Secretaryship of Interim to Marcus. Marcus decided to give both Interim and the SCP a fillip by sending out a mailing to the clergy but, instead of the usual typed sheet, he wanted a properly printed and designed brochure for which he would need typographical help. Somebody told him of a brilliant new man in London, Ruari McLean, DSC, who was then a part-time art director at advertising agency A.N. Holden and a teacher at the Royal College of Art. Marcus wrote to the young typographer but Ruari 'had already found that parsons either asked for one's advice and didn't take it, or took it but were unable to pay for it. I therefore wrote a carefully composed off-putting letter and apparently so annoyed the parson that he asked me to meet him one afternoon at Euston Station, which I did. We inspected each other cautiously. In half an hour a friendship was made which lasted for life.'

The first thing Marcus asked Ruari to design was smart personal stationery, a necessity, he felt, for a budding entrepreneur and journalist. Then came an ambitious range of office stationery, subscription forms, invoices, compliments slips, renewal forms and the brochure for the SCP mailing shot.

Although Ruari complains that 'the number of letters I've had from Marcus can be counted on one hand', there were quite a few in those early days.

'I am hoping to get [the brochure] out by the end of this week, so could you possibly put through a reverse charge personal call to me tomorrow morning.' (No wonder his *Anvil* debts were so high.)

'I enclose an article for *The Anvil* which I shall be most grateful if you can illustrate. We have to go to press early next week because of the Lancashire holidays, so can you possibly manage to do it more or less immediately. . . . I leave it entirely to you to decide on lay-out and size.'

'Would you have time to rough out an idea for a second brochure, . . . the less expensive the better. . . . When we meet again we must discuss the question of your help in lay-out etc.' 'Will you try and think up a brochure to send to church laity, e.g. churchwardens, secretaries of Church Councils, Sunday School superintendents, etc.' 'I now enclose material for a brochure about quite a different matter which I think explains itself. I cannot afford to spend too much on it. . . . I enclose a cheque for eight guineas for part of the lay-out work that you have done. . . . It would be a help to get your comments (as frank as you like) about the *Anvil* lay-out.'

The formal 'Dear Mr McLean' lasted for three letters; thereafter it was 'Dear Ruari', until January 1989 when Marcus wrote to him from the South of France. In March Ruari's reply was the last thing Marcus read before he died.

Marcus's secretaryship of Interim increased the work load – particularly for his helpers. Lilian Oliver was one of the secretaries at St James: 'Marcus was a very kind employer, never critical. He was remarkably natural and modest and thoughtful. He wasn't a person who walked about with a smile, he was quite serious looking. I remember Marcus and Jess going to a garden fête. When they got back I said "What did you do, walk about looking pleasant?" Marcus replied "I just walked about".'

'We worked long hours on occasion. During financial difficulties there were the odd weeks when I didn't get paid, but I always got it in the end.'

In 1949 Audrey Entwistle was asked to join the staff. 'It was a great time. Lilian Oliver sat at a big typewriter at one end of the room and I had MM's little portable. We imported a child of sixteen (I was nineteen, felt terribly grown up), a post girl. A very happy little office.

'Frank Hampson used to come round with his little drawings and strew them over the dining table. He was very kind, I liked him, he was a solid rugged character. He and Marcus seemed to be great buddies.'

By that autumn the sales of *The Anvil* totalled 3,560 and Marcus was deeply in debt. The situation can't have been helped by the eighty-three free copies that went to friends and relations and clergy and laity all over the world. In October Marcus received a remarkably restrained letter from John Sherratt & Son: 'Things are very tight just at the moment and it would be a great help if you could let us have a substantial cheque.'

Marcus was still looking for a buyer for *The Anvil* and, in October, found one. In January 1950 he was able to report in his editorial: '*The Anvil* has been through many vicissitudes during its three years' existence and suffered all the ailments of a young infant. It starts its fourth year under new management and with the stature of a grown adult. . . . It has now, the editor delights to report, been acquired by the well known publishers G. J. Palmer & Sons, publishers of the *Church Times*.'

Bernard Palmer, son of the then proprietor, wrote in his book *Gadfly for God*: '*The Anvil* . . . aimed at a wider audience than a parish magazine, but at one which was not sufficiently informed to want to read the *Church Times*. . . . Moreover, the *Anvil* appeared to have achieved a high standard of popular journalism and to be admirably produced. So that, when in the early autumn of 1949 Morris approached Christopher Palmer with a suggestion that his firm should buy the paper, Palmer and his colleagues were tempted into agreeing. . . . Morris asked £1,500 in cash for the *Anvil*. In the end he agreed to accept £1,250 with a three year contract to continue as editor at a salary of £200 per annum. But there was an escape clause in the contract allowing the board to abandon publication at an earlier date "should this be judged advisable".'

Christopher Palmer also thought that the purchase of *Anvil* would 'bring us into touch with authors and cartoonists hitherto unknown to us and perhaps in the future we may be able to use one of the *Anvil* cartoonists for the *Church Times*.'

Under the new owner the paper was glossier and there were pages of photographs. Alan Jefferson had taken over from Hampson as the principal illustrator. Frank designed his last *Anvil* cover for the March 1950 issue – he had other things on his mind by then. The Ecclesiastical Insurance Office took a full page advertisement but Cannell was no longer on the back cover; it was replaced by Southlands, The Perfect Non-Washable Collar.

*Anvil*'s money problems were not solved by Palmer's takeover. Christopher Palmer wrote to Marcus, 'The losses on *The Anvil* are very much more than I had expected. . . . It might be some months before we could really increase the circulation so as to obtain a larger revenue from advertisements. . . .

'Although I am the Managing Director of this company, my actual shareholding is not very large and some of those people who obtain beneficial interest from the profits of the *Church Times* are people who have extremely low incomes. . . . Though I should be perfectly prepared to make sacrifices from my own pocket, I cannot do it where others are concerned. . . . I gather that the printing order for the April issue has been increased to 9,000.'

*The Anvil* lasted only a few months longer. Bernard Palmer wrote, 'Efforts both to boost circulation and to whip up the support of advertisers got absolutely nowhere. . . . The board was losing money on *The Anvil* at the rate of £4,000 a year. . . . For a time it toyed with the idea of turning *The Anvil* into a parish-magazine inset; but Morris was against the idea and in any event there was too much competition in that particular field. There was no prospect of being able to sell the paper as a going concern to another publisher; so, at its meeting on 27 July 1950, the board reluctantly decided to suspend publication.'

The September issue was the last. Marcus's editorial said: 'It is with very great regret that we have to announce that with this issue *The Anvil* ceases publication. . . .

'*Anvil* has aroused a considerable amount of interest and approval and has been reached by many who were not in the habit of reading any other kind of Christian literature. Our experience over the last four years has . . . proved the need for some such magazine, and letters we have received from many different parts of the world show that it has been appreciated.

It makes it all the sadder that we must cease publication at a time when *The Anvil* appeared to be on the verge of achieving its purpose.

'But the last four years has also shown that no magazine of this kind can hope to succeed fully or gain the circulation necessary for it to pay its way without a much greater measure of support from the Clergy and Church people generally.'

So the last issue of *The Anvil* appeared with a cover illustration of, appropriately, harvest time under a setting sun. Forty-six pages of glossy paper; photographs showing that the best things in life are free, gratis and for nothing; illustrations by Harold Johns and John Ryan; books reviewed by Chad; a full page cartoon by Thelwell (Workers Unite! Down with Tyranny and Oppression and Free Deck Chairs for the Workers!): a far cry from the eight-page St James' Magazine.

Bernard Palmer: 'There is a curious little postscript attaching to the story of *The Anvil*. The G.J. Palmer directors were nothing if not optimistic. They still hoped that the magazine might be relaunched at a later date, and therefore decided to retain ownership of the title. So, after it had ceased publication in 1950, every issue of the CT contained in the imprint at the bottom of the back page the words "*Church Times* (with which is incorporated *The Anvil*)". This continued till the end of 1983, when it was announced that a new evangelical magazine was shortly to appear with the same title. I gently pointed out to its publishers that the title *The Anvil* was the property of my own company – a fact they had overlooked. But I offered to sell it to them for a nominal sum – and the title changed hands in return for a modest donation to the *Church Times* Train-A-Priest Fund.'

Marcus always remained somewhat irritated that the Church authorities had not been more help with *The Anvil* and the SCP but 'one thing of importance for the future did emerge from the Society: we began to discuss the question of a paper for children with a Christian content.

'This subject had been vaguely in my mind before. There had been a section for children in *The Anvil*. The Bishop of Blackburn had urged the need for a paper of this kind and there had been some discussion on the subject in the Church of England Children's Council. I had looked at a children's comic produced by the Roman Catholics in America which used strip cartoons. The idea had been slowly germinating in my mind and it grew quickly after those SCP meetings.'

In his *Anvil* editorial in February 1949 Marcus had written: 'Do you like the idea of a Christian children's comic – as exciting and absorbing as those the children clamour for now? That is one of the projects being prepared by the new Society for Christian Publicity started by your editors and now supported by many well-known clergy and laymen. It is already drawing interested enquiries from all over the place.'

Jess said that the idea came while they were waiting for a train to Liverpool on Birkdale Railway Station. 'The only stuff for children on the railway bookstall was awful American comics. The man on the stall agreed that it was terrible but there was nothing else to sell.'

# Chapter Eight

31 January 1949. The *Daily Mirror*. 'A comic with a serious aim.

'A new children's comic is likely to be on the bookstalls soon; its publishers, the Society for Christian Publicity. "It won't be a dull comic just because it's religious," said the Society secretary, Revd Marcus Morris of Southport, yesterday. "Everyone says 'Why doesn't the church do something to put itself across?' We are the first group to get down to that. We are here to issue propaganda not for the Church of England, but for Christianity." '

That little piece of over-optimistic reporting brought to St James' vicarage a very smooth journalist called Norman Price, who lived in Southport and worked on the Sunday *Empire News* in Manchester.

Norman Price 'reckoned Marcus was on to something' – this was a story which would sell. They would write it together. 'Comics that take horror into the Nursery' was given a prominent position next to the editorial in the *Sunday Dispatch* of 13 February. It described some of the illustrated stories contained in comics brought to the vicarage for Marcus's daughters by a well-intentioned parishioner:

'The front-page serial shows Arab pirates capturing a half-naked girl in trousers, brassière and bolero, who is gloatingly displayed to the crowd. The back page shows her sitting with arms bound in a rowing boat while a hired executioner rows her across a river and kills her with a sword.

'It is a magazine with 175 flawlessly vivid drawings that start with gangsters shooting a girl in the stomach, having the heroine twice bound and gagged, finally dumped in a bath of cold water to drown.

'One of the detective heroes of my own boyhood is now – I was dismayed to see – on sale to children with a front-cover illustration of a girl, naked to the waist, pitched overboard from a ship's porthole.

'This is the home market. American imports include "Fearless Fosdick" in which a character murders a group of six policemen with a machine gun, and a series "Fairy Tales for Juvenile Delinquents".

'Horror has crept into the British nursery. Morals of little girls in plaits and boys with marbles bulging their pockets are being corrupted by a torrent of indecent coloured magazines that are flooding bookstalls and newsagents.

'Have parents really bothered to study them – these weekly and fortnightly "comics" that sons and daughters from seven to seventeen years old are devouring?

'Not mere "thrillers" as we used to know them, nor the once-familiar "school stories". These are evil and dangerous – graphic, coloured illustrations of modern city vice and crime. Any school child with a couple of pennies can buy them.

'Latest crime figures in the Metropolitan Police area show a 33.7 per cent increase since 1938 in child criminals of nine years old – and nearly 40 per cent increase among children aged ten.

'I blame much of this on their "comics". As soon as a child becomes old enough to read, he enters a new world of horror and vice, where there are no apparent morals and certainly no holds barred.

'It sickens and frightens me. Even in the lisping little nursery comics for the tiny tots the cute little animals seem mostly to be bashing each other's heads or stealing each other's sweets and cakes.

'Surely there is adventure enough for any boy or girl in the lives of men like Grenville of Labrador? And some of the daily dangers St Paul met would make even Dick Barton look like a cissy. . . .

'I shall not feel I have done my duty as a parson and father of children until I have seen on the market a genuinely popular "Children's Comic" where adventure is once more the clean and exciting business I remember in my own schooldays – not abysmally long ago. Children are born hero-worshippers, not born ghouls. They will admire what they are given to admire.

'It is up to us – whether or not we go to church each Sunday – to see they get a glimpse of what really brave men have done in this world, and share laughter that comes from the heart – not from the gutter! '

The style is the journalist's, the opinion Marcus's – he was later to write that he found those final paragraphs a little embarrassing to read, although not having changed his mind about the sentiments.

The article created an immediate impact and letters poured in to the vicarage from all over the country, applauding Marcus's stand and suggesting that he do something about the problem.

From Tunbridge Wells: 'Though an agnostic, I obviously must agree that your protest is entirely justified.'

Manchester: 'As the parents of a girl aged eleven and a boy of eight, we fully appreciate the seriousness of your remarks, as our children have from time to time brought these species of sensational literature into the house.'

Cardiff: 'I read your article to a meeting of our TUC Women's Guild members and it was admitted that the majority of the mothers had never bothered to look at the comics which their children read. This, I think, will be remedied from now on. I sincerely trust your article was widely read and that it will be the means of making people more interested in the literature their children are given to read.'

Wells, Somerset: 'Why can't some decent Christian organisation publish for children cheap books at once palatable and wholesome?'

King's Lynn: 'I shall be interested to hear news of the Christian comic as the present type of so-called comic has been banned at the school to which my children go.'

Wolverton, Bucks: 'I must say "thank you" for what you have written. You are the first man I have known to put his finger on one of the gravest sources of juvenile crime.'

E.C. Jennings, Pinner: 'For a long time, I have been waiting for someone like yourself to call attention to the rotten state of the so-called "comics" of the present time and now, with the publicity that will follow your attack, you can, if you will, do something to make it "stick". I am a cartoonist and, if you say the word, I shall be more than glad to pile in and produce, with your help, the sort of comic paper that the children of the country are entitled to read.'

Authors wrote complaining that publishers refused to look at 'wholesome and harmless' stories, many people requested specimen copies of Marcus's proposed comic and Lutterworth Press asked for further details.

Marcus said later: 'The publication of the article, the interest aroused and possibly the twenty guineas I received from the *Sunday Dispatch*, all set me thinking hopefully along the lines of strip cartoon.'

Marcus decided that he didn't have the wherewithal to produce an entire children's paper, but that he and Frank Hampson could easily manage a wholesome yet adventurous strip story. Norman Price thought that a strip cartoon written by a vicar would be a good gimmick and suggested trying to sell one to a Sunday paper. Marcus later explained: 'When Frank and I got interested in the strip cartoon idea, Frank was very keen on it. I wrote the story and he did the illustration for a strip called Lex Christian, which was not really for children, but for adults.

'Frank turned out to have a really brilliant strip technique. Even at that early stage we went quite a long way towards evolving the character of Dan Dare, but Lex Christian was a tough fighting parson in the East End of London.'

Marcus and Frank were pleased with the result and Norman Price sent them to see Terence Horsley of the *Empire News*. They thought their strip cartoon infinitely superior to other samples he showed them. Horsley was enthusiastic and encouraging but suggested that their strip needed a little more work on it and they should come and see him again. Before they could do so, he was killed in a gliding accident on 24 April 1949.

The idea of a children's paper took hold again.

Marcus wrote in 1958: 'Shortly after Horsley died, I went to see Frank in his house at the other end of Southport. I remember the scene and my words very vividly because the decision we took that day was crucial.

'I said, "Frank, we're wasting our time on this idea of a strip for a Sunday paper. Let's forget about it and go back to the original idea of a paper for children, consisting mainly of strips. I know it's much more difficult, but I'm sure it's the right thing to do."

'Frank's reaction was one of enthusiasm. At that moment *Eagle* was conceived, though the birth pangs had yet to be faced and the labour would be long.

'From May 1949 Frank and I gave all the time we could spare to working on stories and ideas and features. We worked in a kind of informal collaboration which is hard to define. Both of us were quite inexperienced at that kind of work and there was a great deal of trial and error.

'To begin with we turned Lex Christian into a flying padre, the Parson of the Fighting Seventh. Then one day, after re-reading C.S. Lewis's science fiction novel *Perelandra*, I said to Frank that I thought Lex Christian should leave London and go out into space. I remember telling Frank to get him to Venus and I would take over from there. Frank got him to Venus without much difficulty and I didn't take over; Frank continued to work on the story and the characters. The name Lex Christian didn't seem quite right and we thought up a large number of alternatives. I think it was Frank's wife Dorothy who came up with Dan Dare. He was the first parson to be launched into space.'

The strip based on the life of St Paul, which was to be the back page of the dummy, emerged from the same process of trial and error. 'I said one day that St Paul's life with all its colour and vigour and incident was just the kind of thing which would serialise effectively. Frank took it up. He wasn't a churchman or a student of the Bible but I have no doubt that St Paul's boldness and courage attracted him. He did a lot of research into the historical background, I roughed out the story and we had our second strip. For the rest of the contents I just drew up what subjects I thought would interest young children – some text, some adventure stories, sport, and wrote some of the scripts.'

All this extra work didn't leave much time for Frank's silk screen printing business and the piecework he was earning on *The Anvil* was not enough to keep his family so Marcus paid him a salary of £8 a week out of his own stipend.

*The Anvil* still had to be produced and Frank's partner, Harold Johns, was brought in to help. Harold was a quiet and self-effacing man and a talented watercolourist – one of his wartime paintings is in the Imperial War Museum. As well as helping Frank on Dan Dare, he produced his own strips for the dummy. It soon became clear that he as well as Frank would have to go on a salary if Marcus was to retain their services.

Harold Johns brought in J. Walkden Fisher, one of a 'gang' of local artists, who was at that time designing for a toy firm. 'Fish', as he was known, produced a series of intricate diagrams and drawings of man-made and natural phenomena, and the Hiawatha story in black and white strip.

The first dummy of *Eagle*, produced early that summer, contained two colour pages of Chaplain Dan Dare of the Interplanet Patrol, Dan in an RAF-colour uniform, dog collar and swirling white cloak. The second major colour strip was two pages of 'Secret City' featuring Jimmy Swift. On the back page was 'The Great Adventurer', the story of St Paul. There were two half-page funny strips – 'Joe from Strawberry Farm', and 'Ernie, Always Unlucky', drawn by E.C. Jennings who had written from Pinner in response to the *Sunday Dispatch* article. There was an Editor's Letter, Railway News, Model News, Competitions, a page and a half of stories and Fish's 'World of Wonders'. Frank made three photo-copies of the dummy and coloured them in.

The name of the magazine had been the subject of much discussion between the Hampsons and the Morrises; it has always been said that Dorothy Hampson came up with *Eagle* after gazing at a church lectern.

Marcus was, by the spring of 1949, in very deep water financially.

'Even my kind and understanding bank manager was losing patience with me, but I couldn't believe that it was a time for caution. I was sure that our idea would eventually turn out to be a great success. Even on the brink of bankruptcy or imprisonment for debt I was willing to back my conviction and did so again when, in order to keep Frank in Southport, I had to raise his salary. If Frank went I knew the idea would go too.'

Frank had also found himself in financial difficulties and went to London to see one or two big agencies. They liked his work and could use it. Frank went back north to tell Marcus that he'd been told he could earn £1,000 a year in London. Marcus had no choice but to increase Frank's salary and he offered to pay him an extra £2 a week. This was nowhere near those prospective London earnings, so Marcus was relieved and grateful when Frank said that he shared his belief in the children's paper and would carry on; £10 a week would be just enough for him and his family to survive for the time being. Marcus agreed to raise this to £12 in August and to £20 by the following February (having faith that he would have found a publisher by then).

By the end of May Marcus was paying Frank 53 per cent of his Church stipend; he owed the *Southport Guardian* over £600; his bank account was heavily overdrawn. Norman Price, ostensibly so helpful, was unwilling and possibly unable to come up with any money. He thought that they were on to a winner with the children's paper but that *The Anvil* was little more than a millstone round their necks. He suggested that they form a publishing company to take over *Anvil*, which would then be suspended for a period. Marcus would be managing director, with Norman devoting himself to compounding with creditors and raising funds: 'I think you will agree that, although I lack your own undeniably brilliant conception and leadership, I am likely to have a far more balanced and stringent hand upon the communal purse-strings and will be able to buy to better advantage.'

The terms of his proposal were so heavily weighted in Norman's favour that Marcus would have nothing to do with it, particularly the idea of suspending *The Anvil*.

'You are asking me to give up what I consider to be the most important thing that I have been doing to date, presumably in order to increase the Company's chances of profits. In return for that you offer me, in effect, £80, i.e. £5 a week to Hampson for four months.

'I may say that I should have felt a good deal more sure of your co-operation in the future if in these last few months you had really done some practical work to help me. I believe you could, with the expenditure of comparatively little time and no money, have made use of your contacts to get *The Anvil* publicity and advertisements. . . .'

Norman replied, 'The features agency was for the purpose of supplying the company with Lex Christian. . . . It might also of course have been used for Frank to sell his comic strips to me, after having first bought his scripts from you – and my selling thereafter to the company – all for no other purpose than dodging taxation.'

Although Norman continued to be involved on the periphery for some months, they never again worked closely together. Marcus was later to say that 'he is a very smooth, slippery customer who sails very close to the wind'.

Still somewhat ingenuously convinced that forming a company would relieve some of his problems, Marcus went to see a solicitor who had been recommended to him by his former colleague. The solicitor was 'an elderly man, scruffy and tall with eyes which didn't rest for very long on anything – least of all on the eyes of anyone talking to him. He always carried a dirty mackintosh. If he had offices in which he interviewed clients, I never discovered where they were, as we always met in the waiting-cum-tearoom at the Central Station in Manchester.'

For the sum of £90 he formed a limited company, Anvil Publications Ltd (also called at one stage Astra Publications; the prospectuses are virtually the same), which Marcus naïvely supposed people would rush to invest in. The prospectus declares, 'The company is being formed to publish popular Christian periodicals which have a wide appeal to the man in the street whether church man or not.

'In particular, the Company proposes to publish a new children's coloured "comic" paper, which will be of a much higher and more mature quality than anything published in England and in appearance and format will be modelled more on the American comic papers which are so far in advance of our own. Retail price 3d. First-class illustrators and well known children's story writers have already been engaged and the first issue is practically complete in dummy form.

'A circulation of 100,000 a fortnight is hoped for within a few months . . . the comic will show a profit at a circulation of 60,000. At 100,000 the profit should be £200 a fortnight.'

Marcus's first approach was to those people who might be assumed to know something about him.

The Church Assembly Children's Council had been talking about the necessity of some kind of illustrated magazine for children and the Bishop of Blackburn had expressed some very precise views on the subject.

Marcus asked Miss M.G. Bartlett, Secretary of the Council, 'whether you think that it would be worthwhile approaching the SPCK or some other Church publisher with a view to their taking it over, wholly or partly. I have no very high opinion of the SPCK and am reluctant to have much to do with them but possibly you and I together might be able to convince them that here is something really worthwhile. And it would have the added advantage that there need be no watering down of the Christian element in the comic paper.' Miss Bartlett was sympathetic and supportive; the Council gave the magazine its backing, but no money.

Canon John Collins suggested that Marcus talk to the head of the Church Missionary Society, Kenneth Grubb, who had been involved with the Society for Christian Publicity. Grubb regretted that 'I do not think we could undertake a project so ambitious as that which you have in mind.'

The next line of attack was the publishing companies. Wills & Hepworth, who produced Ladybird children's books, said that they were not big enough to take on a fortnightly publication. On 1 July, Marcus wrote to Edward Hulton at Hulton Press, but got no reply.

From a public telephone box just off Fleet Street, by Temple Bar, he telephoned Sir Neville Pearson, Chairman of George Newnes. Amazingly, he was put through to Sir Neville and his enthusiasm must have been infectious as, to his great surprise, Pearson invited him to his office. After the meeting with Pearson and his fellow director, E.D. Lush, Marcus was optimistic. He wrote to Mr Lush, 'To begin with we plan to publish it fortnightly with twelve pages of which eight will be in full colour, produced by photogravure. But we can supply the material for weekly publication. . . . It is intended for children between the ages of nine and fourteen, but it may well attract a large adult readership as such papers do in America. . . . Though it will be a Christian publication in the sense that it is being produced by Christians and will stand for Christian values and standards, there is certainly no intention of making it a pious or conventionally religious paper of the Sunday school type. On the contrary, we want it to appeal equally to children who have no contact with religion. Our first aim, therefore, will be to make it as attractive, original and exciting as possible. I believe that the Bible strip as we have treated it will have a wide appeal, but we shall probably alter the hero of the "Dan Dare" strip and will no longer make him a parson.'

While Marcus was hoping that Newnes would supply financial backing, he was also alive to the possibility of their acquiring ownership of *Eagle*, retaining him as editor. But Newnes expressed doubts about paper supply; no new periodicals or magazines were permitted if they used more than sixteen hundredweight of paper in a four-month period. In view of his difficulties in getting paper for *The Anvil*, Marcus seems to have been a trifle optimistic about bending the rules governing Paper Control Orders. He told Lush that John Sherratt & Son, who had agreed to print *Eagle*, had ample supplies of paper. 'If, however, we were to be bound by the Paper Control Order to which you refer, I had intended in the first place to apply for a licence for additional paper. . . . We planned if necessary to acquire another publication with the requisite paper allowance.'

Lush replied, 'There is ample paper available if one has the permission to use it. . . . I agree that there is provision for special licences being granted but having regard to the competitive nature of your proposed publication I personally rather doubt whether such an application would be successful. Your other suggestion of acquiring another publication is, of course, a solution.'

Nothing more was heard from George Newnes until October, when Mr Lush decided 'that the economics of the journal are not sufficiently attractive to us to warrant proceeding any further.'

Meanwhile, Marcus wrote enthusiastically to Mr Morgan of Williams Deacons Bank 'I am glad to say that the arrangements for the new Company are practically completed. . . . I have had one definite offer of help and have made contact with several people who are interested and are just waiting to see the necessary documents. When I went to London on Monday last with dummy copies of our proposed comic paper I was very encouraged by the enthusiasm it met both from the Church authorities and from various people in the publishing world.

'I don't think we shall have great difficulty in raising the necessary capital. . . . I have had to keep paying out in order to have something definite to show those whom we are approaching to support us. . . . I am very grateful for your patience over this long period.'

But Mr Morgan's patience was tried too far. 'The whole business is getting out of hand and you have no right to continue to issue cheques when you know quite well that your limit is £450. We were also very surprised to hear that you still have outstanding bills. Under no circumstances can we allow any further advance and these bills must remain where they are until you can put your hands on a decent sum of money. We should not like to return any of your cheques but we shall be compelled to if you continue in this manner.'

Marcus wrote a passionate two-page reply. 'The matter is being dealt with in the only possible way, i.e., by the formation of the Company which will take over my publications. . . . I already have £500 promised. . . . I am going down to London tomorrow night for several appointments. . . . I have no doubt at all that we shall raise the capital because our proposed children's paper is very definitely a commercial proposition. . . . I have the official support of the Church Assembly Children's Council. . . .

'I imagined that it was because you appreciated the situation that you have allowed me to increase my overdraft. . . . I am so near completing my plans that it would be more than unfortunate if I was prevented from doing so now. I have no other assets or property which would realise the amount needed and the payment of my creditors therefore depends entirely on my success in forming this company. . . . I should be glad if you could see your way to allowing me a little further latitude.' And the splendid Mr Morgan complied.

The first board meeting of Anvil Publications Ltd took place in the vicarage in July. Marcus and Lionel Lister elected each other as Secretary and Chairman, with Jess as a director. The occasion was productive of a great deal of hilarity, but not much else.

Lionel was Captain of Formby Golf Club where John Moores, founder of the vast Littlewoods Pools empire was a member. Armed with an introduction and the dummy of the children's paper, Marcus went to see Moores on 26 July. Mr Moores expressed a kindly interest and said he had no doubt that his young daughter would like a paper of this kind. He would be prepared to back it and would spread the word around. He agreed to lend Marcus £1000. 'I was a very happy man when I left his office, relieved at this apparent solution to all my financial problems.'

This elation was short-lived. On 4 August, Marcus wrote to John Moores at his home in Freshfield, near Southport, 'You were kind enough to say that I might use your name as one financially interested in the project. . . . Since your name carries such weight I have taken advantage of your permission and mentioned your interest to a number of other likely supporters. Since as a result of a telephone conversation with your Publicity Manager, Mr Ayers, I now understand there may be some doubt about the situation, I should be most grateful if you could spare the time to see me again for a few minutes at your convenience.'

9 August, to Revd Marcus Morris: 'I certainly never authorised you to use my name as a "backer" to encourage others to interest themselves in your proposed venture. On the contrary, I expressed grave doubts as to its success, having regard to the resources at your disposal and the competition you would have to face. So much so, that I asked Mr Ayers to see you and, having done so, he confirmed my apprehension.

'Forgive me for saying so, but I take grave exception to the manner in which you have apparently thought fit, quite unjustifiably, to "cash in" on the strength of my name.

'I must, therefore, ask you kindly to leave me out of account in your further consideration of the matter of your children's "comic" paper.'

12 August, to Mr John Moores: 'I must confess to finding myself more than a little perplexed by your letter of Wednesday. And considerably astonished at finding myself accused of misrepresentation.

'I am not in any doubt about the facts and they hardly appear capable of being misunderstood. On three occasions you used the words: "You can rely on £1,000 anyway" and on the third occasion you added "whatever Ayers thinks of it". As you went to the door to speak to your assistant you remarked "You can say I am putting some money into it, if that will help". I naturally assumed that the words were used in their normally accepted sense and that you meant what you said.

'At the close of my conversation with Mr Ayers (of which you do not appear to have been fully informed) he assured me, so far from expressing grave doubts, "that he would do his very best for me" in suggesting that you gave some financial support so long as it did not entail any extra work or worry for you. When he spoke to me on the phone from London he expressed his regret at not persuading you into being associated with us. He informed me that I should be receiving from you within the next day or so a cheque for £250 which, however, was not to be used for shares.

'It is somewhat confusing to receive two such conflicting promises – and then to discover that both are to be abrogated.

'You can rest assured that I shall make the situation perfectly clear to those to whom I have mentioned your name.'

12 August, to Lionel Lister, Esq: 'I enclose a copy of a letter I have received from Moores. I really feel pretty angry with him. His letter is nothing but flagrant lying – the exact reversal of what he actually said to me.

'I suppose that's that, and I only hope that it won't embarrass you in your relations with him in the future.'

18 August, to Revd Marcus Morris: 'I am extremely sorry that there has been this misunderstanding between us, and that your recollection of the facts does not correspond with mine. Nevertheless I feel that no useful purpose will be served by any further argument.

'However, there has quite obviously been a genuine misunderstanding and, rather than you should feel in any way aggrieved, I am enclosing my cheque for £250 and would ask you to accept it with my best wishes for the future success of your venture.'

Marcus's immediate reaction was to send the money back. He was angry at having been misled and falsely represented but, when he had calmed down, he admitted that he badly needed the money. He swallowed his pride, banked the cheque and wrote to John Moores expressing his thanks.

He then went the rounds of the other rich citizens of Southport. His reception was always friendly, sometimes vaguely condescending; occasionally the politeness almost hid the conviction that he was mad or at least more than usually eccentric, even for a Church of England parson.

No more cheques came in and the overdraft started to mount again.

With writs hovering from the *Southport Guardian*, Marcus realised that he would have to give up any idea of keeping the project under his own control and would have to try to sell it to someone who would employ him to edit it and Frank to draw the strips.

He packed the dummy in his briefcase and caught the train to London again.

On Sunday nights, after a full weekend of parish work, services, sermons, baptisms, weddings and putting *The Anvil* together, Marcus took the train from Liverpool and spent the next four days in London, staying with Jess's sister and brother-in-law, the actors Ruth Dunning and Jack Allen, on the top of Campden Hill, Kensington.

'A young chap I met who was someone in the film business put me in touch with John Myers, publicity manager for J. Arthur Rank. Sir Arthur, I knew, was interested in making religious films for children and he was as keen as mustard on Sunday schools. It seemed hopeful. I even saw the great man himself once, in the largest office I had ever come across. It seemed a long walk from the door to his desk. Again I received sympathy, but no cash. John Myers advised me to go and see Montague Haydon, Editorial Director of Amalgamated Press.'

So Marcus went to Fleetway House full of hope and told his story, which he now had off pat. Montague Haydon's reaction was civil, guarded and pessimistic. 'I think I puzzled him. He was not quite sure what to make of this dog-collarless parson from the North of England who was trying to sell him a comic and he was suspicious of what I was really up to.' In September Montague Haydon returned the dummy with a note: 'I have taken a good hard look at the enclosed dummy of *Eagle*. It is bright and it is good, but no brighter and no "gooder" than our average juvenile. So I don't know what we can do with it except send it back to you.'

Marcus wrote: 'With Kemsley Press I utterly failed. I didn't even get as far as Lord Kemsley, then owner of *The Sunday Times*. I was seen by an underling who got the idea into his head that I was asking for a donation for charity. With great charm he said, "I am sure you will realise that his Lordship has many calls on his purse." He was a silly little man, I forget who he was.' It was Denis Hamilton, who later became Lord Thomson's right-hand man and in charge of *The Times*.

'I went to see T.E. Boardman Ltd which was a bold move as they were already importing the very American comics which had inspired me to attempt something better and less harmful for children. They liked my idea and considered it quite seriously for a time before telling me they didn't want it.'

He saw John Walter, General Manager of *The Times*, and Lord Camrose, proprietor of the *Daily Telegraph*; Mike Wardell, editor of the *Sporting Record*, for some reason expressed an interest. Marcus talked to the editor of a children's comic, *Merry-go-round*, at publishers Martin & Reid, but the bogey of paper rationing again reared its ugly head.

'My journeyings round publishers' offices seemed endless, yet though I felt depressed and disheartened and exhausted I never lost my basic confidence. And always, at the back of my mind, the thought of my debts drove me on. I also received much-needed advice and encouragement from Jodi Hyland, who was now firmly established in women's magazine journalism in London.'

Lutterworth Press, publishers of *Boy's Own Paper* and *Girl's Own Paper*, whose advice Marcus had sought in 1947 regarding *The Anvil*, were very keen to take *Eagle* on: 'Of the need of such a periodical there is no doubt. The excellence of your approach and the high standard of its execution greatly impressed.' Lutterworth couldn't see any way of overcoming the obstacle of paper rationing in view of 'the immense quantities of paper that would be needed successfully to launch the publication. . . . I can only hope that you will be successful in finding another publisher who will find it possible to finance you until such time as paper becomes freer.'

In October Marcus remembered Hulton Press and his unanswered letter. This time he paid a personal visit and was shown into the office of Ronnie Dickenson, one of the Assistant General Managers. Ronnie was, according to Marcus, charming and courteous – and sufficiently interested in *Eagle* and 'Chaplain Dan Dare of the Interplanet Patrol' to ask Marcus to wait. Ronnie showed the dummy to the General Managers, John Pearce and Maxwell Raison, and Marcus was invited to see them. 'I told them who I was and where I came from and explained my proposition to them. They said, "We would like to look further into this. Will you leave your dummy with us for a few days?"

'I did so and returned to Birkdale to see my solicitor and try to appease my printers. I was on the edge of bankruptcy, the loss of my job and probable defrocking. My downfall would have been complete. Desperate to get help I returned to London and went to Church House, to the Church of England Finance Committee.'

The Secretary to the Committee, C. Sorden, was entirely sympathetic, but every penny the Committee had was already earmarked.

'After a pause, he said, "Tell me about the last people you saw. Hulton Press – they're Roman Catholics, aren't they?" I said they were; he picked up the telephone and asked someone what they thought about the Hultons. When he'd listened to the answer, he told me, "You go along to the chapel at the end of the corridor for a quarter of an hour and I'll see what can be done." I went to the chapel and sank to my knees and prayed very hard. When I returned to Mr Sorden he said, "I can't give you any official help, as you know, but I'm willing to give you my own personal cheque for £250, if that's any good to you." '

Marcus found it difficult to express his thanks for this very noble gesture, which was given without any guarantee or security from him or anyone else. He was able to return to Birkdale and mitigate the printers' wrath and postpone the impending writ. (Mr Sorden's loan was repaid in January 1950.)

On 10 October, a week after the visit to Hulton Press, a telegram arrived at the vicarage from John Pearce: 'Definitely interested. Do not approach any other publisher.'

# Chapter Nine

Edward Hulton was the third of his name to own a publishing company; his grandfather had built up the (then) largest newspaper office in the world at Withy Grove, Manchester.

The second Edward Hulton also prospered and by the age of twenty-five had largely taken over control of his father's company. In 1909 Edward junior started the *Daily Sketch* – the first illustrated morning paper in this country. In 1919 he was awarded a baronetcy, but didn't enjoy it for long; he died in 1925 at the age of fifty-six. The sale of his fourteen periodicals to Allied Newspapers Ltd realised £6,000,000.

The baronetcy died with him. He had married in his youth a Miss Turnbull, daughter of a Manchester solicitor. It is recorded that she divorced him and that he subsequently married Millicent Warriss. It was to Millicent that a son, also Edward, was born in 1906 – but his parents were not yet married.

Sir Edward, Bart., died while his son was at Brasenose College, Oxford. The young man immediately caused a sign to be put up on his door: 'Sir Edward Hulton, Bart.'. He was deeply humiliated when he was told to take it down. It is said that his only ambition from then on was to get himself a title.

On his deathbed, Sir Edward is reputed to have asked his secretary and right-hand man, W.J. Dickenson, to look after the family. When the young Edward came into his inheritance in 1936, Dickenson was able to show his devotion by helping him to form his own publishing company, Hulton Press.

W.J. Dickenson brought in Maxwell Raison, who in 1934 had founded *Farmers Weekly* which, with its brilliant editor, Malcolm Messer, became the backbone of the new Hulton company. They obtained the *Nursing Mirror*, started *World Review* and, in 1938, bought the humorous pocket magazine *Lilliput* from its founder, Stefan Lorant. Stefan enlisted Tom Hopkinson and between them they produced *Picture Post* in September of that year. In 1939 the company launched *Housewife*, a pocket-sized magazine for women.

In 1941 Edward Hulton, although brought up a Roman Catholic, married for the second time. Nika was a Russian princess whom he met in Paris where she was living with her husband, a young man on the fringes of journalism. According to Tom Hopkinson, 'Teddy' gave the young man a handsome cheque to disappear off the scene; others have said that Nika was a courtesan – a high-class prostitute, ruthless and ambitious.

The general consensus of opinion is that Teddy was a kind and well-meaning man but totally incapable of running anything. His political opinions were apt to veer sharply; from being a Chamberlain supporter in 1938, by August 1945 he was writing a resounding welcome to Clement Attlee's new Labour Government. Eighteen months later he wrote to Tom Hopkinson that 'I am totally at a loss to know why *Picture Post* should become more Soviet than the Soviets themselves.'

In 1944 the company bought *Leader* magazine and towards the end of the war Tom Hopkinson, Maxwell Raison and W.J. Dickenson decided that, to combat the threat from wealthy American magazines, they should start buying up picture libraries. The Rischgitz collection and the Gooch collection were the foundation of the Hulton Picture Library.

By 1949 Maxwell Raison and W.J. Dickenson had been joined on the management team by John Pearce, Ronnie Dickenson (W.J.'s son) and George Ravenscroft, and Hulton Press had become a public company.

When Marcus appeared on their doorstep, Pearce and Dickenson were grappling with a number of problems. Although *Farmers Weekly* was doing splendidly (and is still going strong), sales of *Picture Post* were dropping. *Housewife* was ailing. *Lilliput* had lost over 150,000 copies since the first half of 1948, during which period *World Review*'s circulation nearly halved. *Leader* was not doing well. The company's profits had dropped by 20 per cent in a year.

So fate, or the God that Marcus believed in, decreed that his persistence should take him to a company that needed a major boost, had the vision to see the possibilities of *Eagle* and the courage to gamble on an unknown provincial parson.

Ronnie Dickenson could be justly proud that he took that first step of showing the dummy to John Pearce: 'There are many, many people who say they saw it first – but they didn't – I did. Success has many fathers.'

The telegram from John Pearce caused jubilation in Southport. The Morrises, Hampsons, Walkden Fisher and Harold Johns went to the Belle Vue Hotel and celebrated. Fish was unaccustomed to alcohol and went for the most innocuous-looking drink in the bar; he got tipsy on Green Chartreuse.

Further interviews at Hulton Press followed. John Pearce told Marcus that, at that first interview, they had barely believed his story. As soon as he'd gone they sent out for a copy of *Crockford's Clerical Directory* to check him out. Pearce and Raison had also questioned Marcus about their existing publications; John Pearce commented later, 'You know, one of the things that impressed us at that interview was that you seemed to know a good deal about our publications and had decided if not always flattering views about them. It has always been my firm rule, that if anyone comes to see us about a job and has not taken the trouble to find out what we publish, we are not interested in them any more.'

There has been vociferous debate as to how Hulton Press found themselves with enough paper to launch *Eagle*: Derek Lord, who worked on *Leader* before joining *Eagle* as general editorial assistant, is one of those who says that *Leader* was closed down to provide the paper for *Eagle*, but Ronnie Dickenson refuted this. It is more than possible that the company's paper surplus was caused by the falling sales of *Picture Post* which, according to Ronnie, 'ate paper'.

Throughout its life *Eagle* bore the legend 'Eagle Magazine with which is incorporated The Merry-Go-Round'. *Merry-Go-Round* contained such edifying characters as 'Slim Jim our Priceless Pearl Pincher', 'Tosh the Posh Spiv' and 'Professor Pip and his Magic Pop Gun'. Marcus had talked to its editor during his search for a publisher: 'I remember that he rather mournfully told me that the question of getting paper allocated for the purposes of a children's paper would prevent us from ever getting going with *Eagle*. It is rather ironic to reflect that *Merry-Go-Round* was bought and absorbed for its paper quota and its title incorporated with *Eagle*. I certainly don't quote this fact with any sense of satisfaction – completely the reverse – but it underlines the strange hazards of the situation in those days and of the odd irony of life in general.'

In his unpublished autobiography, John Pearce wrote, 'I was glooming about my routine business when Ronnie Dickenson came into the room and said there was a clergyman with the idea for a children's magazine wanting to see me, and that I ought to see him.

'My immediate reaction was that we would certainly require a clergyman for the apparently inevitable obsequies of *Picture Post* and probably Hulton Press as well, but that his arrival was premature. . . . My second thought was that we had enough troubles without adding to them by publishing a notoriously unprofitable type of publication. Newsagents did not like children's magazines. Advertisers did not like them. Not even children were keen on them. Further, Hulton Press needed a mass circulation publication to cope with its difficulties.

'But Ronnie Dickenson was persuasive and I looked at the mock up of this publication which was called *Eagle*. And behind its obvious superficial inadequacies this dummy showed a spark of genius, but it had to be captured and put into a viable commercial form if it was to succeed at all and if it was to help solve the multitudinous unseen problems of Hulton Press. If we could make a success of *Eagle* we would solve our unique surplus paper ration and maybe make some much-needed money. We would also give our mildly demoralised circulation and advertisement departments something to do with fresh hope behind it. At no time did we set out to do good. . . . I showed the dummy to Vernon Holding our Circulation Manager and asked him if he could sell it. He said, in effect, that he could sell a million copies a week, and said it with enormous enthusiasm.'

Pearce and Raison called down Tom Hopkinson, now editing *Picture Post*, to get his views. Sir Tom revealed in his autobiography, *Of This Our Time*: 'They placed in front of me the paste-up of a magazine for boys quite unlike any I had ever seen. . . . Unlike most dummies, this was not an amateurish affair with one or two pages carefully drawn and the rest hazily roughed in. It was complete from first to last with coloured drawings to scale and all the captions and articles readable and in place. But what chiefly distinguished it was the impression that the editor understood what he was doing. I knew very little about boys aged eight to twelve but I could see that the editor had mentally identified himself with them and appreciated what they wanted almost without having to think.

' "Well, what d'you make of it?" Raison asked.

' "I've been looking at dummies on and off for the last 15 years," I said, "but this is the first I've ever seen of which I'd say 'Hire all the people who produced it and start publishing it as soon as possible'."

' "We can't do that," objected Pearce. "He's a clergyman".

' "Well, he seems keen to become an editor," I answered. "So the thing is to hire him a good curate or two, and let them run the church services while he gets on with the magazine".'

Marcus was told to go away and produce four more dummies to make sure the first one wasn't a fluke. Back in Southport, he and Frank worked feverishly with the team they had assembled, including the writers Vernon Noble, Edward Beal, Elleston Trevor (later to write such books as *The Killing Ground*, *Flight of the Phoenix* and, as Adam Hall, *The Quiller Memorandum*, subsequently blockbusting films) and his wife, Jonquil. But it was the artists who made the most impact on *Eagle* – Frank, Harold Johns, Walkden Fisher and E.C. Jennings were soon joined by others.

James Beetham had been a fellow student of Frank's. He worked on the dummies, but decided that he couldn't stand the uncertainty of the life and joined a Liverpool advertising agency instead. 'Frank always worked terribly intently in a slow methodical way, smoking a pipe. His attention to detail was unbelievable. He was single-minded, very purposeful, a supreme draughtsman. He had a seething contempt for things that weren't as he wanted.'

One of three artists who had been recommended to Marcus by Mr Wedgewood at Liverpool School of Art was a young man just finishing a teaching degree course, Norman Thelwell. Frank went to see him there and roped him in. Thelwell's work had already been published, in *London Opinion* and *Men Only*. He remembers visiting the vicarage one Saturday to see Marcus and having his toes run over by a number of small tricycles – in spite of which, he agreed to produce drawings for *The Anvil* and for *Eagle*. Thelwell's first two drawings for *Anvil* appeared in January 1950, one a full page showing an irate Father Christmas stuffing toys down a central heating flue. In June he drew a small boy remarkably like 'Chicko 'playing at making atom bombs on his mother's drawing room carpet.

The full-page strip he produced for the dummy of *Eagle* was 'Pop Milligan', the story of a family of barge people on a Liverpool canal. Pop didn't make it into the first issue, but 'Chicko' did – and lasted until 1961. Thelwell went on to achieve great fame as one of the most amusing and prolific artists of his generation.

Jos Armitage (Ionicus), who taught at Wallasey School of Art, came to see Marcus through an art agency. He produced a full-page black and white strip, 'Albert Hall', the story of an heroic office boy. Albert too didn't make it into the first issue, but the eight episodes were published in *Eagle Annual* Two. The eccentric 'Professors Meek and Mild' also appeared regularly in *Eagle Annuals* and Ionicus provided illustrations for *Girl Annuals*. Unfortunately that, on the strength of 'Albert Hall', Ionicus gave up his job: 'Five minutes later, "Albert Hall" failed – that's the sort of risk you have to take.'

The team managed to put together three dummies, which was enough to convince Pearce, Raison and Dickenson that they had a winner on their hands and, at the beginning of November, Marcus and Frank and the rest of the gang were on the Hulton Press pay roll.

The company agreed to pay off the most pressing of Marcus's debts and asked what salary he wanted: 'Greatly daring, I asked for £1,500, a big step up from my vicar's stipend. John Pearce did not demur. I tentatively suggested that we might have a royalty from the profits of *Eagle*. Pearce replied, "It's a bit early to talk about that. Let's wait and see what happens when the paper comes out." In my innocence, this seemed very reasonable to me. I had no legal adviser at the time and lost any chance of making some real money. But I never thought very seriously or for long about money. I was only too relieved to have paid off my debts and was excited that, at long last, my children's paper was to be published.'

His creditors were relieved as well. Mr Morgan of Williams Deacons Bank wrote on 28 November, 'We were very pleased to receive your cheque for £1000. . . . It is very satisfactory to find that our efforts to help you over a long time have now born fruit and we wish you every success in the new venture. We shall . . . be glad if you will keep a keen eye on your accounts.'

By April 1950 Marcus was actually in credit – by some £3 – at the District Bank and was able to cancel a guarantee for £70 given by Eric Cook.

Marcus should certainly have had a solicitor to look after his interests. By the end of 1950, when Herbert Bart-Smith became his legal representative and life-long friend and adviser, it was too late to do anything about the question of copyright and royalties for either Marcus or Frank.

It was this fact more than any other that led in later years to Frank becoming bitter, and resentful of Marcus. But as David Harrison of the Southport School of Art said to us: 'It is an indication of Frank's character that he wrote, "I waited to see . . . what was to be done for me and I waited and waited. I went to see the Hulton Press management who upped my pay to £50 a week, or £2500 a year, presented me with a service contract confirming that the copyright in Dan Dare belonged to them. They gave me a lot of assurances – and vanished." How could they vanish? They were all still there in Shoe Lane.'

James Beetham commented that 'if Frank had not insisted on taking a large salary from Marcus, Marcus would not have had to "sell out".'

In fairness to Pearce and Raison, they obviously wanted the best deal for the company and *Eagle* was, after all, an unknown quantity; it might have flopped dismally.

There was no question in November 1949 of Marcus resigning his living in Birkdale; he would continue as before, spending the week in London and weekends administering to his flock. Hulton Press provided first-class sleeping accommodation on the overnight train to and from Liverpool, a pleasant change from third class.

The new editor was given a small office at 47 Shoe Lane, next to Edward

Hulton, who would pass through and grunt as if unsure who Marcus was and why he was there. Marcus was to learn later that the initial silence from Hulton Press was due to Edward Hulton's innate lack of business sense; if he didn't want to answer a letter, he just ignored it. Marcus wrote, 'I remember not very long after I arrived at Hulton Press saying to John Pearce "Does the Chairman know we are producing *Eagle*?" and Pearce replied, "Oh ... yes ... yes ... I must remember to tell him." I am not sure whether Pearce said that to amuse me or to let me know who was running the company.'

Twenty years later Marcus and Jess bumped into John and Mary Pearce in Marrakesh and they had dinner together. Mary recalled, 'It was very touching, Marcus kept saying to John, "This is entirely thanks to you for starting me off in the direction I took," which I thought was very generous minded.'

Tom Hopkinson: 'I was expecting a black-coated, black-suited figure with reverse collar like my father or clergyman brother [Stephan], but Morris proved to be a very smart, dapper, young to middle-aged man, slight, fair-haired and outwardly hesitant, but soon revealed the essential streak. He gave the impression of knowing quite as much about journalism as I did. He was very much a man of the world. When I said that his plans in general looked excellent – particularly the adventures of Dan Dare, that space-age pilot still remembered with enthusiasm by millions of middle-aged men – but that the adventures of St Paul at the back of the paper seemed incongruous – he replied, "If that is not included, then I shall not produce the magazine".

'Hastily I backed down to admit St Paul's adventure. Morris himself I nicknamed "Father Martini", not because of any propensity to drink, for all I knew he might well be a teetotaller, but because – well-dressed, controlled, decisive – he appeared all set for publishing success and therefore for the life of high finance, good restaurants and first class aeroplane travel which not many clergymen, I think, find themselves in a position to enjoy.'

Marcus was very grateful for the early help given him by Tom Hopkinson. 'Not only was Tom kind and encouraging but he taught me some editorial tricks which would not have occurred to me. I was very much a new boy and a beginner. I planned to have two features on the centre spread, it was too big a space just for one. It was Tom who said, "make sure that the top half is deeper than the bottom half"; I would have put them straight across the middle.'

Sir Tom told us: 'I can't think I would have been much help. I probably knew things like placing the advertisements in certain parts of the paper, keeping the pages you value most clear; a picture page shows up much better if it's opposite a text page, on the whole the right hand page is the important one. The left-hand page is apt to be the conclusion of something else, the top half of all right hand pages are the points to which the eye goes naturally.'

To begin with, the only other assistance Marcus had was from his secretary, Rosemary Phillips (now Corbett), who had been working on *Strand* magazine with Macdonald Hastings. Rosemary says, 'Marcus and I started the whole thing. Life was exciting, never dull. He was bossy, demanding and time didn't mean anything to him so we were often working terribly late, particularly before the whole crew got hired.

'I always found Marcus and Chad Varah fairly naughty. I used to think, my word, these two churchmen, they're terrible, but fun. Very flirtatious.'

Frank Hampson now needed a studio and found one in Churchtown, Southport, a converted bakery built on to a house in Botanic Road, for which Hulton Press paid 15/- a week. The Bakehouse was quite large but not overly luxurious: corrugated walls, flagstone floor; the ovens and the coal store were still intact, there was a sink, a one-bar electric fire, an outside loo – and lots of draughts; they worked by the light of two 'daylight blue' bulbs. The studio is now a shrine for *Eagle* fans.

Meetings between Marcus and Frank were usually at the vicarage in the evenings or at the Hesketh Arms, Marcus with his gin, Frank with his beer. Marcus's visits to the Bakehouse were mostly confined to accompanying visitors or bringing urgent news; there was no telephone in the studio.

Hulton Press had decided to launch the magazine in early April 1950, and Frank and Harold Johns set to work to complete the first few episodes of 'Dan Dare', 'St Paul' and 'Rob Conway' (metamorphosed from Jimmy Swift of 'Secret City'). It was an impossible task for just two people. Marcus advertised in the *Daily Telegraph* for 'an assistant artist for a new venture in Southport'. First to answer the ad was a former Wren, Jocelyn Thomas (later Pattinson), who had recently graduated from Hereford Art School. Marcus and Frank both liked her work and took her on as colourist.

Joan Porter (née Humphries) happened to be in Southport and was introduced to Frank. She joined the team as general assistant; she photographed the (live) models, undertook copious research and made costumes.

Fish designed and built models – helmets, guns, spaceships, vehicles – for the artists to draw. David Harrison called Fish's contribution to *Eagle* immense. 'He made models of spaceships, including Anastasia, Dan Dare's favourite, which went on show all round the country. A local undertaker made a special box to pack them in, which cost £6, more than the models it contained. Fish would use any bits and bobs – jewellery, little lights, model trains; the only thing he had to buy was glue. He did a big table-top layout of Space Fleet Headquarters. Without those models they wouldn't have accomplished what they did.'

Not everything in the dummy was considered suitable for the finished product and Marcus had to find other artists and writers to produce the rest of the magazine. Since Hulton Press insisted that the operation remain absolutely secret this was no easy task. He approached literary and artists' agents but, as he was unable to tell them which publishing house he was acting for, some of them took a lot of convincing that their clients would get paid.

One of the first artists to provide a feature was an assistant art-master at Harrow School, John Ryan. He remembers his first meeting with Marcus in his office 'guarded by a very pretty secretary'. John had never done strip cartoons before, only illustrations; he came up with an historical strip, 'Bad King John'. Marcus looked at the first episode, his left shoulder twitched and he said, 'If you draw me something really funny I will publish it'. John was most offended as he hadn't intended the strip to be amusing. However, he went home and drew 'Captain Pugwash' who, he said, 'leapt out of the page'. Marcus accepted it on the spot and although the brave captain didn't last very long in *Eagle*, it is the only original strip from the magazine to have survived to this day. In fact, 'Captain Pugwash' has become one of the most successful cartoon characters ever.

Marcus approached Alan Stranks, the writer of *PC49*, a very successful BBC wireless serial about a bobby on the streets of London. Hultons bought the publishing rights and Alan found an artist, Strom Gould (later to be replaced by John Worsley). Alan's daughter, Sue Ray said, 'My father loved writing for children, he had the imagination, and he was a great storyteller. PC49 was based on a village policeman, the copper on the beat. Alan was great mates with high ups at Scotland Yard, they liked '49' because it was authentic and gave a good image. Alan did a number of scripts for Dan Dare as well, when Frank Hampson was sick.

'Marcus became a great social friend. Much midnight oil was burnt, many a good party held. Comics were banned at my boarding school, but because my father wrote for *Eagle* I was allowed *Eagle* and *Girl*. That gave me great street cred at school, great kudos.'

John Worsley was the creator of Albert RN (the dummy naval officer which helped a prisoner of war to escape), and a gifted artist: 'Alan Stranks used to drive me up the wall, he'd produce his script about two days before Marcus needed it and I had to work all night to get the drawing done. But we knew each other well, we were happy working together.'

Marcus went to see Learie Constantine, whom he had interviewed for *The Anvil*, and asked him to do a series on cricket, which was illustrated by Alfredo and later by Jack Daniel.

J. Spencer Croft, a commercial artist in Southport, was asked to write and illustrate scientific articles and Marcus's young protégé from Birkdale, Bill Todd, helped out on 'Dan Dare' and with drawings and fillers. Chad Varah was persuaded to write a serial story and was also given the task of ploughing through the many manuscripts that began to pour in after the launch.

Ruari McLean introduced his parish priest, the Revd Guy Daniel: 'Ruari suggested that I send my typescript of "The Odd-looking Bicycle" to the editor. He was interested and he bought it, but never used it.' After that Guy sold one or two stories which were used in the Annuals, and provided scripts for cartoon strips including the series 'Their Names Made Words'. Ruari himself was charged with overseeing the overall look of the magazine and advising on layout and typography.

John Pearce, Marketing Controller George Cooper and Sales Director Patrick Henry sat down with Marcus to discuss advertising opportunities. Marcus was very definite that any advertising had to be in character with the magazine and to be something rather unusual. George Cooper says: 'The challenge was to find a company which would put up enough creative money. Pat Henry found the Wall's Ice Cream people and we agreed an adventure series in full colour. We would produce the page and they would have input into the content. It had to do a job for them, but it would be done by artists selected by the editor. Marcus was anxious that any advertising would be very carefully controlled.'

Marcus naturally chose Frank Hampson and his team to produce this very important page. As the workload at the Bakehouse increased, more artists were found: Greta Tomlinson (recently finished at the Slade art school) answered an ad in *Advertisers Weekly* and joined in February; Bruce Cornwell and Terry Maloney also arrived early in 1950; Eric Eden, another student from Southport College of Art, a little later.

Although the dummy had been called *Eagle* for some months, the name still hadn't been finally agreed. 'At first it was suggested that it should be included in *Picture Post* and called *Junior Post*. I didn't like this idea one little bit and resisted it strongly. The name was dull and unimaginative. My idea was a new one and must be produced as a new entity. Everyone who had anything to do with the project made suggestions. It was Frank's wife Dorothy who had suggested putting the name EAGLE on one of the dummies – and *Eagle* it became. It had a good look about it, it could be drawn effectively and could easily be used as an emblem or badge.' It was certainly a better name than *Jumbo*, a title which was bandied around for some time.

Frank was asked to design a logo for the magazine, using as a model the top of a large brass inkwell which Marcus had bought at the White Elephant stall at a vicarage garden party and which sits on the desk as we write this. But among Marcus's effects is a series of hardback books, called *Eagle Omnibus*, published by Edinburgh House Press (later absorbed into The Lutterworth Press) between 1945 and 1949, telling *True stories of Real People* such as Florence Nightingale,

*The model for the* Eagle *logo?* Eagle Omnibus, *published from 1945 to 1949.*

William Wilberforce and David Livingstone. The drawing of an eagle on the front cover bears an uncanny resemblance to the *Eagle* symbol. It is hard to believe that these books can have been in Marcus's study at the vicarage and had no influence on the design of the magazine's trademark. Neither Chad Varah nor Ruari McLean have seen the books before or know anything about them. Of course, coincidences do happen. . . .

Hultons had always used Curwen Press for their design work and to them went the job of designing the title to go alongside Frank's black and gold eagle. Ruari McLean says, 'I have never discovered why it didn't work out. The job was given to an able girl typographer who I can only suppose did not take the job seriously, or was not interested. Her design, which Marcus showed me, was so uninspired that he was free to ask me to have a go myself!'

Marcus was by now installed in a flat in Mayfair, where Ruari sketched his ideas on the back of an envelope.

'I remembered a typeface called "Tempest" which seemed to have the right visual connotation. It was strong, it had movement, the curves which ended the crossbars in E and L seemed to suggest eagles' wings. Marcus liked it. Berthold Wolpe, the designer of "Tempest", now lived in London and we asked him to draw the word EAGLE in these letters.

'From then on I was hired as typographical adviser to *Eagle* at a starting salary of £5 a week. Marcus asked me to find somewhere in London that we could share (his family were in Lancashire, mine in Essex) during the week. I found a flat in South Audley Street, a few minutes' walk from my office in Mount Street. Marcus was not perturbed when we discovered, after moving in, that all the other floors were occupied by tarts.'

While Ruari was at the ad agency or teaching, Marcus was engaged in editorial planning and commissioning artists and writers. In the evenings Ruari laid out the text and marked it up for setting, and designed the titles of the strip cartoons choosing, appropriately enough, a typeface called 'Cartoon'.

'When I arrived back at the flat after work I usually found Marcus briefing an artist. To begin with, Marcus went to the leading strip artists but the best of them were busy, so he had to try artists who had never drawn strips before. He would explain carefully what he wanted but all too often they came back not with what they had been asked to do, but what *they* thought was right.

'If, as quite frequently happened, they finally refused to be told by a young parson who had never edited anything except a parish magazine how *Eagle's* strips should be drawn, they found themselves dropped.'

Marcus and Ruari were soon working the same sort of night-time hours as their neighbours; Ruari counting words, calculating column widths and pondering type sizes while Marcus was sub-editing typescripts, concerned with every syllable, every letter, every punctuation mark.

'We were often still at it at two or three or even four in the morning, at which time I was ready to agree to anything; but Marcus never let anything go until he was completely satisfied. He would consult me about a comma or a hyphen and argue about it endlessly, cursing me for being lazy if I said it didn't matter. I cared about English too, but I didn't have Marcus's stamina. It slowly dawned on me that, for almost the first time in my life, I had the privilege of working for a man who knew exactly what he wanted.'

While the editorial contents of the magazine were taking shape, John Pearce was trying to find someone to print it. The only printing process that could cope with eight pages in full colour and a million copies a week was photogravure. There were two printers at that time who had the capacity: Odhams Press published many competing magazines including *Illustrated*, the deadly rival of Hultons' *Picture Post*; Sun Printers of Watford, who printed *Picture Post*, were looking for business from Amalgamated Press, the largest publisher of children's comics in the country. They agreed to quote for *Eagle*, but did so rather half-heartedly and rather too expensively.

So John Pearce turned to Eric Bemrose, a printer in Liverpool who had broken away from his family firm to set up on his own. Bemrose didn't have the right presses but, being an engineer as well as a printer, said that he could make them in his factory in Kirby from bits and pieces of other machinery. John Pearce wrote: 'Faith, which is presumably a large part of a clergyman's business, must have been provided amply by Marcus Morris to Eric Bemrose and myself when we agreed to print *Eagle* at his plant at Aintree. He knew he could not print it. I knew he could not print it. All of the interested publishing and printing industry knew it as well. So we decided to go ahead. He did it because it was his chance into the big time. I did it because we had to do something. He was an excellent engaging rogue, a superb printing technician and entrepreneur.'

Eric Bemrose asked for guarantees from Hultons, obtained some money of his own and began to build the necessary machinery. The ten-bank rotary printing press was designed and built in about twelve weeks; additional staff were taken on and trained to use it.

Michael Bemrose had joined his father's firm when he left the forces in 1947. 'It took us three eight-hour shifts, twenty-four hours a day, seven days a week to produce a million copies a week. We had 200 staff. It was like that for a long time until we got other presses. For the first issues we couldn't chromium plate the cylinders to make them hard and run longer. I think we made ninety-six cylinders for the first issue. You couldn't buy chromium plating vats, you had to make them.

'We had a lot of trouble with the colour to start with. All the colour correction was done by hand, it used to take one man forty hours to correct a page. The colour of the first issue was terribly pale because it took us so long to print it. The old Crabtree folder was too big so we had to cut the edges off a million copies a week until we could make one of our own the right size.

'The paper used to break because the parcels were tied with sisal and bits of it would get in with the waste paper which was swept up and sent back to the mill.'

George Cooper recalls visiting the printing works not long after *Eagle* was launched: 'This long machine had great bolts sticking out all over it with great big nuts on the ends; no-one had had time to tidy up the machine and cut the pieces off. Marcus was as amused about it as I was. I've seen new machinery come in but never as close to the deadline – and it was good quality.'

Some people have claimed that Bemrose bought his machinery from Germany – well, he didn't – it was all home made.

Meanwhile, another machine was getting into gear – the Hulton Press publicity department. This was to be a big launch and no expense was spared. In December Hultons' advertising agency Coleman Prentice & Varley were brought in, with their public relations subsidiary, Voice & Vision. John Metcalf was in charge: 'The first thing I thought was that this was a genuinely new kind of magazine which would be an enormous problem because comics were banned in schools as the general view was that they were bad. We had to make plain to everyone that *Eagle* was absolutely different.'

Marcus produced a list of mainly Christian organisations that could be approached for publicity. It was then realised that the proposed launch date would be in Lent; not wanting to antagonise the religious bodies, they decided to put off publication until after Easter.

John Metcalf called in his friend James Hemming, an educational psychologist. Between them, they contacted a large number of schools to canvass opinions. James says, 'I'd worked in industry and always liked a new challenge. I said to Johnny, "I'll take a dummy round and show it to a number of head teachers and soften them up." Normally they were against comics. I wanted to get a small group of heads to say "This comic is on our side". I went mostly to secondary state schools which is where I thought the blockage would come from.

'Marcus said we ought to keep permanent contact and could I join them. I said no, I already have a job. He said, "I'll fix you up with a secretary and a desk and you can come in one day a week. It'll be quite flexible, if there's one day you can't come in that's all right." So that was the arrangement. As far as I was concerned it worked like a charm. I kept an overview on the comics in general, looked at every issue, made comments on anything I thought was going a bit skew in terms of principles. I insisted on no stereotype baddies.'

James and Marcus agreed that Germans, Japanese and other foreigners were not to be 'villains'; in any group of children, one or two should be, in today's jargon, from ethnic minorities; religion or preaching must not be obvious but the moral values for which the paper stood should be implicit in every page.

Bernard Audley (now Sir Bernard) was a trainee at Hulton Press, one of thirty-six lately come down from Oxford and Cambridge. His first sight of Marcus was 'on stage' being introduced to a mass of advertising people and sales reps. In his address at Marcus's memorial service, Bernard said, 'Marcus on stage did not fill the representatives with confidence. Slim, youthful-looking and diffident, he didn't even exhibit that "nervous affability" which C.S. Lewis, one of his favourite writers, identified as the hallmark and protective colouring of the young clergyman. Nervous perhaps, but offering none of the communications skills which sales executives even then were coming to expect of editors. As the managers and reps filed away for their off-the-record debriefings in the Two Brewers and the Black Dog the mood was not one of unalloyed optimism.'

Bernard told us, 'They introduced Marcus to this hard-bitten bunch and he, in a somewhat faltering way gave this summary of what the new publication was to be and he didn't seem to me very convincing. It was probably his first encounter of that kind. He had no pulpit to protect him.'

Frank Monkman was with CPV and also remembers that first meeting of Marcus and the mediamen. His first impression was that Marcus was 'missing a couple of gears in terms of drive and initiative, he seemed shy and a bit of a negative character. In fact he wasn't. He outlined his philosophy and answered a lot of questions off the top of his head.'

An assistant account executive at CPV, Ellen Vincent, was told to get some promotional photographs of the vicar. 'The secrecy remained and meeting the man himself was a difficulty. Eventually I was ushered into the presence. I had expected a comfortable figure in a tweed jacket, grey haired, and maybe smoking a mellow pipe. What I encountered was a slim young man, fair haired, dressed in a natty grey suit. He had a quick nervous manner and was obviously a chain smoker. I would say he was, at that time, slightly ill at ease, as he had not yet come to terms with the mechanics of magazine production. He handed me a photograph of Dan Dare for advertising purposes in about twelve different sizes. I told him that one negative would be enough. . . .

'The next time I saw MM he was sitting at his desk surrounded by sacks of letters, all to be answered. It was then, desperate for help, that he asked me if I'd like to join his staff. I jumped at his offer and when he asked me what salary I wanted I doubled my CPV one – he agreed without a murmur!'

Vernon Holding had lunch with his old friend Stephen Williams, a producer with the BBC, and asked his help in looking after Marcus, because 'you know how to handle vicars as your father's one'. Hultons paid him an unofficial honorarium as a consultant and he was closely involved in setting up the Eagle Club. Stephen told us, 'When Marcus came down from Birkdale we took him over to the Two Brewers where he was tactfully told that he shouldn't ask for a double whisky; the person who was buying would say "would you like a large one?" There was a lovely interview in one of the American papers which ended, " 'I'll have another double scotch' " said the vicar.'

'We were working on the organisation side, contributing various suggestions. The main ideas were Marcus's. He thought up the MUGs. The three of us, Holding, Dickenson and I were there to turn his ideas into practicalities. He wasn't very practical.'

Using a coded name, market research was carried out. Women's groups, educational, religious and social community groups were approached to establish their reactions to a strip cartoon magazine.

Ideas for the launch came in thick and fast. One bright idea was to send up 100,000 balloons, each carrying a token entitling the finder to a free copy of the first issue. Voice & Vision spent two days experimenting with balloons: filling them with hydrogen, timing their ascent and working out the best colours to hold public attention. They even checked regulations with the Air Ministry and local government. It soon became apparent that the logistics of blowing up 100,000 balloons and keeping hold of them, to be released all together, were insuperable. A less ambitious scheme was substituted, with a few balloons released from the roof of CPV, the furthest to travel winning its finder £5. The winner was French. Another experiment, carried out on a vacant site owned by Hultons, was flying a kite to which leaflets were attached. The result was a lot of litter in Fetter Lane.

Marcus suggested releasing a golden eagle from London Zoo. This was capped by a proposal to drop Marcus by parachute into Hyde Park.

In the end it was decided to base the campaign on the theme of 'Hunt the Eagle'. Nine 58-inch high *papier maché* eagles (with a four-foot wingspan) were commissioned, designed by sculptor Norman Cornish, based on the inkwell eagle. They were painted with gilt and mounted on eight (one was kept as a spare) hired Humber Hawk cars, which were also equipped with loudspeakers. (It is said that Norman Cornish didn't know what his design was for until he saw one of the cars on the road.) One million tokens, to be exchanged for a free copy of *Eagle*, were designed to look like bank notes. They would be distributed by the cars throughout the country, with separate arrangements (no gilt eagles) for Northern Ireland, Eire, the Channel Islands and the Isle of Man (which had to make do with the wholesaler's van).

This scheme was not without its problems. Wind resistance and weather proofing of the eagles could only be estimated, as the models couldn't be shown in public before the launch. The loudspeakers were located under the bonnets of the cars; five of them were burnt out by the heat of the engines in the first few days of the tours.

Worried by the great variety of local bye-laws nationwide, Voice & Vision consulted the Home Office and Arthur Cain sent a personal letter to every Chief Constable in the country. Hultons' solicitors foretold hundreds of summonses for obstruction; but the only restriction that emerged was a polite letter from the Chief Constable of Portsmouth requesting them not to use the loudspeakers in the vicinity of the town's cemeteries. 'We had a briefing at the Arts Theatre for all the drivers and interviewed all the blokes who went with them to hand out the tokens. They were nearly all university students or young people from Hulton Press who were willing to keep sober.'

£9,500 was set aside to fund 'Hunt The Eagle'. £21,000 was allocated for national press advertising, which was aimed more at parents than their children.

The third spearhead of the campaign was the sending of copies of the first issue, together with a letter from the Editor, to parents, teachers, clergy and youth organisers, so that children would see *Eagle* in their homes, schools or clubs, and adults would see that *Eagle*'s standards were acceptably high.

The postage costs of this mailing were estimated before the first *Eagles* were printed; unfortunately, the weight of the printing tipped the scales –

and 130,000 halfpenny stamps were needed to put that right. In all, nearly twenty different types of direct mail letter were sent out. The response surprised even Voice & Vision; most of the replies received were congratulatory.

In a somewhat contradictory vein, Hultons' 'Most Secret' report on the launch stated: 'Great care is being taken in all our letters and interviews to avoid adults forcing *Eagle* Magazine on their children's notice as a suitable comic, so as to leave the initiative of buying copies in the hands of the children, thus avoiding the danger of children themselves damning *Eagle* as "the teachers' paper".' Endorsement was also to be sought from youth clubs, women's institutes, JPs, the Scout movement, the British Legion, doctors, education inspectors, the Boys Brigade, dentists, district nurses and children's aid organisations. One young Voice & Vision employee to be drafted on to the task of knocking on doors was Edward Douglas-Scott-Montague, third Baron Montague of Beaulieu, whose first job (at £3 a week) this was.

At the beginning of April Hulton Press took the momentous decision to resign from the Periodical Publishers Association. Since November Hultons had been trying to persuade the PPA to allow them to sell the first four issues of *Eagle* on sale or return. The PPA finally refused: 'The over riding consideration at the moment is the maintenance of paper supplies . . . any kind of waste – whether in the form of returns or free copies – must be ruled out.'

John Pearce issued a statement: 'With the use of gifts and other inducements, which are permitted and used under PPA rules, it is possible to persuade people to buy a periodical they have no desire to read. Hulton Press chose sale or return because it puts the onus on the editorial content and the publishers.'

Victor Holt of the National Federation of Retail Newsagents told us, 'The wholesale distributors sided with the PPA. The PPA then arranged for the question to be raised in the House of Commons. Harold Wilson, President of the Board of Trade, replied . . . that he saw a clear distinction between allowing SoR for a short period in order to launch a new publication and a general resumption which the country could not afford at the time.

'In the event *Eagle* was such a success that unsold copies were practically non-existent.'

As the launch date approached, rumours emerged that Beaverbrook Newspapers were to launch a children's paper (to be called *Laugh*) a week before *Eagle*. They had approached Bemrose and been refused. An agent had been cagey when Marcus tried to buy a TV feature from him; the *Express* had got there first.

In anxious conference, Hulton Press decided to advance the publication date of *Eagle* by a week. John Metcalf started a counter-rumour: publication of *Eagle* was to be delayed due to problems with the presses. Marcus sent Rosemary Phillips to see Beaverbrook and, if possible, put him on the wrong track.

'The butler showed me into his drawing room. He was obviously trying to be friendly, thinking, this will be a pushover. I tried to make him think that our plans were very laid back, that there was still lots to do, and he seemed to believe it.'

'Will the eagle stay on?' The Humber fleet is made ready for the launch

Tension began to mount; could they keep it a secret until it was too late for the *Express* to do anything about it? Could Eric Bemrose meet the new deadline? Marcus flew up to Liverpool to do some last minute editing. He was terrified. 'I hate small aircraft. I felt very strongly that *Eagle* was not worth it. I didn't feel any better when they told me they weren't quite ready to start the printing. If I had come by train I would just about have been in time. I was not, I reflected, the Dan Dare type, even if I was a flying parson.'

Bemrose had already been working to a very tight schedule. The week's advance in publication made life even more frantic. When the paper was fed into one end of the machine for the first issue of *Eagle*, Bemrose was still tightening the bolts at the other end. (This story is regarded as apocryphal by some people. Michael Bemrose confirms that it is, in essence, true.)

Marcus wrote, 'I can't remember being terribly excited as publication day approached. Perhaps things had been so tense for so long and so much had happened in the past year that I simply didn't have the energy. Others felt the tension, but I didn't share it with them. Our side of the work was complete, the art work, the stories, the features, the competitions, the gimmicks. Everything was there, all that had to be done was for them to be printed and sold.'

There were orders for more than a million copies of *Eagle*; Bemrose had promised 900,000.

The print run started on 27 March; the presses were manned twenty-four hours a day. The Humber Hawks went out on the roads on 3 April. Lord Montague drove one; Charles Pocklington, from Hultons' publicity department, was manning another: 'I covered Liverpool. It was pretty grotty in those days. In some places we got bricks thrown at us. We didn't hand the tokens out as we were supposed to, we went down the roads throwing them out of the window because you didn't dare stop.'

The drivers of the Humber Hawks were offered a daily bonus to keep to schedule, with an additional bonus if they brought the cars back with the eagles in good condition – each driver was given a tin of gold paint and fixing spirit for running repairs.

The Voice & Vision report on the launch states: 'We had printed one million tokens and the experts advised us that not more than ten per cent would be handed in. In fact, only 460,000 were distributed and over 350,000 were exchanged.

'We encountered many cases where parents and children said they already had a token and refused to take a second one. This illustrated a basic honesty in the British people which is pleasant to experience. On the other hand there were several cases where individuals did try trading in the coupons. It was not possible to prevent this, but it indicates that the spivs will get into everything.'

Amongst all the hectic preparations, Marcus still had a parish to run and *The Anvil* to edit. Even as publication day approached, Marcus was still taking the Friday night train to Liverpool, back to his neglected parishioners. The weekend before the launch was Easter. As Marcus and Ruari prepared to return to their respective homes, Ruari remarked how pleasant it would be for them both to have a long relaxing weekend with their families. 'Marcus gave me a bleak look and said that perhaps I didn't realise that the Easter weekend was the busiest in the Church's calendar.'

Over the next three days, Marcus had nine services to conduct, five of them on Easter Sunday.

Publication day was Friday 14 April. Eric Bemrose had kept his word and produced 900,000 copies. The newsagents, who had been kept in ignorance of the new date for as long as possible, were ready and waiting. The 'Hunt the Eagle' tokens covered the country. Edward Hulton gave a tea party for the families of his London staff – the children had already been made Honorary Members of the Eagle Club, so that they could promote the Club at school.

Marcus wrote: 'I have tried to remember where I spent that Thursday evening but I can't. Friday, publication day, I do remember. I wandered in and out of the management offices as the telegrams came in from reps all over the country. The first report said "Sales are steady" – for a few minutes gloom hung over the office. Then they all said the same thing; *Eagle* was selling, *Eagle* was selling. By mid afternoon we had a success on our hands.'

That night Marcus, Ruari and Guy Daniel went out to dinner together. Guy remembers Marcus saying, 'The time it's taken to get the first issue out, now think, we've got to do this every week in future.' He was appalled by the thought.

# Chapter Ten

The triumph of the first issue was followed the next week by near-disaster. Eric Bemrose's magnificent printing machine, which had coped so valiantly with 900,000 copies, broke down and for a while there were fears that the second issue would not appear at all.

Only 300,000 copies went out and instead of telegrams of congratulation, Hulton Press was inundated with screams of complaint. *Eagle* could have died in infancy; the news trade enquired whether the company was deliberately trying to ruin the previous week's enormous success. Somehow things were smoothed over, the newsagents appeased. Advertisements were taken out in the national press announcing, 'There is a national shortage of EAGLE – but more copies are coming soon!' By the third week the machines were back to normal.

There were other alarums and excursions: Derek Lord 'arrived at the office one morning to hear the startling news that a whole issue of *Eagle* – dispatched in its giant leather bag to Eric Bemrose by rail the evening before – had failed to reach the printer. We had visions of spending the next couple of days and nights, together with all the artists, preparing a duplicate issue, but were saved in the nick of time when the bag, its contents safe and sound, was found at the bottom of a lift-shaft at Liverpool's Lime Street station.'

Ruari McLean recalled, 'Once a week Marcus and I made a final paste-up of the complete issue, parcelled it up and took it to Euston to send it to the printers by rail. We often went out for a meal before going to the station. One week Marcus and I drove into Soho and parked, leaving the *Eagle* dummy in a briefcase in my locked Austin 7. When we returned the briefcase had gone. It was never seen again.'

Fortunately, that issue, the seventh, was the first to have been duplicated. Had it happened earlier, there would have been no *Eagle* that week but 'Hulton Press had provided the facilities we had for so long been demanding, to copy everything photographically before it left London. It was possible for us to make a new dummy next day, in panic, but with complete accuracy.

'It was at about this time that Marcus was in the General Manager's office being congratulated on the latest issue of *Eagle*. "How far ahead are you?" said the General Manager. Marcus looked puzzled. "Well, we're just about to start on the next issue. Is that what you mean?" The General Manager nearly had a fit. "Spend any money you like," he said, "but for God's sake get as far ahead as you can – you should be six or seven issues ahead." '

The first issue of *Eagle* now looks pale and washed out compared to the beauties of later years when printing techniques advanced and paper improved. But at the time it was bright and colourful and completely different from anything else that had ever been produced. Frank Hampson's drawings of 'Dan Dare, Pilot of the Future', on the first two pages were less intricate than they were to become when his team grew and facilities improved but they were, nonetheless, remarkable in their clarity and style. The story that developed was futuristic and exciting: an interplanetary space fleet including Dan, his faithful batman Albert Fitzwilliam Digby, his boss, Sir Hubert Guest, scientist Professor Peabody ('Jumping jets! Sufferin' cats! A woman!') and French and American co-pilots (Frank wanted a Russian as well, but was dissuaded by the management) set off for Venus in the hope of finding food for a starving Earth. There they encountered the evil green Treens and their over-lord, Dan's arch enemy, the Mekon.

The second picture serial was 'The Adventures of PC 49'. Readers complained that he didn't look like Brian Reece who played him on the wireless. Next came a page and a half of text story, 'Plot Against the World', 'A gripping new serial by Chad Varah', a humorously written but rather improbable tale of a young hero stumbling across a wounded man in a cellar, wounded man disappears, young heroine gets kidnapped, hero's dead cousin reappears. . . .

Also on page five was 'Captain Pugwash', 'The story of a bad Buccaneer and of the many sticky ends which nearly befell him'. Introducing the old sea dog, John Ryan detailed Pugwash's three particular belongings: 'His plank (for walking), his compass (for navigating), and a very special box (invariably locked). He also had a wife, who was far more terrifying than Pugwash, but good at mending socks.' He was much more disreputable-looking than in his later manifestation as a television star.

Learie Constantine's 'Cricket Coaching' appeared next, demonstrating The Stance, above two quarter-page advertisements: Biro described prehistoric picture writing, number one of 'A short history of writing', while Ovaltine offered a simple picture quiz and an invitation to join The League of Ovaltineys.

Another page of text followed: 'The Spies Who Saved London' – 'First of a series of real-life spy stories told by Bernard Newman'. It was the tale of British and Polish spies discovering German bomb-making installations and the subsequent RAF Peenemünde raid.

Then came Spencer Croft's 'Professor Brittain Explains:', drawn by John Croft (actually, one and the same), explaining the mysteries of radar, with an invitation to readers to send in any questions or problems to the 'Professor'. Opposite this was 'Seth and Shorty – Cowboys', written and drawn anonymously in colour, 'A tale of heroism and hardship in a lawless land – South-West Texas, sixty years ago'. Good old-fashioned cowboy and indian stuff, not very well done. 'Cortez, Conqueror of Mexico', the colourful story of the Spanish Conquistadores, drawn by William Stobbs, replaced the awful cowboys four months later.

The centre spread contained the first of Leslie Ashwell Wood's 'exploded drawings', showing the workings of The New Gas Turbine-Electric Locomotive due to run on the Western Region. He wasn't the first artist to use this technique; the magazine *Scientific American* featured a cut-away drawing of a skyscraper car park, by W.B. Robinson, in 1919. Similar drawings of motorcars and ships (such as the SS *Queen Mary* by G.H. Davies) appeared in the *Illustrated London News* and elsewhere in the 1930s.

Having trained as a draughtsman, Ashwell Wood became a designer in an aircraft factory and drew cut-aways for *Modern Wonder*, Odhams's scientific paper for boys, which folded in 1939. He had a knack of predicting forthcoming developments in engineering. The Aircraft of the Future which he drew for *Eagle* in 1951 became reality almost forty years later when a very similar aircraft took to the air. The Atomic Sub of the Future, featured in May 1952, was launched in America in 1954.

Ellen Vincent recalled, 'Leslie, a modest man, would arrive with his drawing tucked underneath his arm and explain all the various details . . . it was my job to take him over to the Two Brewers. I don't think he ever failed us. We received regular D Notices from the Ministry of Defence telling us not to publish certain things for security reasons and we were very keen to beat them to it with an exploded drawing of the Swift aeroplane. Old Leslie put together a very fine detailed technical drawing which came out bang on time for the Swift's first flight. The telephone rang: "How did you get the information? Haven't you read your D Notices?" The civil servant was perfectly agreeable and said, don't do it again. Leslie was extremely flattered and chuckled into his beer. When I asked him how he had done it he said "Oh, just by putting two and two together".'

Gerald Palmer drew some of the cut-aways. He remembers when 'one of the freelance artists we used illustrated a Phantom fighter plane breaking the air speed record at ground level on one of the desert test runs. He was given a photograph of the plane by the American Embassy with the names of all the crew painted on the side. Unfortunately, as 10,000 children realised, the names were painted on after the run.' Walkden Fisher also contributed a number of drawings for the centre spread over the years.

Below the cut-away was a Belgian strip bought from André Sarrut – the story of Sir Marlborough Mouseworthy, the greatest hunter of all time, and his brave protégé, Skippy the Kangaroo. In 1951, this spot was occupied by the first published English translation of Hergé's Tin Tin, 'The Story of Ottakar's Sceptre', which was subsequently published in book form.

The next two pages featured 'Heroes of the Clouds', by Captain Brian Nicholson DSO, 'an ace of the First World War' and his son Squadron Leader Dick Nicholson DFC, a test pilot. Below it was 'Discovering the Countryside' drawn by John Dyke and opposite were 'Real Life Mysteries', telling of the disappearance of the liner *Waratah* in 1909, drawn by William Stobbs. Two quarter pages of advertising completed that page: the Ministry of Transport on crossing the road, and Cadbury's Corner Quiz.

Page fourteen featured 'Making Your Own Model Racing Car' and 'Sporting Personalities' and then came the Editor's Page in which Marcus introduced the Eagle Club: 'The Eagle Club is going to be one of the most important features in the paper and we've got a pile of ideas for making it a really good club to join. It has very definite aims and standards.'

He listed the Club rules, which included enjoying life and helping others to enjoy life, and making the best of themselves. 'They will develop themselves in body, mind and spirit. They will tackle things for themselves.' Members had to lend a hand to those in need of help. 'They will not shirk difficult or dangerous jobs.'

Most of these aims would be laughed at nowadays – and imagine asking youngsters to do dangerous jobs – the health police would be appalled!

Membership of the Club cost one shilling and for the first four weeks the *Eagle* badge was free; thereafter it cost 6*d*. The first hundred members were given free trips to Farnborough Air Display, the Silverstone Grand Prix, the West Indian Test Match or the Highland Games, depending on where they lived.

Sixty thousand children applied to join the Eagle Club in the first week. The staff couldn't cope with all the shillings, so Stephen Williams arranged for Littlewoods to sort out that first rush for a modest fee. 'They were used to handling money, so everything was transferred to them and it all came back, neat and tidy, in one large cheque. People were beginning to write in saying "My son sent in 1/- a fortnight ago and he hasn't heard anything".' Marcus had to appeal for patience in the Editor's Letter.

Fan Keith Howard remembered, 'On the second page of the little orange and red membership booklet . . . is the Certificate of Membership. It has my name and the date of acceptance slotted into the appropriate spaces in a brisk but neat fountain-penned hand stating that I was elected at a meeting of the Presidential Board held at Shoe Lane. In my naïve youth I fully believed that they must have put aside much of their valuable time just to talk about little me. . . . Now and again I give the old *Eagle* badge an airing . . . it is interesting to note the reaction it causes.' Simon Garrett concurred: 'It's good to know I wasn't the only one who imagined a special meeting to elect him a member. Nor did I participate (apart from cricket coaching). One didn't need to; simply having so much on offer was enough to engender a sense of belonging.'

By August 1950 there were 100,000 members and the price of *Eagle* went up to 4*d* 'due to a 15 per cent increase in the price of paper and the cost of running the Eagle Club'.

The next development in the Eagle Club was to become a MUG. Marcus wrote: 'That may sound a rather strange thing to become. This shortly is what it's all about: There are really only two kinds of people in the world. One kind are the MUGs. The opposite of the MUGs are the Spivs – also called wide boys, smart guys, hooligans, louts or racketeers.

'The MUGs are the people who are some use in the world; the people who do something worth-while for others instead of just grabbing for themselves all the time. Of course the spivs snigger at that. *They* use the word Mug as an insult. "Aren't they mugs?" they say about people who believe in living for something bigger than themselves.

'That is why someone who gets called a MUG is likely to be a pretty good chap. For one thing, he's got to have guts because he doesn't mind being called a MUG. He *likes* it. He's the sort who will volunteer for a difficult or risky job and say cheerfully, "Alright, I'll be the Mug". That doesn't mean he is stupid. It means he's got the right ideas and doesn't think it is at all clever to be a spiv-type.'

Readers were told that they had to be nominated by someone like a school teacher, parent, or club leader; claims would be investigated and special certificates and badges awarded to those who qualified. There was a certain amount of confusion at first, boys were nominating themselves, or thought they had to rescue people from drowning. One father wrote in to complain that his son was spending all his time by the canal, waiting for someone to fall in. So a pamphlet was brought out defining the rules and aims.

The Editor's Letter, which first had Marcus's name printed below it in November 1950, to be followed by the famous signature in August 1951, was usually written by Ellen Vincent. It described forthcoming events, enjoined readers not to rob birds' nests, or throw stones in crowded places; to send unwanted toys and comics to hospitals and foreign missions, to contribute money for those who couldn't afford the 1/6d club entry fee, to take care using bows and arrows. The letter sent birthday greetings to royals, explained religious festivals and generally acted as a mildly moral guide with a touch of humour.

The editor's page contained a Competition Corner which offered a 10/6d National Savings Certificate for the best outline for a strip-cartoon story – were they trying to save on staff? – and 10/6d to the first correct solution of a picture crossword. There was also the first appearance of *Chicko*, Thelwell's marvellously anarchic and quiffed small boy.

Charles Pocklington, who later became Assistant Art Editor, said that the editor's page was extremely difficult to design. 'You had to get so much information in. We had a competition every week to see who could get the least overmatter. We were setting four and three-quarter point [type size] which is very bad for children's eyes. Throughout my career, if I've mentioned that I've worked on *Eagle*, I've been regarded with awe.'

As Editorial Assistant, Derek Lord organised Competition Corner. 'It was hand to mouth to begin with. I had to learn quickly. When a sub-editorship became vacant I applied for the job and Marcus said "I don't see why not". He always favoured women, it hadn't occurred to him that a male on his staff would be right.'

Pages sixteen and seventeen of the first issue carried a text story by Moore Raymond, 'Lash Lonergan's Quest', a tale of derring-do in the Australian outback, and two more ads – for the Army Apprentices School and Rowntrees Fruit Gums, featuring 'Ronnie the Gumster's Trick Time'.

The Frank Hampson team's strip, 'Rob Conway', now made his appearance; an Army Training Corps cadet coming to the rescue of a one-armed man being mugged and thereby getting involved in strange adventures in Asia. Opposite this was the Wall's Ice Cream advertisement feature, in colour: 'Tommy Walls The Wonder Boy', also drawn, at this time, by the Frank Hampson team. The Wall's 'W' sign is almost as well-remembered now as Dan Dare. This first story was (almost) the only one in which magic played a part: Tommy, having eaten Wall's ice-cream at lunch, makes the 'magic W sign' and flies *à la* Superman to save a sabotaged jet plane from crashing. Thereafter, Marcus and James Hemming decreed that, unlike Superman, success must be achieved by effort, stamina and intelligence rather than magical powers. In the second issue, Tommy saves a friend from drowning: 'That Wall's I had when we started out has given me the extra energy I need for this effort' and the 'magic W' becomes the 'lucky W'.

The final page was, of course, 'The Great Adventurer', the story of Saint Paul, unchanged from the original dummy. This was also scripted and drawn by Frank Hampson and his team, although later, Chad Varah was to take over the writing and Norman Williams the drawing, for that and many other back page stories.

In Issue Two, the spaceship approaching Venus blew up and double crown posters advertising *Eagle* asked the vital question: 'Will Dan Dare Reach Venus?'

Two days later Marcus received a letter from the Assistant Secretary (formerly Chairman) of The British Interplanetary Society: 'I think this might amuse you. Yesterday I was lecturing at the Royal Geographical Society on the problem of interplanetary navigation, with Sir Robert Watson-Watt in the chair. During the subsequent discussion one of the speakers was Dr D.H. Sadler, head of the Nautical Almanac Office. After a highly technical series of remarks about position-finding in space, meteor statistics, etc, he ended up by asking, "*Will* Dan Dare reach Venus?" The other speaker (Dr Atkinson, Chief Assistant at Greenwich) was sure that he would; but I expressed fears that he might encounter space-pirates!'

By 10 May, Arthur C. Clarke had been commissioned by Marcus to write a synopsis for Dan Dare. He was a fast worker: Marcus received it by the 11th; it was accepted on the 12th and expanded by the 19th into three episodes of 1,500 words each. A rewrite was requested on the 25th, and despatched to Marcus on the 27th. For all of this, Arthur C. Clarke received 30 guineas. Unfortunately he cannot remember which the episodes were! Arthur C. was, in fact, instrumental in launching the Treens on an unsuspecting world, by suggesting the outline of their behaviour to Frank Hampson. Arthur thinks he invented the name Treen but isn't quite sure. (It is, in fact, the name of a place in Cornwall and the word for small domestic articles made of wood.)

Clarke's connection with *Eagle* wasn't restricted to Dan Dare. While a student at King's College, London in the 1940s, he had written a number of science fiction stories, one of which was sent by his agent to *Eagle*'s Fiction Editor, Chad Varah. Chad writes in his autobiography, *Before I Die Again*: 'My task . . . was threefold: first to be Marcus's trusted adviser, secondly to write a text serial story and thirdly to read about a quarter of a million words a week of unsolicited manuscripts. I found the last a tedious task. . . . It was a wonderful relief the day I came across two typescripts sent by the agents Pearn Pollinger & Higham which enthralled me, and which I felt sure would appeal strongly to the top 50 per cent of our readership, intellectually. I wrote immediately to the agents offering them double the usual payment and asking to see any other stories by the same writer. He was then comparatively unknown, but is now famous. His name was Arthur C. Clarke.'

On 4 August 1950, 'The Fires Within' was published in *Eagle* under the pen-name Charles Willis.

Later that year Arthur was contracted to write an eight page episode of Dan Dare for *Eagle Annual* at three guineas a week. His 'work-book' for the period states that this was suspended – again, Arthur can't remember why or if his story ever appeared. He remained a consultant to *Eagle*: his records show that on 19 September 1951 he sent a detailed letter commenting on the Red Moon story. On 3 October he wrote to Frank Hampson at Marcus's request and on 12 October to Frank Hampson at Frank's request. For this Arthur received £8.10*s*.1*d*, but we have been unable to discover (and Arthur can't remember) what was in these letters. Arthur says that he has instructed that his archives be kept secret until fifty years after his death.

In 1953 Clarke contributed a four-page article entitled 'Is Space Travel Possible?' to the *Dan Dare Space Book*.

The second issue of *Eagle*, as well as being short of copies, was shorter in pages. This was explained in the Editor's Letter in issue three: 'You will see that this is another 20-page issue of *Eagle* – like the first one. For the time being, we are planning to make it 20 pages one week and 16 the next. This is because of the difficulty of getting enough paper which is still pretty scarce.'

It was in issue three that Peter Probyn's dotty six-frame strip, 'Grandpa', first appeared and Harold Johns was allowed by Frank Hampson to put his name to 'Rob Conway'. From then on, it was produced by Harold and Greta until they ran out of ideas for a story line and brought it to a halt rather suddenly in July. Greta explained, 'Frank started "Rob Conway" but had no story line for it. I was thrilled to death to have our own strip. We took the poor chap to Tibet because we wanted to draw Tibet and then we couldn't think how on earth to bring it to an end. We thought of some fatuous ending which was obviously cobbled together.'

*Eagle* was soon being used in the classroom as a teaching aid and by model-making fathers. One lad wrote that twenty-seven out of the thirty-two in his class were Eagle Club members. It was reported in the *Lancet* in October 1950 that a doctor read *Eagle* on his rounds and the *Norfolk Chronicle* wrote of a rector recommending *Eagle* to his parishioners. The *Daily Worker* noted that students were replacing the *Daily Express* with *Eagle*, and the *World's Press News* that *Eagle* had been banned in South Africa. WH Smith's *Trade Circular* reported in April 1951 that an envelope had been delivered to Hulton Press addressed only with drawings of *Eagle* characters and the message 'Mr Postman, sort this one out'.

*Eagle* was sent to soldiers in Korea and to refugee camps, and was apparently read by the star in a film called *Valley of Song*.

A letter from a religious community said, 'You may be interested to know that the Superior of this Community has a high opinion of your paper and is reading one of your serials as a weekly relaxation!'

From an orthopaedic hospital: 'Every child reads your paper. The *Eagles* that arrive here are immediately booked about six deep and the owners of copies relieve general anxiety as to the welfare of Dan Dare etc by

*The un-addressed letter that found its way to Hulton Press*

broadcasting new developments in the plot at the tops of their voices.'

Geoffrey Grigson on the BBC Home Service said of Dan Dare, 'One of the best things since *Twenty Thousand Leagues Under the Sea.'*

In a radio broadcast about heroes, Dan Dare was called 'The newest superman – a much more up-to-date character than any of his comic strip ancestors. . . . He is a man we can easily believe in, with a masterly control of all the gadgets of his scientific age.'

The Headmistress of Barham School, Wembley, was an ardent reader: 'At least one confiscated copy of *Eagle* is passed around the Masters' Room each week. All the teachers read it, and the periodical is regarded as ideal reading for children (and teachers). Miss Boto (school secretary) was quick to point out that confiscated copies are, of course, returned after school hours.'

Wolf Mankowitz wrote 'A Hero of Our Time, A note on Dan Dare', for *Books of Today* in 1951: 'This need for a hero in well over a million schoolchildren is currently satisfied by Colonel Dan Dare . . . a superman of the Welfare Age. . . . With the coming of Dan Dare, the Marvos and Wondermen, Garths and Mandrakes, have had to retire to whatever markets they can find. . . . Besides Dan Dare they have only the quaintness of Chelsea Pensioners to recommend them. . . . Professor Peabody, [is] a pretty tomboy to whom the rest of the crew together with the bulk of the readership harshly objected until Hampson assured them that Dare would in no circumstances fall in love.'

Dan Dare was mentioned in Parliament. George Holt wrote in the *News Chronicle* that 'Earl Jellicoe, Lord Shackleton and Dan Dare did their best together to put Britain into the space race yesterday. Earl Jellicoe told the House of Lords he had spent the previous afternoon in the historic library of the House, "spellbound" by Dan Dare's adventures. Lord St Oswald confirmed that he and Lord Conesford had found Earl Jellicoe there "working diligently through a pile of brightly coloured space-fiction literature."

' "You may smile at space fiction," Lord Jellicoe said, "but I think it is closer to reality than some of us may suppose. It shows that to the younger generation space represents the glamour and adventure of science."

'He and Lord Shackleton, the great explorer's son, urged the Government to go into the space race seriously, as a matter of priority, but the Earl of Onslow, for the Government, could only promise "some sort of state-ment" in the fairly near future.

'Which seemed to leave Dan Dare with a clear field for the time being.'

Hulton Press were receiving thousands of letters a week from all over the world, from parents, grandparents and teachers, as well as enthusiastic children. Marguerite Mincher and Jessie Starke were drafted in from the correspondence department of *Picture Post* to deal with them. The readership was not confined to middle-class public schoolboys (or girls), there were letters from the sons of chimney sweeps as well as old Etonians. The careers feature 'He Wants To Be . . .' gave advice to would-be bricklayers and plumbers as well as doctors and solicitors.

*Eagle* received an amazing diversity of questions: 'Was Pericles the same person as Hercules?' 'Please send me full details of all the ships, guns and aircraft, etc used in HM Forces, as this will be useful for a notebook I am compiling' 'What is the shape of bricks used in building factory chimneys?' 'What are the times of departure of all main line railway engines from London?' 'How can I compile a space magazine?' 'What was the origin of the Ashes?' 'How can I save my pocket money?' 'How can I avoid losing my hair ribbons?' 'How can I help spastic children?'. Marcus and James Hemming felt strongly that the children must not be fobbed off, they deserved to be given the facts. Eventually four women were employed just to answer the letters.

For some questions they supplied print-outs with addresses to write to for further information; others called for more ingenuity. One child wrote that her goldfish had jumped out of the bowl and been on the floor all night and when she put it back it started swimming and was this a miracle? Answer: 'It was very surprising.' A reader asked how the Mekon got his shirt off to wash it; another wanted to know how nitroglycerine is made into cordite. Raymond Miller wrote from Surrey, 'Dear Marcus Morris, I am sorry to trouble you but can you please explain to me shortly Einstein's Theory of Relativity?' A small boy wanted to know what to do about mouldy frog-spawn.

One lad wrote in asking for advice on keeping mice. He was sent what was thought to be a satisfactory reply; a month later the mouse arrived through the post (dead) with a request for a post mortem.

Some of the children were right clever-dicks: a girl of ten sent in her remedy, with illustrations, for weightlessness in space; a boy pointed out a mistake in 'The Romance of the Moon', 'The nearest heavenly body to Earth is not the moon but a tiny asteroid called Hermes'.

Another wrote that he had always been a dim-wit in science, but as the articles in *Eagle* were written in easy-to-understand language, he was beginning to see the light. A teacher wanted centre page illustrations for use in school. The story of Mark, the youngest disciple, was pinned to a school wall every week – though one parent thought it was anti-semitic. A Sunday School teacher was amazed when all her class managed to answer the curate's questions on the resurrection: 'The small boy beside me – aged eight – said "We know all this – it was in *Eagle* this week".'

Someone wanted a tramcar on the centre page: 'Surely this vehicles [*sic*] have done more good for humanity than, for instance, a BRM car? So please can one of your excellent artists remedy this ghastly omission?' An adult pointed out that any boy using a transmitter, as offered in the Relda Radio advertisement, without a licence, was liable to prosecution. Another wanted to know if the features on prehistoric animals and insects had been published in book form as he found them very useful as visual aids. The chairman of a motor racing club in South Africa asked for back numbers containing pictures of sports and racing cars to decorate his club room. Three readers sent in a 2/- postal order, saying 'We hereby enclose this small Consulation. And hope it will be useful.'

In 1959, a reader who had taken *Eagle* since it first came out wrote to express admiration of the colour pages. He was now training as an artist at the College of Arms and he sent in his version of Dan Dare's coat of arms. He said that *Eagle* was more useful than encyclopaedias as a reliable source of illustrations of animals, insects, birds, prehistoric animals and fossils.

Pauline Patterson had belonged to the St James' Youth Club in Birkdale for a short time. She didn't want to pull strings when she went for an interview with the Personnel Manager at Hultons in 1952, so when she was taken in to see Marcus, 'I think he was genuinely quite surprised and delighted. Mr Morris ran things with the same light unobtrusive hand he had brought to the Youth Club.' She started work answering readers' letters before moving on to sub-editing. 'There were some funny letters. I remember one which said "please will you send me an Advice Bureau", thinking it was a sort of desk; it was one of the features. Another said that "the council should choose gratings in the road more carefully because us ladies get our high heels stuck in them. Love from Fiona, aged 8". We got a letter from one of the little princes, Gloucester, I think.'

Ellen Vincent recalled: 'The story goes that Prince Charles was one of our readers. His uncle, Lord Mountbatten, had ordered a subscription for him at Christmas. The phone rang on our emergency line at Hultons on Boxing Day. A rather irate Lord Mountbatten asked what had happened to his present to Prince Charles – no copy of *Eagle* had arrived. All the bells rang and knees knocked. The Circulation Manager, Bob Boyd, was called to deal with the matter. He swore he got hold of the relevant copy of *Eagle*, folded it royally, put the package in the most important looking post box he could find, stood back and saluted smartly. Then he wiped his brow and made his way to the nearest pub.'

When Marcus produced his book, *The Best of Eagle,* in 1977 and sent a copy to the grown-up Prince Charles, he received a letter of thanks saying that the book brought back fond memories.

The Editor's Letter in issue four contained the names of the first twenty-five club members (three of whom were girls) and the first MUGs were announced, whose heroic deeds included going to work in a hospital in Africa, pulling a child from in front of a bus and keeping cheerful in the face of long illness.

The first Mug Of The Month was John Chown, who was stabbed while tackling two burglars. He was also awarded the British Empire Medal and the Scouts' Silver Cross.

By the end of 1951, 339 MUGs' badges had been awarded. They had special tea parties all over the country, visits to Hulton Press and lunch with the Editor, trips to the panto and free holidays.

The first MUG of the Year was John Grimes who, in spite of having a club foot, nursed his mother and dying brother, looked after the household and his younger siblings and studied hard enough to be the only one out of 500 pupils to gain a place at grammar school; 'A hero of everyday life.'

Marcus's father was also awarded a MUG's badge. Phyllis Tomlinson explained: 'Walter wrote to Marcus and said he had got up at 6.30 one morning for a Mothers' Union outing and did he qualify for a MUG's badge for such bravery? Marcus replied that it was not normal to give MUGs' badges to people over eighty, but he was pleased to make an exception for such outstanding devotion to duty. Walter wore it very proudly.'

In issue four Marcus appealed to readers to pass on their copy of *Eagle* to friends: 'The demand has been so great that it is impossible for the time being to supply enough copies to satisfy everyone.'

For some reason, in that issue the 'magic W' reappeared in Tommy Walls, with Tommy leaping for the cab of a moving express train. James and Marcus had somehow allowed the magic to slip through; it may have had something to do with the fact that Marcus was in the middle of moving his household from Lancashire to Surrey.

Early in 1950, Marcus had begun to see that he would have to make a choice: either he was to be a journalist or a parish priest. When he joined Hulton Press he'd thought he could do both. 'It had never really occurred to me that I should cease to be a parish priest. Somehow I had envisaged myself as the editor of this national paper and as doing my work in the parish at the same time. In a way I regarded the former only as an extension in principle of the latter. First and foremost I was a priest of the Church of England; only secondarily was I to be a journalist.'

Marcus had not realised just how big a project *Eagle* was to become, or how intense was to be his involvement and heavy the responsibility he was taking on. He talked it over with Walter who agreed that doing both jobs was unfair on everyone: his parishioners, his family, himself and Hulton Press.

'My father was of the opinion that as I'd gone so far and had given the magazine so much of my energy and thought, it was right to go on with it, and give up the parish. He seemed to be quite happy that I should make this choice; so too was the Bishop of Liverpool whom he took me to see. The Bishop said that he thought I could best exercise my vocation in Christian journalism and that, with *Eagle*, my congregation would increase from a few hundred to a few hundred thousands.'

A special meeting of the St James' Parochial Church Council was held in the vicarage on 6 March with thirty-one members present: 'Mr Morris informed the meeting that after much deliberation and careful thought he had decided to ask the Bishop of Liverpool and the Trustees to accept his resignation from the living of St James as he was taking up a position as editor of a new children's newspaper with Messrs Hultons of London. Mr Morris went on to ask members to accept his apologies for being away from the parish so much during the past few months. He felt that this new venture must be his work for some years at any rate, though he and Mrs Morris would be very sad to leave Birkdale.

'Alderman Charlton said he felt sure he was voicing the thoughts of all present in wishing Mr Morris a successful career in London and continued, saying that he thought it was the right choice to make.'

One can imagine that, fond though they undoubtedly were of Marcus, the PCC would look forward to having a vicar who could be in the parish more than two days a week, and keep his mind on the job!

Peggy Lister had taken over the day-to-day editing of the parish magazine and she included in the April edition 'an anonymous contribution': 'We have to admit sincere feelings of regret and even of disappointment. . . . The value of Mr Morris's work in the parish can be more clearly appreciated if we consider how difficult it will be to find a worthy successor. With a feeling of pride we congratulate him on the progress he has made in quite a new field. With a feeling of sadness we thank him for his great efforts on behalf of St James.'

There were, of course, parishioners who didn't feel quite so charitably about their vicar; who felt that the parish had been badly neglected and that journalism was not a proper calling for a parish priest. They were, perhaps surprisingly, in the minority and were much less vociferous than Marcus's supporters.

He was to say in later years that *Eagle* wouldn't have been possible without the help and understanding of the people of Birkdale.

At the end of April the Morris family said goodbye to Southport. The parishioners gave a party in the Memorial Hall which included 'songs by the Choir, a solo, three part-songs and "On Wings Of Song" sung by Anne Dixon'. Jess was presented with a bouquet of roses and carnations by Mrs Charlton and the Alderman made a speech.

On 30 April Marcus preached his final sermons at St James.

The *Church Times* reported Marcus's departure: 'Until recently vicar of St James' Birkdale, Mr Morris has resigned his living to become editor of the *Eagle*. Having already made his name as the editor of the *Anvil*, he is one of the ablest of the younger religious journalists.'

The Morrises drove south, the car bursting at the seams with a five-months pregnant Jess, the springer spaniel and three children – the youngest daughter with her head swathed in bandages. Even while organising the leaving of Southport, Marcus's preoccupation with *Eagle* was plain to see. A week earlier Sally, aged three, had been running around the house far too fast, as was her wont, and slipped, cutting the back of her head open rather badly on the old-fashioned radiator in the sitting room. With blood pouring down her neck, she went next door to the study where she found her father in consultation with Frank Hampson. 'Go and find your mother' was all the response to emanate from the creators of *Eagle*.

# Chapter Eleven

As the Morrises had been living in a tied Church of England house and there was no money to go towards buying another one, Hulton Press had agreed to find somewhere which would combine a home for the Morrises with a studio for the artists still struggling in the shed in Churchtown. They bought a large Victorian house in College Road, Epsom, for which Marcus paid rent and was given an allowance to cover the cost of domestic help and expenses in looking after the artists. The builders and decorators moved in to transform the old servants' quarters into a studio. The Hampson family were found a house nearby and the unmarried artists were to lodge in a local hotel.

The Firs had a large old-fashioned kitchen with scullery and boiler house, a dining room, drawing room, study and, at the back, a tumbledown conservatory and a ballroom – a wonderful playroom for three rowdy girls. It even had a dais at one end, an ideal stage for the entertainments they delighted in putting on for their parents and anyone else who could be persuaded to watch. The two acres of grounds contained a huge lawn with a revolving summerhouse, a neglected tennis lawn, stables, greenhouse, vegetable and fruit gardens, two rambling shrubberies and two spinneys with eminently climbable trees.

Until the house was ready in July the Morrises lived at the Drift Bridge Hotel on Epsom Downs at Hultons' expense and doubtless to the inconvenience of the other guests.

Former parishioner Marian Widdows wrote to Jess from Birkdale, 'The vicarage has seemed sadly empty since you all went away. One somehow became so used to seeing toys and tables and funny little chairs and things in the garden and invariably being asked most politely to come to tea somewhere in the bushes. . . . The Bishop of Liverpool said some wonderful things about Marcus. . . . A new vicar is going to seem odd in Marcus's place.'

The youngest child, Simon David Edward Harston was born on 30 August. Marcus was delighted; he had always wanted a son. Perhaps he felt hagridden in his all-female household, though he was thoroughly spoilt by them all and life revolved round his needs and wishes.

Peggy Lister, who became Simon's godmother (as did Phyllis Entwistle; Chad Varah and Jack Allen were godfathers) wrote to Jess in October: 'I spent half an hour with old Bundey [the new vicar of St James] yesterday showing him how to edit a Parish Magazine! and as usual I rammed Marcus down his throat and he ended up by saying "Marcus must have been a very remarkable person". I said "He was and is". He also told me that he didn't approve of a tombola for our Christmas Fair. He didn't think it was quite "Church-like" so I very nearly suggested a quiet game of croquet in one corner. I had a word with Dargie on the phone today and her opinion is that he is trying to reform us quietly but she and I refuse to be reformed. . . . Mrs Bundey seemed aghast at the way St James do things, apparently the Bundeys never had cups of tea after meetings etc. Oh well, they will live and learn.'

*Editor and daughters in the garden at Epsom – the girls never seen so tidy before or since.*

Marcus heard from Esmond Corelli. 'I congratulate you heartily on the arrival of the son and heir. I rejoice that the name of Harston Morris will now not perish from the land.

'Secondly to say how sorry I was that the *Anvil* had to pack up. Sad! Although you have, of course, replaced the interest with a much larger one, the first love can never be forgotten. Perhaps it had done its job in acting as a "flair-revealer".

'You and Jess achieved the remarkable in taking me off the shelf, dusting me, oiling the machinery and causing me to function in some extraordinary tasks (me as Isaiah, and Angel, Chadband and Jaques!!!) but can it be done again? I doubt it. Ah well! I hope the babe flourishes, as also the little friendly souls: J, K, and S.'

Life for J, K, and S was idyllic. They had two acres to run wild in; Epsom Downs were just down the road, convenient for riding, and tobogganing in winter. A regular and favourite form of exercise was to climb out of the landing window and clamber over the turreted roof of the house, three storeys up. Although she said later that her heart would stand still at the sight, Jess was remarkably restrained during these mountaineering expeditions, so the children felt no fear and no accidents ensued. Another favourite game was crawling through the tunnels of the next-door-neighbour's huge dog kennel; the Weedens had children of similar ages and allowed the Morrises to watch their television. The younger girl, Mary, was punished for throwing a pair of scissors at Kate, although Kate remembered that it was she who did the throwing. Mary later became the 'fragrant Lady Archer'.

Schoolfriend Margaret Knight-Smith said, 'It was a nice house, you never felt you weren't allowed to touch things or walk on the carpet, we played everywhere. It seemed very bare, there was no furniture in the playroom; we roller skated in there on the parquet floor. I remember raiding our kitchens for tea trays to go tobogganing. I was a bit in awe of Marcus. We always seemed to behave better when he was there. He wasn't strict, he was living on a different plane, very much involved with what he was doing. We had to keep quiet so as not to disturb what was going on. Whatever it was, was always very important.

'Jess was super, you could always talk to her. My father had just died and she was very kind to us.

'We always had such fun that even fancy dress parties weren't that much different. We were forever having meals in each other's houses. When five-year-old Sally ran away and walked to our house on her own during Derby Day and asked the policeman to see her across the road, my mother rang hers – I don't think Jess had got as far as missing her.'

The girls enjoyed making nuisances of themselves in the studio, which Margaret described as 'a different world, very ordered, big drawing boards, machines, spaceships. There was a lot of geometry up there. It was all contrived and arranged, unlike the free space downstairs.' The children also had their uses: Sally sat as model for the Mekon, Lord of the Treens

and terror of the universe, perched on Pop Hampson's shoulders. They all appeared on the front page of *Eagle* in September 1950, photographed with housekeeper Mrs Dempsey (a cousin, she said, of the boxer Jack Dempsey) and her son, representing the family of Batman Albert Fitzwilliam Digby, lost on Venus. Even Puppy achieved fame as the inspiration for a 'space dog'.

Jess had not improved as a housewife (though she was a good cook when she felt like it and a fine needlewoman)

*The Mekon paddling at Southport, May 1949*

and was, anyway, keen to get back to the theatre. So the house was run by a succession of housekeepers and a nanny for Simon. The only housekeeper who stayed more than a few months was a rather fierce Dutch woman, Gureen Glass, who ran the household with a rod of iron and a great deal of affection, which was reciprocated; but even her devotion to the family gave out after a year or so.

Marcus found it 'an administrative convenience' having the Dan Dare artists under the same roof, but the atmosphere soon became tense. According to Greta Tomlinson, Jess told the artists in no uncertain terms that she didn't like people coming and going at all hours. But as a vicar's wife, Jess was used to it. She remembered taking them to task only once; late at night when Marcus had flu she asked them to keep the noise down.

Greta is still a little hostile towards Marcus and Jess: 'Marcus and I always clashed. It wasn't a happy relationship.'

By contrast, Jocelyn Thomas had very fond memories of the Morrises. She did have a vague feeling that the family thought the artists were in the way and that there was a general anti-Marcus feeling in the studio; he was certainly blamed if anything went wrong. But Jocelyn thought that the main problem was probably good old-fashioned feminine jealousy.

Greta's feelings for Marcus are no doubt coloured by what happened to her and Harold Johns in 1954. By then, work in the Dan Dare studio wasn't quite so frantic and, when Harold was approached to do some outside work in his spare time, he thought he and Greta could give it a go, if Marcus approved. Marcus thought that as long as *Eagle* got priority there would be no problem and gave his permission. Frank was horrified. Anybody who wasn't 100 per cent with him, was against him and he insisted that Marcus sack them. Marcus, who needed Frank more than he needed Harold and Greta, had to agree. Greta was astonished that, when they appealed to Frank, he showed no surprise and refused to intervene on their behalf. But it was Marcus who took the blame.

Another member of the team said that 'I remember walking in to a very heated argument between Harold and Frank. Frank was telling Harold off for some inadequate work he'd turned in. Harold was purple with indignation and was not best pleased at being told off with me in the room. Frank thought that Harold and Greta had spent too much time on other work and were being disloyal and dishonest.'

Greta remains loyal to Frank in spite of all the problems: 'I painted Dan Dare on water skis and I couldn't paint water and I had to do it again and again and then Frank stuck a speech balloon over it. He would often come in and say "Scrap that, I've got a much better idea." He didn't care about peoples' lives, he was totally besotted with Dan Dare. We were not allowed to sign anything, it all had to be Frank Hampson except when we were working on the annuals.'

Harold Johns' friends and relations were always annoyed that he didn't get the recognition he deserved and that 'everything was down to Frank'.

Artist Keith Watson, who worked on Dan Dare much later, called Frank's technique 'a factory job. Frank would produce what he called a visual, a

*Rocket lift off – or not! Another less than successful launch in Epsom. . . .*

very complete one, of the two pages. From this photographs were taken; if possible somebody would pose live for the figure positions in the rough and the final work would be done from live models or photos.'

Greta was the model for Miss Peabody; Frank himself was the original model for Dan Dare (he always said that Dan Dare was what he wanted to be, but Digby was what he actually was), until Joan Porter found Max Dunlop; Pop Hampson was Sir Hubert Guest, among others; his wife was Digby's Aunt Anastasia and Digby was based on Harold Johns.

'There was a tremendous amount of background research, reference hunting, character development,' continued Keith. 'One of the vital ingredients along with Frank Hampson's talent, which was *the* most vital ingredient, was the thoroughness and care which had been taken over the presentation.'

Bruce Cornwell, a brilliant marine artist, and Eric Eden, did the technical drawings. Bruce told us, 'When I first joined the studio (the old bakery) I didn't mind the work load – it was new, interesting and everyone was enthusiastic. I saw my bed about three times a week.

'The first bit of friction came after some weeks . . . two of us were banished to a room in a pub some 500 yards down the road. This of course was unworkable – we had no references, no continuity. . . . Protesting was a waste of time and Frank told us to put up with it or go back to London. . . . Marcus had me working on different projects on a freelance basis. . . . He was easy to get along with. He always knew what he wanted and always appeared calm – unlike the basic panics in the bakery.'

Bruce returned when the studio moved to Epsom and continued with the 100-hour working weeks. 'It was worse than before . . . hours of good work would be scrapped at the last minute. . . . I think even in those days Frank was killing himself.

'I was taken off the strip so that I could devote my time to producing a working model of Dan's rocket. After trials and some success I had to show it to Marcus. Even after all this time I can smile when I recall the meeting at Epsom. I set the model for take-off and lit the fuse but, instead of taking off, it travelled along the ground at about 40 mph with the dog in hot pursuit, followed by Marcus. He made the mistake of picking it up and got his fingers burnt.'

Bruce finally left after Frank refused him a short holiday. 'He told me that if he couldn't have a break then neither could I. . . . I never saw Frank again.' He did however, return later to work on Dan Dare with Don Harley and Desmond Walduck.

Jocelyn said that they worked like zombies till 3.00 in the morning and she would often arrive home in tears of exhaustion, but Frank never expected more of his team than he would of himself.

Walkden Fisher had refused to move south, much to his wife Peggy's chagrin, so he was always up and down to Epsom from Southport with his models. He told Peggy that Frank Hampson was a workaholic and nobody could please him, and that the artists were all getting cheesed off. There was a lot of unrest at the time of Greta and Harold's sacking. 'Fish thanked God he wasn't down there, he was out of it. Frank was getting all the recognition, maybe the others felt peeved,' Peggy said.

Dorothy Hampson was liked by all the artists and was very friendly to the Morris children when they went round to the Hampson house to play with

*Surveying the wreckage*

Peter or watch the Hampsons' television. Peter probably saw more of his father than the Morris children did of theirs.

'One got the feeling he was always around, though busy,' Peter told us. 'It didn't affect my life that much, it seemed perfectly normal. I hardly ever went out with my father, there was no social life. Even when people came to the house he'd pop in and say hello and go back to the studio. He was a funny contradictory man. He could be a bit of a hermit when he was working, although he was very sociable and liked talking to people. He was a very intelligent man with a lot of interests, particularly history.

'He had a bed in the studio and would sleep for a couple of hours during the night. It must have been a great strain for my mother, the whole house was directed towards him working. But it was an exciting time, never dull.

'When father was around he was quite often in a bad mood, usually about the reproduction or the printers.'

Joan Porter said, 'Frank was frequently troubled by the problems of reproduction. He tried various methods to assist the quality of the printing and therefore the look of the art work.

'In the early days the colour had to be absolutely clear, totally flat. It was only as we found that Bemrose's reproduction could accomplish much more that the colouring was able to branch out.'

About eighteen months after the launch Michael Gibson became Art Editor.

'I don't think anybody but Marcus would have taken me on. I was an engineer but wanted to get into publishing. It was a joy to work with a team of enthusiasts who really felt we were doing something worthwhile.

'A lot of artists worked through agents, so one didn't actually meet them. We had one or two good agents, like Jack Marsh, who became personally very involved with the paper because it was quite a large proportion of their income. We paid far more than anybody else which meant we got the best artists, but some of them were notoriously bad at not reading the story you sent them, with disastrous results.'

Artists who wrote their own scripts were easier to deal with. John Ryan was one: 'Marcus decided that Pugwash was too young for *Eagle* and he asked me to do something else. My wife Priscilla drew the first picture of Harris Tweed, a skit on her ideal man. He was bone from the neck up. He was based on all the stupid, thick-headed majors I'd suffered under during the war. I drew Harris Tweed with relish, I hated everything he stood for.'

The sub-editors reckoned they had more trouble with the continuity of Tweed's buttons and ties than with anything else in the magazine. 'Harris Tweed, Extra Special Agent' was a pompous bumbling detective with a monocle, who was always saved from his own folly by his sidekick, The Boy.

November 1950 heralded the start of Charles Chilton's great contribution to *Eagle*. He was a very successful writer and producer for the BBC of, among other things, *Riders of the Range*. Stephen Williams introduced him to Marcus and suggested sending Charles to Tombstone, Arizona, to see the Wild West in the flesh. Marcus agreed to pay all expenses and received in return a series of articles, 'Ticket to Tombstone'. The visit aroused a huge amount of interest in Arizona, where Charles was made a Deputy Marshal of Tombstone and presented with authentic cowboy clothes. The Mayor of Tombstone sent a telegram to *Eagle* asking for pen pals for the Pistol Pete Club; they were swamped by so many letters that the club leader had to write and beg them to stop.

The BBC, who owned the broadcasting rights, gave Charles permission to do a strip of 'Riders of the Range' which started in *Eagle* in December 1950, drawn by Jack Daniel. Jack was already well known at the time as a strip cartoonist on the *Daily Express*, but Charles didn't like his dark satanic drawings. 'My style was a bit rigid for what they wanted. We had this idea on the *Express* of basing characters on well-known film stars, which meant you had a reference for them. Jeff Arnold was based on Gary Cooper, one of the baddies on Mickey Rooney. After about a year Marcus took me off "Riders of the Range" and put me on to sports things, Freddie Mills, Learie Constantine, Billy Wright.'

'Riders of the Range' was taken over by Angus Scott, 'a weird fellow' according to Charles. 'I lent him a lot of books and later found he'd torn the pages out.' Finally Charles found Frank Humphris.

'I was running one of the first Country and Western programmes on BBC, *Hill-Billy Hoe-Down*,' says Charles 'and I received a sheet of paper, set out in comic strip, of all my characters in the programme saying, what about running it in the *Radio Times*. They turned it down, but I was so impressed with these drawings I took them to Marcus; I knew he didn't like Angus Scott and was looking for someone else.'

*Marcus and fans welcoming Charles Chilton back from his 'fact-finding' trip to Tombstone, 1950*

Frank Humphris had exhibited at the Royal Academy and the Royal Society of Portrait Painters, had worked in advertising and in a big studio in the west of England and 'the strip technique seemed to come naturally'.

Charles admits that he could never get his copy in on time and once dictated it over the phone from Italy. Frank complained that 'the first stories were a bit simple. After two or three years Charles started to introduce real life stories, Billy the Kid, Sam Bass, Wyatt Earp and the big one, War with the Sioux and Fighting Cheyenne.

'I could really get my teeth into those, I did a lot of research. I drew Billy the Kid from photographs of the actual person. As Frank Hampson had his models around him in his studio, my studio was littered with chaps, boots, spurs, lariats, a stetson. I made my own Western saddle and rode with it in the park. You don't sit in them the same way as an English saddle.'

Humphris' research included hand-tooling his own holsters and belts, and learning to shoot with old handguns and rifles. In 1958 he was made a Deputy Sheriff of Behar County; *Eagle* had found its way to Texas. Some of his work was sold in the US, including his remarkable painting of *Custer's Last Stand*.

'Luck of the Legion' arrived on the centre page in 1952. Geoffrey Bond had been writing radio scripts and his agent suggested that he write about the French Foreign Legion for *Eagle*. A sample script was sent to Marcus.

'Weeks and months went by and nothing happened. They'd lost the damn thing. They eventually found it and Marcus said "we'll have a bash". He knew what he wanted and didn't waffle . . . he wanted cliff hangers and no "with one bound Sergeant Luck was free". He guided me. First of all, he said "no, you're way off beam". I did it again, he said "yes, you're coming". I did it again, "spot on, that's just what I wanted". He was just as definite when I got it right as when I didn't. I respected that immensely.'

The artist was Martin Aitchison. 'My agent had two or three people with *Eagle* and sent me a script about the Foreign Legion. They gave me some pictures from the Hulton Library and told me to go and see a Burt Lancaster film and to make a note of all the scenery and costumes. After twelve weeks they gave me a contract for two years and I was able to get a mortgage on a house. It was very difficult to get references for the Foreign Legion. I used to get letters about the wrong hat or colour. I replied, "a person who doesn't make mistakes doesn't make anything" or "the mistakes in Luck are legion". I got a curt note from Ellen telling me to send my replies through the office in future.

'I only met Marcus twice. One time he said "Your agent is taking a lot of money away from you, leave it to me." He eventually got it down to ten per cent and did it for all the other *Eagle* artists too. I used to change the script sometimes if I thought it was getting weak; Geoffrey complained to Ellen.'

'All writers complain about artists altering scripts,' Geoffrey said . 'Martin didn't alter very much, though I might have got steamed up. In one episode, Bimberg was cooking a string of sausages and the Arabs attacked. I made Bimberg grab a machine gun and stuff the sausages in and fire them. Martin said you can't fire sausages and changed it to Bimberg throwing them.'

Martin later drew *Peter and Jane* for Ladybird Books: 'You could hardly imagine a greater contrast from "Luck of the Legion". The last time I saw Marcus I told him that having worked for *Eagle* was open sesame for other jobs.'

Anthony Buckeridge, author of the Jennings books, which had been broadcast on the radio, told us, 'I was reading early numbers of *Eagle* and was very impressed with the artistic work but not very impressed with the stories they were running. So I went to see Marcus and said I'd like to write a series of school stories with a character specially for *Eagle*.' Rex Milligan was a schoolboy at an ordinary secondary modern in London. *Rex Milligan's Busy Term* was the first of three or four full length books he later wrote for *Eagle* to publish in chapters.

In 1954 George Cansdale, who had been Director of London Zoo, started writing about pets and wild life. 'Marcus approached me and I put up some suggestions. I had my own series on television and when I went to West Africa Marcus asked me to write it up for *Eagle*. We had to be jolly accurate, the slightest error and some child would find it. It was very good discipline working for *Eagle*, very good training.'

George Beardmore contributed hugely to the children's papers: 'My agent phoned to say that my boys' novel *North Wind* had sold as a serial to the new Hulton Press boys' paper. The prestige would be terrific. This book was now my introduction to the furious world that was to occupy me for the next ten years. Marcus Morris asked me to think about writing cartoon serials. I said that it was out of the question, not my parish. His reply was, "This is what I want. Go home and try." One Friday evening Marcus came through to say that he wanted a serial story for *Eagle* with an historical background, the first instalment of which had to be on his desk the following Monday morning. "Jack O'Lantern" was thus born.' It was drawn by Robert Ayton.

The third of the great Franks who drew for *Eagle*, Frank Bellamy, started by drawing advertisements in the magazine for Gibbs dentifrice, 'Commando Gibbs and Dragon Decay', before doing several features in *Swift*. In 1957 Marcus decided to run the life of Winston Churchill on the back page, *Eagle*'s first biography of a living person, and commissioned Frank to draw it; the script was by Clifford Makins. Historical accuracy was vital and Frank went to the Imperial War Museum and Sandhurst, to study photographs, weapons and uniforms; everything had to be vetted by Churchill. The strip was a huge success; Bellamy's art work was displayed in Hulton House and *The Happy Warrior* was brought out in book form. Three special leather bound copies were produced; one was presented to Sir Winston and another to Viscount Montgomery of Alamein. However, not everybody was ecstatic about it. The *Stourbridge County Express* called it 'A strictly non-political and highly glamorised account . . . nothing about his human qualities. . . . In this book he is almost as remote a figure as Dan Dare.'

The headmaster of Monkton Combe Junior School near Bath wrote, '*Eagle* is the only thing of that sort allowed here, but I take exception to the last page and hope it is a printer's error. "Good God". . . is quite unnecessary and even if the First Sea Lord *did* say it – as well he may have! – I see no earthly reason why our boys today should be reminded of it. There's enough of that unnecessary language abroad without excellent *Eagle*'s suggesting it's a normal or noble saying. Sorry to criticize but it's only meant to help and hope it may. Good luck to your elbow you've done a grand job.'

As an afterthought Mr Bryan Morris added, 'Could you come to preach again in 1959?'

Such a mild epithet would hardly be noticed today, even in a children's magazine. It's also amusing to note that when the life of Nelson was serialised, there was no mention of Lady Hamilton, nor of Nelson's long-suffering wife!

Later, Bellamy's imagination was allowed full reign for 'Fraser of Africa', written by George Beardmore, which replaced 'Jack O'Lantern'. Frank had been obsessed with Africa from an early age, but he had never been there apart from a holiday in Algeria. Marcus said that if he had known of Frank's obsession he would have sent him to Africa on a fact finding mission, as he had sent Charles Chilton to America. But Marcus was no longer with *Eagle* by then and Frank's research made up for first hand knowledge. 'Fraser' was painted in the browns and yellows of the parched plains, which gave Eric Bemrose a few headaches and Bellamy had to go up to Liverpool to sort it out.

Clifford Makins said of Bellamy, 'I was struck by his sensitive yet robust style, his fastidious attention to detail and eagerness to portray the intentions of the writer who had plotted the sequences. He was the best of colleagues and collaborators and insisted always, but always, on doing the lettering for the balloons. For Bellamy this was merely an extension of his art work.'

The individual sports hints and profiles were consolidated into the 'Eagle Sports Page' in January 1952. This was organised by Kenneth Wheeler, author of the *Eagle Book of Sport*, and the sports agent Bagenal Harvey, who had most of the leading sportsmen and women of the day on his books. Bagenal would come in to the office occasionally and then disappear until the next party.

Bagenal became a close friend and colleague of Marcus's and at one stage managed his finances for him. There were those who reckoned that Bagenal ruined sport by tingeing it with commercialism and that he was not overscrupulous in his methods of business. At his Memorial Service in St Bride's Church, Fleet Street, it was remarked (in private) that a service for Bagenal's enemies would have filled St Paul's Cathedral; but under his aegis the 'Sports Page' became slicker and far more professional, with photographs as well as illustrations.

A wide range of events was covered, including such esoteric pastimes as Thames Tradesmen's rowing, speedway, King's Cup air race, the Calgary Stampede, sailing, ice-hockey, stock car racing.

Godfrey Evans, Johnny Haynes, Johnny Leach, Danny Blanchflower, Trevor Bailey and Jimmy Hill all took turns as guest editor of the 'Sports Page'. Many sporting personalities of the day contributed: *Eagle* was 'proud to present Patsy Hendren as your cricket coach'. He wrote, 'I have selected five promising boys, all of whom plan to make cricket their career, and they will receive instruction from the masters.' One called Jimmy was coached by Godfrey Evans and Denis Compton. Three years later he was revealed as J Parks of England and in 1960 he too was writing for *Eagle*. A cricket coaching scheme for talented Club members was organised by the MCC and the England Schools Cricket Association.

Jimmy Hill became the magazine's soccer coach and wrote many articles. 'It was wonderful for me, a stepping stone to another life. It was a change from sport, got my feet on another ladder, making me write. My literary training was on *Eagle*.'

Special soccer activities were arranged by the FA and football demonstrations were given all over the country, by the likes of Don Revie and Jackie Blanchflower (Danny's brother), which attracted thousands.

Readers were asked to vote for their Sportsman of the Year – boxer Randolph Turpin won in 1951 and 1952. Stanley Matthews succeeded him in 1953 and, in 1954, Chris Chataway and Roger Bannister tied for once. They were followed by Peter May, Stirling Moss and Bobby Charlton, who won three times running. He wrote in his *Book of Soccer* after his second win, 'Of all the honours I have been lucky enough to win as a footballer, nothing pleased me more than to be elected for two years in succession the favourite sportsman of the readers of the *Eagle*.' He was the last sportsman to be presented with the *Eagle* Trophy; he received his third from Clifford Makins at Wembley just before England's match with Scotland in 1961.

Stirling Moss was adopted as *Eagle*'s own racing driver (although he says he doesn't remember it) and had its insignia on his cars. The magazine reported all his activities and sent him birthday greetings and messages of good luck. In November 1954 he was pictured doing a trial run with Ellen Vincent in a 1901 Albion 'dog-cart', *Eagle*'s own entry in the London to Brighton veteran car rally.

World table tennis champion, Johnny Leach, started his collaboration with *Eagle* by writing 'How to Improve your Table Tennis' in 1952. He later offered coaching to promising young players at Butlin's Holiday Camps. The National Junior Table Tennis Tournament was announced in *Eagle* and *Girl* two years later, backed by the sport's national associations.

The tournament grew from 750 competitors to 10,000 and by 1959 the England junior team was composed entirely of past *Eagle* champions.

*Eagle* became involved with horses in 1956 when Edward Hulton presented a Trophy to the winning County team at the Juvenile Show Jumping Championships at the Horse of the Year Show at Haringey. By 1958 there were thirty-seven teams in the Inter-County *Eagle* Show Jumping Championships and *Eagle* sponsored the British Juvenile Show Jumping team that won at the world championships of 1956 and 1957.

David Langdon's 'Professor Puff and his dog Wuff' graced the sports page for four years, when his accident-prone 'Simon Simple' took over. 'I'd been drawing cartoons for *Lilliput* for many years, so Marcus knew my work and asked me to think up a black and white strip.'

'I thought up a slightly eccentric professor and gave him one of those tasselled hats, a frock coat and a dog. Then I was faced with the problem of what adventures to get them involved in. All I could think of were standard adventures going round the world. Some of them were in a place called Patagonia which I thought was mythical, but there is such a place.' In fact, he sent his Professor to Papagonia.

Macdonald Hastings, ex-war correspondent for *Picture Post* and erstwhile editor of *Strand* magazine, was appointed *Eagle* Special Investigator towards the end of 1950, his brief to undertake hazardous adventures for the amusement of the readers:

'Do you read Dan Dare?' said the Editor.

'You bet I do,' I said.

'Then why can't you do something like that in real life?'

'What . . . Me? Fly to Venus?'

'You haven't got to fly to Venus. Think of all the exciting adventures waiting for you right here in the world.'

'The only place left in the world I can think of which is still relatively unknown,' I said snootily, 'is the bottom of the sea.'

'But that's a splendid idea,' said the Editor.

So Mac went down in a submarine. Then he joined a circus: 'Mr Cyril Mills said that under no circumstances would he try me out as a lion tamer. I said the editor would be terribly disappointed. Mr Mills said that if his lions got to hear what they had missed he was sure that they would be terribly disappointed too.'

He drove a Centurion Tank, tracked down a Golden Eagle's nest with the aid of naturalist James Fisher, became a human firework and a knife-thrower's target. He rode a camel in Morocco, went to Canada as a lumberjack, drove the Canadian Pacific Railway, joined the Mounties and looked for bears. He investigated murder at Scotland Yard, became a keeper at the zoo, visited a lighthouse and went bird watching with Peter Scott.

In 1954 he went off to Africa in search of the little yellow men of the Kalahari – and found them. Mac brought back with him a present for the Editor, a baby crocodile called Marcus, which was too big for the bath at home, so was given to London Zoo, where the Morris family would visit it occasionally.

Max Hastings, his son, recalled, 'He adored doing it, he obviously enjoyed working for Marcus. At school my father had a much higher profile than if he had been writing for a national newspaper because everyone was reading *Eagle*. School in those days was dominated by *Eagle* culture, lots of people belonged to the *Eagle* Club and wore the badge even at quite snobbish prep schools. One was never ashamed of being an avid reader of *Eagle* and a participant in what *Eagle* was doing. I was teased at school about both parents; my mother [Anne Scott-James] was writing a lot about family life and her children in the *Daily Express* and *Sunday Dispatch*.

'My mother said that my father was like a grown up boy scout. He was undoubtedly eccentric. He did the assignments for *Eagle* with absolute pleasure

The front page of the first dummy contained some elements that lasted . . .

. . . but the first issue looked rather different.

Chaplain Dan Dare, before he discarded his dog collar. Sir Hubert Guest was there, but Digby had yet to make an appearance.

Dan Dare's arch-enemy, based somewhat spuriously on Marcus's youngest daughter (who didn't need a flying chair to get around).

Frank Bellamy's Dan Dare (above) was very different from Frank Hampson's, which was the inspiration for *Eagle* fan Peter Brookes' Dan Blair: "David Driver and I first had the idea of a political Dan Dare spoof over ten years ago, but only after the last election did the analogies seem so fortuitously appropriate."

Three colourful strips that didn't make the leap from dummy to first issue. The artists – Norman Thelwell, Walkden Fisher and EC Jennings.

The biggest education project ever
aimed at the youth of Britain.

Lettice Leefe in *Girl* appeared
from John Ryan's doodling.

Priscilla Ryan's ideal man.

Frank Humphris' depiction of Custer's Last Stand.

It's amazing what a Wall's ice-cream can do for you! (The artist was Richard Jennings)

"Haven't you read your D-notices?"

Bimberg throws the sausages.

The famous signature.

Marcus told John Worsley to draw in more bullrushes.

and lack of self-consciousness. I don't think he was ever patronising or condescending to children. It was one of Marcus's most brilliant ideas getting my father to do it.

'What was bizarre about it was that my father was not very physically got together. He wasn't a natural action man; I've still got his Shuttlecock Badge for falling off the Cresta Run at Shuttlecock Corner on an *Eagle* assignment.' Mac was surely not one of those who fall off deliberately in order to earn the badge?

'I remember going to watch him fly in a Tiger Moth at White Waltham, it was miraculous he survived. If I had owned a racing car I would never have let my father drive it for *Eagle*, he was an appalling driver. He wasn't a very good horseman either. I think he injured himself doing the Household Cavalry stunt, put his shoulder out. I'm surprised he didn't do himself more damage. He was already forty-one when he started on *Eagle*.

'He seemed to me as a child to have access to everything. I was terribly disappointed if he couldn't lay something on for me, like a ride on an engine footplate. In 1956 he started doing "Tonight" [for BBC TV] so for the last few years he couldn't do the big foreign trips.'

Instead, Mac wrote a series on ghosts and dreams and real-life mysteries and stories about war heroes. He and James Hemming did a series on space-travel with Ashwell Wood – 'How Dan Dare Got There First'.

The war stories lumbered on until early 1960, but were consistently bottom of opinion polls. The day Derek Lord became Editor of *Eagle*, he went to Clifford Makins, then Editor-in-Chief, and said, 'I really am in charge now?' Clifford said, 'Yes, what do you want?' Derek said, 'Permission to sack Mac Hastings.' Clifford said, 'Go ahead, you do it, I'm not going to.'

Clifford Makins had been introduced to Marcus by Jess's friend Cyril Luckham in 1954 in The Two Brewers in Fleet Street. Clifford had worked with Cyril in the theatre before joining the publishing house Faber and Faber.

Peter du Sautoy of Fabers, where Clifford was working in the accounts department, wrote to Marcus in March that year, recommending Clifford for a job and regretting that Fabers couldn't give him a more exciting one. 'I think he has a real talent for writing, natural intelligence and a lively mind. . . . He has a very likeable personality. . . . There are few people whom I could recommend more warmly.'

Marcus put Clifford to work with Peter Grey, who was in charge of features. After three months Clifford sent Marcus a memo: 'In a week's time my trial period comes to an end. According to my contract, if I have not given notice by that date and you have not given me notice, my engagement is to continue with a month's notice binding either side at a salary to be arranged.

'Well, I am very happy here and enjoying the work tremendously. If you are satisfied do you think there is a hope of giving me more money? Our first child is three weeks away, and we've moved into a bigger flat. All very difficult on £10 a week. I'm not asking you to subsidise my overdraft, but

I would be most grateful for any increase that could be managed.'

By that autumn Clifford was working as Marcus's personal assistant.

He became Marcus's friend, right-hand man editorially and, eventually, Assistant Editor, Editor and Editor-in-Chief of *Eagle*. They were very different personalities; Clifford was much more gregarious and open than Marcus and knew his own worth. He complained about having to go second class when travelling with lowlier members of the establishment, and having to share an office: 'After all, I am, damn it all, your tried, proved, loyal, dogged, wilful, inspired and most individual Personal Assistant!

'And after these three years of your support and encouragement when I have become most willingly and enthusiastically more and more involved in all that's going on I really must ask you to ensure that I have A Room of My Own.' Marcus invariably supported him.

Clifford told us, 'In a curious way he was a very emotional man but he never showed it. His judgement was perfect. It was always possible to talk to the old boy, he'd listen. He was a stimulating man, something about him inspired loyalty. You wouldn't forget a night out with him, I don't just mean going to night clubs and drinking; it was very invigorating, he might not agree with you, but he'd listen to what you said. He'd go very quiet. He's the only man who could shout without raising his voice. I adored working with him, he treated me well, he pushed me on. He said I should take my wife Sheila on holiday on the continent when she got better. When she died of leukaemia he arranged everything.'

After the funeral Clifford wrote to Marcus, 'Thank you for your help last week. No one else – but no one – could have consoled and stimulated me as you did. It came as no surprise of course when you rose so superbly to the occasion but I do thank you from the bottom of my heart.'

In October 1950 Hulton Press held a party. Marcus got up on a table and, assuming his nervous expression, gave a speech: 'This party is to celebrate the fact that for six months a copy of *Eagle* has appeared every week. No one is more surprised than myself – except perhaps the management.' The party was also, in part, to say goodbye to his personal and very attractive secretary, Rosemary Phillips, who had taken another job. Marcus said, 'She has been working for *Eagle* since it began – one of the brightest feathers in its pinions and, so far, unplucked.'

Rosemary told us, 'I was terribly moved by that, and thought it was terribly unlike him to make such a kind remark.'

# Chapter Twelve

Some months after *Eagle* was launched, Tom Hopkinson said to Marcus, 'Don't you think you ought to hit them with both fists? You've hit them with one, the boys' paper; could you, do you think, also hit them with the other, a girls' paper?' Marcus said that he thought he could, that he'd certainly like to try.

Derek Lord: 'We were a bit irritated when Marcus called a meeting and announced that *Girl* was coming up. He said "We'll all have to double up, there's going to be twice as much work to do." There was dead silence. We thought we'd been working pretty hard without *Girl*. Somebody said "How are we going to work it?" and Marcus said "We're not producing collar studs you know, these are important things." He wasn't normally autocratic. But in fact we were all very keen on the idea of another paper.'

Arthur Roberts was taken on as Art Editor. '*Girl* had a bit more planning than *Eagle*, it started off with a proper staff. An art editor was a luxury they didn't have on *Eagle* to start with.'

The history of the naming of *Girl* is somewhat obscure. It is said that a meeting of the Hulton Press top brass decided that a girl's name couldn't be used because they had all been characters in history who'd been raped. No one seems to know who designed the logo. Julia (Toots) Lockwood (daughter of actress Margaret Lockwood, a friend of Jess) says that the head was based on her and a friend – an artist came to her school and spent all day sketching them. The lettering was again done by Berthold Wolpe.

A year and a half after the launch of *Eagle*, *Girl* went on the market with an initial circulation of about half a million.

On the first two pages was 'Kitty Hawke', a female pilot, though not a space one, proving to her dad and his male chauvinist colleagues that she could fly a plane as well as any man. There was a black and white strip school story and two features about girl detectives.

'Anne Mullion', written and drawn in colour by C.E. Drury was a story of smugglers and pirates in Cornwall in the eighteenth century. Duncan Angier remembers going with Ted Drury to see Marcus in his office.

'He had a bishop-like approach to things, quite a serious man, not prone to back-slapping. He told Ted that there were to be no breasts: "You must try to control your salacious instincts," all said with a perfectly straight face and earnest air. I'll never know whether he was serious or just putting us on.'

The centre pages of *Girl* featured Anna Sewell's *Black Beauty*, drawn by Raymond Shepherd, and 'Jacky the Centre Page Girl'. Jacky Curtis, a student at a stage school with Toots Lockwood, went on assignments each week meeting readers and a variety of famous people and once appeared on television's long running programme *Picture Page* with Marcus and Leslie Mitchell. She left to take up a career as a dancer in 1954.

Also on the centre pages was John Ryan's 'Lettice Leefe, the Greenest

Girl in School', the only character in the magazine to last to the bitter end. 'Miss Froth and Miss Tantrum, the two headmistresses, appeared from my doodling. Miss Froth never wore the same outfit twice; Priscilla designed all her clothes.

'At about this time Harrow School offered me the job of head art master. We were about to produce a baby and with the job came a beautiful house in the school grounds and we sat up all night debating whether to take the job or take the plunge. We decided to take the plunge. My parents were horrified, drawing strips instead of art master at Harrow. Thank God we turned it down. I was on a yearly contract with Hultons for ten years.'

A presentation plate of Karsh of Ottawa's photograph of Princess Elizabeth was inserted in the magazine, and 'Captain Starling', another full-page colour strip written by George Beardmore, sailed the seven seas in search of her long-lost father.

The Editor's Letter welcomed *Girl* readers and announced the Girl Adventurers' Club: 'We are planning all kinds of expeditions, outings, visits and holidays for members. And there will be lots of other privileges, which we will tell you about from time to time.' Membership reached 16,000 in six weeks and letters poured in.

On the back page was 'The Story of Miriam, Daughter of the Nile' (sister of Moses), written by Chad Varah and drawn by John Worsley. John found it easier working with Chad than with Alan Stranks, because Chad visualised the strip, setting out the frames himself.

Ellen Vincent recalled, 'Chad Varah had written in his instructions: "Scene by the river with bullrushes – maidens frisking around having fun". The drawings came in, beautifully drawn, with the maidens naked. Gasps and giggles were brushed aside by MM's brisk order to "send it back to John and tell him to paint in more bullrushes".'

Before long circulation started to fall.

'We decided we had made the mistake of not taking sufficiently into account the difference between the masculine and the feminine psychological make-up. The difference is a very real one,' wrote Marcus.

'We had received reports that quite a number of girls were reading *Eagle* and drew the wrong conclusion; we had made *Girl* too masculine. We therefore made it more romantic in its approach, more feminine. I worked on the theory that you should be a good deal more personal in your motivation in a girls' paper. The adventure and the danger can be there but the reason for it must be the search for a long-lost uncle or father [not mother?]. If you can add a fair amount of personal rivalry, jealousy and a very close friendship, so much the better.

'We applied this theory to *Girl* and sales picked up. Before long they reached 650,000 and stayed there.'

Out went 'Kitty Hawke' and in came a school story called 'Wendy and Jinx'. The heading changed too, to match that of *Eagle*. George Beardmore came up with 'Robbie of Red Hall', the story of an impoverished Scottish laird's daughter and 'Anne Mullion' was replaced by the adventures of a Red Indian girl, 'Flying Cloud', written by Charles Chilton.

The *Girl* Picture Gallery included portraits of the Royal Family and cuddly animals and famous paintings which were 'photographed specially for you at the Louvre'.

Animal lovers were catered for by thirteen-year-old Elizabeth Cruft, great-granddaughter of Charles Cruft, and by Barbara Woodhouse.

One of the most popular strips of all was 'Belle of the Ballet'. It was written by the prolific George Beardmore and drawn by John Worsley. 'When I started "Belle" I got a girl from a ballet school to come round so that I could get used to the way they sit. I didn't use her regularly. I wouldn't have had time to draw from models and photos, I wouldn't have thought it was necessary; I had enough knowledge to do it in my head. *Eagle* and *Girl* were a treadmill – if I wanted a holiday I had to get two weeks ahead. But it's a fun memory and it paid the bills.'

George Beardmore was scripting four stories a week and putting up ideas for more. Vicky Knowles, his daughter, told us: 'I can remember Dad's enthusiasm for everything connected with *Eagle* and *Girl* and the many breakfasts spent with the rest of the family trying to find a new twist, or an appropriate ending for a plot. He was a novelist primarily, but working for these magazines became his bread and butter and enabled me to go to a rather high-flying grant-maintained school.'

The highly successful partnership between George Beardmore and John Worsley was succeeded by another when June Mendoza, under the pen name Chris Garvey, took over the artwork. June, now a very distinguished portrait painter, said, 'Marcus was wonderfully kind to me, this beginner with a flair for reproducing likenesses in the illustrated strip genre.

'He cossetted me through the first six weeks of artwork as I had no idea how my work would print. For instance I was being far too "arty" and many of my subtleties would either disappear or jump uncomfortably in the printing. I had to learn to use colour in such a way as to counteract an overdose of, say, reds (boiled faces!) etc. Marcus saw me through all that until I settled and was able to move from as close to John Worsley's style as possible, to my own. . . .

'Marcus never made this inexperienced young person feel inadequate, but I came away fortified with such a back up and the wish to use the new knowledge. He was kind and considerate. He took me out a couple of times, I must have bored him stiff with my wide-eyed naïvety. But he got the work from me, and soon I knew what I was doing and I stayed for five years.'

June did illustrations for the Annuals and drew the back page serial of 'Joan of Arc', scripted by Chad. She also drew 'What's Cooking with Carol and Chris', a feature sponsored by the Gas Council; in *Eagle*, 'Gasology by Mr Therm' explained how gas cookers evolved, drawn by Walkden Fisher.

Jack Blanche, Advertising Manager of *Housewife* and *Lilliput*, who had first met Marcus over large gins and tonic at the Two Brewers, arranged a meeting between Reggie Gregg, Publicity Manager of the Gas Council, and Marcus.

'The meeting was at ten o'clock in the morning and even Marcus was staggered at being offered a large whisky. It was Marcus's job to take Reg Gregg out to lunch once a year and drink enormous amounts, to secure the contract for the following year.'

The result was what *Gas Journal* called 'the biggest educational project ever aimed at the youth of Britain by one industry.'

The first sporting feature in *Girl* was 'Improve your Table Tennis' with Peggy Franks, world doubles champion. June Foulds, the Olympic athlete who worked in the *Girl* office, later took on 'exciting and unusual assignments' like a female Macdonald Hastings. But, on the whole, sport did not feature very strongly in *Girl*; its readers preferred a more artistic form of exercise. In January 1955 *Girl* proudly announced its Ballet Scholarship Scheme, in association with the Royal Academy of Dancing and Sadler's Wells School.

In a letter to members of the Girl Adventurers' Club Margot Fonteyn said that, through the generosity of *Girl*, the Royal Academy would give free ballet tuition to those Club Members who qualified. The *Girl* Sadler's Wells Scholarship was to be awarded to the most outstanding pupils, enabling them to study ballet and finish their education at the Sadler's Wells School at White Lodge in London.

The Editor hoped 'that one day we shall see a great ballerina emerging from the Girl Adventurers' Club'. There were nearly 300 candidates for the London auditions.

Maxine Hooper, a postman's daughter from Orpington, was the first winner of the Sadler's Wells Scholarship. Assistant Editor Jean Crouch said: 'Arnold Haskell, Principal and Director of Sadler's Wells School, thought she was physically perfect, ideal for the corps de ballet; but what we wanted was a future prima ballerina, with more artistry and imagination.'

By 1957 there were 150 *Girl* scholars receiving tuition from the RAD and two studying full time at Sadler's Wells. In 1958 Marcus got what he was looking for – the winner of the scholarship was Lesley Collier (not at that time a *Girl* reader!). She was entered for the scholarship by her ballet teacher, Irene Ayres, who had also taught Maxine Hooper. Lesley was a boarder at White Lodge for five years from the age of eleven and went on to the Upper School. She joined the Royal Ballet Company in 1965, becoming Principal Dancer in 1972. She says that if it hadn't been for the *Girl* Ballet Scholarship she would probably never have become a ballerina. 'I thank my dancing teacher and the fact that the scholarship was there.' She has now retired as Principal Dancer and in September 1995 took up her appointment as Ballet Mistress at the Royal Ballet School.

Marcus had asked Jodi Hyland to help with the launch of *Girl* but, before long, appointed her Assistant Editor (as he had Ellen Vincent on *Eagle*). The Assistant Editors were *de facto* editors, with Marcus in overall control.

Derek Lord, who became one himself, says that they were called Assistant Editors because Hulton Press didn't want to pay them Editors' salaries – and it was Marcus's name that Hultons wanted.

Jodi stayed for about a year. 'I used to get frightfully cross with him on press days. I told him that the paper went to press in spite of him not because of him – he was a most irritating man for trying to make up his mind. He used to walk about rattling coins in his pocket.' Jodi subsequently married Hugh Cudlipp, later Lord Cudlipp and Chairman of IPC.

Rosemary Garland, who worked on *Eagle* before becoming Editor of *Robin*, said, 'A lot of his genius was his indecision – or rather – his studied delay. He used to drive us round the bend but when he had to, he could put decisions through very quickly.'

A journalist who had worked on *Woman's Own* with Jodi, Laurie Purden, joined *Girl* as Jodi's Assistant Editor (the Assistant Editor's assistant editor) before taking over from her. 'The first time I heard mention of Marcus's name, Jodi kept telling me about this extraordinary priest in her home town who was trying to do something with his parish magazine. Later, she got me a job on *Girl*. The interview with Marcus was the most extraordinary I've ever had. Marcus didn't actually say anything. Silence makes you nervous and I found myself blabbering, trying to give him the information that I thought he ought to have been asking me. Whether he liked me, or Jodi put pressure on him, I don't know, but he offered me the job. It was genuinely one of the happiest times of my life. You really felt that you were helping to create something that mattered.

'He could be totally tormenting. . . . When I first went there, he wanted to see what I was doing. When he realised that one had got it, so to speak, he would only see new scripts, new artwork. Occasionally one would go in with a story board and a script and he'd say, "There's something wrong with it," and you'd say, having worked rather hard on it, "What?" He couldn't actually tell you. You had to accept that if he was unhappy about it, he was right and it was up to you to do something about it. You had faith in him. If you hadn't, you wouldn't have stayed. He wouldn't have wanted you there – you had to believe, and we did. We were a terribly dedicated and loyal lot, of a kind you don't get any more.'

Jean Crouch took over from Laurie in 1954. 'I always felt he was a very serious priest, he had a priestly authority. He was one of the few Englishmen who preferred women's company. He didn't really get on with some of the chaps.

'It was a marvellous job; I was in love with it. I trusted Marcus totally, he knew when you'd got it right. Another thing that made him a marvellous employer, he might tear you off a strip in private but while there was anyone else present you had his hundred per cent support. I once rashly told George Beardmore that I was going to replace Robbie of Red Hall. He wrote Marcus a very unpleasant letter. Marcus behaved extraordinarily properly. He wrote a reply, which he showed me, which said very firmly that he hoped we would make it up. It was my first lesson in how to deal with an author. I tried to change Chad at one stage. There was so much violence in his scripts we had to send them back.

'During my time we put in pictures of pop stars for the first time, which caused parental disquiet. Tommy Steele was the first one. When we pictured Harry Belafonte I got some very strange letters about our lovely girls being taught to admire black people. I used to get academic friends, including Christopher Logue, to do the potted biographies on the centre page, a cheaper way of doing it.

'I wrote to Arthur C. Clarke to try science fiction. He got quite interested in a story geared for girls but, when we got down to the nitty gritty, £10 for a thousand words, he said, "I'm afraid my agent couldn't conceive my writing for that", so it wasn't on.'

Jean introduced the first ever fashion page in a children's magazine in 1958. Ellen Vincent's daughter Jackie was one of the models, as was Marcus's youngest, photographed by Bert Hardy. The first ever children's beauty page appeared a month later. Girls were growing up faster.

Shirley Brieger started on *Housewife* in 1952 and went over to *Girl* eighteen months later. 'When I found myself working on *Girl* I couldn't believe it. It was like a club. We used to stay late and play cowboys, just like school. When we had organised tours of school kids round, we'd have to rush round the art department and clear up the beer bottles.

'For "Adventure Corner" I used to go round the country at weekends with a photographer, interviewing kids who'd written in to tell us about their hobbies. David Steen was one of the photographers and Adrian Flowers, Zoltan Glass, Budd Powell. I interviewed all sorts of people from the Japanese Ambassador's daughter, to girls from a prefab in Peckham. No matter what their background, they all wanted to be in *Girl*.'

Jean Crouch said that 'the great difference between the readerships of *Eagle* and *Girl* was the letters. I got 160–170 letters a day from girls. They'd write about anything, their geography mistress, their pets, holidays.'

Several girls declared their intention of becoming missionaries after the serialisation of Mary Slessor's life. One wrote: 'My friends and I agree that *Girl* is the only comic which has grown up with us. Other comics talk down to the reader, whereas *Girl* treats its readers as equals.' A mother wrote in asking for a *Girl* belt for her daughter. 'Although she is thirteen she has never been to school owing to lung trouble and it was *Girl* who first interested her enough to try to read. Up till then no other weekly paper helped in any way.'

Debby F. wrote, 'If a boy and you are alone together and the boy suddenly kisses you without warning is it better to say afterwards "Thank you" or murmur the boy's name softly or say nothing and act as though the action had never been performed? (or anything else you can suggest?) Please publish question and answer quickly because I am very worried.'

Marcus confessed himself stumped by that one – the letter went to James Hemming.

They received so many problem letters from girls that a regular feature was started. 'Each week we'll deal with problems of general interest in "What's Your Worry?" No readers' names will be printed, so if you've got a personal problem or there's something on your mind, just write to us about it and our experts will see what they can do to help. It doesn't matter how big or how small your worry is. . . . If you'd like a private reply by post we'll arrange that too.'

James Hemming dealt with all the letters from girls with psychological or sex problems. James's assistant, Pat Jackson: 'The kids would often say "please don't write back to me because my parents open my letters and I don't want them to know that I've asked you". We would put something in the paper under a general comment so that we would hope that the child would read it and recognise that it was her problem that was being dealt with. It was very sad sometimes, children who'd been interfered with by their fathers or uncles, didn't know anything about sex, had the most curious ideas about where babies come from. We were the first children's paper to address this kind of problem.'

In 1956 James wrote his thesis for his doctorate on adolescent problems. 'The input of letters that came in from readers, especially *Girl* readers, provided valuable data. It was rather sad; a lot of them couldn't go to their parents about things that were worrying them, so they had to write in. We had a robust correspondence.'

The third children's paper, *Robin*, was launched on 28 March 1953, advertised as 'A happy new magazine for boys and girls'. It was aimed at children up to seven or eight and hit the target straight away with a circulation of 450,000, which it consistently maintained.

*Robin* was bright and cheerful, with 'Andy Pandy', a popular television puppet, in colour on the front page (he could only be seen in black and white in his alter ego). The centre pages were also in colour, featuring 'The Robin Scrapbook' (pictures to cut out and keep) and two strips, 'The Magic Wellingtons' and 'Johnny Bull'. There was a Zoo Corner, rhymes, cartoons, short stories, the 'Robin Reading Strip' and black and white strips including 'Tom The Tractor', 'Princess Tai-Lu' (a Siamese cat), drawn by Ann and Janet Graham Johnstone, daughters of the artist Anna Zinkeisen, 'Bingo, Bango and Bongo' (three monkeys), 'Mac and Maggie' (a dog and his girl) and 'The Flower Pot Men', like 'Andy Pandy', in colour and on licence from the BBC.

The Editor wrote: 'Dear Boys and Girls, Here is number one of your new paper, *The Robin*. I hope you will like it very much. You will enjoy reading about all the friends we have found for you.'

One of the most popular strips was 'The Woppit', the adventures of a small bear. The real Woppit belonged to the speedboat ace, Donald Campbell, to whom it had been given by his friend, Peter Barker, who was in charge of merchandising for the Hultons' children's papers. In 1959 a photograph of Donald Campbell was shown on the Editor's Page of *Robin* with his

Woppit, which he took everywhere as his mascot. It was with him when he died in Lake Coniston in 1967; the Woppit survived the crash.

Marcus's family became quite involved in producing *Robin*. Jan wrote a short story for the second issue and Jess contributed the half-page strip 'The Twins Simon & Sally', obviously based on her two youngest children, which caused a certain amount of teasing at school.

Jess also wrote the back page story 'Richard Lion', who lived in a village called Gay, with his parents Dr and Mrs Lion and friends Henry (a kangaroo) and Pug (a pug). Jess had a very fertile imagination and an unexpected talent for science fiction. She invented the Universal Do-It-All Robot and the Carshiplane, a very versatile vehicle, as well as a machine which goes there and back to see how far it is.

Jess frequently got behind with her scripts and others had to step into the breach, including daughter Jan. The Assistant Editor sent a plaintive letter, 'Two scripts [were] written in your absence by Rosemary Garland. We had no idea you were going on holiday and a major panic resulted. Could you please let us know in future when you intend going away so that we can get scripts in advance?'

*Robin* readers were almost as prolific letter writers as their elder siblings. One wrote that 'you don't have much bad things in *Robin*' and another asked 'Please do the story of Ulysses. I like cement mixers as well.'

*The Times Educational Supplement,* 3 April 1953: '*Robin* represents the departure from the old hyphenated convention in comics for the undersevens, and the good intentions of the publishers and of the editor are apparent in more ways than in teaching its readers to read.'

David Holbrook, the eminent academic, author and poet, disagreed and compared *Eagle* and *Robin* unfavourably with folksongs and nursery rhymes.

But in *New Era*, June 1953: 'I hope the publishers will be encouraged to produce a similar magazine for the 7–10 year old children.'

They were. It was decided to bridge the gap between *Eagle* and *Robin*.

Marcus: 'Frankly I don't think I did very well with *Swift*. I was a good deal preoccupied with other things at the time and had lost some of my earlier keenness and enthusiasm. Producing papers for children was getting to be rather a habit and perhaps I was becoming bored. Certainly the edge seemed to have gone from my editorial ability. For *Swift* more than for any of the others I should have had all my energy and imagination about me.

'The target was small and hard to hit. We had to be careful to keep within those narrow limits so as not to compete with *Robin* or *Eagle* and *Girl*. The paper was aimed at boys and girls; we had decided that their interests at this age were still the same. Maybe we were wrong.

'When it came out *Swift* seemed to lack the life and attack of the others. It never had the success we hoped for and achieved a circulation of only a quarter of a million. It lost money, but at least it retained readers.'

*Swift* was launched on 20 March 1954, backed by yellow birds on the tops of cars going round London in a watered-down version of the *Eagle*

*A* dedicated *Robin* reader –
*Simon (the dirty knees were*
*normal )*

launch. John Hughes remembered ignoring rude remarks like 'what yer
selling, mate, bird seed?'

Vanora MacIndoe, daughter of Sir Archibald, the renowned plastic surgeon,
met Ellen Vincent at a party and was told that Marcus was looking for
someone to run *Swift*. 'I went into his office and there was this dour man.
It was very difficult to get him to smile; he sort of chewed them up and
swallowed them. He asked me all sorts of questions to which I didn't know the
answers like, "Can you type?" – "no". "Do you know anything about type-
setting?" – "no". "Do you like children?" – "not particularly". And he offered
me the job at £1,000 a year, which I couldn't refuse. He was afraid of
having anyone who knew more than he did. He liked to teach them his way.
He didn't want anybody saying, "no, this is how it's done". Everybody
was an amateur. You got dropped in the deep end and had to get on with it.
Occasionally he would ask to see the dummy and say if he didn't understand
a story or it was boring. He was always right, his instinct was infallible.

'He protected us all from the Hultons; he wouldn't have us messed around'.
Ellen Vincent recalled that Marcus once warned her not to encourage flirtatious
talk from Edward Hulton; his wife could be a dangerous enemy.

*Swift* was pretty much the mixture as before. 'Tarna the Jungle Boy'
was followed by 'Nicky Nobody', an orphan boy who never seemed to go
to school. 'Educating Archie' and Peter Brough were brought over from
the BBC by Stephen Williams, and the Wild West was represented by 'Tom

Tex and Pinto'. There was the usual 'Make Your Own' feature, a puzzle and a short story, and a number of comic cartoons – 'Roddy the Road Scout', 'Sammy and his Speed Sub', who went about rescuing people, and 'Our Gang, Tubby, Teena and Titch', drawn by Dennis Mallett. The centre pages featured John Ryan's latest creation, 'Sir Boldasbrass', a dotty mediaeval knight, a predecessor of 'Sir Prancelot'. History was represented by 'Paul English', cabin boy to Sir Walter Raleigh, while religion came in with the story of 'The Boy David'.

The back page featured a colour strip serial, 'The Sign of the Scarlet Ladybird', sponsored by Ladybird children's clothes.

The tenets adhered to in *Eagle* seem to have been abandoned in *Swift*; there were quite a lot of magical or even miraculous solutions, especially in the 'Scarlet Ladybird', which involved gangs of kids going round in Ladybird clothes exposing their labels. They went in for rather a lot of armed warfare too. Small boys wrote in to object when Chinese pirates were portrayed eating chop suey – a dish invented in San Francisco.

The first issue of *Swift* provoked hundreds (not thousands) of letters to the Editor, and 'a great rush to join the Swift Club'. Before long *Swift* underwent major surgery with new features and layout. 'Captain Pugwash' took over from 'Sir Boldasbrass' and 'The Swiss Family Robinson' appeared, drawn by Frank Bellamy, who went on to do 'Robin Hood' and 'Monty Carstairs'. Michael Bentine contributed 'The Bumblies' 'as seen on TV'.

'Marcus and I met somewhere,' Michael recalled. 'He said he was a fan of the *Bumblies* and would I like to do some for *Swift*. I said I couldn't do it because I was off to Australia, so my brother Tony did them. They were my own design and I did the master drawings, then Tony did them most beautifully, he's a very fine draughtsman.'

In 1955 the Editor's Letter claimed that *Swift* was read all over the world; old *Swifts* were wanted in the Bahamas 'to help coloured children to read'! Later that year Charles Chilton and Frank Humphris contributed a new cowboy strip. By 1957 Sammy (now a space cadet) had reached the moon and looked very like a junior version of Dan Dare. Robin Hood was joined by Maid Marion and Tarna acquired a girlfriend called Peggy, no doubt to appease female readers.

To celebrate the launch of *Swift* Hulton Press took a large room at the Criterion overlooking the lights of Piccadilly, and gave a party for all the staff. The secretaries performed a can-can under the personal supervision of the Editor. Stephen Williams got a professional can-can dancer to teach them the steps and they had *Swift* emblazoned on the seats of their knickers. James Dreaper was then one of the first graduate management trainees at Hulton Press together with John Hughes, Jack Layborn and Peter Sargent, son of Sir Malcolm.

'Bernard Audley and Keith Kotch were our mentors, we were shoved round all the departments. Bernard knew I played the guitar and asked me to compose something for the party. He said it wasn't funny enough, so we knocked it up together. He gave me the best lines and I put it to calypso music.'

## The Marcus Morris Calypso

Here's a calypso sung without cynicism
About a sudden success in journalism,
And how, in the course of four short years
Came the fulfilment of some good ideas,
Which did away with some of the worries
Of the Reverend Mr Marcus Morris.

He was vicar of Birkdale in Lancashire
Which you might think was a quiet career,
But he knew the sort of comics that the children should get,
And his parish magazine was very much in debt.
And this accounted for the worries
Of the Reverend Mr Marcus Morris.

So in the summer of 1949
He created something new in the comic line
And he produced a full sized dummy
Of a paper to please every daddy and mummy.
But still this did not cure the worries
Of the Reverend Mr Marcus Morris.

So he came to London with his plans complete
And he tried to sell them in Fleet Street.
But all the publishers told him he was mad
And his overdraft was still as bad.
So wondering if he was to fail
He went back again to Birkdale.
But then to eliminate his distress
Came acceptance from the Hulton Press.

Thus was founded the *Eagle* comic
The effect at once was quite atomic.
It put all our rivals in a whirl
And was followed the next year by *Girl*.

Editorial staff grew with great intent
Along with the arrival of Ellen Vincent.
And then to shed some editorial burden
*Girl* was put on the shoulders of Laurie Purden.
And between them they probably increased the worries
Of the Reverend Mr Marcus Morris.

Then things really began to shift
With the births of *Robin* and then of *Swift*.
More pretty ladies joined the show
Including Miss Garland and Miss MacIndoe.

So now in 1954
It's like the Windmill on the second floor.
The atmosphere is like Queen Charlotte's Ball,
It's a wonder that the comics come out at all!
And this is paramount among the worries
Of the Reverend Mr Marcus Morris.

Now the moral of this pleasant tale,
Is if you make a good comic you cannot fail.
But you'll always need the backing of a genial sultan
Like the well-known Mr Edward Hulton.

Also if you want the comics to sell
You must get some pretty ladies on the staff as well;
As in a doctor's or an editor's estimation
Ladies is good for the circulation!
So there they sit like a heavenly chorus
Round the Reverend Mr Marcus Morris.

# Chapter Thirteen

On *Eagle*'s first birthday there were two pages of profiles and photographs of the main editorial staff and contributors; Marcus was the only one without a hobby.

In August the Editor told readers that he would pay for their contributions to *Eagle* and by September they were flooded with them. Ellen Vincent recalled that quite a few children sent in Tennyson's poem *The Eagle*, signed by Mum as little Johnny's own work. In November 1952 the page of readers' efforts included a cartoon depicting 'The *Eagle* Artists' Nightmare' sent in by sixteen-year-old Gerald Scarfe.

The following year Ingersoll ran a competition in *Eagle* to design an advertisement for its Dan Dare and Riders of the Range watches, 'The Ideal Christmas Gift'. One of the runners-up was fifteen-year-old David Hockney of Bradford. It was won by Gerald Scarfe: 'I remember two men arriving at home with a package of goodies – I've still got the *Eagle* watch. It was then I realised I wanted to go on winning competitions. It was a wonderful, wonderful moment. That inspired me to go on publishing my work and hopefully getting more money for it.'

Competition prizes became more exotic: winners went to BBC TV studios, the Royal Tournament, the Festival of Britain, had a flight to Le Touquet. Bicycles proved so popular as prizes that it was decided to award one a week – one of them was won by a girl who asked rather plaintively for a ladies' model. Somewhat unfairly, when a boy won a bike in a *Girl* competition and said 'thank you very much, but please may I have a boy's bike', they changed the rules; from then on only girls were allowed to enter. Of course there were also more mundane prizes like Dan Dare braces and radios, a month's supply of Wall's ice cream and special *Eagle* and *Girl* cricket bats and tennis rackets from Slazenger.

Within three years of its launch the Eagle Club had 200,000 members and

*The winning competition entry (left) by Gerald Scarfe (age sixteen), and David Hockney's (age fifteen) runners-up entry.*

Eagle *prizewinners, where are they now?*

those whose birth dates were printed on the Editor's Page could choose a free gift. The Morris children were rather peeved that their birthdays never seemed to appear, but they would find the odd free gift in their Christmas stockings.

The following year Vice-Presidents were appointed; Neville Duke, Stirling Moss, Denis Compton, Stanley Matthews, Godfrey Evans, Trevor Bailey and Leonard Cheshire headed the Eagle Club. The task cannot have been onerous, as Stirling Moss could not remember it; Dame Beryl Grey, who was Vice-President of *Girl* with Anna Neagle, Odette and Pat Smythe, wrote to us that, 'I do not seem to have many clear recollections of the period during which I had the honour of being a Vice-President. So I am sure that the duties were minimal and that it was very much an honorary position. I think that it was the first position of that kind that I held. . . . I know that I was very proud to be associated with *Girl*.'

At the beginning of 1954 *Girl* launched the Star Adventurers Badge and *Eagle*'s MUGs were replaced by the Silver Eagle Badge and Star; some people thought that the MUGs were just a little too pi and the name rather

*The* Eagle *canoe – the Editor remembers his technique*

off-putting. Gerald Creed (formerly Trace) from Bath, who was awarded his MUG's badge in May 1952, told us that he was teased about it at school and would definitely have preferred to be called a Silver Eagler. He is now being teased by his young receptionist.

The *Eagle* Holiday Scheme began very early on, with the aim of providing cheap holidays for children who wouldn't normally get one at all. Charles Chilton, who took *Eagle* holiday-makers and prizewinners to the *Eagle* camp at Little Canada on the Isle of Wight, said, 'All I had to do in the evenings was to dress up in my cowboy set and help with the entertainment.' The Editor went too and was photographed paddling the *Eagle* canoe, wearing a suit, showing that he had not forgotten the technique after nearly twenty years.

The first holiday abroad, with *Eagle* paying half the cost, was to Sestrière in the Italian Alps. For nineteen guineas per child, six parties of thirty readers had nine days of skiing, skating and tobogganing. The trips were nerve-racking experiences for the Hulton staff who were detailed to look after the children. Charles Chilton remembers that 'one of the boys was a girl called Pat. We had to find her a separate room. All the boys were in one long dormitory.'

Joan Harvey took a party to Austria for two weeks' winter sports with two headmasters and their wives. 'The place we stayed was terrible and didn't supply enough food. One young man was homesick and cried and wouldn't go out, until he fell in love with one of the girls – by then he'd sent a telegram to his mother begging her to bring him home.'

There were trips to Paris and Brussels and holidays in Yugoslavia, Germany and Holland. They became a regular feature as prizes and special offers and provided many youngsters with their first taste of foreign travel at a time when most people couldn't afford it and there were very tight currency restrictions.

Another staff member who looked after prizewinners on their trips to London was Keith Motts: 'It's amazing how parents were willing to let their children come on their own, although we always met them at the station. We only lost one child; I saw a girl off at Liverpool Street and at about 7p.m. we had a call from her parents, she hadn't come home. It turned out that her boyfriend had met her at the next station and taken her away for a couple of days.'

The *Monas Herald* reported that the best seats at the Isle of Man TT Races had been reserved for *Eagle* prizewinners and that three Manx prizewinners would act as hosts. John Russell and Marcus accompanied the readers on this jaunt. According to John, Marcus blew the entire weekend's expenses on the first night. John had to phone the Company Secretary and get him to wire some more. 'He said "How much?" I said, "Three or four times what you originally gave me". That was my first taste of Marcus's spending.'

There was a cowboy quiz to win a ranch holiday in Arizona. Arthur Roberts recalled, 'For this competition they picked out the top dozen and interviewed them in the office. What they wanted was a photogenic boy who would be good for publicity.'

It was won by Alex Keep, a bus driver's son, who was labelled *Eagle*'s Ambassador to Arizona. He was seen off at London Airport, wearing an *Eagle* Riders of the Range outfit, by a posse of cowboys. On arrival at Phoenix, Arizona, he was met by Hopalong Cassidy and a battery of press cameras.

For a 'Thrill of a Lifetime' competition with a prize of a holiday in Africa, the winner's accompanying parent was vetted too, so as not to disgrace the magazine by getting drunk and disorderly or making racist remarks. When Barbara Christmas, daughter of an RAF officer, won a trip to New York she was a gift to the PR men – her arrival was heralded in the papers with the headline 'Christmas comes early to New York'.

*Girl* ran sewing and knitting competitions, short story and poetry competitions, which attracted thousands of entries. But by far the most popular were the painting competitions.

The first nationwide painting competition was run in *Girl* in 1954, with prizes worth over £1,000 and weekly awards for the most interesting paintings. There were 11,000 entries. Two years later an Editor's Letter claimed that they had received 'so many pathetic letters from boys' they were extending the competition to include readers of *Eagle* and *Swift* – the number of entries increased to 52,000.

The judges were to be 'art experts' – rather an understatement to describe the Principal of the Royal College of Art, the President of the Royal Academy, the Principal of St Anne's College, Oxford and the Curator at the Victoria and Albert Museum. In the following years distinguished judges included James Fitton, Sir Ralph Richardson, John Betjeman and Ruskin Spear.

In 1958 Professor Sir Albert Richardson enthused, 'We were very much impressed by the high standard of all the entries. All the paintings exhibited are remarkably good and show a lively sense of colour and movement.' He and Henry Rushbury, Keeper of the Royal Academy, 'trotted joyfully among the 300 selected works for a couple of hours this morning liking almost

*The distinguished judges of the painting competition including Marcus, John Betjeman and art editor Arthur Roberts (third from right)*

everything they saw,' according to the *Eastern Daily Press*, Norwich ' "Look at that," said Sir Albert, "What a composition for a boy of his age. It's a bit like a Sickert.". . . A Scottish girl might have been mystified to learn that her rather brash landscape was a bit too much like Jack Yeats for everyone's taste. "But the sense of colouring in all of them," muttered Sir Albert to Mr Rushbury, "It's terrific when you think of it." '

The top prize every year was a trip abroad – sketching in Belgium and Holland, a holiday in Lloret de Mar, trips to Moscow and Leningrad, to Venice and Florence.

Jean Crouch met Nika Hulton in Venice with some of the winners. 'She was extremely unpleasant and kept making malicious remarks, but Sir Edward entertained us to a delicious lunch. Going to Venice was one of the perks for organising the competition. Jenny Nicholson, Robert Graves' daughter, was there; she organised an impoverished sprig of the Italian nobility to teach everyone to row a gondola, with lots of photos. I behaved quite irresponsibly in Venice and put the children on a plane and didn't come back with them. Marcus tore me off a strip, in private, but when anyone else was present he defended me.'

The *Eagle* winner in 1960 was Paul Riley, one of the youngest people ever to have a painting accepted for the Royal Academy.

The visits to Bertram Mills Circus began in 1951 with thirty Club Members attending a dress rehearsal. *Eagle* booked hundreds of seats every year in various parts of the country. Prizewinners were invited to spend the day behind the scenes, meet such stars as Coco the Clown and 'help' in rehearsals, then have lunch with the Mills brothers, Cyril and Bernard. Special nights were arranged for *Eagle* and *Girl* readers and when the Editor attended he would make an appearance in the ring. One year the 'Mekon' (aka Paul, the Hulton Press post boy) and 'Dan Dare' performed, to the delight of the 2,000 *Eagle* and *Girl* readers in the audience. Marcus and Jess took their offspring (and friends) every year and after the show would bribe them with money to spend at the fun fair while they went off for drinks in the VIP lounge. Much riotous behaviour ensued (at the fun fair, not in the VIP lounge).

Jan to her godmother: 'We went to Olympia for Bertram Mills circus. We were given some free tickets for the fair while Mummy and Daddy had drinks with Cyril and Bernard Mills. About an hour after we had been told to meet, Mummy and Daddy emerged from the Press Room. Then our loving parents sent us home in Mr [Alfred] Black's chauffeur-driven Bentley while they went off to eat some place in London, telling us to "find ourselves something to eat, *dears*" and then go to bed and no nonsense. We have been well trained to know when we're not wanted. When we got home at about midnight we got something to eat and went straight to bed.'

In 1951 Marcus decided to put his dog collar to good use and it was announced that a special carol service for *Eagle* and *Girl* readers would be held in St Paul's Cathedral on 22 December. It may have been his friendship with Canon Collins that secured such a prestigious venue but as Chad says, 'You could get anything for *Eagle*. I've never signed so many autographs in my life as at those carol services.'

St Paul's was overflowing that Saturday, with 3,000 people trying to squeeze in; only state occasions had attracted such a large congregation before. The doors had to be left open so that people standing on the steps could hear the music. Marcus conducted the service in his black cassock, white surplice and stole, and three Eaglers, Rupert Scott, Philip Hughes and Philip Belgeonne read lessons. So too did Marcus's eldest daughter – in time all his progeny read lessons in St Paul's, as did those of Chad Varah, Ruari McLean and Malcolm Messer. The best part of the day for the children was the party at Shoe Lane afterwards, rampaging up and down the building in the antiquated (and probably dangerous) lifts.

Marcus described that first carol service as perhaps his proudest moment of the *Eagle* years: 'Apparently the head virger said to the Dean, "Well it comes to something when you have to get a comic paper to fill your cathedral for you." It was very impressive seeing all those children.'

The following spring, Marcus was asked to preach at St Paul's and received a note from Edward Hulton: 'I was very interested to hear that you preached at St Paul's last Sunday. I am aware that this is no mean honour and would like to congratulate you on it. You might at the same time pass my congratulations on to EAGLE – for having such a distinguished Editor.'

In 1952 Marcus became an Assistant Stipendiary Curate (Honorary Chaplain) to St Bride's Church in Fleet Street and was invested to the Guild of St Bride's in 1954. When the church, which had been bombed during the war, was re-dedicated in the presence of the Queen and Prince Philip, Marcus read the Gospel; his children were given the day off school to attend and were lunched at the Ivy afterwards.

Marcus frequently took services (which were held in the crypt until the restoration was completed) for the Rector, Cyril Armitage. Mrs Armitage wrote to Marcus when Cyril died: 'He had a soft spot for you and your family – you understood one another.' Dewi Morgan, whose impressive mien and long white beard caused one of Marcus's grandchildren to mistake him for God, succeeded Cyril and became a close friend.

At Christmas 1952, carol services were also held in Manchester, Bristol and Portsmouth Cathedrals, Birmingham Parish Church and St Giles' Cathedral, Edinburgh, all with readers taking part. By 1954 they were extended to Belfast Cathedral and St John's Church, Cardiff and readers complained that they couldn't get tickets for St Paul's.

John Littlejohn was circulation rep in Northern Ireland and was asked to arrange the service in Belfast: 'It became obvious during the next few weeks that his reputation among the ecclesiastical community was of such a high stature that it was almost supra-denominational. I found it very easy to obtain the co-operation of all churches and schools in promising to send parties of their children to the carol service. I honestly believe that any lesser man than Marcus Morris could not have "harmonised" the people of Northern Ireland in the way that he did.'

When Marcus arrived, frozen and in need of a drink, John was startled by the sight of his tie, 'pink, red, white and wide enough and bright enough to dazzle the other occupants of the lounge. . . . I certainly warmed to this tall, rather flamboyant man who was to lead the carol service at the Cathedral in less than an hour – in front of around a thousand children, teachers and ministers of both denominations. . . . As he emerged from the gents . . . his tie had miraculously changed to a dog collar. . . . The carol service was a stupendous success. . . .

'At the reception for members of the choir and their parents Marcus held court and must have chatted personally to everyone there and shook hands with everyone as they departed. Then with a sigh of relief and a broad smile, he suggested we deserved another drink. . . . He popped into the cloakroom and re-emerged sporting his lurid Picasso-style necktie. . . . We found to our horror that most of the parents, teachers and ministers were still outside waiting to say goodbye to Marcus. . . . You can imagine the looks of astonishment as their eyes fell on the vision that had replaced the dog collar.'

Durham and Glasgow Cathedrals were added to the roll; by 1957 they had to hold two services in St Paul's to meet the demand and Liverpool Cathedral joined the list – after a certain amount of opposition from our old friend Dean Dwelly. Marcus had written to his father five years earlier, 'You may be interested to see the letter I have had from Dwelly in reply to my letter asking for a Carol Service in the Cathedral. We have had permission to hold it again in St Paul's and I am hoping to arrange it in other Cathedrals. It is rather a pity that Liverpool won't play. If you get a chance to get a crack at Dwelly about it I should be very grateful.'

Peter Cooper, Marcus's administrative assistant, took over the organisation. 'Clifford Makins and I did it together, went and saw all the Deans. We would go and drink bottles of wonderful Burgundy in order to discuss it properly. We'd get hysterics if we were interviewing Dean Dwelly in Liverpool. The Provost of Portsmouth put at the bottom of his letters, "Pray for me as I pray for you"; it became a catchword we taunted Marcus with. Dean Matthews was very helpful; he wouldn't have objected if we'd embroidered "Buy Eagle" on the back of his surplice.'

By 1959 Marcus was taking twelve carol services all over the country, aided and abetted by Chad Varah and local Bishops. It was a punishing schedule and meant that Marcus often arrived home in the early hours of Christmas morning too tired to enjoy the day with his family. Jan wrote to her godmother again, 'On Christmas Eve Daddy came back from a carol service at Edinburgh looking very seedy. He preached at the morning service at St Bride's on Christmas Day and then, just before Christmas dinner, Mummy sent him to bed with a temperature of 103. All he had instead of turkey and Christmas Pud was soup and about half a glass of champagne.'

Another year, 'the New Year's Eve party went on till about 3.00 a.m. No one got up till about 11.00 apart from Daddy who got up at 6.00 because he had to go to Bristol for a Carol Service.'

*The Times Educational Supplement* got quite carried away: 'London has perhaps never seen such splendour in simplicity as in the carol services which have been held in St Paul's on the last two Saturday afternoons.

'They were children's services, but not just that. . . . There was no doubt on Saturday about the response of the Rev Marcus Morris's readership. This was their service and they came in their hundreds – perhaps literally their thousands – beautifully turned out, and bringing the family with them. The whole huge serenity of Wren's church was loud with their singing. It was packed, not merely to the doors but to the roof.

'There were children in the choir, children down the length of the nave, children under the great dome and children in the galleries at the back. . . . Lastly the ancient majesty of the great hymn "O come all ye faithful". Hundreds of children hit the last verse and sang in exultation as they were bidden until the citizens of heaven would have been hard put to it to match their soaring offering of praise. . . .

'Some of them read lessons, in a modern translation, as clear as a bell and with devoted care. One diminutive tot got through some difficult bits about King Herod with the greatest of ease. . . . A wonderful idea and an experience which may be remembered when Saturday's cherubims are escorting their own grandchildren.'

It was not to be. In 1962 there were no *Eagle* carol services in St Paul's; instead, three were held in St Pancras Church and others in eight provincial cities. They were the last.

While he was touring the country taking carol services, Marcus also made appearances at Christmas parties. Charles Chilton, dressed in his cowboy outfit, entertained the readers and taught them the *Eagle* song, 'Spread Your Wings', which was written specially for the magazine by John Jerome:

> Spread your wings,
> Spread your wings,
> You'll find the World is full of wonderful things;
> Spread your wings,
> Learn to fly
> And seek adventure in the sky.

> You'll find your cares look small, far below you
> And the clouds will fade from view;
> There'll be a rainbow shining to show you
> That the world belongs to you!

> Your heart will
> Be so gay, every day
> So full of happiness it sings;
> The sky's your highway
> Take the skyway
> Like the eagle
> Spread Your wings.

It was at one of these parties that an anomaly was found in the Club rules – no age limit had been set and young Eaglers were startled to find a middle-aged, balding man wearing shorts and scout uniform, singing away in their midst. He had paid his sub, he was a club member, he was entitled to be there. After that the club was open only to boys.

In January 1951 *Eagle* took one of the largest stands at the Schoolboys' Exhibition in the Royal Horticultural Hall, Westminster. It was the forerunner of the great Hultons' Boys and Girls Exhibitions at Olympia which ran every August from 1956 to 1962. Most similar events were held during the Christmas holidays to compete with pantomimes and circuses but John Myers (who had joined Hultons from the Rank Organisation and whose idea the exhibition was) and Marcus recognised, from bitter experience, that there were a lot of bored children at the end of the summer wanting something to do.

Over 200,000 of them flocked to the first one, breaking all attendance records for Olympia's National Hall. It was called the most comprehensive exhibition for young people ever staged. There was a British Railways scale model railway system, an electronic computer, full-size Maserati, a submarine, a puppet display. There were competitions to win a flight to Edinburgh and back by BEA, and treasure hunts. For the girls there were nursing, cookery and make-up demonstrations and a stand showing life behind the scenes of a ballet company, which was visited by Margot Fonteyn and Alicia Markova. *Housewife* put on the first ever fashion parade for teenagers, with teenage models.

There was a Club Room for members which, according to *Ad Weekly*, was 'run on austere Pall Mall lines. The premises were comfortably furnished with lounge chairs, a table with magazines and writing desks. Apart from the commissionaires on the door to check club membership and keep out parents, there was no adult supervision.

'The children behaved with the decorum of life-long members of the Atheneum. Thousands of names were neatly recorded in the visitors' book. Not one scrap of litter was left on the premises nor one magazine taken away.'

James Dreaper helped to organise the second exhibition, which put him off them for life. 'It was really hard work. Seventy per cent of exhibitors signed up immediately, the Army, Navy and Air Force, the Gas Board, the banks. It was the final 30 per cent that counted if we were not to have a colossal loss. I always got the impression that Marcus was a reluctant participant in the exhibitions. There was a rota of Hulton Press people meeting VIPs. The Dagenham Girl Pipers came one year. They filled themselves with scotch and wandered round for about two hours. Every time you thought they'd gone you could hear the skirl of pipes.'

The Exhibition was opened that year by Sir John Hunt, which was considered quite a coup as he was still very much a hero. Harry Secombe did the honours in 1958 (and again in 1961), holding up the traffic in Kensington by arriving on a mechanical elephant called Min, which had a motor cycle engine in its tummy. Harry was so densely mobbed that he had to escape through the National Coal Board's model of a working mine.

*Daily Sketch*: 'The National Coal Board is spending £6,000 to show the boys of Britain what the mines offer them by way of a career. . . . The coal industry's biggest single problem is that it still can't persuade enough young men to see in coal mining a worthwhile twentieth century career.'

But Eric Fenner in the *Socialist Leader* castigated the exhibition for not having enough career stands, complained about the armed forces always having money for recruitment, the Coal Board for showing the latest machines for putting miners out of work, and the amount of litter on the hall floor.

(The *Socialist Leader* had already had a go at the children's papers: 'The Hulton Group, which claim to have cleaned up the comics, insert religious propaganda into their children's papers. Militarist and religious propaganda may not be so terrible as the brutality pictured in the "horror" variety, but they are anti-socialist and therefore anti-social, prejudices being pumped into our children.')

The *Glasgow Evening Times* reported: ' "This is murder" groaned the desperate young man on the Boosey and Hawkes stand. . . . "They're not supposed to touch these instruments." He hauled a French Horn from a boy who had just produced a noise like Auld Nick on a Saturday night. By now a crowd of urchins was banging away at guitars, several saxophones were on the go, cymbals clashed, and trumpets blared. It needed the combined efforts of two artillery men to stop one youngster using an AA gun as a merry-go-round. There are roller cycle races, a full size cricket net where boys in rig can face up to our Test cricketers. A real helicopter with whirling blades and even "working" spaceships and sputniks with room inside for human beings.

'In the midst of such a hurly-burly as firing ranges, accident prevention demonstrations, conjuring tricks, and film excerpts, the little Church of England chapel strikes one as incongruous. . . . As well as being shown how to operate a potter's kiln and how to play chess. . . . They can find out how to look after their teeth and their pets, where to get the latest match box labels; and they can talk to Donald Campbell, who is there with his record-breaking boat *Bluebird*, only too happy to answer questions about his forthcoming land and water speed bids.

'They can also see, beside a 40ft model of HMS *Bulwark*, a glass-sided tank in which real frogmen are working. The only stand that was being neglected was the National Trust one advertising "Places of Historical National Interest".'

Marcus renewed his acquaintance with snakes, in the person of a large python, at George Cansdale's Pets Corner. Denis Compton and Godfrey Evans were clean-bowled by a fourteen-year-old schoolgirl in the cricket nets. Vivien Leigh and Sir Len Hutton were there on behalf of the Spastics Society.

Peter Barker was put in charge in 1958: 'We had trouble with old men and young boys. We used to get colonels out of the lavatories and put them in taxis, pay the fare and tell the drivers to dump them in the middle of Hyde Park. It didn't happen often, but we didn't dare let it get into the press. I always think that managing the Boys and Girls Exhibition was the most difficult assignment I have ever attempted.'

A team of eight-year-olds challenged all comers at chess and there was a tiddly-winks contest. Children could have painting lessons in a mock-up of a Paris artist's studio; there was a Dan Dare space walk and a parents' oasis. In 1959 an Emmetland Railway appeared before embarking on a world tour and in 1960 youngsters could cut their own discs and enter a talent competition – Cliff Richard was one of the judges.

In 1959 it was opened by Frankie Vaughan; more celebrities put in appearances: Beryl Grey, Anna Neagle, the Lone Ranger, Pamela Brown, Brian Johnston, Peter West, Freddie Mills, Eamonn Andrews, Jack Warner, Barbara Woodhouse, Johnny Leach – and the Morris children were introduced to many of them.

The *Spectator* was haughtily dismissive of the whole thing, but the end of its report was rather disquieting: 'The big battalions of the Forces of the Crown had the whole place drenched in martial music and all their favourite toys on show – a twenty-five pounder field gun, a Daring Class destroyer, a section of a Vampire jet and some glamorous Guardsmen. Recruiting officers, casual and watchful as tarts, stood by to enrol any adolescents seduced by their pretty weapons.'

The article provoked a letter stating that 'any agreement signed hastily by a boy is legally binding and does not need parental consent'. One hopes that no over-enthusiastic sixteen-year-old took the Queen's shilling at the Exhibition and lived to regret it.

Holiday Playtime started in 1955: 'It's fun, it's free, it's by the sea!', a promotion to boost sales of the papers in the summer. John Russell said, 'It was so successful that resorts were coming to us and we had to set up a separate department.'

At towns all round the coast, *Eagle* and *Girl* readers carrying current copies of their paper could claim prizes in a 'Spot The Face' competition. Games with thousands of prizes were organised on specially set aside parts of the beach: sack races, egg and spoon races, three-legged races, running races, sandcastle competitions, talent contests, sing-songs.

*Spread your Wings*, *Eagle*'s own weekly radio programme on Radio Luxembourg, started in November 1954, organised by Stephen Williams who, although at that time with the BBC, had set up Radio Luxembourg in 1933 (and who fifty-eight years later made the final announcement on the station when it closed down). The compère was Robbie McDermott, Denis Compton talked to Marcus Morris, the guest star was Max Bygraves, and there was a 'Luck of the Legion' serial story and a competition, followed by 'Dan Dare's Space Adventure'.

There were personality interviews, a quiz between *Eagle* and *Girl* Club Members, to find 'the Best Brains of Britain', and Steve Race's band became 'The Eagle Orchestra'. It was called the 'best boys' radio show'.

In celebration of its second birthday *Eagle* linked up with its namesake, the aircraft carrier HMS *Eagle*. The Editor sent darts and dart boards and a crib board with the *Eagle* symbol to the crew and copies of *Eagle* were supplied every week. They were sent a piano with an engraved plate inscribed 'Presented to HMS Eagle by the readers of *Eagle* Magazine'.

Graham Mottram, curator of the Fleet Air Arm Museum, wrote to a fellow *Eagle* fan in 1986, 'I regret that our records do not run to maintenance records of ships' pianos . . . but we have a pretty shrewd idea of their ultimate fate. . . . It was something of a tradition to catapult a piano over the side on party night or returning to harbour.'

In May 1959 the ship went into dry dock for three years. The Editor said that when it put back to sea the friendly links would be renewed; contact was made again in 1964, but by then *Eagle* was a very different magazine.

And then there were the annuals, books and off-shoots. Hulton Enterprises was started in September 1950 and hardly a week passed without the planning and production of new toys. More than sixty *Picture Post/Eagle* educational film strips were distributed to schools all over the country; at the 1951 Harrogate Toy Fair several exhibitors featured *Eagle* toys.

Peter Barker said, 'John Myers and I were still at Rank in 1950 and we suggested to Hulton Press that they should exploit Dan Dare. The only company that did licensed merchandising at the time was Disney, so we pinched a Disney contract and found out about the legal side. Hultons said we would have to pay our way fairly quickly; if they were going to take us on we had to get licences signed on Dan Dare.

'A Dan Dare space gun was the first idea. We had belts, cameras, glassware, jigsaw puzzles, story books – a tremendous range of things. Everything was taken to Marcus for his approval. Riders of the Range went well, PC 49 hardly at all, policemen weren't in with the toy trade at that time. Harris Tweed was very small – tea towels. Walls did their own publicity. We couldn't do much with the Centre Spreads, though we did try to get them into books at one time. Dan Dare was easily number one: we had space ships, guns, helmets. It was very successful, we made a lot of money for Hulton Press.' But not for Marcus or Frank Hampson.

The *Church of England Newspaper* reported that 'Advertisers today say they can sell anything to children, even soap, if only it can be represented as part of the equipment of Dan Dare.'

There were twenty-seven licencees making Riders of the Range braces, bootees, mouth organs and accordions, Dan Dare projector-viewers, *Eagle* stationery, card games, Range Rider pistols, holsters, badges and spurs, greetings cards, cowboy outfits, balloons, ray guns, lampshades, all sold through the magazine.

There were *Eagle* books galore. As well as the Annuals there were books of hobbies, modern wonders, aircraft, balsa wood models, railways. *The Times* reported that the *Eagle Book of Cars and Motor Sport* was 'a good deal better value for money than most'. There were *Eagle Sports Annuals*, *Dan Dare Stamp Albums*, the *Girl Book of Wonders*. *The Eagle Book of Records and Champions* came out as 'an entirely new idea' in October 1950, well ahead of *The Guinness Book of Records*. *Luck of the Legion* and *The Three J's of Northbrook* were brought out as novels, as were *Belle of the Ballet*, *Wendy and Jinx* and *Susan of St Bride's*.

The Annuals made careful note of future events: *Eagle Annual* gave full coverage to space satellites six weeks before the Russian launch.

By 1959 the *Eagle* empire had grown and overtaken everything else at Hulton Press; a party in the Café Royal for those directly involved numbered a couple of hundred people – and parties were thrown at the drop of a hat.

Ellen Vincent wrote, 'We were moved from our rather cramped and insignificant little offices on the top floor . . . and as we became more important we eventually got very fine, roomy offices on the second floor. . . . From the beginning there was an ambience of fun about *Eagle*. . . . There was an air of youthful hilarity about the whole concept. . . . This happy note ran through most of the years that *Eagle* was in existence and under the editorship of Marcus. Champagne flowed at the slightest excuse.'

Life in Epsom became increasingly strained for Marcus and Jess as the tension between them and the artists grew. The Firs turned out to be very inconvenient and expensive; the allowance paid by Hulton Press by no means covered the running costs. They needed a smaller house and Jess wanted to be nearer the action. In April 1953 the Morrises were on the move again.

Marcus bought a house in Hampstead Garden Suburb. Later that year, recognising that he had been put to great expense, Hulton Press agreed to acquire the leasehold for slightly more than he had paid. Marcus was to rent the house back from the company on an assured tenancy and the company agreed to pay for a garage and a second bathroom.

The Oak House in Wildwood Rise was built of Dutch brick in about 1910 and was a severe disappointment to the three girls – a small suburban garden, no turreted roof and one (almost) inaccessible oak tree to climb – but there was Hampstead Heath, which was not then beset by muggers and rapists (just the odd flasher) and a tame squirrel called Charlie.

The children were sent to Byron House School in Highgate (former pupils included Sir John Betjeman and Elizabeth Taylor) and in due course the three girls went to South Hampstead High School for Girls at Swiss Cottage. Simon was sent to Highfield School near Liphook at the age of eight and then to Marlborough, which delighted Marcus, as he had been turned down by them thirty-odd years earlier.

Jess was working regularly again, but getting staff to look after such a disordered household was difficult to say the least. Gureen Glass went with the family to Hampstead, but left in August that year. Terry arrived at the end of September; Jan's and Kate's diaries recorded the chaos:

24 January 1954: *Terry left yesterday and today was rather unsettled.*

31 January: *Bridget leaves and Francis and May come.*

28 February: *Francis and May leave.*

14 March: *Kathleen and Joan come.*

A Dutch couple, Mary and Alex, actually stayed for about a year. They were fond of the family but eventually decided that the Morris household did not offer them enough scope for their talents.

In January 1956 it is revealed that Mina and Alphonse have been in residence since the previous August.

29 March: *Mina and Alphonse left today thank goodness.*

6 April: *Maria and Carmine came today.*

By 1958 Maria and Carmine and Amelia and Antonio had come and gone.

6 January: *Maria came* [a different Maria, it was all very confusing].

17 February: *Maria out. Giovanni came at last. Can't speak a word of English.*

29 June: *Got Dad's supper. Mummy's in Manchester doing a broadcast. Can't listen because our radio's being mended.*

13 July: *Maria and Giovanni leaving. Won't stay till Mum finds someone else. Have to get our own breakfast etc.*

17 July: *Stayed at home from school to look after Pop because ill in bed and Mum out at rehearsals. Did housework most of day.*

18 July: *Kate stayed at home to look after Pop. Sally felt ill. I brought her home from school.*

23 July: *On Saturday Mummy didn't feel very well so she stayed in bed. On Sunday Simon went to bed with a temperature. On Monday and Tuesday Kate stayed home from school to look after them and today and tomorrow I am. Yesterday Mrs Mason came to try us out.*

11 September: *Mrs Mason went.*

18 September: *Miss Johnston came this afternoon.*

19 September: *Got up early and went downstairs. Miss Johnston had walked off.*

27 September: *New Italians came today. Anna and Conrado.*

26 October: *Mum had a row with the Italians and they're leaving tomorrow.*

1 November: *Two girls came, Claire and Hazel. I think they're students.*

23 December: *Claire and Hazel left.*

They were the last of the live-in, walk-out helps. Jan was coming up seventeen and she and Kate were quite capable of running the house, though they baulked at it occasionally. Thereafter, Jess employed a daily, Mary Suffling, who stayed with the family for over ten years.

'I really liked the job, became part of the furniture. Yes, it was chaotic.' Mrs Suffling would often come back in the evenings and weekends to help with parties, take Simon for walks and sew on his school name tapes: 'Jess never got round to it.' One morning Mary smelt burning and eventually traced it to Marcus and Jess's bedroom. 'The bed was on fire with both of them in it. The children used to be left alone a lot. When I turned up in the morning they'd be going to school or arguing the toss, half dressed, having breakfast, house like God knows what. They were sleeping alone in that big house.'

She remembered the time when the girls woke to find a large policeman in their bedroom; Marcus and Jess had come in late and left the car doors and front door wide open – the police thought the house had been burgled.

'Jess hadn't got a clue. I think in the theatrical world they're like that. I asked Jess if my National Insurance was being paid and she said it was all being seen to. Of course, when I left it hadn't been seen to at all. I was so fond of everybody I just let it go.'

Jess wrote to Jan in November 1959, 'I went to have my hair done today and when I got back I found a Harrods man in the drawing room putting up the curtains – I'd forgotten to lock the door, wasn't it lucky!'

Ruth and Jack were concerned about the children's welfare but, as Jack said, 'They all seemed pretty normal.' For a time there were problems with Simon because he wouldn't speak English, but would pick up whatever language the staff spoke.

The one person Jess could always rely on to jump to the rescue during these years was Ann Shaw, who had been her closest friend since the 1930s. She was a tower of strength and would come and stay at the drop of a hat to be with the children or to comfort Jess (or Marcus) after a particularly acrimonious row – when she would say 'Get them together in bed and it'll be all right'.

Letter from Jess to Marcus in California, December 1955: 'I watched your plane go off into the confused darkness of the runways from the airport manager's office. It's odd how even then, although still within waving distance, one felt that the three thousand miles were already between us. There is a terribly empty feeling in not hearing the Pathfinder [Marcus's car] coming round the corner. . . . I miss you quite dreadfully. There seem to be so many acres of the Great Bed of Hampstead when the other half is empty!. . . . We are very thrilled as Constance [Spry] is coming to have dinner with us [Jess and Ann] one evening next week.'

In spite of their enjoyment of each other, Marcus and Jess both strayed from the marital bed. Jess was jealous of many of the women in Marcus's orbit, not always without reason. In the mid-1950s, he had a serious affair with one of his 'pretty ladies' and Jess came close to walking out. Such a scandal would have been disastrous for the children's papers; Marcus ended the relationship and Jess was persuaded to stay. It was rumoured that the young woman tried to commit suicide, but she later married and she and Marcus remained friends, lunching and dining together regularly until Marcus left London on his retirement.

Odette Fasquelle was a journalist working on *Réalité* in Paris in the 1950s and was introduced to Marcus by Mrs Hulton. 'I needed to meet *Picture Post* people for *Réalité* and I knew Nika Hulton through a friend. Marcus was wonderful with her. She respected him very much. I saw him sometimes trying to calm her down.

'Marcus was always speaking to me about his wife. When I was in London he would help me in every way, so when he came to Paris I would help him. One time he said he wanted to buy some pretty underwear for his wife. We went to look together. He said they weren't naughty enough, so we went to Pigalle and got the naughtiest.' Of course, they may have been for one of his pretty ladies.

'He could apply himself to any subject. He talked very little, when we were together I did all the talking. I remember in the office several people were having a discussion, he wouldn't say a word, then in the end with a quiet voice he would just give the solution.'

Their father's success and greatly expanded circle of acquaintances meant an exciting social life for the Morris children; at *Eagle* do's they were treated like VIPs. They went to recordings of 'Spread Your Wings'; Charles Chilton, who produced The Goon Show, invited them to a performance and introduced them to the cast. They had the best seats for a recital by Paul Robeson in St Paul's.

The family went to charity cricket matches, there were frequent dinners at the Ivy and other West End haunts of Marcus's, and visits galore to the theatre, which were much more fun when one could go backstage and meet the stars. 'Went to see *Large as Life*. Met Harry Secombe at stage door by his request, he wants Pop to go and have drinks with him. Went to Quaglino's, danced with Daddy.'

One summer Jess took Jan and Kate to Paris for a long weekend to prove to her extravagant husband that it could be done for less than £25.

Kate and Jackie Vincent, Ellen's daughter, appeared on television with Marcus, Peter Twiss, the test pilot who held the official world air-speed record, and Moira Shearer in a discussion about careers.

Jackie remembers the excitement of those days, spending her school holidays in the office, 'the highlight of the holidays, I always felt I was in the middle of everything. My mother loved her days on *Eagle*. At the time she said "I can't believe I'm paid to go in there" she was so happy. They had some marvellous times at Wildwood Rise. I remember one party, John Arlott was there absolutely smashed, but terribly funny. Marcus was greeting people as they came in and John pushed him out of the way. He went on all evening saying how do you do to everybody.'

The house was frequently full of celebrities: sportsmen, actors, writers, artists; Marcus and Jess were enthusiastic and expert party givers and the children were all roped in to help.

Marcus's constant refrain on these occasions was 'There isn't enough to eat and no one will come anyway.' Many friends attended the New Year's Eve parties every year for nearly thirty years. They started when Jess, alone with the children in Wildwood Rise (Marcus was away taking carol services) invited a total stranger to 'first foot'; Theo Cowan was taking a breather from the party across the road given by Roma and Alfred Black. Alfred and his brother George were theatrical impresarios and Roma (née Beaumont) had been a star with Ivor Novello. They had two younger children around the same age as Sally and Simon and the families soon became friends.

'Marcus always seemed quiet and reserved, he took a lot of breaking down. He was very intense, very hard-working. The children had a bohemian up-bringing, but weren't badly behaved. They didn't always have clean clothes. We had some people for drinks, Monty Mackie and A.E. Matthews. Suddenly Simon appeared in his pyjamas. He stayed quite a while, nobody missed him. It was a happy-go-lucky atmosphere, but we didn't live in each other's pockets. At Christmas we were backwards and forwards, and on New Year's Eve we used to dance like mad, up and down the road.'

Jan wrote at the end of 1958: 'On Christmas Day we were twelve. On Christmas Eve a fuse blew – Daddy had popped off to Edinburgh for Carol Services so I got Mr Black. He mended the fuse and had a drink and then his sister Pauline and her husband Mickey Ashton (from a famous circus family) came too and Mickey helped us to put up the Christmas tree. The Blacks and family came over for drinks again before dinner on Christmas Day. In the morning everyone in Wildwood Rise including Mum and Dad had gone next door.'

Next door was Spaniard's Field, at the end of Wildwood Rise, a large house into which Pip and Norman Gregory and their three children moved in 1956.

'Jess was the first person to come to the front door and welcome us and ask us over for drinks. She was a very shrewd lady, very intelligent – and I never heard her say an unkind word about anybody. We used to come home late at night and the study light would be on, Marcus was still working.

'Jess and Sally disturbed the robbers when we were burgled. The police said they shouldn't have come in, they might have been shot. There were rats under the Morrises' garden shed which used to play in our garden near the pond. Jess said they were water rats, nice and harmless. Eventually we got the Council in and they were appalled. It was the untidiest house – the children threw things around and Jess never did any housework.' She was too busy.

She was in *It's Never Too Late* at the Strand Theatre with Celia Johnson and Phyllis Calvert, did a number of broadcasts from Manchester and began to appear in ever more television plays. One of the first was *Missing from Home*, which was transmitted just after Jan had gone AWOL for a day and the police had been called to look for her. It was good publicity for the play.

When ITV started in 1955, Jess and her sister Ruth became known as 'The Detergent Sisters Dunning' – Jess advertising Persil, Ruth singing the praises of Tide. Their appearances prompted Quentin B. Dobson to pen a verse:

### MONDAY IS DUNNING DAY

Sisters, sisters,
> Never were there such detergent sisters,
For laundering by Persil I'll abide,
> While she washes all her clothes in Tide.

Sisters, Sisters,
> Never were there such divided Sisters,
She uses Persil in her tub;
> Tide is what I use as I rub.

Lord, how it's urgent
> For us to keep selling detergent
And Lord help the washdays
> That come between us and our soaps!

The sisters were more deeply divided than the poem suggests; they never acted together, but Jess did appear with her brother-in-law, Jack Allen, in *The Army Game.*

*Manchester Evening Chronicle*: 'The Dunnings are doing well. Now that success has come to them the Sale-reared sisters are past the first bloom of youth. But they have matured into a couple of fine TV lead players. You saw Ruth, the one-time BBC TV Mrs Grove, in *The Hot Summer Night* three weeks ago [for which she won a Best Actress award]. Tomorrow night, Jessica follows her forty-seven-year-old elder sister to the Manchester ABC TV studios for the Armchair Theatre presentation *To Ride a Tiger.* . . . Miss Dunning – Jessica, I mean – averages a TV play a month, mostly on BBC.'

After the televising of *Before the Party*, the *Bradford Telegraph & Argus* reported: 'Dame Sybil Thorndike and Sir Lewis Casson . . . were overshadowed by the more vital characters so excellently portrayed by Jessica Dunning and Robert Flemyng.'

Marcus's single foray into showbusiness was when he cut his first, and only, disc – narrating *The Coronation and What It Means*, with script by Stephen Williams. It was recorded in St Margaret's, Westminster and launched at the Schoolboys Exhibition in January 1953.

Robert Treddenick of the *Tatler* was quoted in *Eagle*: 'I do not believe there will be anything to better this record. By its very simplicity it can touch the hearts of everyone the world over and surely that is praise enough.'

# Chapter Fourteen

At the opening of the new Scottish National Library in Edinburgh the Queen and the Duke of Edinburgh were being shown the Periodicals Section. The Duke of Edinburgh was examining rows of highbrow and obscure journals when he saw a copy of *Eagle*. 'Ah,' he said with an air of relief, 'we do at least take this one in our house.' [1958, origin unknown]

The initial payment made to Marcus by Hulton Press, much of which was in the form of a loan, had saved him from bankruptcy but didn't cover all the debts he had incurred when starting *Eagle*. By July 1950 he was asking his bank for an overdraft and by November he was in debt to the company to the tune of £2,100. Over the next year or so he received irregular payments totalling nearly £3,000 but, as he wrote at the time, 'When the idea of *Girl* was first mooted I was told that that would be an opportunity of making a capital payment to me to cover both *Girl* and *Eagle*, but instead there was a long argument extending over several months as a result of which I received a contract dealing only with my salary as Editor of *Eagle* and *Girl*. Instead of a capital payment I received a series of loans which I am now having to repay at a higher rate than I can afford.'

Not only had Marcus underestimated his debts but he had not realised that everything he received from Hulton Press to pay off his debts would be liable to tax – and surtax. He was now paying the price of not keeping proper records: the tax man asked him to separate his expenses into those incurred as a clergyman and those which 'refer to secular duties', and pointed out that Marcus's phone charges had increased by £30 in two years, 'presumably the reason for this is the fact that the telephone has been used considerably more.'!

There were constant niggles from Marcus about reneged agreements; Hultons complained about his expenses. Marcus felt that, as the company repeatedly ignored his requests to discuss royalties, he was entitled to some recompense. He wrote to the General Manager: 'The impression has been given that I have been continually asking for additional sums of money, loans etc., as a result of my own personal over-spending. . . . What I am asking for is not an act of charity, but a reasonable reward for the contribution I have tried to make to Hulton Press.'

In the words of Bart Smith in 1953, Marcus wanted 'to remove any suggestions which have been made of his financial irresponsibility or that he has made or is making exorbitant and unjustifiable requests. It would seem that the most that can be said is that Mr Morris lacks commercial sagacity.'

After more nagging by Marcus and Bart Smith, in 1955 Hulton Press acquired the copyright of Marcus's signature for £7,250 (£2,500 of which was a loan) the first (and only) real money Marcus made out of Hulton Press, apart from an increase in his salary to £5,000 p.a. (of which 45 per cent went in tax). The copyright deal was a recognition of Marcus's increasing responsibilities in the company and avoided surtax. The Trade Mark Certificate is decidedly fishy; the signature on it, and on the Editor's Page at the time, was not Marcus's (unless he wrote it with his right hand – he was left-handed). It was registered in the name of Marcus John Harston Morris (*sic*), 'in respect of pamphlets, newspapers, circulars, booklets, book and periodical printed publications' for seven years. The 'real' signature was back in *Eagle* by the end of August.

Hultons had made valiant attempts at curbing costs. George Ravenscroft and John Pearce appealed for more flexibility in the departmental use of staff and a reduction in the amount of overtime. 'Messengers are very frequently sent in taxis when they might as well travel by tube or bus. . . . Instruct your staff to use the cheapest stationery and to be sparing with it. . . . Please instruct a junior member of your department to ensure that lights are turned off. . . . There are far too many trunk calls to Bemrose in Liverpool. . . . No first class travel warrants will be issued to anybody travelling fifty miles or less.'

'The salaries of Frank Hampson and assistants are higher than the salaries of the Editor and assistants. The present cost of this army is £240 per week. I ask, not without considerable alarm, if we have now reached the maximum? I ask, not with much hope, what possibility there is of reducing the increase in the charges we have been paying to outside help on Dan Dare? . . . Fisher is still receiving £15 per week (charged as your assistant and not Hampson's). When is he going to be sacked?' He wasn't.

A memo from John Pearce to Heads of Departments was headed HARD TIMES: 'The travelling expenses of the Editor and his supporters . . . are going to be charged to Editorial Expenses. . . . If it won't harass the Editor too much, it would be better to estimate the cost of his lecture visits, budget for it and charge it as a separate item in the Publicity Budget. Certainly any expenses of the Editor in attending functions connected with Sales Promotion should be paid for out of the Publicity Budget.'

No wonder Marcus got his figures in a twist. (Edward Hulton wasn't much better. One year he decided that the company needed a more exciting Christmas card and asked Marcus to commission Charles Mozeley to paint one. The result, a beautiful depiction of angels in gold, reds and blues, duly arrived at the Chairman's office. Edward was most enthusiastic about the painting until his wife informed him that it was hideous.)

Jean Crouch said, 'Marcus got through cash at an alarming rate. His expense account over a weekend could look like the national debt, but there was no one like him for getting your budget. If it was a good idea he would say go for it. The *Girl* ballet scheme, for instance, must have cost a fortune, with not a great deal back for it.'

Peter Cooper started at Hultons working for Malcolm Messer on *Farmers Weekly* which, apart from the children's papers, was the only magazine making money. Peter recalled, 'On my second day Malcolm said "There's one man in this organisation you've got to meet." I said, "Edward Hulton?" He replied, "No, no, he's far more interesting than that." So we went up and that was the first time I set eyes on Marcus.

'In 1956 I joined him as Executive Assistant. He said, "You don't know anything, you'd better have a title that makes other people think you do". He made me go with him to every meeting and take down notes which he never read.

'He held his own among the giants of Fleet Street without the faintest difficulty. They used to drink with Marcus in the cellar of a little restaurant across the road. The editors of *The Times* and *Telegraph* and *Mail* and *Express* all knew Marcus because he had this unique stage that he'd created for himself.'

Peter was quite expansive on the subject of Marcus's finances: 'Expenses were the most interesting area of Marcus's operation. There was a special teller in the accounts department, George Kenwood, whose job was solely to look after Marcus's expenses. Nika engaged a specialist in administration and management, John Gittins, a colonial civil servant and in one of her periodical hates of Marcus, she thrust into Gittins's hand a pile of Marcus's expenses and said "I don't believe he can have spent that amount of money, you will go to every one of these restaurants and have exactly what he had and see if it comes to that amount." Gittins was Presbyterian, pompous, unused to high living and drink, so most of the report was incomprehensible. He gave up after a while, he became so ill.'

Memo from J.W. Gittins to Marcus Morris, 1958: 'I should be glad to know how many people were present at each meal, . . . to be informed why it is necessary invariably to go to the most expensive restaurants in London at a time when revenues from your papers are falling and when everyone is making an effort to economise wherever possible.

'I cannot see the slightest justification to lunch and dine continually at these restaurants and I must ask you therefore in the interests of the Company if in future you will be good enough to reduce your expenses so that they may be comparable to those of other Heads of Departments.'

John Gittins also complained to Marcus about the expenses of his staff. Clifford Makins, Peter Cooper and Peter Barker were accused of spending too much on lunches, while other staff were castigated for using taxis instead of public transport. Marcus's habits were obviously catching.

Marcus had a series of accountants, none of whom managed to sort him out. One such, Tom Mason, suggested that Bagenal Harvey should take over Marcus's finances.

Peter Cooper said, 'Bagenal gave Marcus cash every week. I think Marcus had an acute and astute idea of the value of money, it was very simple to pretend that he didn't, it meant that somebody else took care of it; not that somebody else paid the bill, he was never mean. He never tried to take money for himself; he just couldn't understand why there wasn't an endless supply, mainly for entertaining.'

Marcus was out to lunch and/or dinner practically every day with contributors, job applicants, editors, advertisers. He took his dentist, Cyril de Vere Green, to dinner to discuss the Dental Health poster competition. He took his beautiful young editors to lunch, one at a time. He signed the bill at the Ivy, Boulestin, the Mirabelle, Casanova, the River Club, the Savoy, Wheeler's, the Gargoyle, L'Escargot, Pigalle, Maison Prunier.

Peter Barker thinks it was probably he who introduced Marcus to the Empress Club. 'He was a great man for going out. We used to go to Rule's and Les Ambassadeurs, El Vino's of course at lunch time for champagne. Marcus had all the attributes of a great editor and a great playboy. He was a chameleon, he changed from one to the other so fast. I can't say I've ever seen him drunk. I've seen him have a skinful, he used to become very quiet. I don't think he ever raised his voice; I've never seen him really angry though I've seen him be ruthless with stupid people.

'One Saturday night Marcus decided he wanted to go out on the town. He got me to ring up two girls who lived in Dolphin Square. We all had champagne then went out to dinner in pairs and agreed to meet up at a night club. At about one or two we all went back to Dolphin Square for a nightcap. Everything was above board, there was no sex going on. Between two and three, Marcus decided he'd go for a walk on the embankment, at which point he told me he was preaching that day in St Bride's. Getting on for four o'clock I went to find him, he was fast asleep on a seat. I thought the best thing for him would be a Turkish bath. I put him into a taxi and rang up Peter Cooper and said "Your master ought at this moment to be sitting in a Turkish bath at the RAC Club. You'd better get up now and get down there and see that he gets to the church." Which he did, gave him black coffee, put dark glasses on him. I'm told Marcus gave a diatribe on the subject of sin.'

Ruari McLean wrote: 'Marcus liked living well. He reckoned that his talents had earned him some of the douceurs of life. I was lucky in having what I preferred to call a hard head and we had a certain amount of hilarity at our dinners. I never saw Marcus drunk and only once do I remember seeing him slightly flushed. What I do remember is a series of meetings in night clubs (there was a sort of convention among the higher executives in Hultons that you could never conduct serious business during the day, and the best time and place was the Gargoyle at two in the morning) when I watched tough advertising types plying Marcus with champagne or brandy or both, thinking that this inexperienced young parson was an easy victim; after the eighth brandy it was Marcus who was still cool and collected and it was they who were on their knees.'

One lunchtime, 'While we were sipping our gins-and-tonic he wrote down a list of the seven deadly sins and marked both of us. He reckoned that he himself was guilty of six out of the seven. The one he acquitted himself of was accidie, sloth. He said he knew what was wrong with himself but not how to cure it. He was no longer interested in just editing children's papers; he had no ambition to improve the world, but he did want to exercise his own power and talents. Should he leave the Church? It was a serious question. It would have been the Church's loss if he had left it, but he stayed.'

Arthur Roberts said, 'My wife and I went to the Two Brewers one night and the place was nearly empty. Marcus was on his own which was very rare; none of his cronies was there. He came straight over and joined us, very friendly, most uncharacteristic.

'He always listened to what Clifford Makins said, so anything we had to communicate was best done through him. Clifford said to Marcus once that he wasn't in touch enough with his staff, he was a bit too aloof. One day he appeared in the art room, a great big open plan place where all the letterers worked. Clifford led him from desk to desk like the Queen at a garden party. He stopped and chatted to everyone. They were very startled, some of them had never spoken to him before, some didn't even know who he was; they looked at one another with a wild surmise after he'd gone. It probably did some good, they said "that was nice, fancy him coming round like that". He didn't do it more than once.'

Pat Jackson took over the editorship of *Girl* from Jean Crouch: 'I was a member of a Youth Club in Kilburn and Marcus came and talked to us about *Eagle*. He was a very interesting and persuasive speaker, it made a tremendous impression. He had the most wonderful smile, his approach was very casual and informal. Everybody took to him immediately.

'I was mad keen to become a journalist and I asked him if there was any chance for me and he said, "When it comes to the point write to us and we'll see what we can do for you". So when I left secretarial college I wrote to Hulton Press and got a job as sweeper-up of floors, opener of letters, licker of stamps. Marcus said, "If you keep your eyes open and look for opportunities there's no reason why you shouldn't become a sub-editor". I became assistant secretary and sub to Rosemary Garland on *Robin* when it started, then worked for James Hemming for a couple of years on the problem page, then sub-editor on *Girl*.

'I didn't see Marcus around the office a lot, but whenever there was a cause for celebration like the birthday of a paper or something new coming out there would be a champagne party for all the staff and Marcus was always there. They were impromptu and hilarious, working there was like working amongst the family. There was the most tremendous spirit. We all believed fervently in what we were doing. A kind of ethos pervaded the place that stemmed from Marcus, Chad and James, who were all marvellously friendly, understanding, interested people. We all had this common purpose, a feeling of dedication to something tremendously worthwhile.'

Despite the informal atmosphere, standards of work had to be kept high. 'If you let a spelling error slip through you were on the carpet next morning, delivered in very firm tones. That very friendly accessible side was not apparent in the office. He appeared to be more shy than anything else. I don't think he was remote because of any notions of self importance. He always had a smile whenever you met him. I suppose I thought it was sad when he was no longer "the clergyman" because of the effect he'd had on me when he was still going round wearing a dog-collar. That talk Marcus gave at the Youth Club changed the course of my life totally.'

Anita MacFarlane (née Dent) was introduced to Marcus by Clifford Makins and worked at Hultons one day a week answering letters. She also worked for John Betjeman: 'Marcus wanted to meet Betjeman so we set up a lovely lunch at Rule's with John, Marcus, Clifford and me. Betjeman ordered the claret and Marcus used to go back there for lunches and drink the same wine till there was none left.

'I think a lot of people were jealous of Marcus. They were disapproving because he was a Rev and successful with women. It made Betjeman laugh; he always called him Rev Marcus. People are always much more excited when I say I worked for *Eagle* than for Betjeman.'

Beth Davisson was Marcus's secretary for eighteen months in 1952–3. 'Marcus wasn't always easy to work for. His hours were quite difficult. He wasn't a very good arriver in the mornings and tended to take rather long lunch hours. He was never the worse for wear afterwards and he then liked to work late in the evenings, which I didn't mind – it wasn't a nine to five job. Sometimes he didn't want to be bothered with people, or with what he considered to be frivolous points, he thought people should get on with things themselves. He knew what he wanted and saw that he got it, and he was usually right.

'I wouldn't have said his expenses were particularly high for the sort of job he had.'

Not all his secretaries were so forbearing. Liz Gregory: 'I left him at one point; I got fed up with him. He was giving me far too much aggro, coming in at 5.00 p.m. and doing a day's work. He was getting very demanding and rather awkward.

'Marcus always had problems about money; he was appalling. I was having to do all these expenses and was terrified. You had to make it all up. I did a lot of private and personal work, including the milkman who was constantly ringing up and saying if you don't pay the bill I'm going to take you to court. I paid most of the household bills. Jess was pretty busy at the time. You had to be prepared to do anything for him.

'He could be very difficult when he wanted to; once or twice he got pretty sharp with me. People who are brilliant are difficult to work for. It was very good training; if you could work for him you could work for anybody. I liked him, I found him attractive, he was fun, and he made life interesting. You couldn't be a wimp, you had to stand up to him.

'When I got married, Marcus wrote an ad for a new secretary which was typical of his humour: "Fleet Street Editor with prominent publishers requires hard-working secretary. This man is exacting. Indispensable qualifications are coolness, initiative, mind-reading, good shorthand and typing speeds. Five day week, at times hours are long. This is an interesting and stimulating job with high salary for right applicant." '

Gloria Dunn answered that ad: 'I was there in 1957, but not for long. He got rid of me because he realised I didn't approve of his expense accounts.

I can't accuse him of fiddling, in those days it was considered tax avoidance. The girl who was there before me taught me the dodges.

'I had to make sure there were vast quantities of drinks in my filing cabinet. He generally came back from lunch and lay down on the sofa and had a sleep. It was very irritating, he tended to call me in at half past four to take dictation and expected the letters to go out. I made it clear that I wasn't going to work late. Anybody who was well organised wouldn't be doing their work at 4.30 p.m. they'd do it at 10.30 a.m.

'He tended to be surrounded by yes-men and yes-women. He was very witty and talented and kind, but I didn't see that side. He didn't like me and the feeling was mutual. I found him very cold and unfriendly. In the staff club upstairs Marcus always ignored me completely.

'I should think that he was remarkably difficult to live with. He distanced people; it depended who you were. You could see him switching on the charm. I think I didn't like him because he didn't respond to my charm.

'He was a great snob. My husband was Chairman of the Arts Council and when Marcus saw us in their box at Covent Garden, he gave a tremendous double take and was much nicer to me than he'd ever been before, which was rather satisfactory. He preferred me as Lady Cottesloe than little miss nobody.'

Christine Bernard met Marcus through Wolf Mankowitz who was married to her best friend. She took over *Swift* in 1958: 'I enjoyed it immensely on *Swift*. Marcus was enormous fun, under that gloom and doom he was very funny. We all got on well in a quiet sort of way with him, nobody was singled out for special attention, he was sweet to all of us. He was a very hard man to dislike. Everyone was nice to Marcus because he looked so troubled and worried. When you knew him better you knew it was just his expression.

'I said to him once "Why are you always so sad?" which took him back a bit. He leant across the table and poked his finger at my cheek and said "You've got those muscles there, look, you smiled. I haven't got those muscles, I can't smile, it's very difficult for me, it hurts."

'Marcus put up with some fairly eccentric people quite uncritically. Maybe because he was eccentric himself. I found him impeccably well-mannered. He was never rude, but could be pretty preoccupied. He was always on the ball if it was a question that needed an instant answer. He was very good at letting you get on with it. Clifford threw his weight about a bit more. We didn't take too much notice of him. One was inclined to say, "Oh shut up Clifford, write it yourself if you don't like it." You wouldn't dream of saying that to Marcus.'

From Marcus Morris to Deaconess Phyllis Entwistle, 21 March 1955: 'Everything goes on much the same here. Jess is being kept pretty busy with various jobs for television and films, and I find life fairly hectic now I am looking after *Housewife* as well as the comics. The children are all flourishing, and send their love.'

Marcus was asked to become Managing Editor of *Housewife* in 1954. Instead of an increase in salary, which would have attracted even more income tax, the company, rather unwisely perhaps, gave him an account at Harrods with which to buy furniture at the company's expense; he was guaranteed a business trip cum holiday abroad each year; Jess was given a car (a black Ford Consul). Like so many of the promises made by Hulton Press, this arrangement didn't last long and, within eighteen months, Marcus was being billed direct by Harrods. He was usually late in paying, which resulted in statements being sent to Hultons; Company Secretary Jim Halliwell dropped a hint: 'I think it is very unwise for these statements to be constantly sent to Hulton Press, as the impression which arises therefrom is that Hulton Press are paying for your wife's personal purchases. I do not think that this impression is good for you or for Hulton Press.'

But Halliwell wasn't unsympathetic: 'I fully realise how much you are doing, particularly with the added burden of *Housewife*. On the other hand, I have a directive which requires me to keep expenses down and, as you incur higher expenses than any other executive I cannot avoid writing to you about them. You probably haven't realised how they mount up.'

And to the General Manager he wrote, 'Mr Morris assures me that he is doing his best to keep expenses down, but he finds it impossible to cope with the pressure of work except by making business appointments for lunch and dinner.'

*Housewife*, no longer pocket-sized, had been through various metamorphoses and by 1954, under the editorship of Olive Jones, it was fading fast. Jack Hargreaves, Editor of *Lilliput*, was moved over to try to inject some life into the magazine. He decided to change it completely, using fiction left over from *Lilliput* and commissioning articles by academics. The circulation fell still further.

At the beginning of April Marcus had written to Vernon Holding: 'I would regard this as a temporary assignment in the first place, lasting until such time as I have done the required job satisfactorily, or that it becomes clear that I cannot do it. I should still regard my primary function in the firm as being in charge of the children's papers. . . . I am not afraid of going into a hornets' nest. . . . I may be able to soften some of the stings. . . . I should prefer to avoid any friction with the person responsible. This depends on when and how he is told. . . . The person in my department who is being discussed in this connection will have a very valuable contribution to make. . . . I think it would be better for her to wait to go over when I can at least offer some kind of "protection".'

The person needing protection was Laurie Purden, whom Marcus intended to install as Editor in place of Jack Hargreaves. Jack retained a lifelong antipathy towards Marcus as a result.

Laurie had been Assistant Editor on *Woman's Own*, 'even so, it was very brave of him to give the job to a twenty-five-year-old. I happened to be one of the few professional journalists he worked with. He consciously didn't want them. He deliberately chose people who were going to be right and understood what he was trying to do. Although he wasn't able to express it, which was one of the difficulties, he had an absolute instinct for what was right and what was wrong.'

Pam Glanville started as secretary to Olive Jones and worked her way up to Chief Sub, eventually, through Marcus, becoming Beauty and Features Editor. 'I was terrified of him, but I was immensely happy there. Everything was so beautifully run and organised, one had a totally free hand. He wasn't glowering over one's shoulder all the time and criticising. I never heard him be destructively critical. Laurie ran the show and he was happy with that.

'When Marcus came to *Housewife* he revolutionised it. He turned it into a sophisticated intelligent women's magazine that was readable, that people felt comfortable with. The combination of Laurie and Marcus was magic. I think it was the flexibility he brought in which made everybody on the magazine happy.

'The only time I suddenly saw Marcus as nearly human was when I had my leaving party, he and Clifford came and sat at our table and he told me I looked like Gina Lollobrigida; for the first time it was a flirty thing and suddenly that impassive face had changed, the barrier came down.'

Audrey White, now Lady Wardington, was Fashion Editor of *Housewife* for six years. 'I met Marcus at one of Peter and Cherry Barker's parties. He said they were looking for a fashion editor and did I know anybody, and I said there must be millions who'd love to do it, I'd love to do it. Magically, to my amazement, I got the job having had no office experience at all. All I'd ever been was a photographic fashion model.

'I knew about fashion and knew all the photographers and models and the fashion houses, but I hadn't the faintest idea how you put those things together. After two months of absolute nightmare I went to Marcus and said it's hopeless, I can't do it, I can't cope, I don't know what I'm doing. He sat thinking about it then said I must give it more of a try. So I stayed and found it easier.'

Audrey used the Morris children as models and once a year photographers would take pictures of the girls for the *Girl* diary. This was in response to readers' complaints that a man couldn't possibly know about girls. To anyone acquainted with the family the sight of the three, smartly dressed in their school uniforms, sitting primly on father's lap, must have raised an eyebrow. They and some of their friends also modelled for advertisements for prizes, annuals and free gifts. It was cheaper than using a model agency.

Audrey: 'I remember Marcus saying he was worried about his image, he felt he needed a new overcoat. We had lunch on this overcoat. I don't think he was vain, just the opposite, he was unsure of himself, needed reassurance. That was the only time he came to me for fashion advice. We decided on a camel hair coat. I remember those days being very funny happy times.

'I asked him what he did at weekends and he said nothing, he used to stay in bed on Sundays with absolutely nothing to do. That seemed to me amazing with young children.' And it wasn't true; there were usually drinks or lunch parties on Sundays, not to mention services at St Bride's, or at St Jude's in Hampstead Garden Suburb, or at Hampstead parish church.

In 1955 there was an attempt to involve Hulton Press in the new world of commercial television. In January a subsidiary, Hulton Visual Productions, was set up to make and advise on TV programmes. Marcus wrote to Peter Barker, 'We want to be sure that with the features in the comics we have got TV rights wherever possible, but we also want to try and keep our clutches on contributors themselves from the point of view of appearing on television, to try and ensure that if, for example, John Ryan or Charles Chilton do anything for TV they do it through Hulton Visual Enterprises [*sic*]. I don't think at this stage we can offer them any retaining fee, but we might be able to get them to agree to give us the first option of handling them.'

The company put in a bid for one of the original independent TV companies, covering the North and Midlands at weekends, based on Hultons' contacts within the media, farming, children, general humour. The funding would come from Hulton and other big investors.

The first meeting to consider the Hulton tender was attended by Marcus and Peter Barker representing the children's papers and *Housewife*, Lionel Birch and Denzil Batchelor for *Picture Post*, Bagenal Harvey for Hulton Visual Productions, John Myers for Hulton Enterprises. Bernard Audley and Kenneth Adam represented the management. The report stated that 'The meeting was unanimous in believing that the greatest strength of the Group would lie in its knowledge of and performance in the children's field.

'Characteristic Northern variety must figure. . . . It should be possible for *Picture Post* reporters to become the Mayhews and Murrows of tomorrow. Trevor Philpott was thought to be particularly suitable in this respect.'

Marcus wrote on behalf of the Children's Department, 'We are convinced that it is possible and desirable to present to children the exciting and adventurous material they demand while at the same time confronting them with the right social and personal values.'

Proposals for children's programmes included dramatised Bible stories and carol services presented by Marcus, real life adventure stories, children's discussion programmes, elementary science and appearances by personalities such as Denis Compton, Macdonald Hobley, 'and many others who are connected with us'.

Dan Dare, Jack O'Lantern, Belle of the Ballet, Harris Tweed and Lettice Leefe were scheduled to make appearances. George Cansdale, Mac Hastings and 'Professor Brittain' would all take part.

There would be women's programmes, political discussions, and farming and the countryside would be given fifteen minutes 'without attempting to rival the fabulous success of *The Archers*'.

Sport was to have three periods during Saturday. 'We are struck by the absence of any regular Saturday afternoon sport in the ABC schedules. . . .'

Edward Hulton, Malcolm Messer, Vernon Holding, Kenneth Adam and Marcus represented Hulton Press at the interview with the Independent Television Authority on 23 August. The following day Kenneth Adam sent a memo to all those involved: 'You will like to know that Sir Kenneth Clark's introduction to our hearing yesterday was that the programme suggestions in our application had seemed to the Authority to be the best they had received. 'For your information, the Chairman's speech at the hearing made a very considerable impression.'

So what made Edward Hulton change his mind?

Sir Bernard Audley told us, 'Our application and tender was virtually awarded. I saw a letter from Sir Kenneth Clark, who was chairman of the ITA, to Edward Hulton saying how bitterly disappointed he was that Hultons had withdrawn the application, which was by far the best they'd received. If Hultons had secured that contract, with the depth of talent they had, they would have been one of the leading programme contractors in the UK and made the kind of money that Granada has made. Folklore has it that most of television was peopled initially by Hulton trained men and women who found themselves new jobs in 1955 when commercial TV started. There was suddenly a brain drain from Hultons – which there would not have been had the policies and strategies at Hultons been right.'

George Cooper was one of those who left the company after failing to persuade the Hultons to take up the contract. 'I had a lot of meetings with Nika; if she wanted something Edward would go along. The Authority were prepared to give them the contract, but the Hultons thought it would compete with their business. Nika was in New York with Bernard when I gave my notice to Hulton.'

Marcus was in New York as well.

Bernard: 'We went to the States with Nika. Marcus and I remained the firmest of allies. Malcolm Messer was with us. The first night we were there we swore a solemn oath that we would not be divided on any issue by this woman who would seek to spread alarm and despondency. We would present a solid front. Then Malcolm went off to see farmers in the mid-west leaving Marcus and me to deal with Nika and the Duchess of Westminster, the awful Loelia Ponsonby. We used to go round Harlem together in a limousine, looking at the terrible scene outside. Then we would go to the theatre. We went to see *The Chalk Garden* which to Marcus and me was utterly incomprehensible. Marcus had the temerity to say so in his rather diffident way to Loelia Ponsonby. She said "You and I don't speak the same language," to which I said, "Thank God for that". Marcus just disappeared into his beer, he didn't offer any challenge. His silence was more eloquent than any comment.'

Marcus wrote to Jess that 'most of the time is spent dancing attendance on Nika – until she gets launched in "society". It's all rather like a circus with Malcolm, Bernard and me as performing seals.'

Bernard continued: 'Marcus and I couldn't wait to get away from the oppressive presence of these two ghastly women, so we took off for Hollywood where we were looking into stories for *Picture Post* and *Eagle*. I'd got a wide brief and so had he. We were well looked after in Hollywood by Bob Ballin, hero of the Hucksters. Bob booked us into the Beverley Hills Hotel; when we got there our room was full of flowers. Bob Hope's PRO looked after us. Bob Hope came in, and Cary Grant; we were moving around among the stars. We were entertained on the set of *Carousel*, every night we'd go to the Brown Derby or Romanov's or Crescendo or the Interlude.

'It was there that I realised that Marcus had infinitely more stamina than I had. By about 3.00 in the morning I'd be ready to go, but Marcus was not, he'd stay up most of the night. He'd say, "What are you flaking out for, you're much younger than I am". He had immense stamina. Maybe a popper or two kept him going. He had hollow legs; I can drink but I wasn't in Marcus's class.

'Gresham's Law states that the Bad drives out the Good. Marcus turned it on its head. He was one of the few people who could do it, the Good actually drove out the Bad. For that to happen in Fleet Street is unique.'

1955 was a busy year; Marcus was asked to create a new Sunday paper in colour, to be known as the *Sunday Star*.

Peter Cooper: 'Once the idea grew that there was room for a Sunday paper no one was in any doubt who should be in charge of it. Clearly, the editorial genius of Hulton Press.'

Marcus wrote about the new venture, 'No criticism of our present Sunday papers *qua* papers intended, but Sunday journalism is a hot house of habits and clichés, even the best of the Sundays desperately seek new formulas, new lay-outs, new ideas, new personalities, new lights in old chancels.

'The appeal of the *Sunday Star* is the advent of full colour – the first time in a Sunday newspaper. I have heard this called a gimmick. Well, yes, but a gimmick which will probably become a commonplace in news photography before very long – a gimmick which in, shall we say, ten or even five years' time, no real national newspaper can afford to be without.

'The more important fundamental aspect is the content. Is it not true that there is a real need for a Sunday paper which steers a course between the presentation of the sensational and cynical side of life on the one hand, and the reactionary and the fatuously optimistic side on the other?'

According to the 'Ideas Committee', the *Star* was to be 'a reasonably clean paper, fit for all the family, with a positive attitude in its weekly message. It would not exclude glamour, medical advice, astrology etc., but it would search for additional overseas ideas to help its impact.'

Features were to include The World at a Glance, Politics for the Unpolitical, Leading Questions to Leading People, The World of the . . . postman, dust-man, policeman etc., Teenage Table Talk. The paper would embrace such topics as entertainment, sport, music, books, hobbies, health, gardening, cookery, fashion, science – and news.

Marcus prepared a dummy assisted by some of the staff working on the children's papers. He approached Norman Thelwell to do a cartoon in the style of Giles, social comment rather than political, and experiments were carried out to see if colour pages could be duplicated in London quickly enough for transfer to Bemrose in Liverpool. Costings were made (734 guineas for pictures alone in one dummy), but they didn't include any increase in salary for the newspaper's editor.

Edith wrote to Marcus in February 1956, just before Walter's retirement, 'It is a shame to worry you with our affairs when you are so very busy with your newspaper! If Hultons don't consider you more they will "kill the goose that laid the golden egg". It is too much altogether to expect from one man. You will have to strike! We are looking forward to seeing the *Sunday Star* – even *Punch* mentions it!'

All the top names in journalism were in and out of the office. A team was sent to Monaco to photograph the wedding of Prince Rainier and Grace Kelly; the photos were processed on the plane back and a dummy distributed to the newsagents by the weekend. Unfortunately that was as far as it got.

Victor Holt was Assistant General Secretary of the National Federation of Retail Newsagents at the time: 'Hultons announced the *Sunday Star* as the first colour Sunday newspaper, but . . . it was apparent to the retail trade that it would be a periodical, prepared mainly during the week and containing only a minimum of news.

'The retail margin on Sunday newspapers was considerably lower than that on periodicals and the NFRN saw the danger of a precedent being created . . . the National Council voted unanimously not to support the *Sunday Star* if published as a Sunday newspaper. . . .

'I suspect also that there would have been resistance from the Sunday newspaper publishers at an attempt by a known publisher of periodicals to enter the Sunday newspaper field. . . . I am of the opinion that Hulton Press could not have failed to anticipate some opposition, but were tempted by the prospect of very great rewards had they "got away with it". Had I been the publisher I too would have been tempted to have a go.'

Hultons were certainly well aware of the problem. A memo from James Hemming said, 'Skilful writing could make features seem immediately topical in spite of the production lag.'

Nevertheless, the company responded angrily: 'In our opinion the Federation's decision constitutes a very real threat to the whole industry. It means that no one can produce a new Sunday newspaper. . . . It is a disastrous situation if the initiative in launching new publications no longer lies with the publishers.'

Norman Thelwell said that when the project collapsed 'Marcus called me into his office and asked me if I'd mind foregoing my fee. I was a bit shocked about that, I thought it was unfair as I'd done the work. Marcus said, "That's perfectly all right, I just thought I'd ask".'

Marcus (and everyone else involved) was extremely disappointed, angry and frustrated at this waste of time and effort. He wrote, 'The idea was to give the people a positive, forward-looking paper they could enjoy without the ordeal of being written down to and treated as morons. As for the trade, we felt that here was a golden opportunity to stimulate their inert response to the present Sunday papers with a powerful bright new publication which would certainly bring them profit.'

In September 1956 Marcus wrote to his father, 'I have to go to East Africa on business for three weeks on Sunday next. I am going to Uganda first and then down to Kenya, Tanganyika and Rhodesia.' This was a fact-finding trip made with Keith Kotch, to explore the possibilities of a colour magazine for Africa.

The dummy was called *Wonder* and contained a somewhat patronising mix of hints on how to write a letter, a sports page, a simplified cut-away, news from other parts of Africa and comic strips, including 'David The Boy King', with sub-titles – an African version of *Swift*. The Editor was Marcus Morris, but this was yet another aborted project.

The journey wasn't completely wasted; Marcus brought back a new dance, the High Life, which he taught to his daughters. Postcard from Kampala, Uganda, to Jessica Dunning c/o BBC Birmingham: 'We are terribly busy seeing people all the time and it's all very respectable. No high life. . . . Hope you're being good Darling.'

Jess replied to Meikles Hotel, Salisbury, 'Me, I'm being very good; I jolly well hope you are – I notice you disclaim High Life, but say nothing about Low Life! . . . I'm writing this in bed, with your briefcase as a rest – in fact I've been going to bed with your briefcase for the last week – a curious perversion. I miss you quite *dreadfully* – although it's only nine days since the best bit of pillow-craft we've ever had. . . . '

At the company's 1957 AGM the Chairman cut the dividend and reported a slide in profits from £298,000 to £36,000. He blamed the losses on reduced revenue from *Picture Post* and increased costs of production. It could also have had something to do with the money wasted on the *Sunday Star* and the cost of his new office building in Fleet Street. The foundation stone of Hulton House had been laid in May 1955 and it was reported in *Picture Post* to be the first building erected in Fleet Street since the war; Ruari McLean designed the lettering on the fascia. Hulton House was opened on 14 February 1957 with a luncheon at which the Lord Mayor of London and Marcus gave speeches. Edward Hulton had just been awarded a knighthood by Harold MacMillan.

Not long afterwards, Vernon Holding, by then General Manager of the company and a good friend of Marcus's, was dismissed after an acrimonious row with Nika. Marcus took Vernon's side in the dispute, which did not improve his relations with the Hultons. They began to mistrust him; he began to think of leaving, even toying with the idea of moving to the *Express* or the *News of the World*. He started to feel isolated when another friend, Assistant General Manager Keith Kotch, left to go into partnership with Holding.

James Hemming wrote to Marcus in May: 'After the way you have been treated it would not be unprincipled for you to take any course of action to escape from the intolerable situation in which the Hultons have placed you. . . . I cannot but be apprehensive. . . . It might be felt by people not knowing the inside story that you were betraying something of value in order to secure your own future. . . . The bugger of it is that there is no way of getting the truth across in these situations. . . . If you were to stay, there should be a direct act of approach to the Hultons on your part. . . . Once the paranoic attitude in relation to you had been cleared, they would become less dependent on boot-lickers.'

Everything seemed suddenly to be going wrong with the company and the Hultons turned on Marcus as a scapegoat.

In 'a direct act of approach', Marcus agreed to join an Administration Committee 'although I recognise that such Committee must be regarded only as "first aid" treatment in what is essentially a very difficult situation. My main object, of course, is to serve the best interests of the Company, but you will recognise that I must always reserve to myself the right to have my own opinions which may not necessarily agree with those of yourself or the other members of the Committee. In this sense the position I have now agreed to take on is outside the competence of my Service Agreement.'

The other members of the Interim Management Committee were John Myers, Len Spooner and Jim Halliwell. Marcus insisted that accurate minutes were kept of the meetings; between March and the end of July they discussed the purchase of venetian blinds, the possibility of buying a bookshop in Nairobi and a publishing company in Eire, the sacking of a member of staff for peeing in a desk drawer while drunk, the distribution of *Studio* and *Art & Industry* magazines and the purchase and sale of company cars. They also 'agreed that JH write short letter accepting resignation of Frank Hampson. Agreed that we can cope adequately (and perhaps more cheaply) without Epsom studio (2/4/57).'

Three days later Frank Hampson telephoned to withdraw his resignation and the Committee agreed to explore his proposals for the development of Dan Dare. The syndication of early Dan Dare strips in black and white was one possibility.

One of the Committee's main topics of discussion was how to save *Picture Post*. It had been losing circulation since Tom Hopkinson was sacked in 1950 in a dispute with Edward Hulton over a feature about the Korean War. Editor had followed editor, all subject to the Hultons' whims and none was strong enough to stand up for himself. Advertising was being sold on Audit Bureau of Circulation figures of 740,000 copies, but only 520,000 were being printed. When the new ABC figures were due out, a true report would have halved the advertising rate.

Nika had attempted to sell *Picture Post* the previous year. She held clandestine talks, accompanied by Len Spooner, with a Swiss company; she even asked Trevor Philpott to put together a proposal for revamping the magazine, but the discussions came to nothing. *Picture Post* staff photographer John Chillingworth was ordered to go with them on one of these trips to Switzerland; he thought, to provide her with his travel allowance. When she told him of her plans and said that his future with the magazine was assured, he went home and resigned.

Peter Cooper said, 'Nika became frightened. If she'd weathered the storm *Picture Post* would still be alive today. Hulton was in a combination of alcoholic and sexual slavery to her. He did whatever she wanted.' She offered it to the *Sunday Times* as a colour supplement and to *Paris Match*, with her husband as editor-in-chief. Negotiations foundered because she conducted them herself.

The thirtieth meeting of the Interim Management Committee on 15 May 1957 was informed that the Chairman had decided to close *Picture Post* without delay; it was left to the Committee members to inform the unions and the staff. Edward Hulton publicly blamed increased costs, wage rates and commercial television.

In June the Board passed a vote of thanks and confidence in the Interim Management Committee but, at the end of July, it was reported that the Chairman (in effect, Nika) was contacting staff over the heads of the Committee, as well as making announcements in the trade press. The IMC was doomed.

Marcus was by now also running the Projects Department and the Book Department.

Confidential memo from Clifford Makins to MM: 'Just before lunch today, Rumbold [John Rumbold, Nika Hulton's assistant] – on Lady Hulton's behalf – asked me to do a personal report on WREN. This had to be done immediately for immediate presentation to her Ladyship by 2 p.m.'

*Wren* was to be a paper for girls aged eight to eleven. '*Girl* is now definitely slanted towards the older girl between thirteen and sixteen. . . . Would the paper succeed if we lavished on it all the energies and special skills and know-how which the Children's department under Marcus Morris undoubtedly possesses?! . . . Personally I think it would go. Marcus Morris I believe is understandably more cautious but I know he thought quite highly of this first dummy.'

There was talk of producing an adult strip cartoon magazine 'which makes it possible for the average man to assimilate the news and information in an easy and quickly-read form' and Marcus suggested a magazine for teenage girls. Advertisers were becoming aware of the spending power of that age group, 'I am hoping to persuade my Board to consider the matter again.' Perhaps he was influenced by his own now-teenage daughters.

Other ideas included a weekly science comic for ten to fourteen-year-olds, a science magazine for twelve to sixteen-year-olds and a monthly science magazine for fifteen to nineteen-year-olds. James Hemming talked about a paper for boys aged sixteen to twenty-five: 'Now seems to me to be the time to get going. A gap already exists; this will be widened by the coming legislation against imported comics. . . .'

By November 1957 there were twenty-two projects in hand, including *Teenager, Weekender, Woman, Young Man, European Trade, Children's Book Club, Hobbyhorse*, a 'make and do' magazine and a shopping magazine. Later, a dummy was produced for a space magazine.

At the beginning of 1958 Marcus was asked to undertake the Managing Editorship of *Lilliput*, a position he held for only a few months and for which he was paid £500. James Hemming had written to him the previous July, '*Lilliput* is tatty at present. . . . It is over formularised and hasn't an idea in it anywhere . . . so immature that it . . . writes down about women. . . . The robust, the Rabelaisian, the complex in man-woman relationships do not appear. . . . I have little doubt that you can knock it into shape.

'You are now inching forward into a quite new position in the firm. To fill this role effectively you will need to be left as free as possible for top-level editorial planning, but yet you must not get completely cut-off from the papers and projects for which you are responsible.'

Marcus knocked *Lilliput* into shape and increased its advertising revenue, although nothing could be done for its circulation due, Marcus thought, to lack of investment.

In February 1958 the Management Committee was dissolved and it was publicly announced that Sir Edward Hulton, as Chairman and Managing Director, had appointed Marcus and Len Spooner as his Chief Executives 'and has asked Lady Hulton to work with them in the same capacity', responsible to the Chairman and the Board of Directors.

Peter Cooper told us, 'Meetings of the Executive Committee were quite incredible. Lady Hulton was a panther, a tigress, her language was appalling and she was not above physical assault. She encouraged Halliwell to buy an expensive house and then sacked him; she scratched his face from forehead to chin.' She also threw a typewriter at John Rumbold.

When Tom Hopkinson left Hulton Press in 1950, the *Observer* wrote: 'Hopkinson is not the first editor to find that Hulton alternates between long periods of accepting advice, and sudden irrevocable decisions of his own.'

There had been the night of the long knives in January 1953, when four directors (W.J. Dickenson, John Pearce, Maxwell Raison and Bertram Ogle) had been forced to resign from the Board when they tried to prevent Nika interfering in the business. Marcus suffered his own knife in the back when, in the autumn of 1958, Sir Edward informed Marcus that he wished him to give up management and concentrate his activities on the children's papers. He wrote that 'it is unfair to expect you . . . to devote part of your time to management'. Naturally enough, in view of all his past experience and responsibility, that didn't suit Marcus at all.

Horrified by Hulton Press's declining profits (down to £11,000 the previous year), Nika had started looking round for a company that could take it over. What the Hultons didn't need was a Chief Executive to get to know about their negotiations and, possibly, interfere.

There was an unsatisfactory exchange of correspondence between

Marcus and Edward Hulton, in which Hulton refused to spell out exactly what he wanted from Marcus. Marcus pointed out how difficult it was to 'make a worthwhile contribution to the firm' when 'it is known throughout the firm that you no longer seek my advice'. He said that staff morale was generally low and that 'there is a limited future in comics such as *Eagle*. . . . The comics are not sufficient by themselves to occupy my interests and energies. . . . I would now like to devote my energies . . . to adult journalism and to editorial management. . . . It may be necessary for us to consider terms for my leaving Hulton Press.'

In December Marcus arranged a meeting with Sir Edward, at which he proposed to offer his resignation unless he was given an increase in salary, was made a Director (which he had first suggested three years before), was given editorial control of all Hulton publications apart from *Farmers Weekly*, all restrictions on outside activities were removed, and he was allowed to develop new projects.

The meeting never took place, owing to the offer made by Odhams for the shares of Hulton Press.

# Chapter Fifteen

The late 1950s and early 1960s were years of great turmoil in the newspaper and magazine publishing business. In 1958 Amalgamated Press, the largest magazine publishing house in Britain, had been bought by the *Daily Mirror* group, run by Cecil Harmsworth King, nephew of the founder of Amalgamated Press, Lord Northcliffe. The purchase included children's magazines such as *Jack and Jill, Playhour, Girls' Crystal, Tiger, Lion* and the *Children's Newspaper*. Not long before this takeover, Odhams Press had made an abortive attempt to obtain part of Amalgamated.

Hugh (now Lord) Cudlipp, at that time second in command to Cecil King, wrote in his book *At Your Peril*: 'Out-manoeuvred, outbid, the angry board of Odhams Press searched elsewhere. . . . Barely two months after the news that Amalgamated was firmly in the *Mirror*'s bag, the boards of Odhams and Hulton Press issued a joint announcement that Odhams were making a £1,800,000 offer for the entire capital of Hulton Press.

'By this take-over Odhams signalled that they were preparing and were eager for the great competitive struggle heralded by the *Mirror*'s capture of AP . . . the notable children's comics . . . would strengthen Odhams in one of its weaker fields.

'Hultons' shareholders were no doubt delighted by this development. For a long time the firm had been hovering between profit and loss, and the previous year no dividend had been paid.'

On 14 March 1959 Odhams wrote to the Directors of Hulton Press (Edward, Nika, Malcolm Messer and E.J. Lowman) formally offering to acquire the company. As Edward and Nika between them held nearly 59 per cent of Hulton shares, they made about £1,000,000 out of the deal.

In his memoirs, *Strictly Personal*, published in 1969, Cecil King wrote: 'Sir Edward Hulton, from his contribution to publishing, must have derived a fortune of not less than two million for himself and his family. Others whose contribution to the publishing industry might seem as great have enjoyed no such spectacular rewards.' The *Daily Mail* reported that Edward's fortune had increased to £3,000,000.

As Sir Bernard Audley put it, 'The Hultons became starved of cash and destroyed a company which was put together by W.J. Dickenson, Max Raison and Stefan Lorant, using Teddy's father's money. What had been put together by others they dismantled. All the things that people had identified with, taken such pride in, given their lives to, were sold off like a mess of potage.'

Nika was allowed to keep the trade and technical papers – *Production Equipment Digest, Garage and Transport Equipment* and *Shipbuilding Equipment* – the first controlled-circulation magazines in this country, which had been started by George Cooper. (In 1979 Bernard Audley bought the magazines, together with the name Hulton Press.)

In May Odhams added George Newnes (fifty publications including

*Woman's Own, Homes and Gardens, Country Life* and *Tit-Bits*), to their stable, becoming the world's biggest periodical publishers.

Odhams' newspaper the *Daily Herald* quoted the company's chairman, A.C. (Pat) Duncan, as saying, 'We shall certainly carry on everything that is running successfully. I do not anticipate staff being reduced, or anything of that sort, but I am not making any promises.'

Marcus not unreasonably assumed that Odhams would make him an offer of a directorship of Hulton Press. He went to see the Chairman of Odhams and asked more or less what he had been going to ask Sir Edward. Pat Duncan was unable or unwilling to make any promises. Ruari McLean wrote, 'In his first interview with the Directors of Odhams, Marcus was told that they were sure they would get along all right together "provided you run along our tram lines".

' "The trouble is," Marcus said to me afterwards, "I am not a tram." '

There was worse to come.

In February, before the takeover, Frank Hampson had been offered a job by Amalgamated Press at twice his Hulton salary. As Marcus explained later to Len Spooner, 'Frank brought this offer to me on 5 March and after some discussion I persuaded him to refuse it.

'In return for his refusing I agreed that (a) He would be given three months' [paid] holiday as soon as it could be arranged. (b) That one of these months should be on a business trip to America at the Company's expense. (c) That he should come off Dan Dare. (d) That in future he should draw for us only one page per week – in colour or black and white – of a completely new story.

'It seemed to me – as indeed it still does – essential that Amalgamated Press should be prevented from obtaining Hampson's services with the considerable attendant publicity advantage to them.'

Marcus wrote to Frank, 'I will send a proper detailed letter of agreement next week. This is just to confirm briefly that it is agreed that you be released from drawing Dan Dare as soon as this can be arranged and that after three months' leave, you then will be responsible for providing one page a week for EAGLE, either black and white or colour. 'You will retain the services of Joan Porter and you will be free to do other work, except for other children's papers.'

Frank wrote on 14 April, 'Many thanks for the prompt despatch of the cheque, which has already been put to use. . . . With regard to the USA trip I suggest that I should go as soon as possible after handing over the strip. I will then be right out of the way while everyone is discovering that I did everything wrong – the inevitable fate of any person handing over any job after ten years! . . .

'May I suggest that I should have three main objects to accomplish over there: (1) To investigate production methods in the Cartoon studios of Walt Disney, The Lone Ranger Organisation and individual cartoonists such as Milton Caniff and Hal Foster. (2) To collect material from both the story and pictorial angles for future strip stories. (3) To obtain any experience it may be possible to arrange of Rocket firings and development work at US testing grounds. This on the grounds that this has been my "field" for ten years, and may well turn out to be so again. (I would also like to take some of my original Dan Dare pages with me and see if I could get some authoritative advice on how we could adapt to attack the American Market – I still have that bee in my bonnet.)

'For the main purpose of my visit – the stimulation and refreshment of my creative faculties, I would prefer a sort of circular tour by train and/or coach to darting hither and yon in airplanes, which are pictorially bankrupt. . . . Best wishes, Yours, Frank. PS. Would, of course, postpone the US trip until later if there was any chance that you could accompany me yourself.'

On 7 May Marcus wrote again to Len Spooner: 'With reference to the memo I sent you about Frank Hampson and his trip to America, I have had a note from the Company Secretary to the effect that it is "beyond his competence" to carry out my instructions [to book Frank on a ship to the US].

'I had certainly assumed that this matter was an editorial one and that since in fact it arose before the Odhams take-over was announced, could be proceeded with. However, if you feel that this should be raised with Odhams perhaps you would be good enough to do so.'

On the same day Frank wrote to Peter Cooper regarding arrangements for the trip, 'My friend Sam Mann, in Quebec, will be delighted to put me up [on condition that] Dorothy should accompany me. This has already been suggested by Marcus, but I am still trying to persuade Dorothy that she can, in fact, leave Peter for such a period. I am now more hopeful of succeeding.'

The following week, Marcus had a meeting with John Walters, the new Acting General Manager of Hultons, to discuss the trip and met with a flat rejection.

Afterwards, he wrote to Walters emphasising the main points of his argument, 'There was no question of "blackmail" on Hampson's part. Indeed, the trip to America seemed to me – and still seems – a reasonable concession to make, since he was not asking for any more salary. . . . I therefore gave my promise to Hampson. It seems clear to me that a moral and probably a legal obligation exists. . . . Frank Hampson . . . is certainly the best strip cartoonist in the country.'

Marcus also wrote to Charles Shard, Joint Managing Director of Odhams: 'Since I have known Frank for many years I was able to persuade him to reject the offer at the very last moment, because I felt that it would have been a very great loss to us and a very great triumph for Hugh Cudlipp, who is planning a new boys' paper to compete with *Eagle*. . . .

'This decision was one which I felt, and still feel, was entirely within my authority as Editor and in the best interest of the papers I edit. . . . I could not agree to my promise being dismissed in this fashion.

'I find it incomprehensible that a matter which affects my personal integrity should be dealt with in such a cavalier fashion.'

We have no record of Charles Shard's reply, but Frank didn't get his trip to America. Odhams managed to wriggle out of the deal on the very flimsy premiss that the agreement had not been in writing. Frank wrote to Marcus: 'Your news came as a bombshell. Unfortunately I am so tied up with the amount of work that has to be completed by this weekend, that I cannot possibly get away from here. I'm having to summon every last ounce to cope. I have, however, written to John Roberts [his solicitor] as you suggested.

'It seems unthinkable to me, after all the lifeblood I've poured into Dan Dare, that the firm should even contemplate welching on arrangements for which I turned down a three year £22,500 contract.'

Bart Smith agreed that Marcus had been quite within his rights to negotiate with Frank: 'It seems clear that Hampson . . . has been prejudiced. . . . If any proceedings are taken by Hampson against Hulton Press then I presume you would give evidence on behalf of Hampson.'

Marcus needn't have felt so guilty, however, since it seems that the deal between Frank and Amalgamated Press wouldn't have materialised anyway. According to Joan Porter, AP wanted Frank to produce a whole new children's magazine, from ideas, to visuals and the actual drawing. Frank didn't want to be lumbered with the whole production, but felt he could produce a magazine if he didn't have to draw.

Leonard Matthews, in charge of the negotiations for Amalgamated Press, told us: 'I heard that Frank wasn't very happy. We had several sessions; Frank said "All right, I'll leave and come over". He was offered £7,000 p.a., more than I was getting as a Director, more than the head of the group, who was incensed. I said if we want him we've got to pay for him. Frank got more and more difficult about it. When I told him we were looking forward to having his drawings he said, "My drawings? I don't draw any more, I have artists working for me." I said, "If we're going to pay you all this money, I don't want other artists whose services I can obtain a lot cheaper if I want to, I want you as an artist." He said, "I'm not going to do any more drawings." That was that.'

So Frank stayed, unhappily, at Hulton Press.

Just as distressing to Marcus was the threatened loss of his home. As part of the deal between Odhams and the Hultons, Edward and Nika were given the option, for three months, to buy the house in Wildwood Rise. Marcus thought that this clause was inserted out of spite. The Hultons didn't take it up, but the whole matter created uncertainty for the family, and it left a nasty taste.

During that spring and early summer edicts came down from on high with monotonous regularity. Executives were forbidden to take company-owned cars abroad on holiday; the practice of signing restaurant bills 'will cease . . . with immediate effect'; the Accounts Department decided that Marcus had been under-charged for rent of The Oak House for the past four years and, probably the last straw for Marcus, 'In keeping with the practice of the Odhams Group, you will in future draw fixed expenses at the rate of £1,500 per annum, payable monthly. This puts you in line with all the other top Executives in the Group.'

Marcus replied to John Walters: 'I have already made it clear to you that there were certain arrangements in existence as between myself and Hulton Press which were part of an overall arrangement, and your present requirements do not accord with those already existing.'

Marcus's expenses for 1958/59 covered entertainment, travel (mainly to carol services and speaking engagements), hotel accommodation and foreign trips, including a family holiday. His expense account had been agreed with the Hultons to mitigate tax liabilities; such a drastic decrease meant, in effect, a substantial loss of salary.

The acrimony between Marcus and senior Odhams management increased by the week. Marcus wrote to Walters in June, 'I cannot be a party to any arrangement whereby promises solemnly given are broken deliberately.

'Your attitude in the Hampson matter, coupled with the general directions I am now receiving, are wholly inconsistent with the implied terms of my Service Agreement with the previous management of Hulton Press. These arose, not out of goodness of heart, but substantially because I gave to Hulton Press assets which now have a capital value of hundreds of thousands of pounds.

'In the circumstances, it seems that I have no alternative but to ask that we part company. It is obviously in the interests of all concerned that this should be done amicably.'

By the beginning of August, relations between John Walters and Marcus had deteriorated to the extent that Clifford Makins was appointed Editorial Advisor to Walters, over Marcus's head, and to Clifford's embarrassment. Marcus wrote formally to the Joint Managing Directors asking to be released from his contract, which still had some three years to run.

Throughout August they argued about the terms of release, the main sticking points being the arrangement with Hultons to sell The Oak House to Marcus at a written-down price and the repayment of the £2,500 'loan' in relation to the sale of the Marcus Morris trademark. In spite of a letter from Vernon Holding confirming that the 'loan' was in fact cash to be paid free of liability, Odhams refused to honour the agreement.

After a month or so of acrimonious correspondence Marcus agreed to a vague, unpaid, consultancy and Odhams waived both repayment of the so-called loan and an undertaking not to be associated with women's magazines. The company no doubt realised that Marcus could have done serious damage to the children's papers if he had been so minded. He left Hulton Press on 30 September 1959, just short of ten years after John Pearce sent that telegram to Southport.

Peter Cooper said, 'We didn't have much time for a whip-round, but I managed to get enough to buy him a silver Dunhill lighter with MM engraved on it. At his goodbye party Paddy Campbell turned to me and said, "There's the Reverend Benzedrine." He was at the time popping a couple of pills as was his wont.'

Jean Crouch thought that Marcus was treated abominably. 'The new owners wanted to get him out. The Accounts Department would refuse his expenses and send them back through the office, not even in an envelope, so everybody could look at them. His expense account was where it hit him. Maurice Richardson said the sell-out was like being castrated and orphaned all at once. Everyone gathered in El Vino's. I decided that my time was limited. Odhams had *Girlfriend*, I knew that *Girl* wouldn't last long. But the readers made such a fuss, they kept it going.'

Charles Pocklington reckoned that 'trouble with the management came just before Marcus left. We'd go in to him and outline our grievances; it was felt right down to the lettering artists. Marcus would listen to everything you said and you'd get no answer. You felt he appreciated what our problems were and understood them but there was nothing he could do about it.'

On 31 October 1959 the *Eagle* Editor's Letter was signed Marcus Morris for the last time: 'This is probably the last Editor's letter I shall write to you. After nearly ten years, I am giving up my position as Editor of *Eagle* and its companion papers.

'But your favourite "Comics" will go on as before – and I am sure will continue to flourish. They are in the good hands of people who have worked with me for many years to make your papers as exciting and interesting and enjoyable as you tell me you find them. The traditions and the quality we have established will be carried on.

'Meanwhile, thank you for your support and friendship – and for your many thousands of letters. Good luck to you all.'

*Eagle* fan Graham Page can still remember the shock he felt on reading those words: '*Eagle* without Marcus Morris? It didn't seem possible. . . . I was relieved that *Eagle* was indeed in good hands.'

The 'good hands' were those of Clifford Makins, who became Editor-in-Chief of the four children's papers. According to Charles Pocklington, 'Clifford was terrific. He was much more approachable – we had more meetings with him than with Marcus. Clifford was more hands on – and fighting to save it. We did a lot of work with Derek Lord trying to launch another *Eagle*, called *Galaxy*. That was how desperate we felt about it.'

Marcus didn't immediately sever all links; there were carol services booked, talks, competitions to judge, a review of the *New English Bible* to write for *Eagle*: 'You will find reading the New Testament now no more difficult than any of the good modern books you are used to reading. . . . The Bible was not written in order to be beautiful. It is not the fine-sounding language that matters. What matters is what it *means*. The important thing is to have the Bible in plain English which does not hide the truths it tells behind a barrier of beautiful out-of-date language.'

He changed his mind later.

Marcus only managed to take five carol services that year; he wrote letters of apology, 'As I hope Chad Varah explained to you, I have just taken on a new job and, on that particular day, it was impossible to get away.

'I am however keeping up my connections with the children's papers and hope to be able to do some, if not all, of the carol services next year.'

The Dean of Manchester replied, 'From what you say I gather that the new ownership is not likely to dispense with the services which have now become an annual event.'

Jess wrote to Jan: 'Has anyone told you about the carol service? Sally and Simon did well, though Simon I thought not quite as well as last year. Why *will* they give that embarrassing Annunciation reading to the smallest boys? It's so *long* too. Sue Messer was splendid and made the best spoonerism for a long time – you know the appalling "modern" translation they use – which for Luke 2 runs "She gave birth to her first child, a son". And Sue said "she gave birth to her first son – a child". It was very funny and she didn't bat an eyelash. There were no high jinks after the service, tea, but no rushing up and down in lifts – Odhams can't afford the electricity! Or drinks for the grown-ups!'

Marcus had been asked to script the life of Christ for the back page of *Eagle*, to be drawn by Frank Hampson. But he was too busy getting to grips with his new job and turned to the Revd Guy Daniel.

Guy was only too pleased to supplement his stipend by scripting what would be a long running serial, even though Hulton Press couldn't let him have a by-line; it was Marcus's name they wanted. 'Up to a point I resented not getting a by-line, but I was writing for money and it brought in £10 a week, which paid the school fees. If I'd known Marcus was getting £20, I might have asked for £15. He did a certain amount of revising to start with but after the first few weeks he was happy to let me carry on.'

'The Road of Courage' ended, appropriately, at Easter 1961, after fifty-six weeks, and Guy asked Clifford Makins for a chance to do another script. Clifford said that it was still Marcus's prerogative to decide what went on the back page. Marcus decided that Guy should do the story of Sir Walter Raleigh, drawn by Robert Ayton, and this time Guy and Marcus had a joint by-line.

The last collaboration, if that's the right word, between Guy and Marcus was the *Robin Bible Stories* which were brought out in two volumes, Old and New Testament, by Longacre Press in 1961 (copyright Marcus Morris, for a change). 'I didn't do the whole lot, Marcus's father did some.' Walter (who was paid in bottles of whisky) sent in his copy in his own tiny handwriting but did not get a by-line – and neither did Guy: 'I was disappointed in them, they were just a re-hash of the old Bible stories which anybody could turn out; but it was what was wanted.'

Whatever the shortcomings of the text, the illustrations by Ann and Janet Graham Johnstone were delightful.

'The Road of Courage' was (almost) the last strip that Frank Hampson drew for *Eagle*. He was sent to Palestine to research the scenery and the atmosphere and the people, although, as Guy Daniel said, Palestine had changed a lot in 2,000 years. Frank no longer had the big studio, but he still had Joan Porter, who was interested in the era and undertook most of the research. She found suitable models and costumes, took photographs and coloured Frank's visuals. She compiled a notebook of items and locations to be checked by Frank in Palestine. Frank became totally immersed and fascinated, checking and noting and sketching. A television programme in 1991 on the life of Christ showed illustrations from Leonardo da Vinci, Michelangelo and Frank Hampson's 'Road of Courage'.

When there was talk of bringing it out as a book, Guy, Frank and Joan wrote and suggested that they should have a share of the proceeds. Bagenal Harvey was not at all happy about that; he was then acting as Marcus's agent.

But Marcus wrote to Frank,' You probably know that Odhams have the option [to publish 'Road of Courage' as a book] which must be exercised within a year. If they do publish it they will pay me a royalty, and it may be possible to persuade them to pay you one too, although you are on the staff. If this is not possible, I will share my royalty with you.

'If, on the other hand, Odhams don't take up the option and I can find another publisher to do it, then you, like myself, would be paid whatever royalty the publisher concerned will let us have. Out of this royalty we, of course, shall have to pay a royalty to Odhams for the right to do the book. Assuming that we each receive equal royalties from the publisher, then presumably we shall equally share the pain of the royalty to Odhams.'

In the event the book never materialised; Marcus approached two publishers in the mid-1960s, who both turned it down. In 1981 a facsimile edition was brought out by a small publishing company, but no royalties were forthcoming.

The regime under Odhams was not draconian; things continued more or less as before, although the Clubs were discontinued at the beginning of 1960 and the Girl Ballet Scholarship Scheme was ended; Odhams decided they were too expensive. They had also decided that the Hampson studio in Epsom cost far too much.

Keith Watson joined the Dan Dare team only a year or so before it was disbanded: 'Frank Hampson and Marcus Morris were my heroes. After six years of drawing Dan Dare for my own amusement I finally got up the nerve to apply for a job on *Eagle*. It was a very exciting experience to meet two almost mythical figures. Frank was looking to expand the Dan Dare studios, he had ideas of branching out in other directions including an animated film of Dan Dare.'

When Frank gave up Dan Dare (the last episode to be signed by him came out in August 1959), 'The rest of the team were moved to Hulton House to work under Frank Bellamy. He was told by Marcus to change Dan Dare, to give it "a new dimension". So Bellamy did his first page and radically changed it and Marcus and Clifford didn't think it looked enough like Dan Dare and gave it to Don Harley to change and work on. Bellamy was shattered by this. He didn't believe in Hampson's factory system, he believed in one artist sitting at his board. Bellamy was a brilliant artist, but Dan Dare had been more than just the skill and talent of one artist. The thoroughness and care was being lost.'

'When it was announced that Marcus was leaving Hulton Press, I was crestfallen. He *was Eagle*, he represented everything that *Eagle* stood for. While he was in charge, *Eagle* was always going to be *Eagle*. It seemed to be a very ominous development. The day he left he came round the office and shook hands with people. I was concerned that he might not be pleased with me because of our disagreements about Dan Dare, but he shook hands and smiled, and for the first time I saw the warm and friendly side of him. In that minute I got to know him better than I had in two years.'

October 1959 saw the culmination of another of Marcus's fights with the Odhams hierarchy – *Swift* was amalgamated with *ZIP*, an Odhams comic. Marcus was against the merger and many readers agreed with him. One wrote, 'I don't like *Swift* since it changed editors.'

Derek Lord took over the Assistant Editorship of *Eagle* from Clifford. 'We got on quite well; Odhams weren't that bad, they let us get on with it.'

But catastrophe happened when Fleet Street again became a battleground.

In the autumn of 1960, the new Chairman of Odhams, Sir Christopher Chancellor, offered the company's newspapers to Roy Thomson (later Lord Thomson of Fleet). Thomson suggested a merger of the two companies and was turned down flat.

Odhams then proposed a takeover of the Mirror Group's Fleetway periodicals and magazines, which in turn was countered by a proposal from Cecil King for a merger of the Mirror and Odhams. Chancellor revived the talks he had been having with Roy Thomson. By the end of January 1961, Odhams and Thomson Newspapers had agreed a merger. The following day, the Mirror Group made a takeover bid for Odhams, topping Thomson's offer considerably. Roy Thomson withdrew from the battle.

On 22 March 1961, after increasingly hostile negotiations and questions in Parliament, it was announced that 90 per cent of Odhams shareholders had accepted the Mirror group offer for the company. Odhams, and Hulton Press, had been gobbled up.

This takeover destroyed Hulton Press. From being a small, friendly, exciting, go-ahead company with twelve publications (including *Sporting Record*, *Disc*, *Football* and *The Studio*), Hulton Press became an insignificant part of a conglomerate, the International Publishing Corporation, which produced over 200 magazines, newspapers and 'juvenile' publications. *Eagle, Girl, Swift* and *Robin* were now lumped together in the Mirror's Fleetway division with such comics as *Jack and Jill* and *Lion*.

Derek Lord: 'The takeover was fought valiantly by the Trade Unions, with the help of several MPs, and I remember attending a huge meeting sponsored by the National Union of Journalists at Westminster, to try to find means of halting the thoroughly undemocratic creation of a monopoly.'

Christine Bernard, who was editing *Swift* and *Robin*, remembers heated meetings of the NUJ. She was convinced that the Union didn't put up enough of a fight to protect its members. When the NUJ backed down Christine threw in her union card and never rejoined. The Mirror Group were forced to take on existing Odhams staff, but too often in inferior positions in the hope that people would resign. 'I was very sad to leave the papers, I loved them. I think I was offered a job on the annuals, but I couldn't bear to be doing anything else so I resigned.'

Clifford described it as 'a time of real hell. I was left with a bloody shambles.'

Leonard Matthews was in charge of the Mirror's Fleetway children's comics when the Mirror took over Odhams. He said that Cecil King asked him what he was intending to do with Hulton Press and the *Eagle* group. Matthews replied that he was in charge of Fleetway juveniles and nothing to do with Hulton Press. ' "Oh yes you are," said Cecil, "last Friday you were elected a member of Hultons' board." "Nobody told me," I said. "I'm awfully sorry, that's the way things are done here," replied Cecil.'

Leonard Matthews says that he didn't take a lot of interest in the *Eagle* group. 'I acquired it and left it alone. I didn't seek to impose any form of government. They were doing very well without me and I took a back seat. I tried not to interfere with the editorial, I don't remember having anything to do with the content.'

But other people involved saw things differently; Derek Lord claimed that, 'backed by the Mirror men, such as Cudlipp – who knew a lot about daily newspapers but nothing at all about children's weeklies – Leonard Matthews wormed his way into a personal takeover of our four titles and imposed his autocratic rule upon us.'

Matthews sent a memo to Clifford Makins: 'I have informed the Managing Editors that there is no reason why they should not meet you to discuss any matters. I suggest that this will be a happy working arrangement.'

Clifford replied that he would arrange for three Fleetway executives 'to enlarge on their ideas with Miss Garland, Mrs Jackson and Mr Lord'. He added that he had reservations about certain proposed changes; that colour pages should be used exclusively for editorial and that four and a half pages of advertising in a 20-page issue was excessive. 'If we allow advertising "greed" to keep in step with bigger issues we shall be right back where we started from.'

Shirley Brieger called the new management 'the gangsters from Fleet Street. When Marcus was there we called them magazines or papers. When Fleetway came we felt we were working on comics. If you were working on *Robin* you went to *Chick's Own* and found a story from 1936 and up-dated it – that sort of thing went on. The market place dictated, the ideals went out of the window. I think they thought we were caught in a time warp. We moved to a building in Longacre where *The People* had their paper store. Max Clifford and Graham Marsh were the office boys. After the takeover the number of staff declined.'

In May Matthews wrote that he would be 'taking up residence' at Longacre the following week.

Pat Jackson had taken over *Girl* from Jean Crouch: 'The *Daily Mirror* rep came and told us that all kinds of changes were being made and that we were to let it be known that the changes were coming from the Editors and not directives from higher up. We were all totally appalled at this, we all resigned *en masse*. We really cared about those papers, they were extensions of ourselves. We couldn't bring ourselves to work with watered down versions of the best children's papers there had ever been.

'We were not impressed with anything about the new organisation. The little man in the brown suit, who thought of himself as Napoleon, came and had us all lined up and walked up and down the row telling us that things were going to be different from now on. He had the audacity to refer to James Hemming as a dirty old man who liked reading little girls' problems. We were totally affronted.'

James Hemming: 'After Marcus left I was still under contract. They got hold of my secretary and said they wanted to see the letters I had copies of. Whoever was in charge faced me with one of my letters, in which I had tactfully said, "Well, obviously your Mummy and Daddy are very worried about you, but you must realise you're a person in your own right and remember that if they're cross with you it may be because they're anxious. What you need is someone to talk to." Absolutely straight down the line stuff. But he said, "We could be hauled over the coals for this." I said, "Why?" He said, "That letter is turning the child against its parents, we can't have someone like you around. Out." So I went to say goodbye to my secretary and went home.

'That was the appalling difference. Marcus had the interests of the readers at heart. He saw everything I wrote because he signed the letters and he hadn't the slightest apprehension about being frank.'

Clifford wrote to Matthews, 'I regard Mr James Hemming as an invaluable member of this organisation. His price is low and his quality high – a very rare combination. . . .'

The following day Matthews replied, 'In my opinion we are taking too much upon ourselves to run such a feature as "What's Your Worry?".

'Frankly I am astonished to learn that a member of the editorial staff of a girl's [*sic*] comic (because, all prestige matters aside, GIRL is fundamentally a comic) should take upon himself the very tricky and unauthorised task of giving guidance on sexual matters to an eleven years old girl. . . . In my opinion this letter of Hemming's is irresponsible, if not wicked.

'We, as editors of children's comics, are not authorised in any way whatsoever to give advice on such intimate matters to young children and we are wrong in the first place to encourage the readers to write to us on matters of this nature.

'Readers' letters are all very well – I encourage them in fact – so long as they are concerned with the ordinary everyday life, such as school, sport, entertainment etc. Will you please, therefore, give instructions to cease the "What's Your Worry" feature . . . and bend our energies to one task only, to entertain our readers.'

Clifford was furious: 'Your memo seems to me to be most unfortunate in tone. To call Hemming "irresponsible" and "wicked" betrays an attitude of mind which, quite frankly, is beyond my comprehension. I protest, most vigorously, against your "order" that the "What's Your Worry" column cease forthwith. Meanwhile the unique and excellent work of Hemming is on file – should you wish to see more of it. . . .

'I should like to know if the matter of consulting me is purely a formality. You have been fair and generous on several matters but I am left with an overwhelming impression that my opinions are valued only in so far as they fit in with your own.'

As Dan Lloyd, the new Chief Sub, said, 'Fleetway rooted out most of the stuff people bought *Eagle* for and put in a lot of the rubbish they had in their morgue. Some of that was originally black and white, and had to be coloured up to be introduced as a marvellous new feature. *Eagle* lost all the appeal it originally had and that was reflected in plummeting sales.'

In May 1961 Leonard Matthews was planning more changes for *Swift/ZIP*. Clifford was not at all happy and wrote to Mr Shard, 'I think it is a mistake to eliminate reading matter almost entirely. . . . We have always encouraged children to *read*. . . . I do not agree with Matthews' assertion that boys are not concerned with written stories until they reach the age of ten or eleven.' Shard agreed with Clifford and told Matthews that 'A short, simple story, set in fairly large type, seems to me an essential ingredient.'

By the time the New Look *Swift* appeared, Clifford had resigned.

Marcus wrote to Clifford twenty years later: 'You made a great contribution to the children's papers. I'm sorry you had to fight such battles after I left with the appalling people who moved in.'

Clifford replied, 'I'm never quite sure why you gave me a job all those years ago, but you lifted me from oblivion and made a first-class journalist out of me. . . . As I grew more adroit and experienced and met the "best" of them, I knew without doubt that you were, by a mile, quite the most outstanding editor I have ever known . . . [When] the Hultons packed their bags . . . and the Shards and Gibsons and unspeakable Matthews moved in . . . the only relief was Hugh Cudlipp. He kept asking me out to lunch at the best restaurants in Soho. Finally he roared with laughter and said "You'll never get on with these buggers".'

Dan Lloyd remembered the astonishment of Val Holding, Clifford's replacement, when he asked how much some of the script writers were being paid for working on *Eagle*. 'His eyes popped out of his head, they were getting £30 instead of Fleetway's £10. From then on, Fleetway rates were going to apply. Top notch people like George Cansdale fell away. Bagenal Harvey's sports page didn't survive the takeover. His salary would have been enough to raise the blood pressure.'

John Ryan was on an annual contract. 'When this unpleasant character slid in, I can't remember who he was, the hatchet man I think, I went to see him and said my contract's up for renewal and he looked at me and said, "We don't like contracts, John". That was it more or less. That was when I started edging rapidly into television.

'I had an exhibition of Captain Pugwash and other items on the South

Bank some years ago. Marcus walked round and came up to me and said "You know it is an extraordinary thing, but of all the features we produced in *Eagle*, Captain Pugwash is the one that has survived. One would never have thought so." '

Charles Pocklington didn't last long with Fleetway. 'They wanted to put another art editor over me, a production editor. We had a special way of dealing with Bemrose. You had to use a list of specific colours. If you went out of that range the printers had trouble. This chap said, "I'm sorry, we're not going to work that way, the printers will have to change." I resigned there and then. Clifford had just left. Within a year of going to Fleetway it fell apart, it hadn't got heart in it any more. They didn't realise the bag of gold they'd got in human effort and attitude.'

According to Christine Bernard, some of the artists blamed Marcus for the destruction of the children's papers although, as she said, he couldn't have done anything about it. 'They resented all the work, time and care they had put into the magazines. They felt squeezed dry and thrown away. Men who'd worked their guts out on *Eagle* couldn't get jobs, they just about starved.' Including Richard Jennings, to whom she was briefly married: 'We got married on a very decent salary and three months later we had virtually nothing. Richard never really got over it.' Some of the artists became designers in publishing, some went to *Readers Digest* and Ladybird Books.

Derek Lord said: 'Leonard Matthews talked about stopping the haemorrhage of *Eagle*, which was a load of nonsense because the circulation was still 500,000 in July 1961; *Girl* was about 360,000, they were still doing very nicely,' – in spite of a seven week long printers' strike, which resulted in falling circulations all round; there were only two issues of *Eagle* between 20 June and 29 August.

'They put "The Last of The Saxon Kings" on the centre page, old stuff, historically inaccurate. I said it was warped history, with the Saxon hero swinging from a castle chandelier to break glass windows with his feet, and not the sort of thing we normally published in *Eagle*. Leonard Matthews said, "It would be an awful pity if you're not going to stay with us." Next morning I put in my resignation. Everyone was doing the same thing, one after another. They lost all the editors and art editors in a matter of weeks.

'That was the end of it all. We had letters by the sackful, thousands every day, saying "What are you doing to our papers?" Mrs Starke in the correspondence department came and asked me to help answer them. I said "No, I can't find answers for all these wretched people who've brought this on their heads. They perpetrated this, they must answer the letters." They were all letters of complaint, the readers were horrified. They were not prompted by the parents, you could tell that, the kids were furious. They knew the difference between something worthwhile and not. "I'm afraid it will be the end for me if you continue with the new edition." "Getting rid of the centre spread is a tragedy. It made *Eagle* unique." "Please bring back all those interesting, colourful, education articles we used to have."

"The Last of the Saxon Kings lowers your high standard, the drawings are enough to make your original artists weep." "I am horrified to see the centre page delegated to the back page. I am thinking of cancelling the paper." "Please return *Eagle* to its old form as soon as possible." "You have ruined the high reputation of *Eagle*, it has degenerated into a comic." In the case of *Robin* it was the parents who wrote, saying things like, "My child is heartbroken".

'The Fleetway people couldn't understand it at all, they never understood that the children's papers were successful because of the quality. They had no idea a child reader could be so perceptive. They were just in it for the job of turning out comics.'

Within months the circulation of *Eagle* fell by 150,000 and continued to plummet. By 1962 the combined print order of *Eagle* and *Girl* was less than 500,000.

But Barry Cork, a member of Matthews' staff, who became Editor of *Girl* in 1961, described Leonard Matthews as 'the most outstanding man in children's publishing at the time. His turnover of new magazines was incredible. He was brilliant, a most aggressive merchandising character. It's not fair to say that when the dead hand of the *Mirror* fell on the Hulton Press papers they wrecked them in no time at all. *Eagle* and *Girl* were very much of a time and that time was passing. What people forget is that they folded in the sixties when the people who bought *Girl* were maturing at a fantastic rate. Teenage papers were coming out. Stories of Belle of the Ballet and Mary Kingsley spreading the word in Africa were totally alien to what they wanted. We kept *Girl* going, trying to catch up with the times but it didn't really work. *Eagle* had the same problem. Technology was catching up with Dan Dare, what had been fantasy was now reality. It was a very difficult period.' Yet Bunty, launched in 1958, with stories of school, ballet dancing and air hostesses, is still going strong.

Derek Lord: 'Frank Hampson was pushed in late summer 1961. He used to come up and bind on about contracts and all sorts of things. There was nothing we could do about it, or anybody else, it was absolute chaos, Fleetway were frightful. Frank went over the top, he was in a bad way. He was so naïve. He thought that if you signed on the dotted line you had a contract for life. He didn't take into account that when Fleetway moved in everything changed overnight.'

Leonard Matthews described Frank as 'a difficult fellow, always moaning and groaning and complaining. At that time there was a lot of difficulty about artists who wanted royalties. I was approached by several. I said I could understand, so next time I give you a commission for a picture strip, instead of paying you £50 for the page, I'll pay you £5, I'm only buying one use, you want all rights after that. Artists said they wouldn't be able to sell anywhere else. I said it was no concern of mine, fees are for all rights. I think these days original drawings have to be returned to the artists.'

Gerald Palmer: 'The law changed, I think, in 1967. All the publishers suddenly realised that they owned the rights to reproduce but not the actual art work. They've been trying to find the artists and give them back their work.'

Harry Bishop, who drew 'Tarna' for *Swift*, knew Frank Hampson well: 'In 1961 or 2, I found out that we lived near him. I found him a very ill man. He was embittered, disenchanted. He felt right from the start that Marcus had usurped the creation of Dan Dare and *Eagle* and had built his career on it whereas Frank had slowly slid downwards.

'Artists are hopeless at business, we must blame ourselves, but Frank blamed everything on Marcus, he felt he'd been betrayed. He felt that Marcus had let him down because he thought that Marcus was in a position to fight for him. He blamed Marcus for selling *Eagle* to Odhams.

'The copyright for Dan Dare should have been Frank's, this is what upset him so badly. He could have gone on and made something of Dan Dare in his own right, he mentioned a film to me. These days he would have made a fortune.

'After *Eagle* Frank had nothing to go on. He was washed out, wasted. He worked for me for eight to ten weeks on a "Gun Law" story, which was scripted by Alan Stranks. We were working together when Alan died. But Frank quarrelled with me as well. I gave him the script and asked him to do pencil drawings which he did, but he got so involved he started bringing in the finished drawings in ink, all ready for production. This was not what I intended because our styles were different and it would have shown. His horses were inclined to look like rocking horses and my horses looked real.'

Peter Hampson was too young at the time to know exactly why or when things went sour between Frank and Marcus, but from as far back as he can remember, he wasn't allowed to breathe Marcus's name. 'I had the feeling that Frank resented Marcus's later success.'

But Keith Watson said, 'The build-up of the Marcus Morris versus Frank Hampson antagonism is in danger of careering out of control. It was inevitable that Frank Hampson and Marcus Morris should need to be in their own individual departments.'

After 'The Road of Courage', Frank illustrated a few books for Ladybird under Douglas Keen. 'As an admirer of his work, of his imaginative approach and thoroughness in research, I was happy to be able to pass work to him.' Frank then went to Ewell Technical College doing illustrative work and visual aids for lectures. He was much happier when he moved to Epsom College of Art taking life classes.

Jack Daniel also went to Epsom College of Art as a teacher. 'I thought I was going to cash in on the fact that Frank Hampson had been there. There was a glazed silence. I got the feeling that Frank had walked in and expected to take the place over. Apart from the fact that they didn't like the way he assumed that all the kids would throng round him, which they did, in his particular way he could draw them all under the table. He had this way of asserting himself by saying, "If you can't draw a thing in five minutes you can't draw it at all". These fine art chaps didn't like that.'

Frank toyed with a few other ideas for strips and did one for the National

Coal Board and ads for Bovril. But most of the ideas he came up with were not what the publishers wanted; his style was becoming old fashioned. Peter thought that Frank was also afraid that the same thing might happen again and he would be back in the nasty world of big business, which made him a bit half-hearted about his projects. In 1970 he developed throat cancer and was ill for a long time. Heart attacks and strokes followed and he was never fully fit again.

In August 1961 Marcus wrote to the Deans and Provosts of the Cathedrals which had welcomed him so enthusiastically for carol services: 'Recently . . . the papers have come under the control of the Daily Mirror Group and Mr Makins has now left his position as editor.

'Since these services have been of particular personal concern to me (even though I was not always able to take them all) I thought I should write and let you know that I shall not be associated with them any more.'

Others were writing to the press. James Hemming wrote to *The Times Educational Supplement* and other educational papers saying that he wanted everyone to know that he was no longer identified with the Hulton children's papers.

Guy Daniel to the *Church of England Newspaper*: 'The true-life back page story in *Eagle* has been abruptly dropped; it was written by a couple of parsons and therefore was presumably suspect – since it is rumoured that one of the charges the new owners make against the previous policy of the papers is that it was "too religious". Other signs abound, but perhaps enough has been said to warn parsons and parents that these four are not what they were.'

*Swift* died first. Frank Humphris drew a sort of mid-west Superman: 'When the *Mirror* bought Odhams they ruined it completely. I still had to work, I did a thing called "Blackbow the Cheyenne". A young doctor put on a war bonnet and for some reason nobody recognised him when he came to their rescue.'

More space was taken up with advertisements; war stories appeared; there was an editor's letter beginning 'Hello Chums'; Tarna the Jungle Boy aged ten years in a week and became a violent thug.

In March 1963 *Swift* was merged with *Eagle*.

*Girl* was the next to go. There were endless 'New Looks' and pages of pop. Lettice Leefe grew up and was no longer 'The Greenest Girl in School'; on the centre pages Belle and Mamie, no longer 'of the Ballet', went into television.

Many features were written by Sally Brompton, the youngest member of staff. 'My main qualification when I joined *Girl* was that I'd actually read it from the first issue. It was wonderful in the old days. I used to write all the pop columns. I would go along to *Ready, Steady, Go* every week and interview the stars.'

In 1964 the Beatles appeared on the front cover – eight pages were devoted to pop stars. A strip called 'Minx and Her Friends' was obviously aimed at younger readers. *Girl* didn't seem to know where it was going. In June they had the audacity to claim that *Girl* cost thousands of pounds a week to produce; they certainly weren't spending the money on the contents.

On 3 October 1964 the last *Girl* appeared. 'Exciting news for all readers.

*Girl* joins *Princess.*' *Robin* struggled painfully on, but by 1962 had lost its innocence and seemed to be aiming for an older market. In 1966 several earlier features were repeated; in 1968 they repeated a story from 1967.

'Richard Lion' appeared for the last time in May 1967 and the following week *Robin* was renamed *New Robin and Story Time.* 'The Woppit' had been replaced by 'Super Bear', the teddy from outer space.

*Robin* finally came to a grinding halt on 25 January 1969: 'Next week *Robin* and *Playhour* come together.'

*Eagle* suffered more than the others, though its death throes were only a few months longer than *Robin*'s.

The exploded drawings and 'Luck of the Legion' disappeared from the centre page, to be replaced by Derek Lord's *bête noire*, 'The Last of the Saxon Kings', indeed a dreadful strip, first published in 1954 in *The Comet*. Even more sacrilegious, 'Dan Dare' was forced to share the front page with 'Men of Action', featuring various sportsmen. One ray of light was the serialisation of C.S. Forrester's *Hornblower* drawn by Martin Aitchison. 'Harris Tweed' became Super Sleuth and later suffered a further indignity by being called Super Chump.

In March 1962 there was a sudden and complete transformation. Out went 'Storm Nelson', 'Riders of the Range', 'Harris Tweed' and all the other old favourites. On the front page there was one frame of 'Dan Dare'; the rest of it was inside in black and white, very badly drawn. A strip biography of Monty of Alamein, by Clifford Makins and Frank Bellamy, lasted four weeks. At the end of March, for the first time ever, there was no 'Dan Dare' on the front page; from then on, one frame appeared there occasionally to remind readers that Dan was just about alive and kicking. The whole thing was very messy. Page lay-outs changed from week to week, features would come and go. Apart, that is, from the exploded drawings on the back page, many by Ashwell Wood.

New Looks came and went and the price went up. Of the twenty-four pages, only six were in colour and six were advertisements. Particularly poignant was a page which featured an ad for the Army drawn by John Worsley and a Bovril ad drawn by Frank Hampson. The one bright spot, pictorially, in all the dross of badly drawn, violent strips, was 'Heros the Spartan', a fantastic tale of ancient times, drawn by Frank Bellamy.

In 1963 'Dan Dare' resumed his rightful place on the front page 'by popular request' and the following year it was announced that the adventures of 'Dan Dare' were also appearing every Sunday in *The People*. The comic *Wham*, launched by Fleetway, had a strip called 'Danny Dare', 'Dan Dare's greatest fan'. *Eagle* claimed to be the only paper catering for the young male who has grown out of comics. Rather a misleading statement in view of the paper's comic contents and the fact that a month later it became *Eagle & Boys' World*.

In April 1965, when *Eagle* was fifteen, Bob Bartholomew was named as Editor. Bartholomew, who had been editor of *The Children's Newspaper*, had a more sympathetic approach and tried very hard to bring *Eagle* back from the brink, but to no avail. New Look followed New Look.

At the beginning of 1967 Dan Dare was made controller of Spacefleet and his manual was to be published in *Eagle*; a good excuse for running old stories. In December 'Dan continues his exciting memoirs by telling for the first time of a strange adventure that befell him one Christmas'. That pathetic and badly drawn story ended a bare month later. The next week 'The Man From Nowhere' was re-hashed from the original art work. Dan Lloyd had 'the onerous job of getting a Dan Dare story which had run for two years in the early 1950s and compressing it into six months. The frames were cut out and remounted on new paste board and the whole story rescripted.' He did the same thing with 'Mark Question' which was regurgitated as 'Mark Mystery'. That 'act of vandalism', as he called it, was his last job on *Eagle*.

Graham Page wrote in the *Eagle* fanzine, *Eagle Times*, in 1992: 'Those who worked during the Golden Age are proud to have done so and are keen to share their experiences with us; but those who contributed to *Eagle* from 1962 were "just doing a job" and have no wish to revive memories of it. This is certainly true of Ted Cowan, author of "Cornelius Dimworthy", "Blackbow", "UFO Agent", "Billy Binns". We shall never get him to write anything for our magazine.'

On 26 April 1969 Dan Dare's (re-hashed) adventure, 'Rogue Planet', ended. The following week *Eagle* was merged with *Lion*. Only Dan Dare had survived (just) from the first issue. The death throes were over, the reincarnations had yet to come.

Post Script:
News International acquired Eric Bemrose's printing works in 1969 and the company was wound up in 1991. The Deputy Archivist and Modern Records Manager of News International went up to Liverpool and spent a week sorting out surviving records. There was very little left. The workforce had been laid off and 'obsolete' documentation had been destroyed.

# Chapter Sixteen

On 1 April 1958 the Managing Director of the National Magazine Company in London wrote to the President of his parent company, the Hearst Corporation, in New York.

Ben McPeake was beginning to contemplate retirement: 'I believe that younger people with new ideas should come in and be capable of meeting the changing publishing conditions and so continue to expand what is now a valuable property. . . . Just now I don't think there is anybody on our present staff who could take over. . . . I don't think any of them particularly want responsibility (they would all like titles!), mainly because high taxation prevents saving and so there is no real incentive. Expense accounts are so closely checked by the income tax inspectors that they do not now provide the incentive they did a few years ago and if we get a Socialist Government again, the "Directors" will become almost public enemies. . . .

'I think we need a youngish man – preferably with several children as I always think that having to feed several mouths encourages ambition – who can look forward to an active future of fifteen or twenty years. If he is American, he should be able to understand the British and their national peculiarities and if he is British, he should be capable of understanding American enthusiasm and drive. . . .

'One Britisher does occur to me as a long shot possibility – he is a brilliant man but a distinctly odd character. He is now with Hultons and he pretty well runs the outfit as far as he is allowed by Lady Hulton, but I know he is not too happy and is, I believe, sewn up on contract for a couple of years. He is Marcus Morris and has a brilliant creative mind. He originated the Hulton children's papers and also the annuals and he is now re-organising the whole outfit. Perhaps he would be worth considering in a year or so. (He is in the early forties and has four children).'

Richard E. Berlin replied, 'I do agree with you that a younger man should be installed and brought along . . . to a spot where he could work under you, such as I have done with Deems, with the idea of his taking over. . . . I would rather not appoint an American in England.'

In 1910 the American newspaper magnate, William Randolph Hearst, bought his first British property, *Nash's*, a successful pocket-sized 6d fiction magazine, which had been started just a year earlier by Eveleigh [or Evelyn] Nash. In 1912 Hearst installed a forty-two-year-old Belfast journalist, J.Y. McPeake, who had been the first man to use Marconi's wireless telegraphy to report a current event, as Managing Director of his National Magazine Company.

Just before the First World War, McPeake purchased *Pall Mall*, which he merged with *Nash's*, and *Vanity Fair*, which was published for only a few months due to paper shortages. *Nash's Magazine* flourished, even during the war, when the cover girls by Harrison Fisher were used as 'pin-ups' by the troops in the trenches. In 1917 J. Y. was joined by a thirty-one-year-old woman journalist who had been secretary to Lord Alfred Douglas on *The Academy* (a literary weekly). Alice Head became Assistant Editor of *Nash's*, which attracted most of the literary lions of the day including Rudyard Kipling, John Galsworthy, George Bernard Shaw, H.G. Wells, Arnold Bennett, G.K. Chesterton and W. Somerset Maugham.

In 1922 McPeake and Alice Head launched the English version of the Hearst Corporation's *Good Housekeeping* and, two years later, J. Y.'s sons joined the company; the younger, Brendan (or Ben as he was known) on the advertising side and Alan as Art Editor of *Good Housekeeping* and Fiction Editor of *Nash's*. The Good Housekeeping Institute was opened at Wellington Street, Strand – 'a practical testing station for all kinds of domestic appliances'.

Later that year J. Y. died and Alice Maud Head, to the lasting chagrin of Ben and Alan, was appointed Managing Director of Hearst's British subsidiary.

In 1925 Hearst decided he would like to have a country house in Britain and Alice Head was instructed to buy a castle; she found the fourteenth century St Donat's Castle in South Wales. Over the next few years a number of simple alterations were made: mains water and electricity were installed; a bathroom was planned for each bedroom (sixty of them); the North Court was reconstructed into eight bedrooms each with a marble bathroom. Fireplaces, screens, tapestries, roofs, portcullises, armoury, chapel, banqueting and assembly halls were transported to Wales from all over Europe, not to mention countless pieces of antique furniture. Three hard tennis courts were constructed and a heated sea water swimming pool was built on the old tilting ground between the castle and the sea.

By 1927 the National Magazine Company was profitable enough to buy the twenty-six-year-old two shilling antique collectors' monthly, *The Connoisseur*. This was to be a great asset to Mr Hearst in his acquisition of art and antiques; he cabled to Alice Head in April: 'Your accounts are wonderful they cover all my art expenditures and that means a lot thanks and congratulations I hope to see you this summer.'

In 1929 the British edition of *Harper's Bazaar* appeared, a high-fashion magazine, with Alan McPeake as Art Director. Unkind critics at the time said that the four million strong queues outside the labour exchanges would 'no doubt find it interesting reading'. Mr Hearst thought that *Harper's* would provide a British vehicle for the acting career of his mistress, Marion Davies.

In 1938, with the fortunes of the National Magazine Company looking less rosy (*Nash's Magazine* had been forced to close in 1937; Alice Head put it down to the success of *Picture Post*: 'Young Mr Hulton's new pictorial weekly has made an excellent start. It is so good that it ought to succeed brilliantly.') and with war imminent, Hearst instructed Alice Head to stop the renovations (only about a quarter finished) and sell St Donat's. Some of the contents were easily disposed of, but nobody wanted to buy a castle. It was eventually sold in 1960 to Atlantic College.

By the following year Alice Head was losing control of things. When the war started in September she panicked and took the staff of *Good Housekeeping* and some of the accounts department, down to St Donat's for safety. Elsie Cannon, at the time Assistant Editor of *Good Housekeeping*, recalled that 'the butler obviously found us a very poor substitute for the Hollywood stars and celebrities who had attended Hearst's parties in happier days. It was all rather an inefficient muddle'; they returned to London two months later. The castle was then appropriated by the Army for the duration of the war.

It must have been from St Donat's that Alice cabled to Hearst in New York saying that, unless they were prepared to lend financial aid, it would be necessary to sell or liquidate the business at the end of the year. Tom Buttikofer was sent to London and found, to his horror, that next to no accounts had been kept for months. He informed Alice that her contract would not be renewed and appointed Ben McPeake, by then Advertisement Manager of *Good Housekeeping*, to follow, at last, in his father's footsteps.

By March 1940 Buttikofer had 'generally re-organised the affairs of the Company to bring them under proper control so that the Company is now being operated on a policy similar to that covering our American companies.'

He was ably assisted in this by an elegant and beautiful temporary secretary, Mrs Kay Thomas, née Islip, with whom he was reputed to be having an affair. After about a year Buttikofer returned to the States, leaving Kay to be secretary to the new Managing Director.

Kay's second husband, Jack Brebner, was involved with the Ministry of Information during the war and *Good Housekeeping* produced helpful leaflets, including such gems as *Economical Catering for Home and Communal Use*, *100 Best Ration Recipes*, *Cakes and Puddings for Wartime*, *Forces Knitting* and *Thrifty Wartime Recipes*. Hearst were still unsure of the company's viability and, in 1942, Ben McPeake went to New York to plead Nat Mag's cause. According to Erica, Ben's widow, 'Ben certainly had his heart and soul in Nat Mag. One can almost say that he risked his life when he travelled from London to New York via Portugal, returning in a small Norwegian boat at a time when the U boat war was at its height. I remember that Richard Berlin gave Ben *The Complete Sayings of Jesus* as a parting gift in New York!'

The 1950s were a time of expansion and consolidation for the National Magazine Company. Ben McPeake, encouraged by the success of the wartime booklets, established a Book Department which brought out children's books and, in association with *Good Housekeeping*, a series of 1/6d booklets. In 1953, Gwynne Ramsey, Editor of *The Connoisseur*, introduced Ben McPeake to George Rainbird, an ex-advertising man who, two years previously, had set up a publishing imprint with Ruari McLean.

Rainbird, McLean Ltd produced books for other publishing houses to market; their thirteenth was *The Queen's Silver*, produced in 1953 for *The Connoisseur*. It was the beginning of many years' successful collaboration with Nat Mag.

Rainbird, McLean were also at this time collaborating with Hulton Press on producing *Eagle* and *Girl Annuals* and books such as the *Eagle Sports*

*Annual* and *Learning to Cook the Girl Way*, which was put together by Joy Law (née Spiro).

Joy ran the Rainbird, McLean office in Wyndham Place, a converted flat, where George and Ruari would stay during the week and from where they conducted various extra-marital affairs. At weekends they would lend the rooms to their friends – including Marcus. Joy used to go into the office early on Monday mornings: 'I remember more clearly than anything Marcus's wonderful golden yellow silk damask dressing gown – very eighteenth century. The bathroom would be smelling wonderful. I said, "Marcus, if you don't get the hell out of here so that I can air the place and actually turn this into an office and not a bordello I will scream". The young woman had left rather earlier.'

In 1953 Ben McPeake became ill and gave power of attorney to Kay Thomas, who was soon appointed a Director and General Manager of the company. By the late fifties Kay was pretty well in the driving seat. As well as being beautiful and elegant, she was also tremendously ambitious, with a good business brain and a strong character. She was unpopular with many of the staff, except her few close associates. A senior executive who joined the company in 1959 said, 'Kay Thomas was reputed to be the highest paid woman executive in the UK. She had worked her way up by her bootstraps and done very well. Many people had respect and admiration for what she achieved and some sympathy for what she had to do to keep her place on the ladder, but very few people liked her.'

According to another former executive, 'Morale was bad when I joined the company in 1958. Everyone went in fear of Kay Thomas.' But Joan Robinson, who ran the company's switchboard for thirty-six years said, 'The girls just all adored her. She was so fair, and marvellous to us.' Joan's husband, Jim Lucas, first met Kay in 1947 and chauffeured her for nearly thirty-four years. He was very fond of her and was one of the few people Kay would agree to see towards the end of her life. 'Ben McPeake was an outstanding man in many ways, but hid himself away from the staff – any queries were always referred to Kay. It appeared that Kay was running things; she was in the firing line, where Ben didn't want to be.'

But Ben didn't tell her about a meeting he had in March 1958 at George Rainbird's office. George Rainbird was by now a close friend of Ben McPeake. They had the same tastes in food, wine, art and antiques; while Marcus didn't have the same interest in art and antiques, he was certainly fond of good food and wine – no doubt a contributory factor in *his* close friendship with George Rainbird, to whom he had been introduced by Ruari McLean. Their relationship even survived a brief affair between George and Jess.

Knowing that Marcus was getting increasingly frustrated at Hulton Press and aware that Ben was beginning to look around for a successor, George decided to play Cupid and invited them both to lunch. Ben didn't know quite what to make of Marcus but, encouraged by George, decided that Marcus was possibly the man to carry Nat Mag through the sixties and seventies.

The letter to Richard Berlin followed and more meetings with Marcus. By October 1958 Ben's solicitor was talking to Marcus's solicitor and, at the end of November, Marcus and Jess spent a weekend at St Donat's with the McPeakes and the Rainbirds. Marcus had been in two minds about leaving Hulton Press, but Edward Hulton's decision to unseat him from the management team tipped the balance. He needed fresh challenges and, with the takeover of Hultons by Odhams the following March, the decision to accept Ben McPeake's offer wasn't as difficult as it might otherwise have been.

Jan's diary for 18 September 1959: 'Pop home about 8.30. Over dinner Pop discussed future. He is leaving Hultons at the end of the month. Has to decide whether or not to buy the house. He said we've got to keep it tidier if we want to live here. New job means Pop is now short of money, but in the end hopes to be director or something. . . . Pop warned us not to say anything to reporters who might phone about Pop leaving Hultons.'

Kate recorded: 'Daddy left Hulton Press today, it's going to be funny without *Eagle* etc.' Marcus and Jess took a short holiday in Majorca. While they were away the usual financial crises erupted at home, with the milkman refusing to leave any milk until his bill was paid.

Marcus had complained to his accountant earlier in the year when both the electricity and telephone were cut off. 'I have also had two lawyers' letters about unpaid bills. Since I had left everything in your hands I knew nothing about any of these things until it was too late. I am wondering whether now that your business is expanding so much, you are unable to give the attention required to my somewhat complicated affairs.' On this occasion, seventeen-year-old Jan, in charge of the household, managed to get a cheque rapidly dispatched, but the accountant later landed in gaol.

As Marcus wasn't due to join Nat Mag until the end of the year, he and Ben McPeake had a series of secret meetings at George's new office in Charlotte Street and at Ben's home in Hampstead to discuss the new job and familiarise Marcus with the company's magazines. It was also arranged that he should visit New York to get to know Richard Berlin.

Although Ben had told Berlin in 1958 that there was no one on the staff suitable to succeed him, there were, apart from Kay Thomas, two other Nat Mag executives who had thought they might have a chance of being appointed Managing Director; Company Secretary Bill Jackson and Circulation Director Allan Boddy had both, according to the former, received hints to that effect from Ben.

It therefore came as something of a shock to Bill Jackson to receive an invoice for bottles of whisky that had been delivered to a Mr Marcus Morris on board the *Queen Elizabeth* en route to New York. This was the first intimation anyone in the company had that an outsider had been appointed – it is perhaps not surprising that when Marcus arrived at the office in Grosvenor Gardens he found the senior executives somewhat antagonistic towards him.

Marcus berthed in New York at the beginning of November and spent a month getting to know the Hearst executives. He had discussions with the

Publisher (business manager) of *Popular Mechanics* in Chicago regarding the feasibility of a British edition. Marcus wanted something which would interest young men when they grew out of *Eagle*. 'There is room,' he suggested, 'for a popular magazine for the man in the street, who is increasingly interested in the achievements of modern science and their practical application to himself,' – perhaps a surprising proposal from someone for whom changing a plug was a major production. The dummy he produced, provisionally called *Science Illustrated*, was received enthusiastically in New York, but the British advertising agencies were not interested.

Marcus talked to Richard Berlin about the necessity for Nat Mag to move to bigger, centralised premises (there was mention of renting Hulton House in Fleet Street, but Ben thought that the staff wouldn't want to move from Victoria). They discussed the possibility of Eric Bemrose's taking over Nat Mag's printing from Sun Printers and talked about arrangements for Nat Mag to repay a loan from Hearst, dating from before the war. There were meetings with Circulation Director Bill Campbell about the falling sales of *The Connoisseur* and with the Executive Vice President of the Magazine Division, Dick Deems, about the ongoing problems of *Harper's Bazaar*.

At Berlin's suggestion Marcus flew to the west coast, visiting Los Angeles and San Francisco, before returning home on the *Queen Elizabeth* through a storm of such ferocity that the ship had to heave to and portholes were broken, which didn't worry Marcus in the least; it was flying that terrified him.

Marcus officially joined National Magazines as Editorial Director and Managing Director Designate on 31 December 1959 on a three-year contract. He may not have expected that, having escaped from one ferocious female, Nika Hulton, he was to spend the next six years at loggerheads with another. Kay Thomas deeply resented Marcus's being appointed over her head. As one executive put it, 'Kay had everything her own way until Marcus joined the company. Her nose was put out of joint.' Another said that, 'Kay saw Marcus as an interloper – she wouldn't have minded someone from within the company.' A third reported, 'It is said that when Marcus arrived, Kay announced, "Bill and I run this company, and I will have that man out within a year".'

During one early trip Marcus made to New York, Kay wrote to Richard Berlin saying that Marcus wasn't suitable to take over the company; the letter was shown to Marcus – it is no wonder that he became somewhat hostile towards her. Susie Babbington, Kay's assistant for some years, says, 'Kay asked me to work for Marcus because she wanted an ear to his office, but he didn't take to me because he knew I'd worked for Kay. I never came across anybody who didn't like her apart from Marcus. He was very devious. Kay was very open and found that difficult to deal with.'

Bill Jackson says, 'I got on quite well with Marcus at the beginning. The friction between Kay and Marcus was very much Ben's creation.'

Bill and Marcus first met over a drink at the Directors' Club; Marcus had to leave to catch a night train to Scotland to conduct an *Eagle* carol service. The *Eagle* mantle wasn't easy to cast off. When he returned from the

States one of his first tasks had been to judge a Heinz 'Cowboy's Breakfast' painting competition with Harry Corbett and Sooty. There were still numerous speaking engagements booked at schools, colleges, scout groups, mothers' unions – many of which now had to be cancelled, some at appallingly short notice, although Chad Varah and Clifford Makins filled the breach on a number of occasions. Jess wrote to Jan, who was in Austria, 'Daddy is settling in to the new thing. He gets up every morning at 7!!! and off and away before 9!! Quite exhausting, but very good for us all.

'We went and had a drink with Clifford and Caroline, who are getting married next Friday. . . . I, unfortunately, shan't be able to be there as I am rehearsing!!! At last, *Flowering Cherry* for Tennants, a tremendous part. Mac says I got it in the face of great opposition – I'm very thrilled, very frightened, they're paying me a lot of money.' Marcus urged Jan to come back a few days early to see the play – he was very proud of Jess's career.

*Flowering Cherry* (with Michael Hordern and Andrew Ray) went out on ITV in February 1960 to great critical acclaim. Cecil Clarke of H.M. Tennant wrote, 'Thank you for last night and for your lovely performance. People have been phoning in to say how much they enjoyed it and how wonderful they thought you were.'

Later that year Jess was on stage in the last of Noel Coward's straight plays, *Waiting in the Wings*, about life in a retirement home for ancient thespians (based on the still-thriving Denville Hall, run by the Actors' Charitable Trust). The very distinguished cast was headed by Dame Sybil Thorndike and Sir Lewis Casson; they opened in Dublin to thunderous applause. The Master himself attended the first night and the family were introduced to him; Jess's dressing room was, as usual, awash with red roses.

Margot Boyd, who plays Marjorie Antrobus in Radio Four's *The Archers*, and Jess were the youngest members of the cast and both were rather reserved, which drew them together. 'She was in a frenzy the whole time about her family and husband. She was always exhausted, coping with Marcus's success. She was dearly loved by the whole cast, they were enchanted by her being so beautiful, gentle and sweet. She wasn't one to push herself forward, but she stood her ground.'

The play closed in March 1961 after a successful West End run.

Early in 1960 Marcus started to refuse invitations to preach and speak outside London, although he gave a number of lectures arranged through the Foyles Lecture Agency. One invitation he did accept was to open the seventy-ninth annual fête at his old parish of Weeley. He also found time to write an article on children's books for the *Sunday Times* and was persuaded by Anne Scott-James to write a piece for the *Daily Express* on parenthood entitled: 'I'll tell you why I'm a selfish father'.

'My four children can do what they like, as long as they don't get under my feet. At least, more or less.

'I object to them making a racket when I'm trying to get an afternoon sleep. I object to them messing around in my study, and not putting back the books they borrow.

'I object to them scattering their clothes all over the bathroom, and leaving lights and gas-fires blazing in empty rooms.

'They can drink if they want and smoke if they want (they don't particularly want to). They can go out with boy friends and come in when they want. We ask them to let us know, as a matter of courtesy, where they are going when they go out. And we've advised them not to walk alone on the [Hampstead] Heath – and told them why. [They walked home from school alone across the Heath every day.]

'There are no rules. I don't believe in them and they don't work. The children just get bawled out if they are a nuisance to other people. [True! Jess's frosty look was most effective.]

'I've never read them to sleep at night, or played rousing games of hockey with them. I dance with the three teenage girls because I enjoy it and happen to be better at it than most of the young men they are likely to meet. [Very much better than any of them.]

'I believe that children are not some special category of creation. They are just like you and me – only younger. And they need only two things. One, a secure background against which to grow and that, in practice, means a father and mother living together in a home. Two, the minimum of protection against the more serious mistakes. But not protection against life. Sooner or later, they are going to find out what life is really like, and try to come to terms with it. And the sooner the better.

'To be squeamish and over-protective arouses an unhealthy curiosity. . . . Personally, I don't particularly want my children to be a credit to me. (In fact, they are such that I'm proud of them, but that's accidental.) I would prefer that they should be a credit to themselves. It's up to them what they make of their life.

'You mustn't impose even your hopes on them. It's an unfair strain on a child to let him feel he has to live up to what his parents expect of him. [An echo of his own childhood?]

'And it seems to work. They are not in revolt. There is nothing (much) to revolt against.

'They are, in fact, sane, normal, mature and free. They will talk to us about anything at all – thank God. They ask questions – and don't have to accept the answers. . . . They are different people, not shadows or replicas of us.'

Marcus mentioned letters from Jan describing her love affairs in Austria (whither she had been sent to learn German) and twenty-minute kisses in the moonlight; this brought a flood of letters to the *Express* – and astonishment and disbelief from Jan's friends. Jan was equally astonished that her friends were afraid, or disinclined, to write to their parents on such interesting topics. She wrote to Jess, 'It's awful not having anyone to tell absolutely everything to. . . . '

What Marcus doesn't say in this article is that his children, although allowed (or forced) pretty well to bring themselves up, nevertheless received a great deal of love from their parents. Friends and neighbours thought that they were neglected; they never thought so themselves, although they were sometimes a little envious of friends who could invite people to tea and be sure of homemade cakes and jellies and sandwiches. At one stage, the Morris children had only a poached egg each for tea every day for months.

They did think at times that they were put upon. Jess to Jan: 'Kate is being simply splendid, cooking well and cheerfully. She can do shepherd's pie and tripe and fries a very pretty piece of liver. . . .'

Marcus was appointed a Director of Nat Mag a month after he joined the company and in March was elected a Fellow of the Institute of Directors; in April he attended his first Nat Mag board meeting. He reported that using Bemrose to print *SHE* and *Vanity Fair* would save the company some £7,000 but negotiations foundered when Eric Bemrose died later that year and his successor's estimates rose. In July, Marcus spoke at the Institute of Public Relations' conference on 'The Public of the Future', in support of the youth of the day; he believed that the younger generation would grow up more mature, more knowledgeable, more sophisticated and more sceptical than their elders.

Later that year he became involved in controversy when he criticised the Archbishop of Canterbury, Dr Fisher, during a sermon at St Bride's in Fleet Street. Fisher had rebuked the Bishop of Woolwich, John Robinson, for testifying in favour of the book at the *Lady Chatterley's Lover* trial; Marcus opined that 'People were perhaps thinking that the door was opening and that a breath of fresh air was being let into the Church. But the Archbishop very quickly put a stop to that "nonsense". The door was smartly shut and the public image of the Church was back where it was before.'

When this was reported in the press, together with Marcus's statement that he would not object to his three teenage daughters reading *Lady Chatterley*, he received a number of rude letters, including one from a man in Dover who proposed sending a copy of the book to Marcus's daughters 'and later endeavour to discuss with them certain passages I choose to select'. Marcus dealt with this smartly with the help of a dismissive letter from Bart Smith (who entirely agreed with the Archbishop). The three girls had already read the book and found it rather boring.

At the beginning of 1960 Marcus was joined at Nat Mag by his old ally from Hultons, Jack Blanche.

By the previous summer, Jack had been as fed up with the new regime as Marcus and, without knowing that Marcus was also talking to National Magazines, applied for the job of Advertisement Director.

In the course of initial interviews, Jack heard that Nat Mag were also looking for someone on the editorial side; he told Marcus, who pretended he hadn't heard of them. Four or five weeks later Marcus told Jack that he was going to New York. On his return he enquired how the job application was going; Jack replied that he'd been told he was on a shortlist of six.

Marcus said, 'Well, in New York you're at the top of the list.' Jack joined the company three months later and was warmly welcomed by Marcus, who said, 'I'm going to run editorial, I want you to run advertising. You can do what you like as long as I know and agree.'

Another old Hultonian to join Nat Mag was Margaret Hamilton, who had been Keith Kotch's secretary. She joined Marcus as his PA after an interview over lunch at the Institute of Directors when, unbeknownst to Margaret, the Martinis he bought her were doubles. 'He didn't bat an eyelid when I confessed "I hate to say this, but I think I'm drunk".' She became his right-hand woman and confidante, until she left in 1965 to join the probation service.

One of the first major problems that Marcus encountered in his new job was the Good Housekeeping Institute and its Seal of Approval.

The Institute had grown into a non-profit-making limited liability company independent of *Good Housekeeping* magazine and was best known for its Seal of Guarantee. The Complete Classified List of Seal Holders for August 1960 contained 1,073 entries, from Aga cookers (price from £115) and British Warm rubber hot-water bottles (6s 6d), washing machines, floor coverings (Florafoam Kumfy Mats from 19s 7d), gardening tools, furniture, paints, distempers and floor dressings, to food products (O-So-Lite self-raising flour, 8d per 1lb) and kitchen equipment (Owl rubber bucket silencers, 1s per pkt).

There was no question of the Seal being awarded in exchange for the promise of a large (or small) advertising budget, but the accusation was occasionally levelled, which led to one of the many rows between Marcus and Kay Thomas, who was Chairman and Director of the Institute. In 1963 a small London diocesan magazine called *The Bridge* inferred this very thing. Kay Thomas immediately, and without reference to Marcus, instructed the company's solicitor to fire off letters to the Revd Timothy Beaumont, the magazine's publisher; to the Bishop of Southwark, whose diocese it covered, and to the parson who wrote the article, threatening legal action and demanding substantial damages. Marcus was furious. It was not so much that Mervyn Stockwood and Timothy Beaumont were friends of his but, 'Much more seriously, it seems to me utterly wrong that a lawyer's letter, with a demand for damages, should have gone to a parson who may perhaps be earning £700 to £800 a year and was clearly writing out of ignorance, and to a well known bishop. If it were to become known that such a letter had gone out to these people it would, in my opinion, be extremely damaging to the name of *Good Housekeeping* and the Institute and would make us look ridiculous.'

*The Bridge* published a full retraction and apology, but Kay asked if Marcus's personal relationships with the Church were more important than the interests of the company 'and, had the offending paragraph appeared in a commercial publication, would you still have interfered?' Marcus replied, 'My concern was not to protect the Church (which does not need my help for that) but to make sure that in this case the Institute was protected. . . . My whole point was that the procedure adopted was the wrong way of going about it in these particular circumstances.'

Tempers were raised and fuses short on the question of the Seal because of the publication in July 1962 of the Government's Molony Report on Consumer Protection, which had been scathing about the reliability of the Institute's methods of testing and the quality of its standards.

There was a final, grudging concession: 'In reaching this unhappy conclusion, we do not imply that the Institute is cynically and deliberately misusing its seal for private profit.'

Kay Thomas protested strongly to the Department of Trade; frantic discussions took place between London and New York; fees to manufacturers for testing were dropped; Phyllis Garbutt, the Principal, decided to retire and Freda Cowall was appointed Associate Principal for a trial year. 'We found that lots of things were sporting the Seal which had no business to. There were files there that hadn't been looked in for twenty-five years. It was like cleaning the Augean Stables.'

One immediate result of the furore was the decision to move the company from the rather cramped conditions of Grosvenor Gardens, where the Institute occupied a dark and dingy basement, to a modern building in Vauxhall Bridge Road, the other side of Victoria Station. The Institute was given a large area on the eleventh floor, with all mod cons, and the company's other magazines, with the exception of *Harper's Bazaar*, were brought together under one roof for the first time.

With bigger premises and an expanded staff, Freda and her team struggled for two years to redeem the Seal, against increasing competition from The Consumers' Association and its magazine *Which?*

In the end Marcus and John Miller, General Manager of Hearst, decided that the Seal had outlived its day; it was suspended and the Institute incorporated into the magazine. John and Marcus thought alike on most things and it was the beginning of a long and close friendship. They had first met at a cocktail party in New York and, on the briefest of acquaintanceships, Marcus and Jess were invited for the weekend to the Millers' country house in Pennsylvania. At a dance at a local inn, 'Marcus and Jess cleared the floor – everyone stopped and watched them,' according to Bunny Miller.

Willie Mae Rogers, Principal of the American Good Housekeeping Institute, came to London in an attempt to mediate between Marcus and Kay, who had fought tooth and nail for the Seal. Willie Mae told Marcus that 'I am about to say some things to you, which are straight from my heart, and I hope you will listen with *your* heart as well as with your mind. You are the key to this entire unhappy situation that exists between you and Kay. I do not know what she did to Ben or you to make you distrust her so, but you cannot allow it to continue serving as a barrier to good working relationships.

'In such a situation one person has to be big enough and unselfish enough to forget personal emotions – and because of your own particular background and your own belief that moral concepts can, and should, apply in business, surely you are the one to do it in this case. If you could bring yourself to just unlock that door between your and Kay's offices, and once in a while pop into her office with a question or a comment or, best of all, a request for help, I truly believe the major problem would be solved. The worst thing that can happen to a woman – in business or elsewhere – is to feel unwanted. Kay feels unwanted and unneeded – and whether or not she deserves to feel so is beside the point. You are the top man and yours is the responsibility for making all your staff feel needed and important. . . . I'm sure I would never have written you such a letter as this if I had not come to feel close enough to you to say what's in my heart.'

Marcus replied, 'I value very much your speaking to me from your heart and I hope you will always do so. I will listen with mine (some think I haven't got one! They are wrong!). But I cannot let my heart rule my head when the interests of the Company and the morale and work of many people are concerned.

'You have perhaps, Willie Mae, heard only one side of the matter. However, I won't go into that. It is not a question of my personal feelings – we can none of us expect always to work only with people who are bosom pals.

'Kay greatly exaggerates in her complaint that she is left out of things. It is in fact difficult to know what other areas of work I can hand over to her. But I will do my best – as I have tried in the past (not very successfully, it seems) – to get along with Kay and bring her into things more. As you say, it is the right kind of leadership and the right kind of working relationships which matter – and it is up to me to establish these.

'I am not, as it happens, a vengeful person and I have no childish desire to "get my own back". I am only interested in the successful running of the Company. Ben's attitude to Kay is an entirely separate matter. He has his own reasons.

'The door between Kay's and my office is not locked. There is a bolt on it in case I should *ever* want privacy – but I have not used it. I know that we must all try to love those who do not love us. I will, Willie Mae, make a further effort – with my heart as well as my mind.'

# Chapter Seventeen

*SHE* magazine, launched by the National Magazine Company in 1955, was the brainchild of Michael Griffiths, Art Editor of *Good Housekeeping*. He didn't want to edit it himself so Joan Werner Laurie, who also worked on *Good Housekeeping*, took it on, while Michael looked after the art side. Brian Braithwaite and Joan Barrell in their book *The Business of Women's Magazines* describe it thus: '*She* was a strong formula magazine with its format and logo owing not a little to *Picture Post*. It was a unique mix of brash and down-to-earth articles and pictures with an inherent thread of British vulgarity. . . . Editorially it was a mishmash of punning headlines, frank sex articles, peculiar photographs and rude jokes. . . . It had the effect of a fast-talking, loud-suited, red-nosed uncle in the rather gentile [*sic*] drawing room of the women's magazines of the day.'

By the time Marcus arrived at Nat Mag in 1960 the trail-blazing *SHE* was well established and successful. In Michael Griffiths' words: 'The women's magazines of the early 1950s just didn't reflect women as I knew them. Of course women have softness, but they are also funny, vulgar and tough. They are in touch with the harsh realities of life. No one who undergoes child-bearing could be anything else.'

*SHE* appealed to a wide range of women – and men. It engendered strong emotions – you either loved it or loathed it and its staff were always strongly partisan. A young Peter Chipperfield, who started in 1958 as an advertisement rep, loved the magazine so much that he took a cut in salary to join it.

Joan Werner Laurie (known as Jonnie) was a brilliant, if somewhat touchy, editor and, apart from the odd bout of artistic temperament, there was little for Marcus to worry about. One of the most notable contributors to the magazine was Joan's lover, the celebrated Nancy Spain ('Newshound Nancy brings you back the latest gossip . . .'), who had at one time been Literary Editor of *Good Housekeeping*. Nancy was a larger-than-life personality – broadcaster, author, journalist – who was the inspiration for the part Jess played (the lesbian journalist) in Noel Coward's *Waiting in the Wings*; Coward was a close friend of Nancy's.

On Saturday, 21 March 1964, Marcus and his family stopped off at a pub in the Cotswolds on their way to the Whichford home of George Rainbird. They bumped into Bill Fine, Publisher of American *Harper's Bazaar*, who told them that he'd heard on his car radio that Nancy Spain had been killed in an air crash at Aintree Racecourse. Marcus rushed to a phone and learned that, as he'd feared, Joan Werner Laurie had also been on the plane. Nancy had been going to cover the Grand National and the small twin-engined Piper crashed, near the Canal Turn, as it was coming in to land; there were no survivors.

Marcus swiftly returned to London. The following Monday brought Marcus a cable from Dick Deems, head of magazines at Hearst, commiserating on their loss and suggesting Ernestine Carter as a possible replacement. There were also letters from British journalists asking to be considered for the Editorship of *SHE* – Marcus put these straight in the bin. Letters of sympathy poured in from readers, publishers, PR companies, magazine wholesalers and retailers, advertisers and agencies and the many charities with which Jonnie had been involved. Offers of help from journalist friends were gratefully received but, as Marcus said in the dozens of letters he had to write, 'Joan Werner Laurie left a very efficient, enthusiastic and well-knit team and everything is now well under control'.

A memorial to Joan was built in the form of a landscaped garden at Chailey Heritage, the craft school and hospital for crippled children, to surround the swimming pool which had been installed with the aid of some £12,000 raised by readers of *SHE*.

The company set up a trust fund for Jonnie's two sons, Nick, aged seventeen and eleven-year-old Tom. It wasn't until he was nineteen and at university that Tom discovered he wasn't Jonnie's son at all; Nancy was his mother.

(In researching this book, Sally asked Auberon Waugh, author of a piece in *Private Eye* in 1973, why he had referred to Marcus as 'a sanctimonious and dirty-minded clergyman'. Waugh telephoned Sally and asked her, with some satisfaction, if she didn't know that she had an illegitimate half-brother. She was a little taken aback by this bald statement but, when Waugh went on to say that Marcus had had an affair with Nancy Spain, she became decidedly incredulous, knowing that Spain was in no way Marcus's type of woman. Further enquiries of Tom elicited the information that his father was in fact Pip Carter, the husband of the novelist Marjorie Allingham. Auberon Waugh wrote to Sally in December 1995: 'I am extremely sorry. Tom Carter has withdrawn his claim to be your father's bastard, even if he ever made it. I seem to remember his making it, but it may be my geriatric memory. What an embarrassment. . . .'

And what a pity that an unsubstantiated rumour (which neither Marcus nor Jess had heard) should have been the basis of such a malicious statement. Jess, who was always upset by spiteful remarks aimed at Marcus, had been very hurt by the paragraph in *Private Eye*. She had a habit of jotting down odd pieces of verse in times of stress and wrote:

'How awful to be Mr Waugh
Not E, nor first A, But Auberon Waugh
Born with a silver sneer in his pen,
Approving of no one at all but hissen.')

Michael Griffiths took over the editorship of *SHE*, promising to do it for six months. None of the applications they received was considered remotely acceptable, until the Features Editor of *Woman's Mirror*, Pamela Carmichael, rather tentatively approached Marcus. Pamela had worked with Jodi Hyland on *Woman*, which may well have influenced him. He said: 'You're the best I've seen so far, but you'll have to get on with a very difficult man called Michael Griffiths. You'd better have lunch with him.'

Michael telephoned Pamela and thought he was talking to a ghost. 'It was very strange. Pamela and Jonnie's voices were very similar; I almost said "For God's sake, Jonnie, get off the line".' Pamela got the job and later married the 'very difficult' Michael Griffiths.

Over the years Mrs C and Mr G, as they were known to their staff, developed a very close relationship with Marcus, despite his rejection of Michael's idea for a new general interest magazine for men, originally titled *Extra*. Marcus was not keen, but a decision was deferred when Jonnie died; Pamela and Michael rechristened it *HE* and obtained the support of Allied Breweries for selling the magazine through pubs. Marcus sat on the idea – he didn't want to deflect any thoughts away from *SHE* and, from past experience, didn't think a general men's magazine would work. Pamela still thinks he was wrong since, at the time, 33 per cent of buyers of *SHE* were men – and many more were readers. 'Marcus had the power of making you very fond of him, even when you were furious with him. I always knew when he was angry with me because he put his monocle in [an affectation he adopted in the seventies]. We used to have rows; we had a terrible scene early on when a marketing man wanted to do a statistical analysis of *SHE* competition entrants. We jealously guarded the privacy of our readers and refused to let him have them. Marcus called me in and said "You're being pig-headed, but I respect your judgement". He was very, very good like that. But he used to say to me "Can't you get Michael to behave?" '

Michael's reputation for eccentricity may have started from his habit of never wearing shoes at work. The story of his having been seen washing the feet of his goat in the office gents is, unfortunately, apocryphal – it was a Scottie dog called Matilda.

'The endearing thing about Marcus was that he would allow you to see his state of mind – most bosses won't', said Pamela. 'You realised he was as full of doubts and fears as you were yourself. It was a remarkable characteristic. Most people would have buttoned themselves up completely and said "I am IT". He didn't – he could share his feelings. I never found him difficult to talk to.'

For the rest of the decade *SHE*, the book department and *Vanity Fair*, were to make up for the continuing losses on *Harper's Bazaar*.

*Harper's Bazaar* had been a financial problem pretty well since it was launched in 1929, except during the war years, when it was appointed by the Ministry of Information to 'exclusively handle fashion portfolio for propaganda in neutral countries'. Paper rationing restricted the magazine to ten issues a year, which were easily filled with advertising. After the war Anne Scott-James, former Women's Editor of *Picture Post*, took on the editorship, handing over to her Fashion Editor, Eileen Dickson, in 1951.

When Marcus joined the company the magazine was well produced, but the overall look was uninspiring and drab, with little to leaven the rather dull fashion, and circulation was falling. Joan Hornsey, who had been Features Editor since 1958, says: 'It was a good magazine, very literate with high standards. But the whole group was in need of gingering up.'

Marcus set about gingering up *Harper's*. He wrote to Dick Deems: 'I have found the editors friendly and co-operative. I have deliberately gone slowly and tried not to impose my views on them too bluntly. I think you wished me to avoid precipitating any crises and I know Ben feels the same.

'We are aiming to improve the quality of production and to make it even more a luxury magazine, but I am also trying to revitalise the magazine as a whole to give it a more definite personality and a more dramatic impact.'

Joan Hornsey was promoted to Assistant Editor and Marcus asked René Lecler, the idiosyncratic part-time Features Editor of *Good Housekeeping*, to double up as Features Editor on *Harper's*. René quickly started to build up a coterie of lively contributors. Robert Carrier, who had written his first article about cooking for Eileen Dickson in the late fifties, became a regular. His monthly food column graced the pages for about a year, until there was a falling out over copyright, and Carrier joined *Vogue*. The cookery column was taken over by Robin McDouall, of whom Marcus wrote: 'He is altogether different from Carrier. He is urbane, sophisticated and very charming . . . and is an extremely nice person.' But Marcus later wrote to McDouall: 'After four and a half years in connection with *Harper's Bazaar* I thought that I had become almost inured to alarms and excursions. But I am afraid I must admit to a deep shudder of horror at reading your recipe for Lancashire Hotpot in the August issue. As a Lancashire man born and bred may I please take issue with you.

'A Lancashire Hotpot *never* uses lamb chops. This is a kind of bastard by London out of Irish Stew. Good honest beef cut into chunks is essential. Further any Hotpot that cared for its reputation would not be without chestnuts and, if available, one or two oysters. This was the Hotpot my mother made and look what a strong boy I am!'

(The subject of hotpot was a running battle Marcus also fought with *Good Housekeeping*. He was never able to convince Carol Macartney, Principal of the Institute from 1966–79, as to the rights of the matter. Robin McDouall conceded: 'Can it be that Lancashire hot pot is like mint julep and varies from village to village and house to house?' The Morris family don't think so.)

The scope of *Harper's* was widened and soon included features on art investment, modern architecture, food, books, beauty and travel.

A typical suggestion from René Lecler was 'Their Graces. It's probably a throwback of my republican upbringing but I have always been fascinated by British dukes. . . . The marriage of Marlborough's droopy-lipped heir to the beautiful Tina encourages me in the belief that dukes have it all their own way. In a world full of peers, mostly uninteresting ones, dukes are something special. Have you ever seen a poor one? Have you ever seen a sane one? After Bedford, Argyll, Marlborough and the unspeakable Norfolk, what else? They float through life doing nothing except looking ducal. Whereas there are hundreds of earls, marquesses and viscounts, there are only thirty-six dukes – the most exclusive band in the world. Why not, if I may sound beastly, have a look at dooks by somebody with a sharp, funny and bad tempered pen?'

The contributors' list rapidly grew to include Malcolm Muggeridge, Compton Mackenzie, Maurice Edelman, Macdonald Hastings, Tom Driberg, Daniel Farson, Kenneth Allsop, Gavin Lyall and Stirling Moss as Motoring Correspondent.

Richard Berlin sent a note: 'I particularly like the bold fashion pages, a woman can really tell something about the clothes portrayed. I have heard any number of complimentary reports . . . about the rejuvenation of *Harper's Bazaar*. My compliments to you as I know you are the one who has been responsible for this change.'

At the 1963 AGM, the Board of Nat Mag (Ben McPeake, Marcus, Kay and Richard Berlin) reported its best result in the history of the company. Marcus became Managing Director and Bill Jackson was elected to the Board. Ben McPeake stayed on as Chairman until his retirement the following year, when Marcus decided that the Chairmanship of the Company should go to the President of the Hearst Corporation. Richard Berlin accepted 'on the understanding that he didn't wish to become involved in the detailed executive control of the company. . . . Mr Morris as Chief Executive would be required to act as Chairman of the Board as his Deputy.'

As Managing Director, Marcus was able to fight a successful rearguard action against the Americans who were keen to change the title of *Harper's Bazaar* to *Bazaar*, as it was in the States: 'The word 'Bazaar' in this country I think has quite the wrong connotation and implies something cheap.'

Circulation and advertisement revenue rose very slightly and the financial position was 'Lousy, but improving' according to an internal memo.

In order to exercise more control over the magazine and because they had a spare floor in the new building, it was decided to move *Harper's Bazaar* out of their lovely Brook Street, Mayfair, offices (where it was the Assistant Editor's job to order coal for the fires and plants for the back garden) into the utilitarian Chestergate House. In October Eileen and Marcus had a very stormy meeting, which resulted in tears and her resignation.

While the search went on for Eileen's successor, *Harper's* was edited by Marcus and Joan Hornsey, who didn't want to become Editor but quietly held the magazine together as Assistant Editor – for twenty-three years. Jane Stockwood, sister of Mervyn, rejoined the staff; Marcus had received a letter from John Betjeman asking Marcus to 'Turn this subject over in your kind heart and mind'. Jane was in need of a job; since she was a first-rate journalist, Marcus found no difficulty in employing her on *Harper's*, where she stayed for many years as a features writer.

Early in 1965 Nancy White, Editor of American *Harper's Bazaar*, suggested Ruth Lynam, Women's Page Editor of the *Telegraph* magazine but, as Ruth was young and inexperienced, Nancy became Editor-in-Chief. Dick Deems asked Fleur Cowles, the American journalist, author, painter and socialite, who had been living in England since 1955, to act as advisory editor. The company provided her with a secretary and office equipment and monthly editorial meetings were held at her chambers in Albany, Piccadilly. By May, Fleur was writing to Marcus cancelling the meetings and demanding that her name be taken off the masthead. It was said at the time that Fleur quickly decided that the magazine was going to be a disaster, but she says, 'It was hard to have any control. . . . I didn't think the magazine was going to be a disaster. . . . I simply reasoned that such an arrangement wasn't creatively fulfilling.'

Shirley Lord, wife of the carpet manufacturer Cyril, had been Beauty Editor since 1963 and Maggie Buchanan became Fashion Editor. Ann Dickenson joined the company as Promotions Editor: 'Ruth was quite unable to control two such forceful and machiavellian women as Shirley Lord and Maggie Buchanan. The tantrums, the rows. . . . I've never met such egos. I think they made Marcus's life a nightmare.'

Having an Editor-in-Chief in New York also created problems. Approval of proofs was usually merely a matter of form, but sometimes a storm blew up, as on the occasion Ruth used a black model on the cover. Nancy White and Dick Deems were outraged and said that it was totally against the company's policy. Marcus fully supported Ruth and said that it was too late to change. The story got into *Private Eye* in a garbled form, with Marcus being accused of racial prejudice; Joan Hornsey says that she and Marcus kept quiet because they didn't want to embarrass Hearst.

In 1965 Marcus installed René Lecler as Travel Editor of *Harper's*, an appointment described by Joan Hornsey as 'an inspiration'. Travel was just taking off and it was the start of a massive increase in travel advertising. René became one of the all time great travel editors, producing huge travel supplements and the successful and idiosyncratic book, *The 300 Best Hotels in the World*.

But Marcus still wasn't happy and said so to Nancy White when she came over for the 1966 Paris shows. '*Harper's* should be concerned, first and foremost, with beautiful clothes, with style and class and impeccable taste. And this must apply to the way they are presented. . . . I believe that a woman who cares about fashion is interested in looking at a beautiful picture of a beautiful dress and she does not need tricks or gimmicks to attract her attention.

'Fashion Editors in general, and photographers too, appear to be saying "We cannot show a picture of a girl in a suit. We must put her on a camel, or hang her upside down from a chandelier."

'I think as you do that we have an able and potentially successful Editor in Ruth Lynam and a good team who are enthusiastic in the face of many difficulties. I want to help and encourage them, not hinder or depress. . . .'

By the following summer Nancy White was no longer Editor-in-Chief. Although Marcus was still publicly supporting Ruth Lynam, circulation had dropped in the two years of her editorship. Ruth says today that she feels she was pushed on to Marcus by the Americans: 'I was too young. I'd had no editing experience – I was a journalist. I had no real idea of what I was doing. . . . There's no way I could have done it without Joan Hornsey – she was simply marvellous.'

Ruth went and Marcus, against his better judgement, bowed to the insistence of Dick Deems and the Editors of *SHE* became Managing Editors of *Harper's Bazaar*.

While Pamela and Michael were inspired on *SHE*, their sojourn on *Harper's Bazaar* was not a success; within three months *Harper's* was transformed into an upmarket *SHE*.

Joan Hornsey described it as a disaster: 'It was like a rich woman's *Woman's Own*. They threw out all the beautiful fashion pictures and introduced masses of columns. They were lovely people, absolutely right for *SHE*, absolutely wrong for *Harper's*.'

Marcus agreed – as did Pamela and Michael – and it wasn't long before Marcus was again on the lookout for someone to perform miracles on the ailing magazine.

In 1968 Michael Lewis, Chairman of Oxley Industries, who had recently bought *Queen* magazine from Jocelyn Stevens (Edward Hulton's nephew), offered to buy *Harper's Bazaar*. Richard Berlin countered with an offer to buy *Queen*.

Michael Lewis declined, but some of the talent that had been collected by Jocelyn Stevens started to move across town to Victoria. Brian Braithwaite, Advertisement Director of *Queen*, who had worked on *Farmers Weekly* and *Lilliput,* was one of them, recruited by Peter Cooper, who insisted on Marcus's paying him a head-hunter's fee, much to Marcus's indignation. One of Brian's first sights of Marcus had been at a party in the Hulton Press office in Shoe Lane. Marcus was dancing sexily with a beautiful young woman while Brian was standing next to another beautiful young woman, whom he didn't know. Brian said, 'Do you know, that chap's a vicar?' The young woman replied, 'Yes, I know, I'm his wife.' Later in the evening, somewhat flushed with wine, Brian was again standing next to a beautiful young woman; Marcus was dancing with yet another of the same and Brian said again, 'Do you know, that man's a vicar?' The young woman replied, 'Yes, I'm still his wife.'

Brian brought with him his young Ad Manager, Terry Mansfield; they both turned down a simultaneous offer from Condé Nast as 'whatever we do at Nat Mag will be a hundred per cent improvement, because things are so bad at *Harper's* and *Vanity Fair*.' With them went Uta Canning, Braithwaite's assistant – the exodus caused Michael Lewis to think of suing Marcus for alienation of staff. Although welcomed by Marcus, Terry and Brian had a less enthusiastic reception from Bill Jackson, who made it clear that he didn't like advertising people and allegedly informed Brian, after two bottles of wine at lunch, that 'Marcus doesn't know anything about running this company. I should have run the company.'

It was well known within the company that the Managing Director and the Company Secretary were always at odds but Bill Jackson says, 'Our reputation of not talking to each other is completely false. We liked to convey that impression – it was useful for people to think we were at loggerheads as we often got information we wouldn't otherwise have got. We couldn't have worked together for twenty-odd years if all the rumours were true. We both knew each other's failings and best points. Marcus was the boss and wouldn't give way, which would irritate me, but it's natural to have arguments.'

While Brian and Terry were rejuvenating *Harper's* advertising, Marcus was introduced by Peter Cooper to Clive Irving, who describes himself as 'a magazine doctor. We played a bridging role, to prepare the ground for later editors. It was a travelling show – we selected people who'd not be on the permanent staff but just work on transition issues. . . . It was up to the company to decide if they stayed or not.'

The team that Clive brought in turned the genteel world of *Harper's Bazaar* upside down. The job of Fashion Editor went to Mollie Parkin with whom Clive was having an affair. Joan Price, formerly on *Queen*, became Beauty Editor. His Features Editor was Sally Beauman, a bright twenty-three-year-old with Afro hair who, she says, 'was so young I didn't know my arse from my elbow'. Art Director was a young, long-haired former *Eagle* fan, David Driver, who found it very difficult working for Marcus because of the awe in which he held *Eagle*'s creator. When Marcus sent the team bottles of champagne to celebrate their first issue, David thought, '. . . how amazing. Every week of my life as a child I saw this signature and now here it is on a personal label.'

With all this talent the 'new' magazine should have worked well (the March 1969 issue was heralded 'The return of the Beautiful Magazine').

But Sally Beauman, now a very successful novelist, says: 'It was a ludicrous situation. There was no editor and Clive, having appointed us, instantly disappeared. We had a very unclear brief from him, except to inject new life into it.'

Initially Marcus stayed at arm's length but, as the weeks went by, he was forced to take a hand. Mollie Parkin was frequently drunk and foul-mouthed, insulting all and sundry, especially Marcus, who wanted fashion photographs that showed the clothes, not the self-indulgent (albeit pretty) pictures that Mollie produced. Many people thought that the fashion pictures in the March issue contained more than a hint of paedophilia. April's pictures were dramatic, but you couldn't see the clothes. Marcus's patience snapped when, for May, he was presented with pictures photographed on sand dunes in Wales – very atmospheric shots, but the outfits were just draperies made up for the shoot. When the proofs were brought to Marcus (who was at home with flu), he hit the roof and telephoned Mollie. She cheeked him once too often and he sacked her there and then.

Another alcoholic, Jeffrey Bernard, was hired to write about horse racing. Sally Beauman had terrible trouble with him, as his copy was always very late and badly written. He turned up drunk in her office one day demanding money. 'I don't know if it was for the next article he hadn't written, or the previous one which had been rejected,' and he wouldn't leave. 'Jeffrey was getting quite violent – threatening, falling down, weeping – Marcus came down and just told him, "You must leave and you must leave now". Jeffrey started railing and Marcus stood quietly and said, "You're coming and I'm taking you out of the building". Jeffrey went with him!'

David Driver left after three issues and went to the *Radio Times*, where he was able to give work to two more of his childhood's heroes – Frank Hampson and Frank Bellamy. David was saddened by the fact that whenever he said anything complimentary about Frank Bellamy to Frank Hampson, Hampson was angry and quite vicious about Bellamy. Bellamy became a father figure for David, but, he says, Bellamy 'wasn't all that pleasant about Frank Hampson, either.'

In the autumn two more ex-*Queen* employees arrived at *Harper's*, Fashion Editor Jennifer Hocking and former Art Director, Willie Landels.

The following January Marcus appointed Willie Deputy Editor. Willie is regarded by many as a genius and he transformed the magazine. One of the first changes he made was to the logo – he altered the typeface letter by letter, one a month; no one noticed. He was not always an easy man to work with, however, and Sally Beauman resigned in high dudgeon. She went to the *Telegraph* for a brief period and was then appointed Editor of *Queen* by Michael Lewis. Unfortunately, nobody told her that Lewis had been holding secret meetings with Marcus. Warned by Willie (who heard it from Adrian Bailey, then Art Director of *Queen*) that Michael Lewis was hoping to sell *Queen* to Peter Cadbury, Marcus jumped in and secured Lewis's agreement to sell the magazine in exchange for £1,000 and the contract to print it, *The Connoisseur* and *Vanity Fair*. By November *Harpers & Queen* had been born, edited by Willie Landels.

The new magazine combined the best of both the old. First thoughts were to call it *Harpers Queen*, but Marcus insisted on the ampersand which would make it truly *Harpers* **and** *Queen*. *Queen* had been a society magazine when it was launched by Samuel Beeton (husband of Mrs) in 1861 and one of the reasons for its success a century later was the society pages written by Betty Kenward, *Jennifer's Diary*. Betty, then aged sixty-four, joined the new magazine with alacrity and continued her chronicling of high society until her retirement, some twenty years later. In 1972 Joan Hornsey retired, Fiona Macpherson became Executive Editor and Ann Barr arrived as Features Editor. It was Ann who, with Peter York, wrote *The Official Sloane Ranger Handbook,* which was in the best seller lists for a year, although it was one of the sub-editors, Tina Margetts, who coined the phrase 'Sloane Ranger'. Humphrey Lyttelton wrote the restaurant reviews, until pressure of musical work forced him to resign; Larry Adler took over but his style didn't suit Marcus, who called it 'terrible and so very vulgar'. He preferred Leslie Kenton (daughter of jazz musician Stan Kenton), who became Beauty Editor and something of a health guru, introducing Marcus to the world of alternative medicines, which he took up with enthusiasm.

Dick Deems, inevitably, wasn't happy with the magazine and called for 'serious reappraisal'; Marcus had to point out that losses had been cut by two thirds since 1969 and that, as *Harpers & Queen* was carrying three times as many advertising pages as American *Harper's Bazaar*, the magazine just needed to be given time.

And with time, Marcus built a very strong team – *Harpers & Queen* became an extremely successful and stylish magazine.

In 1949 National Magazines had re-launched *Vanity Fair*. Braithwaite and Barrell again: 'This magazine must not be confused with the famous old Victorian title noted for its political caricatures, but was in effect a fashion magazine for the shorthand typist and as such was an immediate success. . . . It is surprising that it should have been so successfully launched during a period of clothes rationing. . . . [It] offered the teenager and the younger market exactly what they wanted at prices they could afford.'

During the 1950s *Vanity Fair* had the largest sale of any British fashion magazine but, in the sixties, it began to face competition from Newnes' new magazine *Flair*. In 1963 Marcus recruited his old ally from *Housewife*, Laurie Purden, as Assistant Editor to Phyllis Bayley Van Thal, Editor since the launch. The following year, in a game of musical chairs, he appointed Hazel Evans, Fashion and Beauty Editor of *Good Housekeeping*, in Laurie's place.

Hazel had a difficult time working under Phyllis Bayley, whom she describes as having some enormous hold over the company. Phyl was rumoured to have had an affair with someone at Hearst; certainly Marcus tiptoed very gingerly around her hurt feelings when she thought he was trying to get rid of her. Marcus managed to persuade her to step up to Editor-in-Chief and Hazel took over as Editor.

One of her more unexpected duties was to accompany the boss to E Wing of HM Prison, Holloway. Marcus had become involved in prison visiting through Margaret Hamilton and he dragooned Hazel into going with him to talk to the inmates about fashion. She hated it. 'The girls would put on the gramophone and dance together. Marcus just chatted to them, but they'd pull at my clothes and say, "Is *that* what they're wearing?" I wriggled out of going whenever I could.'

Hazel also fought a losing battle with *Vanity Fair*. Circulation continued to drop and Dick Deems nagged Marcus to get rid of her: 'The magazine does not have the urgency of appeal that seems to be so necessary in today's competitive publishing. I don't think Hazel has what it will take to make a success of this magazine and I think that unless we develop now something that has much more "sock-it-to-me" *Vanity Fair* will go out of existence.'

By 1970 *Vanity Fair* was losing almost as much as *Harper's Bazaar* and, fed up with pressure from all sides, Hazel decided that she'd had enough and asked Marcus to make her redundant; Audrey Slaughter, former Editor of *Petticoat* and *Honey*, took over.

Hazel continued to work freelance for Nat Mag for some twenty years, writing mainly about gardening and travel. In 1971 her book *How to cheat at gardening* was published by Ebury Press. She subsequently started work on a companion volume on cookery but, when she offered it to Ebury, was told it was already being done. Marcus had met a young chef, Delia Smith, at a party; Delia told him that she wanted to write a cookery book, and Marcus suggested the How to Cheat formula. *How to cheat at cooking*, full of recipes using tinned, frozen and instant ingredients, was the start of Delia Smith's amazing career. Hazel was upset but forgiving; Marcus stayed at her house in Morocco on a solitary holiday a couple of years later.

The book publishing arm of National Magazines became very successful through the sixties. In 1961 Marcus decided that, as certain books would not fit the *Good Housekeeping* or *Connoisseur* imprints, he would dream up another one; staff photographer Ken Swain came up with 'Ebury Press', after their offices in Ebury Street. The marketing of the company's books was handed to publishers Michael Joseph. As well as the wide range of *Good Housekeeping* books, there were *SHE* books, sponsored booklets and pictorial encyclopaedias. In 1963, *Tutankhamen* was published jointly by *Connoisseur* and Michael Joseph, produced by George Rainbird, who had parted company with Ruari McLean in 1958. Kay Thomas had written to Marcus, 'in view of the fact that the subject is of such limited interest, I would have thought that the total edition of 20,000 copies is far too high and would suggest that this should be dispensed with'. In October 1963, 150,000 copies were printed; by 1985, over one and a half million copies had been sold worldwide. *Tutankhamen* was selected by the American Booksellers Association as one of the best 250 books published between 1961 and 1965 and a copy was presented to President Lyndon Johnson as a gift for the White House Library.

In 1965 came the joint publication of the Revd W. Keble Martin's *The Concise British Flora in Colour*, studies from life drawn and painted over a span of sixty years. Seven leading publishers had turned the book down, leaving the eighty-seven-year-old parson in despair of seeing his life's work published. His daughter-in-law wrote to the Duke of Edinburgh, who was at the time trying to encourage the country's youth to take an interest in wildlife and, by a series of circuitous routes, the book ended up on George Rainbird's desk. He had no trouble persuading Marcus and Peter Hebden of Michael Joseph that it would be a good investment. They ordered a first printing of 50,000; the first 40,000 sold out within six weeks and it sold hundreds of thousands over the next two to three years. In 1967 the Post Office issued three Keble Martin British Flora stamps. In reply to a letter of congratulation from Marcus, Keble Martin wrote: 'It seems strange that I should be more widely known through [my botanical drawings] which were my recreation only, than through my work as a padre. In the latter I have striven to be a "workman that needeth not to be ashamed". I still take an early celebration every Sunday morning and visit persistently, but not as an incumbent, only as a has-been.'

Ebury Press had three books on the best-seller list in 1966 – *The Waters of Rome*, *The Shell Bird Book* and *Flora* (its second year on the list). Over the next ten years or so Ebury Press and Rainbird published such diverse titles as the *Encylopaedia of Firearms*, *European Bronze Statuettes*, the *Shell Guides to Britain*, *Thorburn's Birds*, *World Theatre*, *Sherry and the Wines of Spain* (written and researched by George Rainbird) and the *Dictionary of Garden Plants in Colour*.

In 1976 the Rainbird role was taken over by Dorling Kindersley who, with fairly hefty investment from Ebury Press, produced the remarkably successful series of photography books which did so much for the careers of John Hedgecoe and Michael Langford. Through the 1970s, they published about twenty titles a year, including *London in Maps* and *The Complete Illustrated West Highland Terrier*! Ebury Press was run for many years by Roger Barrett, who had taken over from Margaret Hamilton as Marcus's Personal Assistant, before Marcus put him in charge of books.

Roger's replacement as PA, Beverlie Flower, also rose higher in the organisation. When Personnel Manager Susie Babbington left in 1969, Marcus told Beverlie that she was going to take over. Beverlie confessed that she didn't know anything about personnel but Marcus said, 'It doesn't matter. I want someone who knows the company – you can learn the rest.' Which she soon did; she also took over the running of Marcus's personal life, helped by Jim Lucas, who had become Marcus's driver in 1968. Between them they organised his shopping and laundry, paid his bills and found the dozens of Christmas gifts he gave each year. Beverlie house-sat when Marcus and Jess went away and bought 'red roses and cello' (cellophane) for his 'pretty ladies'. She also had to cope with one who had a nervous breakdown when the affair finished, but Beverlie took it all in her stride. Marcus was remarkably fortunate in his personal staff; over the years he had many loyal (and attractive) secretaries and PAs, but Beverlie became, and remains, a close family friend to all the Morrises.

Another area of success was the cookery and housecraft books produced by *Good Housekeeping*. The magazine itself had suffered a decline in circulation in the first half of the 1960s. Oliver Robinson, son of W. Heath Robinson, had been at the helm since 1947 and had seen it through some extremely successful years, but the magazine was now looking tired. Marcus wanted new blood, and he wanted Laurie Purden to inject it, but didn't want to hurt Oliver's feelings. So Laurie worked on *Vanity Fair*, waiting for the right time for Marcus to tell Oliver. While she was waiting and occasionally nagging Marcus about the *Good Housekeeping* job, he decided that he needed her on *House Beautiful*.

*House Beautiful* had never reached its target circulation. It had an old-fashioned, 'heavy' appearance; in 1961 Marcus had asked Ruari McLean to advise on layout and presentation, a task that Ruari undertook for all the magazines at one point or another. But even Ruari and Laurie couldn't save it and, in August 1968, Marcus went down to the *House Beautiful* offices to explain to the staff why the company could no longer afford to carry the losses and the magazine was incorporated with *Good Housekeeping*.

By May 1965, Marcus had steeled himself to tell Oliver Robinson that he wanted Laurie as editor of *GH*, and Oliver was appointed Editor-in-Chief. This created a difficult situation for Laurie: 'Marcus caused an awful lot of problems through not taking decisive harsh action. The kindness had a double edge because it could hurt, even though not intentionally. *GH* was going very swiftly down the tubes and I was put in to shore it up. Oliver, as Editor-in-Chief, insisted on coming to my first editorial meeting; to develop a new policy, whichever way you phrase it, is a criticism of the previous editor. In the end, I think Oliver saw that this was an untenable position for him, and Marcus appointed him as Production Planning Director.'

Laurie modernised the magazine and injected interest and style, setting it on its way to becoming one of the great magazines of its day – and a splendid money-earner for Nat Mag. Laurie stepped down due to ill-health in 1973, becoming Editor-in-Chief) and handed over to her deputy, Charlotte Lessing, who had worked on the magazine for some years, having previously also been at Hulton Press, on *Lilliput*.

Laurie was devoted to Marcus. 'He was not an easy man to know. Those of us who had the good luck to get to know him, as Keith [Kotch, her husband] and I did, understood that curious dichotomy of a man of the flesh and a man of the spirit. Women could always get closer to Marcus than men. Very few Englishmen actually like women enough to be confident enough to be at ease with them. Marcus liked women, and he liked good-looking women.

'He wasn't a great communicator and wouldn't be chatty in the lift with someone he didn't know well, but the moment that person got any personal problems, absolute miracles happened. He hadn't a lot of time for whingers, but had an instinct for recognising when a personal problem was important and then he would be supportive to a quite extraordinary degree. To me, this was the man of God coming out. He could never understand that people could find him unapproachable.

'He was a very good student of people, perhaps because he was basically quiet, an observer more than a talker. He was very protective of his editors and kept the Americans off our backs. They were very interfering in the early days; they would jet over if things were good, or if they wanted a trip to London, or if things were rocky. They'd bowl into your office and say "Hi, how are things?" and, in a very British way, you'd say, meaning things are bloody good, "Everything's fine" and watch their faces drop. You had to learn the language of enthusiasm. Dick Deems would worry me sick, but Marcus could handle them and could understand them.

'Praise from Marcus was rare but, when it did come, you felt you'd been given a million pounds.'

Marcus was equally devoted to Laurie and when Keith died suddenly in 1979, even although Laurie was now working for the opposition, Marcus arranged all the business of announcements and the funeral, which he conducted at St Bride's.

'In the early days, Marcus and Keith and Bernard Audley were off to night clubs – always had a lot of fun. We used to delight in making Marcus laugh. He must have been born looking old and normally didn't laugh a lot; when you did make him laugh his whole face – this elderly baby face – crumpled. Between them, particularly Bernard, who teased him dreadfully, they could make him crumple helplessly into laughter.

'You felt able to talk to him about anything – I'm not talking about sex here, but that too, he loved talking about sex. It also allowed you to talk about lots of other things you wouldn't normally talk to people about. He was one of the few people I've ever been able to talk to about religion, a very private aspect of most of us.

'You could ask him about anything, talk to him about anything. He never minimised or put you down and he gave honest responses about whatever it was. He understood women and didn't create barriers, which most men do. He wasn't afraid of talking about emotional things and he wasn't shockable. You never wished afterwards that you hadn't said something or that, because you worked for him, it would make the working relationship different.

'Keith was totally uncommunicative but he could talk to Marcus; I don't know about what, but he felt him equally someone he could trust. It was an element of the confessional. There was a sort of religious element to Marcus that had nothing to do with the Church. He was a good man and perhaps in some ways tormented; the Church can screw up people.

'An interesting thing as an outsider watching Marcus's family develop and grow was that there was an awful lot of family, always what appeared to be a natural, automatic part of his life – he always seemed to be surrounded by family. Jessica and the kids were a very necessary part of his life.'

# Chapter Eighteen

Laurie was right. And while Marcus was battling at the National Magazine Company, family life went on as normal – well, normal for the Morrises.

Marcus and Frank Hampson had both bought their houses from Hulton Press's new owners and Marcus decided to instal central heating in his. At the beginning of 1961 the old-fashioned kitchen and scullery were ripped out and the family scattered to the four winds: Jess was touring with *Waiting in the Wings*, Jan was studying in Paris. Kate stayed with Ruth and Jack while preparing for an audition for drama school, Sally lodged with long-suffering neighbours, Roma and Alfred Black, so that she could get to school. Simon was back at his prep school in Hampshire. Jan wrote to her best friend: 'The house is being knocked about, heaters, boilers, floorboards, walls being knocked down and pulled out. Mummy keeps moving around and Daddy seems to have disappeared.' He was staying with George Rainbird.

By May the house was habitable again and Marcus and Jess went to America for a month while the gardener, Mr Millward, decorated and the girls cleared up. Jan wrote to her godmother, 'Mummy and Daddy went off to New York, on business, they said, but they had a whale of a time, with six days on the way aboard the *New Amsterdam* and weekends in the mountains of Connecticut and in Bermuda. They got full VIP treatment wherever they went – First Class and all expenses paid.'

She wrote to her parents: 'We haven't been doing too badly, but we seem to have spent an awful lot of money – it's all down on paper. . . . Granny M rang last night to see how we were. She seemed a bit dubious that we're all alone but I reassured her. Simon was on good form at the weekend. He was disappointed you weren't there.'

In September Jan confided to her diary: 'Daddy went to Berlin for a day yesterday afternoon but he's not back yet – I hope he hasn't been arrested. Last night Mummy talked a lot about Daddy and how unfaithful he's been since they were married. It's so silly – they're both miserable and unsatisfied and yet they don't want a divorce. They both love each other in a lot of ways, but they haven't any trust or understanding left. . . . I didn't feel anything when she told me of the affairs Daddy has had – I suppose I ought to be shocked and hate Daddy for ever more. I've never, except perhaps when I was very, very young, believed my parents to be perfect – I just love them both equally and unreservedly – there are times when they get me down and I get them down and we hate each other but it never lasts long.'

Jan didn't mention in her diary the affair that Jess had with an artist she met while on holiday on the south coast with Sally and Simon. Ned was very much in love with her and asked her to leave Marcus and marry him. Marcus complained to Jan that he felt desperately lonely but, knowing of her father's peccadilloes, Jan was not as sympathetic as she might have been. After much emotional turmoil, Jess decided that the family was more important – and she still loved Marcus.

In March 1962 the Morrises moved again. It was mainly lack of funds that forced this move; Marcus had spent so much on the alterations to The Oak House that he couldn't afford to live there. But with the children growing up, central London was more convenient than Hampstead Heath. The house was sold and Marcus took a lease on a flat in Oakwood Court, a large red-brick mansion block behind High Street, Kensington, from where they could hear the mournful cry of the peacocks in Holland Park.

The flat was redecorated as befitted a Managing Director Designate and Marcus decided to smarten the family up with new furniture. A boudoir grand piano replaced the old upright, which was lent to a relative, and out went the Victorian mahogany dining table on which *Eagle* had been born. George Rainbird advised reproduction antiques.

In May, Granny Morris died. Marcus was travelling in Africa, looking into the possibilities of magazines for children and young people. The international telephone exchange did a magnificent job in tracing him; the funeral was held in Eric Cook's church in Worle.

That summer the Morrises had their last family holiday together, on the Costa Blanca. Jess drove the family down through France and was extremely glad to meet up with Marcus in Barcelona, whither he had flown. Benidorm was just beginning to be built-up and for Marcus it was not a happy holiday. The luxury house he'd been promised turned out to be a rather grotty bungalow, next door to a night club (forbidden to the girls on their own). The children were quite happy, swimming, water-skiing, sunbathing and exploring the countryside (which still existed then), but Marcus complained in the strongest terms to the holiday company when they returned. He was offered a full refund, but turned it down.

The following year the friendship between Marcus and John Miller, General Manager of Hearst, was further cemented when Sally, having finished a short secretarial course, went to the States for a holiday with John and Bunny, who had a son around the same age. Marcus wrote to a friend: 'I was very sorry that I had to leave your party last night rather earlier than I would have liked. But my youngest daughter flew to New York this morning and I really felt that I had to be with her for a bit on her last night at home, so I sent her and my wife to a restaurant and joined them for coffee. I am sure you will understand.'

When he was eighteen, John's younger son, Mark, came to London for what would today be called 'work experience'. Marcus organised a job for him at Claridge's; he had no work permit and was not paid – Marcus said to him, 'If nobody knows about it, it's perfectly legal'. Mark, a first-class mathematician, later rose swiftly through the ranks of the Hearst Corporation: 'Numbers made Marcus nervous. He and John both understood what was important in publishing – both said you can always buy number crunchers, but truly talented editors are hard to find. Publishing success is not made by advertising sales people or circulation people, it's made by great editors.

Marcus and Dad treated talent with great respect and were able to get the right people.'

Marcus also had a good relationship with Richard Berlin's younger daughter, Christina, who first met him when she was about twelve. 'He always treated me like an adult, nobody else did. We had serious debates about God: I was trying to avoid being a Catholic. He helped me a lot when I was a teenager. He always insisted that I make my own decisions. He would never give me an easy way out, he would never give me an answer. And he always told my parents that they worried too much; he said you've got to misbehave as a kid!

'I remember at a dinner at the Mirabelle, Father was going on about his friend Joe McCarthy and Marcus said, "In my opinion, Dick, Joe McCarthy is the one man in American history who should be shot." Father wasn't used to being contradicted and loved him for it. They could argue and Marcus was never scared of Father, who was quite in awe of his intelligence and *savoir faire.*'

Jess was still busy, appearing in episodes of *Compact*, one of the first TV soaps, set in a magazine office (having visited the offices of *Harper's Bazaar* and *Vanity Fair* to soak up the atmosphere), *Emergency Ward 10* and *Z Cars*, and a number of TV plays. A fan wrote, 'I was just amazed at your beautiful sensitive face, conveying every character of the lonely, frustrated widow. . . . I am still under the sway of that haunting memory of your superb acting.'

In the spring of 1963 Jess joined what became known as 'Peter Potter's Campany of Actors' – a British Council Tour which took in Uganda, Ethiopia, the Sudan, Kenya, Mauritius and Egypt. She was fond of saying that she was the only woman to have played Shakespeare in the Throne Room of the Emperors of Abyssinia, and proud to have been banned in the Sudan for being too sexy (playing Kate in *The Taming of the Shrew* at the age of forty-eight).

While she was away, Jess and Marcus resumed their correspondence habits of the war years. Absence, it seemed, really did make the heart grow fonder.

London, June: 'I had rather too long a sleep this afternoon. I wish you had been here darling! I would have given you our call-sign – the mating call of the greater-bellied morris-bird – known by its Latin name of marcus gintonicus – "Would you like a brandy, darling?" According to the reply – either "I don't think I'd better" or "I'd love one" (or on special occasions "yes, *please*"), you know whether the female is in season or not. Actually, according to the ornithologists, this particular bird – by nature rather shy – is allowed by the male to preen her feathers & show her attractions & without waiting for the male's call-sign, to make her own invitation call "may I have a brandy, please?".

'The female wasn't here today to answer the call (where was she, I wonder?) so I went to my lonesome bed & slept.

'It's strange – since normally I hate writing – I would like to write about all sorts of things – but somehow I feel I mustn't. I have felt from the beginning that this trip for you was a break away from a pattern of life – & particularly from me. A chance to be free – to "do the things you want to do". And so I have had the feeling that I ought not to *intrude* – even by telling you that I love you. It's putting chains on you. I feel that even writing like this may be selfish. I have the feeling that you want to be away from it all for a bit – You deserve it after all you have done for me all these years – my darling, loyal, long-suffering Jessica.

'You said not so long ago that I was your "rock". If you still want that, the rock will always be there – *always* – a bit jagged in places, with nasty rough edges & some soft crumbly bits which flake away when you grasp them – but I think basically a fairly firm rock – & yours if you want it.'

Kampala, July: 'Cor lumme, corblimey, & any other cor you can think of including my own "cor", quod marcus gintonicus semper tenet.

'Darling, I would love you to write *all* your thoughts – as if you could intrude – people can't intrude where they already are – & you're an integral part of me now as you always have been. I've got you, as they say, under my skin. Being away has made me realise this all the more.'

London, July: 'Don't worry about any of us here. Everything is fine & all are fit & healthy. But we are rather like a lot of planets without their sun to revolve around. Perhaps you don't realize how much we all love you & need you & depend on you (or do you? & is it too much of a strain being the sun of a solar system?)

'As I told my latest head-shrinker – who says I *don't* need analysis but just someone to *talk* to – because all my life I've never *talked* to anyone (they've talked to me & I've listened) & as I told him (this sentence is getting rather complicated) – I want to be able to *show* my affection & love for you – to stop being undemonstrative & closing up on myself. Because it is *you* I love & want to spend the rest of my life with.

'I'd love to talk to you – and take you to bed, right now. Why don't we make love more often darling, when we have the chance? Perhaps, because I'm a semi-impotent old man. . . . According to the books it's very usual, at our age, for "the initiative to pass from the man to the woman"! So perhaps you'd better start revealing more of your initiative more often. . . . Only don't start revealing it to anyone else.

'And I want us to have more *fun* together – & talk more – & get closer. Shall we try? We are really very close deep down, aren't we? – I know I couldn't imagine being without you. . . . The girls are all fine and being good and looking after me.' But since he says in another letter, 'I'm shortly going to open the tin of pilchards Sally got for me – I had the baked beans last night after I got back from Highfield.'. . the looking after seems to have been minimal. He made up for it by going with Kay Thomas and John Brebner to Sandown Park races and to Epsom, where they had a regular box, for the Oaks.

In August Jan married Richard Hallwood, nephew of Ann Shaw; for an engagement present Marcus gave Jan a cheque for a hundred pounds with a recommendation to take Richard to Paris for a dirty weekend. As Jess was away until a few days before the wedding, Jan had a free hand with the arrangements, ably assisted by Margaret Hamilton, who also made some of the bridesmaids' dresses. Jan wrote to her mother, 'I asked Daddy how much I can spend on patterns and material and he said he didn't have any money anyway so it didn't make any difference.'

The service at St Bride's was conducted by a plethora of priests – Marcus, Eric Cook and Chad Varah; the reception was held at the Guildhall and the flowers were by Marcus and Jess's friend, Constance Spry. As a mark of appreciation for all that Marcus had done for St Bride's, the choirmaster, Gordon Reynolds, waived his usual fee and the churchwardens offered the choir payments as their wedding present.

Marcus may have been a little disappointed that none of the three girls had opted for university, but he never nagged them about it. Though Jan's godmother, who had known Marcus as a child, wrote: 'Somehow with your parents' brains I rather expected you would have had an academical career. Your father was the most brilliant young child I ever knew and I always knew he would do great things. . . . You ought to have inherited brains from both parents – your father was an infant prodigy. . . . It's surprising how your father's career has changed since the war, I always thought he'd grow to be a Bishop or something big inside the Church. . . . I had hoped for better things and a University education from your father's daughter! . . . from all your letters you seem to be quite a "good time girl" in fact, not at all like a parson's daughter.'

In 1964, Simon passed his Common Entrance exam to Marlborough College, in spite of Marcus's misgivings about his prep school education. He wasn't doing particularly well at Highfield and Marcus wrote to the headmaster, Peter Mills: 'I think very often Simon has been too shy to speak up when he has not understood something. . . . I have pressed him pretty firmly on the importance of working hard to get into Marlborough, but I don't want to go so far as to get him too anxious or depressed about it. . . . In my experience a child is lazy, complacent or casual because the experts who are supposed to teach him have not learned the art of arousing his interest. They very rarely seem to succeed in making the pursuit of knowledge an exciting and fascinating thing for its own sake. They only succeed in making it a bore.

'I found it very interesting to note that during the holidays when he has had a private tutor he has been enthusiastic and has felt that certain things for the first time "made sense". . . . Simon has never once complained about his experiences at Highfield where he appears to have been happy. He has merely expressed disappointment and puzzlement at some of his reports, partly, I think, because he felt he has been letting me down. This is a reaction which I certainly do not want him to feel.'

Mills replied: 'In the past he has behaved like a boy who comes from a home where there is considerable tension and where the boy has not had consistent attention from his parents. In fact, he used to put on an air of

*Marcus conducted Jan's wedding in St Bride's*

rather apologising for his existence. . . . I am not worried about his failing for Marlborough next term as he has made considerable progress this term.'

Marcus commented: 'As to tension and lack of attention you may be right, though I do not really think it is true to any marked extent beyond the fact that there are three other children to attend to as well, and that both my wife and I are engaged in creative, exacting and highly competitive work.

'Certainly the people who have met Simon do not appear to find him a "badly-done-to child" but, in many ways, quite self-possessed and even confident.'

On social occasions Simon always seemed at ease and he had beautiful manners but he also, poor lad, suffered from three bossy elder sisters, who went to a day school, while he was away from home most of the year. And, it has to be said, Marcus and Jess were not good at attending speech days or sports days, quite often cancelling at the last minute. These duties often fell to the girls and to Richard. Marcus also preached fairly regularly at Highfield, which may not have gone down very well with Simon's contemporaries.

In 1964 the Richmond Repertory Theatre, where Sally was working as a student Assistant Stage Manager, put on the premiere of *The Uncertain Heroine* (later renamed *The First Fish*), starring Moira Lister and Paul Carpenter, a Canadian actor who was brother-in-law to Alfred and Roma Black. Sally persuaded her father to become an 'angel'; Marcus took out a £500 investment and inveigled George Rainbird into splitting it 50/50. Unfortunately and sadly, Paul Carpenter died suddenly in rehearsal and his replacement was not up to the part. After the first night at the Savoy, George wrote to Marcus: 'Thank you for a lovely evening – quite a wonderful way of seeing one's investments down the drain – Damn the critics especially Levin – but they may be wrong. Anyway no regrets whatever happens.'

The play was about a wife who hires a call girl to restore her husband's libido. Various publicity stunts were suggested by Marcus, including arranging a fight in the theatre audience and getting the play banned by the Mothers' Union; the stunts didn't come off, but the play did, taking the Morris and Rainbird money with it.

The winter of 1965–66 played havoc with Jess's bronchitis and in February, she, Kate and Sal went down to Cornwall with family friend, actor Rowland Davies, to shake off their winter bugs. Marcus had to make his regular trip to New York – he shook off *his* winter bugs in Eleuthera in the Bahamas, where he had a romantic encounter with a beautiful Mexican singer and dancer, Carmen de la Vega. He left her disconsolate when he returned to New York for another round of meetings. He told Jess that 'this trip has, I think, been more worthwhile than all the others from the point of view of establishing good relationships with Hearst.'

That summer Granny Dunning moved in to the flat in Oakwood Court, as she could no longer manage the stairs at Ruth and Jack's house; she was an awkward guest, who pinched Marcus's favourite armchair and hogged the television. It was a particularly busy time for Jess, with a number of television and radio performances, and she was about to lose the assistance of her younger daughters. Kate decided it was time to leave home and moved into a flat with friends, much to Jess's annoyance, and Marcus gave Sally an early twenty-first birthday present of a one-way trip to New Zealand.

Soon after Sal sailed, on the ill-fated Italian immigrant ship the *Achille Lauro*, Jess played a short season at the Wimbledon Theatre in *Who's Afraid of Virginia Woolf*, with Bill Owen, for which they received rave reviews. Marcus, left with only Granny D for company in the evenings, moved into a flat near Sloane Street.

Jan wrote to Sally in November: 'Mummy rang yesterday and said she hadn't heard from you for ages. Please write and reassure her, you know what she's like. Mummy and Granny are both knitting furiously. I had forgotten that Mummy could knit and she does it terribly well.'

The knitting was in aid of Marcus and Jess's first grandchild, Toby Marcus John (no Harston!), born just after Christmas, much to his mother's chagrin – she missed the New Year's Eve party at Marcus's new pad.

Marcus had felt the need for a place of his own, for a breathing space away from the monstrous regiment. He found one in an unlikely area, the East End of London. A row of half a dozen eighteenth-century sail-makers' cottages in Narrow Street, fronting on to the River Thames near the Isle of Dogs, was being redeveloped by a co-operative led by the author Andrew Sinclair. Marcus leased number 82 and, until the conversion of the interior was finished, lived in Andrew's house, three doors up.

In January Jess left for a three month British Council tour of the West Indies and Granny D went to stay in a residential home near her sister Nell in Fordingbridge. The flat in Oakwood Court was let and Simon stayed with Richard and Jan until he went back to Marlborough. Walter, now living in an old folks' home in Chard, wrote to Jan in some exasperation: 'Where is Marcus now? We have no address in case of emergency. Where is Jessica and when does she come home? What is your baby's name? [He later wrote to say that only dogs were called Toby.] Has he been baptised? When and where? Write to me at the above address and tell me all the news. You might all be on the moon for all we hear from you. . . . Your loving Gramp.'

Jessica was all over the place – Grenada, Trinidad, Antigua, St Kitts, Montserrat and Guyana. She returned home at Easter; Jan wrote to Sal: 'Toby adores Daddy even though he doesn't see him all that often but he usually yells at Mum which is a bit unfortunate. The parents went to NY for a couple of weeks and came back last Tuesday having had a few days in Bermuda. The Narrow Street house still isn't ready.'

Jan (an assiduous correspondent) to Ann Shaw: 'We had dinner with the parents at the Royal Garden Hotel where they're staying until they go to Venice on Friday for the re-opening of the Lido which got flooded last year – talk about international jet set. We'll arrange for Daddy to do the christening when I can pin them down.'

It was a nomadic spring and summer for Jess. She spent occasional weekends at Narrow Street, odd weeks with Jan and Richard and her grandson in Ealing and others at various hotels. Jan to her mother-in-law, August: 'Mummy went to the States with Daddy and when she got back she went to the Royal Garden Hotel where she caught a bug, so she went to Claridge's instead! Then she got a TV part and decided to move to a hotel near the studios. When we got back from France Mummy was staying here until she moved into her house in Ebury Mews. Simon is still with us as the parents are now in Canada staying with Daddy's boss.'

Marcus and Jess had decided that they got on each other's nerves too much to live constantly together, so Marcus bought 54 Ebury Mews and Jess enjoyed setting up her own home in Pimlico. But they continued to see each other frequently, travelling abroad together and visiting each other's houses. Jess also felt, as she said to Maureen Muloch, Marcus's cleaning lady at Narrow Street, that the Limehouse pad 'was Marcus's thing'.

Marcus moved into 82 Narrow Street in May 1967. It was a dreadful mess and Marcus asked Maureen to sort it all out. When she was going through an old chest, she came across a set of priest's robes. She was terrified. All she knew about Marcus was that he was a publisher – she now thought he was a pervert. The following day Marcus asked her to take the robes for cleaning. Shaking in her shoes, Maureen said, 'What are they for?' Marcus: 'What do you think they are for?' Maureen: 'What do you use them for?' Marcus: 'What do you think I use them for?' Maureen (now in a cold sweat): 'Well, they're priest's robes.' Marcus: 'Yes, I'm a priest.' (Maureen thought, 'He's mad as well as a bloody pervert.') Maureen: 'I thought you worked for a publishing company?' Marcus: 'Well, I do that as well.'

Marcus was by this time starting to smile, 'He'd got the feel of the thing by then. He took his bloody monocle out of his pocket and put it in his eye and said, "Do I frighten you?" and I said no. He said "I wear this to frighten people" – and we started laughing and he explained about being a priest.'

Their relationship was thereafter one of mutual affection and respect. 'One Saturday lunchtime, Marcus ushered his guests out on to the terrace saying, "Come outside and let Maureen get on with what she has to do." He didn't say "The cleaner". I appreciated that. Little things like that made me like him – he was a nice man, human. He could wine and dine with the best of them, then sit down and eat beans out of the pan.' Leaving the pan for Maureen to wash, of course.

She worried about his smoking habits – as well she might. He set the bed alight at Oakwood Court more than once. Maureen found an enormous tea tray and put it by the side of the bed. Marcus left her a note: 'Thanks for ashtray, just my size.'

Although Marcus professed to be the fancy-free man-about-town in his bachelor pad, Maureen remembers his being on his own a lot. She found him one morning in the sitting room, head in his hands, crying. It was a fit of depression, he said, nothing special, he was taking tablets for it, but 'I can't bring myself out of it – I don't know what the answer is.' Maureen did. 'The answer is you're living in a bloody great house all by yourself. You should have your family with you.' Marcus replied, 'What, go back to bath towels and washing all over the floor?' But another time he said: 'I've got three daughters and I can't get one of them to come and have lunch with me.'

In an effort to dispel some of the loneliness Marcus acquired a small dog, a Jack Russell. It wasn't a success; Marcus wasn't a doggy person (he wasn't keen on cats, either). The dog was neurotic, hid from its master, and pee-ed on the bed. In desperation, Marcus called in a dog psychologist to 'help your nice but sad little autistic dog to adjust to normal living'. In vain; the dog went back to its former owner. It was a horrid little animal but left Marcus depressed by another failed relationship.

Marcus tried hard to fit the image he wanted for himself at that time. He had a series of transient girlfriends, only one of whom moved in for a brief period: a nurse, a tall slim girl with long legs (of course!) who wanted to be a model and who stole money from Maureen's purse – which Marcus reimbursed, with apologies.

Marcus's old friend, the distinguished journalist Sheila Black, visited him quite often at Narrow Street. 'He was a funny man, because he loved the love of women in the very old fashioned courtier's sense, despite his reputation. I was able to talk to him like a sister. I always got the impression that he had a lot of fantasies for a number of women without consummating them. I said, "What do you do with your freedom, Marcus? You go out with this one, go out with that one, nothing lasts." He said, "No, nothing does last because I think with me love is a fantasy and therefore easily dispelled. The wrong word at the wrong time, my illusions drop and without my illusions I haven't got love." Maybe there was physical consummation, but it was secondary to him. He needed love from them. He was actually much more unsure of himself than he ever gave the impression of being. The moment he moved away from behind his desk, Marcus needed his self confidence boosting.

'During the time they were apart I saw him socially fairly often. No question of it, he was always close to Jessica through it all. I was always sure he'd get back to Jess. He never forgot her. I don't think he told me why they'd split. I think it was his infidelities – or his apparent infidelities – or hers. The only time I discussed it with Jess she said he started it. Marcus said it was an unlikely marriage, showbiz and church, and he never moved into her world and she never moved out of it – even when she gave it all up she still had a sister in the business.

'When he was supposed to be dashing about with women he was often ringing me, saying he was lonely, come and have a bite. If he did it to me he did to others, I'm sure. He wasn't the bachelor gay he was made out to be. But he didn't think physical infidelity ought to break up a marriage. He didn't think it mattered to that extent. He said "Unfortunately it does lead to so much discord, that's what breaks up the marriage." '

In February 1968 Simon was sacked from Marlborough for smoking pot. Marcus was furious, not so much with Simon, but with John Dancy, the 'Master', for not having informed him that Simon had been in trouble before – although, it turned out, only for smoking (ordinary cigarettes) and drinking.

Marcus wrote to Dancy: 'If there have been a number of serious problems with Simon I do not understand why you failed to inform me. You were, after all, made responsible for him and you should have consulted me if you were disturbed about this situation. . . . Simon pointed out to me last evening that as you had only seen him about twice, you were not really qualified to express the view of his character which you did. I think he has a point here.'

There followed a diatribe about the low teaching standards at the school: 'Simon has been bored with Marlborough, as I know have other boys. . . . Because of this lack of a guiding interest, Simon has been uncertain, bewildered and insecure, and it is this that has made him both lazy and rebellious. . . . I wish I had sent him to a good grammar school. I have myself, on visiting Marlborough, sensed a complete lack of inspiration and community spirit. But I did not write [to you] because of possible repercussions on Simon. . . . It is, to me, pathetic that your only recourse in dealing with problems of this kind is to shirk the responsibility you undertook and so to damage a boy's whole career. What you should have done is possibly to have given him a good hiding. . . .

'Simon is, of course, to blame – largely for stupidity, and I intend to be very firm with him. But Marlborough, and certain individuals in it, are also very much to blame.'

Simon's housemaster offered advice about his A Level studies and he received a great deal of support from his erstwhile fellow pupils, who thought he had been made a scapegoat. There were certainly other boys who had smoked pot; Dancy wrote that the ex-pupil who had got Simon into trouble 'realised that it was wrong to introduce another, younger, person to drugs.'

Simon moved in with Jess and Sally (back from New Zealand) and went to a crammer, intent on getting his A Levels. In the summer, he went up to Anglesey to stay with his close friend George, who had been involved in the drug scene at Marlborough and who said he was having problems with his parents. Marcus and Jess had gone on their annual pilgrimage to New York and on to Murray Bay in Canada to stay with Richard and Honey Berlin. When they returned, Simon phoned to ask if he could stay longer with his friend. Jess said, 'Yes, of course, if he needs you.' It was the last time she ever advised anyone to do anything.

On Sunday, 25 August, five days before his eighteenth birthday, Marcus and Jess, together at Narrow Street, received the news that Simon had been killed in a car crash.

Marcus took the train to North Wales. He discovered that Simon, George and a couple of friends had been out drinking with George's mother, Audrey. As the local paper recorded: 'An MG sportscar with three teenagers sitting on the back with their feet on the back seat, when overtaking another car at Brynseincyn, went right over on its offside. It struck a wall, came back, collided with the other car, and went through a fence, throwing the occupants into the field.'

Simon hit the wall; no one else was seriously injured. Audrey later pleaded guilty to causing death by dangerous driving, was fined £50 and banned from driving for seven years. What the newspaper reports didn't say, and what the Morris family were told by George, who very bravely visited them after the tragedy, was that his mother was an alcoholic who had previously killed another person in a motor accident. She was drunk when she killed Simon; George had refused to be a passenger in her car.

Jess was distraught with grief and under sedation for days; on tranquillisers for many years. Marcus, equally grief-stricken, retired behind a barrier of stoicism. Ann Shaw dashed down from Stockport; the whole family moved into Ebury Mews. After the funeral at St Bride's Marcus and Jess went to stay with the Rainbirds on Rhodes, the girls undertook the sorting out of Simon's effects and replying to the many letters of condolence.

# Chapter Nineteen

At the end of November 1968 Jess decided that work might help the healing process. Jan wrote to her mother-in-law:

'The parents seem to be a lot better. Daddy has been marvellous anyway but Mummy has cut down on her tranquillisers and is going to take over the role of Mrs Crewe in *Hadrian VII* at the Mermaid Theatre. [The play of the book by Baron Corvo which Marcus and Jess had first read during the war.] They're both still at Ebury Mews, spending weekends at Narrow Street.'

Marcus had no choice but to return to work, which perhaps helped to keep him sane, although the girls worried that he showed so little emotion and kept his feelings bottled up. The Americans were on the whole immensely supportive and, in November, Ben McPeake was re-appointed as a Director, so that he could take some of the pressure off Marcus.

There were certainly plenty of problems to occupy his mind.

One was *The Connoisseur*, the old-established antiques magazine which had been so useful to Mr Hearst. Marcus asked Ruari McLean to cast an eye over it and he was retained as a part-time consultant to advise and assist on typography, layout and general presentation. The changes brought forth complaints from readers who didn't like these attempts to widen the magazine's appeal. Marcus responded that 'I do not agree that a work of scholarship has necessarily got to look dull, any more than a beautiful woman has to be a half-wit.'

Ruari became Art Editor in 1963 and circulation increased throughout the sixties, largely due to his modernising influence. This led to friction with long-time Editor, Gwynne Ramsey, who accused Ruari of trying to pinch his job.

In 1968 Marcus received a letter from a young journalist asking to be considered for the editorship of *The Connoisseur* when Gwynne Ramsey retired. Bevis Hillier was at that time writing sale room reports for *The Times*: 'I incautiously said that I was sure I could get circulation and advertising above *Apollo*'s [a rival fine-arts magazine]. Marcus replied that there was no prospect of Mr Ramsey's retiring and added rather indignantly that he could assure me *The Connoisseur*'s circulation was much in advance of *Apollo*'s already!'

However, in October the following year, Marcus wrote to John Miller about the need to look for a replacement for Ramsey: 'Bevis Hillier [is] at present PRO to the British Museum and writes regularly on antiques in *Harper's Bazaar*... in my view and in Ben McPeake's he might be a good person to take over eventually.'

When Gwynne Ramsey did decide to retire three years later, he recommended Bevis Hillier as his successor. Ruari moved to Scotland when his office lease came up for renewal, so Bevis found a new Art Editor and set to work putting his own stamp on the magazine.

He spent quite a large part of his time travelling – to the US to meet the American advertisers and collectors, to Bulgaria for an article on icons, to China with a party of *Connoisseur* readers and to South America for a special South American issue. Braniff Airlines provided the flights and Hearst agreed that the magazine would carry a photograph of their aircraft; Bevis refused and Marcus backed him. 'I have never forgotten the principled support that Marcus gave me on that occasion.'

Bevis was a high profile editor but, by early 1976, there had been a considerable downturn in advertising revenue and the relationship between Editor and Managing Director was deteriorating. Bevis was beginning to chafe at the bit and was unhappy with his salary, which he said was less than that of a New York garbage collector. He offered Marcus an ultimatum – double it or he would leave.

Marcus had been increasingly uneasy: '[Bevis] has spent little time in the office,' he wrote to John Miller, 'and a good deal of time contributing to other publications, writing his book, broadcasting and even lending his name and that of the *Connoisseur* to promoting a not very good book club. I am afraid that he has allowed his appointment as Editor at such a young age to go to his head. I had been on the point of giving him a good talking to about several matters.'

Marcus appointed Bevis's deputy, Will Allan, in his place: 'I have told Will that we must get the *Connoisseur* back on its traditional rails, dealing with true antiques and paintings and using the best and most scholarly writers available.'

Circulation had risen to 20,000 with Bevis at the helm, but the magazine had made its first loss in many years. Finances didn't improve under his successor; circulation fell and Will Allan was succeeded by Paul Atterbury, now well known for his appearances on *The Antiques Road Show.*

The *Connoisseur*'s appeal was widened; it became less scholarly and academic; a magazine dealing with 'the best of everything' that might appeal to very rich and discriminating readers. In 1982, the *Connoisseur* disappeared from Nat Mag's orbit entirely; because 70 per cent of sales were in New York, publication was moved to Hearst Magazines.

Meanwhile, Marcus had acquired a second antiques magazine. The *Antique Collector* had been owned by an old lady; when she died her estate put it on the market for around £35,000. In 1974, when the price had come down to £10,000, Marcus bought it and put in Bevis Hillier's deputy at the time, David Coombs, as Editor. The magazine was to be aimed at the average collector, who had not got thousands of pounds to spend, but wanted a magazine with quality and authority.

Circulation rose from 5,000 to over 32,000, but it never made a profit. Marcus nurtured it through to the early 1980s but it was closed by his successor.

In 1975, Marcus bought the *Antiques Yearbooks* from the *Financial Times*, bringing into National Magazines that lively journalist Marcelle d'Argy-Smith. 'Marcus was gentle, but an ace flirt. He made me feel talented. When I first joined he took me to lunch at the Mirabelle; he was a bit fatherly, a bit uncle-y, a bit naughty, but terribly interested in what I was doing. You'd feel awfully good after a lunch with him. You didn't feel threatened. . . . He didn't have the essence of a shit about him. He was incapable of playing the corporate bastard. He wasn't corporate on any level. He believed in his editors – and he was a wonderful dancer!'

A totally different type of magazine, which Nat Mag bought in 1967 from Hulton Publications, Nika Hulton's company, was *Containerisation International* which dealt with container hardware and handling equipment. In three years Nat Mag turned a loss into a profit. In 1976 it became a subscription only magazine and the world authority in its market. It sat oddly with the women's magazines, as did *Environmental Pollution Management*, another controlled circulation publication, which Nat Mag started up in 1971. It was distributed free to 15,000 officials responsible for buying pollution control equipment and its only source of income was from advertising – which wasn't forthcoming.

Marcus wrote to John Miller, 'The October issue will be the last. I hate to have to do this, but as somebody remarked to me, it is perhaps before its time. When governments everywhere really take pollution control seriously and legislate, then perhaps there will be room for a magazine of this kind.'

This didn't stop Marcus from trying again and in 1980 Nat Mag launched *British Shipper*, aimed at shipping managers who controlled some £4,000 million a year spent on freight and forwarding services. It lost heavily from the start, due mainly to the severe recession, and limped along until 1984 when it went down to Davy Jones's locker.

Another strange bedfellow was *Small Car*, which came to Nat Mag as part of a deal struck between Marcus and Timothy Beaumont (now Lord Beaumont of Whitley), owner of Prism Publications. Beaumont, described at the time as 'the richest priest in the Church of England', had acquired *Small Car* in 1963 after it had been turned down by Marcus. Beaumont also bought *Studio,* a contemporary arts magazine, from Longacre Press. A year later he decided that he wanted to concentrate on his religious, educational and political publications and he offered to give the two magazines to Nat Mag: he didn't need money, they were already being distributed by Nat Mag, he was a friend of Marcus's and, as he says, 'I was trying to get rid of an embarrassment. I had taken on too much and *Small Car* was a world I didn't understand.' Marcus wasn't into cars either, but he decided that the slight loss the magazines were making was a better option than losing Beaumont's distribution contract and, against Bill Jackson's advice, made the deal.

The Art Editor of *Small Car* was Charles Pocklington, who had worked on *Eagle*, and the mercurial Australian Doug Blain became Editor. Blain was enthusiastic and full of ideas and didn't give a damn about the sensibilities and susceptibilities of advertisers. He soon came up against the Advertising Manager, who complained frequently and at length to Marcus that advertisements were being withdrawn because of adverse editorial comments about the motoring trade.

Marcus, as usual, supported the Editor, even when a furore blew up over an article that showed how the drink-driving laws were being flouted; the magazine was accused of encouraging drink-driving – which, of course, it hadn't.

The magazine was renamed *Car* and, in 1966, presented the first Car of the Year Award, with an international panel of judges including Stirling Moss (who was also a contributor). The award went to the Triumph 1300; the following year the winner was the Jensen FF four-wheel drive saloon. Throughout the 1960s a loyal and enthusiastic readership kept *Car*'s circulation up; advertising was also steady, in spite of what the business manager described as Blain's 'publish and be damned principles', but what Blain called 'a forthright and critical approach to the cars that are tested'.

Marcus wrote to John Miller in 1969: 'The Publisher was a little worried about the Editor of *Car*'s outspokenness . . . but I think that Doug Blain is a very bright editor and it is his liveliness which gives the magazine its appeal. From time to time I have to get him to moderate his views but I think it would be a mistake to clamp down on his editorial freedom too much.'

But Doug Blain was getting bored and in 1971 he resigned. Before long *Car* was being independently produced by former executives; Marcus sold the magazine to them in 1975. Nat Mag's flirtation with the macho world of motoring was over.

*Studio*, Timothy Beaumont's second gift, was more to Marcus's taste. It was first published in 1893 and was for some years regarded as the bible of modern art but had deteriorated in the Hulton stable before becoming lost in the maws of Longacre Press.

The first thing Marcus did was to call in the ubiquitous Ruari McLean, who said: 'In this whole issue I cannot find any writing that I think is either good journalism or good art criticism. . . . The magazine seems to me to be wildly out of touch with contemporary British painting and art criticism.'

Marcus changed the title to *Studio International*, put the price up and changed it into a modern 'glossy' magazine, 'whereas previously it largely catered for art students and amateur painters, we have been going out for the serious scholars and collectors of modern art and aiming to get in advertisements from modern art galleries throughout the world.'

Losses on the magazine rose by 25 per cent the following year; the Americans, who didn't have the same interest in contemporary art and didn't like loss-makers, insisted that Marcus dispose of it. In 1966 *Studio International* was sold to its printers, W. & J. Mackay, for £12,000, to be paid when it made a profit; it never did.

Another less-than-successful publication was *Womancraft*, bought in 1973. This was a practical householders' magazine, with women in mind; serious text described how to build a car port or an aquarium, construct a shed, keep bees or mend a broken washer. It was Jack Blanche's idea to bring *Womancraft* under the wing of *Good Housekeeping* and Laurie Purden became Editor-in-Chief, with Wendy James as Editor. Marcus explained to John Miller, 'Women over here, both married and single, take it for granted that it is the woman of the house who does many of the "chores" and does not rely on the man to do them for her.'

John replied, 'I never think of the girls being interested in changing the washer, etc., but maybe that would be women's lib.'

Wendy James thought that *Womancraft* suffered from being a poor relation to *GH*: 'Laurie wanted even bricklaying wrapped up in beautiful words. . . . It was ahead of its time – we talked about problems with glue sniffing, we discovered Michael Barry, the "Crafty Cook". *Womancraft* would work today. . . .'

In the seventies it didn't. Although circulation nearly doubled in four years, advertising just didn't come in and losses quadrupled. Marcus wrote again to John Miller: 'This magazine ought to succeed because there is a gap in the market for it, and because in our present economic situation, everyone has to think much more about money-saving and "doing it yourself". I am very reluctant to kill this magazine, but clearly we cannot go on carrying the existing losses. The slump is really beginning to bite now' – indeed, that July, three magazines belonging to other publishers closed – *Nova*, *TV Life* and *AdWeek*.

*Womancraft* was sold to IPC in 1977; it had been offered to Wendy James, who couldn't raise the finance: 'The closure seemed to us very wrong. I was very angry when I had to go and hand it over to my former editor at *Woman's Own*. Marcus said you have to accept certain things; business is about having profits.'

In 1973 the company made the highest profit in its history. In addition to the success of *Good Housekeeping*, *SHE* and Ebury Press, 1972 had seen the launch of *Cosmopolitan*.

In 1965, the author of *Sex and the Single Girl*, Helen Gurley Brown, took over Hearst's failing magazine *Cosmopolitan* in New York. She wanted to encourage the young woman of America to be liberated, to be able to attract men, hold down a good job, make the best of herself and, not least, improve her sex life. *Cosmo* was an immediate, rip-roaring success in America and Dick Deems and Richard Berlin began to think that this philosophy should cross the Atlantic. They met with unexpected opposition from Marcus.

Although Richard Berlin stated flatly that 'Dames are the same the world over', Marcus didn't think so. Dick Deems agreed with Berlin: 'I come over here and I look at British girls, I go to Annabel's . . .' Marcus retorted: 'Yes that's just the trouble – you go to Annabel's, the King's Road, etcetera. You don't go to Manchester or Birmingham – you don't really get a national picture. The British girl is not as open about her life – I don't think she'll respond to open discussion about sex lives. She's more reserved.'

Phyllis Bayley, the veteran Editor-in-Chief of *Vanity Fair*, was more blunt: 'I fear that Helen Gurley Brown has not the faintest conception of the English consumer market. . . . I cannot bear to contemplate the readers we would lose, and the letters I would receive, were *Vanity Fair* to use the five pages on "Facts About Orgasm", the six pages on "Sadism" and the four pages on "I married a Dirty Old Man" that [American] *Cosmo* has published in the present issue. . . .'

Brian Braithwaite, *Vanity Fair*'s Publisher reported: 'Our very loyal readership appear to buy the magazine for its fashion and beauty coverage and seem to accept most of the more "frank" articles introduced in the past year. The Editor has found that the most numerous complaints come in response to articles adapted directly from *Cosmopolitan* – our indigenous "problem" articles seem to be assimilated with little or no complaint. . . . If we were to close the magazine and relaunch it as *Cosmopolitan*, a very substantial investment will have to be made. . . . I still maintain that a much more modest investment can be made on our present magazine. . . .'

Deems wrote again suggesting that Helen Gurley Brown should come to London to help choose a new editor to re-launch *Vanity Fair* 'in the *Cosmopolitan* way'. Marcus's reply was a masterpiece of inaccurate clairvoyance: 'If you mean that we should actually change the title and bring it out as *Cosmopolitan* . . . then it would cost a great deal of money to get it off the ground and none of us here feel that it would have a big chance of success.'

There were many heated discussions over two or three years and Marcus remained unconvinced that *Cosmo* would work in this country. But, in 1970, he was approached by Vere Sherren of City Magazines to discuss the possibility of franchising the magazine. Talks foundered, but they started Marcus thinking that perhaps the time was right for *Cosmopolitan*.

His first task was to find an editor who would meet with the approval of Helen Gurley Brown, who was to oversee the new magazine's conception. Helen says, '*Vanity Fair* was not working. Marcus, who was very loyal to his editors, wanted Audrey Slaughter to be editor of *Cosmo*. So I read a couple of *Vanity Fairs* and Marcus and I had a really screaming discussion at the Dorchester about the fact that *Vanity Fair* was failing. If she were a great editor surely she could have kept it alive. What do I want with her for *Cosmo*?'

Audrey told us, 'Helen took me to lunch and offered me the editorship. Like a fool, I said I would edit it as well as *Vanity Fair*, not instead of. Helen didn't like that idea, so I was out of the running.'

Marcus and Helen interviewed some seventy journalists until they found someone on whom they could agree, the Woman's Editor of the *Sun*, Joyce Hopkirk. Joyce had the right image – ebullient, newly divorced, with a small baby, a hardworking young woman-about-town – and, most important from Marcus's point of view, with very decided ideas about making the new *Cosmo* a *British* magazine. Joyce says, 'I felt passionately that if Helen was going to interfere to the extent that the magazine was going to be hers, it wouldn't have worked. British women weren't quite so desperate as their American counterparts. Brits feel we can survive without a man, whereas Helen's whole philosophy was how to get him and keep him happy. Although some of the ideas were splendid, we needed to have our own people and our own twists on it.'

The launch of *Cosmopolitan* in March 1972, orchestrated by PR man Brian Begg and a new advertising agency called Saatchi & Saatchi, is regarded as the most successful launch of a magazine since the war. Joyce Hopkirk, Brian Braithwaite (whom Marcus appointed Publisher of the new magazine) and Brian Begg travelled the country promoting the *Cosmopolitan* ethos. Begg persuaded Desmond Wilcox to produce a *Man Alive* BBC2 television programme, *Who's Afraid of Helen Gurley Brown*, which was followed by a *Late Night Line Up* devoted to *Cosmopolitan*. This coverage was worth more than any advertising campaign (although the TV commercial was also regarded as brilliant) and *Cosmo* sold out on the first day of issue. The rumour (denied by Joyce) was put around that *Cosmo* was going to publish a full-frontal male nude in the second issue; in fact, the nude, who was Germaine Greer's husband, had his knee discreetly raised.

*Cosmo* wasn't so well received by the media magazine *Campaign*, which called it a 'coy sexual revamp of the old-fashioned get-and-keep-your-man formula which has always been the basis of most women's magazines.' (An opinion shared by Marcus's daughters.)

Much of the publicity centred on the fact that the publisher of *Cosmo* was a clergyman and, to boot, the clergyman who had founded and edited *Eagle*. Was it right, people asked, for a parson to be involved in a magazine that included topics like 'How to turn a man on when he's having problems in bed' and 'I was a sleep around girl'? Marcus told the *Southport Visiter* and other media: 'I have always believed in sex as a good thing and that relationships between men and women can be improved. Too many people have got the idea that sex is only something that you can indulge in when you are properly married, instead of saying it is a thoroughly good thing which should be enjoyed as much as possible. . . . I have never felt any conflict in producing *Eagle* for boys and *Cosmo* for girls. It is other people who find it odd. This is because they misunderstand the Church and what sex is all about.'

Marcus thought it another example of the 'quite extraordinary' attitude people have towards the clergy. 'Some people think because you are a parson you are going to be shocked. But the one person who is unshockable is a parson.'

The *Sunday Times* published a cartoon by Marc which took a sly dig at Marcus the priest and publisher of *Cosmo*. Jess hated it, but Marcus bought the original and it now has place of honour in the loo.

*Cosmopolitan* reached a circulation of nearly half a million by that summer, before settling down at around 350,000. By the autumn Dick Deems was complaining that Joyce Hopkirk was not using enough material from American *Cosmo*.

Marcus responded, '*Cosmopolitan* is considered a hot property by the advertising agencies not least because we have been at such pains to "de-Americanise" it. When we did our small bit of research last year . . . we got the reaction that English women, while believing they had something to learn from French and Italian women, do not believe they can be taught anything by American women about handling men or anything else.'

The following spring Marcus had to look for another editor, when Joyce Hopkirk was offered the assistant editorship of the *Daily Mirror*. He didn't have to look very far; Marcus always liked to promote people from inside the company where possible, and Deidre McSharry, Fashion and Beauty Editor of *Cosmo*, proved an extremely successful Editor for twelve years, winning the PPA Editor of the Year Award in 1981. 'The reason I stayed was to do with the idea I got from Marcus that the individual was more important than the whole, which is jolly unusual in publishing. He really

*Marcus's great friend, John R. Miller, Jr*

believed – which most companies pay lip service to – that the editor is important. You didn't feel you always had to put your best foot forward, which is what editors usually have to do. Partly due to Marcus being a priest, you felt you could talk to him. You could trust him.'

With all eyes on *Cosmo*, it was perhaps inevitable that poor old *Vanity Fair* should be overshadowed. Losses had risen and though Marcus thought Audrey Slaughter was doing a good job editorially, advertising wasn't coming in. The Americans were not willing to give *Vanity Fair* more time and, at in January 1972, Marcus finally decided to close it. But since Audrey had expressed an interest in taking it over herself, should it ever close, he offered the magazine to her, for a royalty; Nat Mag would keep the distribution. Audrey raised the backing she would need, but Hearst changed their minds. Dick Deems told Marcus on the telephone: 'We think that it has value and we think that anyone who is interested in the thing ought to be willing to pay us . . . I can tell you, for example, that John Miller puts a value of £100,000 on it.'

Marcus felt that the value of *Vanity Fair* was simply a matter of the name and the goodwill but, in the face of opposition from John Miller as well as Dick Deems, his hands were tied. At the end of the month *Vanity Fair* was sold to IPC for £40,000, to be merged with *Honey*. Audrey Slaughter decamped with a number of her colleagues, including Shirleys Green, Conran and Lowe, and in a very short time started *Over21*.

John Miller's stance on *Vanity Fair* was one of the rare occasions when he and Marcus disagreed. John had become a very close friend. Since the early seventies, when he became Executive Vice President of Hearst, John had been aware of the antipathy between Marcus and Dick Deems, Richard Berlin's protégé and presumed successor. Berlin's increasing Alzheimers had left Deems with more power and Marcus felt there was a concerted effort on Deems' part to undermine his standing and authority. He became increasingly annoyed at Deems' constant interference in Nat Mag's affairs and felt that his frequent visits to London were unnecessary, costly and a waste of everybody's time.

Dick Deems says, 'I didn't personally find Marcus easy to work with; we were two different personalities. I've always been on the selling side, the business side – always looked for instant results. Marcus by nature was more thoughtful, more depthful, and so we just didn't think alike.' One Nat Mag executive who did think like Deems was Brian Braithwaite, who records that Deems said to him more than once, 'As soon as we get rid of Marcus Morris, you're in.'

John Miller told Marcus to bide his time; Deems was expecting to be appointed President of the Hearst Corporation and 'while that man waits in the wings for the call, he *has* the authority and while he has the authority he obviously intends to exercise it.'

Richard Berlin retired in 1973 and Frank Massi became President until two years later when, to Marcus's delight, John Miller, not Dick Deems, took over. Marcus was again dealing with someone who trusted him.

In 1978 the Deputy Editor of *Cosmopolitan*, Maggie Goodman, and Joan Barrell, its Associate Publisher, went to Marcus with an idea for a new magazine for women and men, *Two's Company*. Marcus felt that it held the germ of a good idea but, remembering that *Extra* had failed to attract the necessary advertising, told them (about ten times, according to Joan!) to go back to the drawing board, as it wasn't right and a unisex magazine wouldn't work. Joan would come out of his office saying, 'Silly old sod, he doesn't know what he's talking about!', but a couple of days later they would realise 'By God, he's right.'

The new magazine was launched as *Company*, aimed at eighteen- to twenty-four-year-old women, as was *Cosmo*, but with its own very distinct editorial personality. It became the second-highest selling young woman's monthly magazine on the bookstalls (after *Cosmo*) and Marcus was very proud of this wholly British venture.

Marcus retained to the end his distrust of general-interest men's magazines *per se*. Stephen Quinn, Publisher of *Harpers & Queen* in the eighties, was keen to start one: 'Marcus was vaguely discouraging over lunch but, being kind and gentle to a younger man, didn't ever say firmly "forget it". He had a resounding capacity to be unbelievably inaccessible, you couldn't know what he thought – he had a byzantine mind. He allowed editors to take sabbaticals, understanding that they might need intellectual nourishment, that an enriching experience could bring something new and more substantial to a magazine.'

Marcus may have been right at the time, but men's magazines are now very popular; Stephen went on to launch *GQ* for Condé Nast and Nat Mag brought *Esquire* over from the States.

In the early 1970s, Marcus decided that Nat Mag should rejoin the Periodical Publishers Association, which they had left ten years earlier; he was assured by members of the Council 'that on no account does IPC have more pull than any other organisation.'

By 1974 he was the Chairman of the PPA's Editorial Committee and the Association's Chairman commented that 'in Marcus's time this very important committee has begun to fulfil the sort of function that it ought to fulfil', that is, to consider the interests and problems of editors. To this end, Marcus organised a seminar at the Howard Hotel in the Strand which was attended by 180 editors – the largest number ever to meet together in London. The seminar's guest speaker was Michael Foot, at that time Secretary of State for Employment, who was heavily involved in trying to legalise the union closed shop in journalism with his Trade Union and Labour Relations (Amendment) Bill.

The editors feared that the closed shop would leave them open to censorship by the union, which could lead to expulsion and therefore dismissal if they disobeyed union instructions. Marcus said: 'There is still time for compromise and behind-the-scenes bargaining. . . . As the psalmist said of the Almighty in psalm 121 "He will not suffer thy foot to be moved". . . . Whatever happens in these next few days . . . the least we can do as editors is to commit ourselves to eternal vigilance, to keep up the pressure to protect our own freedom. Today I believe we must impress on Mr Foot just how we feel and leave him in no doubt. Do not let us be put off by any vague disclaimers that he may produce. . . . Whatever the attitude of the NUJ may be today, we do not know what the attitude will be in a year or two's time.' His words may have had some effect – there is no closed shop in journalism.

Marcus resigned from the Editorial Committee in 1980, feeling that 'I have been on it a long time and I think that now is right to make way for a younger man.' He retired from the Board of the PPA in 1982 and was elected a Vice-President.

Marcus came up against another government department in 1973. During a period of price freezes, he decided to raise the advertising rates on *Cosmopolitan*, *Harpers & Queen* and *Good Housekeeping*, because the magazines' circulations were much higher than the figures on which the rates were based. At a meeting with the Minister of Trade and Industry, Geoffrey Howe, and his officials, Marcus argued that the increases had been put into effect six months before the freeze was announced and, as they were justified by increased circulation, they were not really price increases at all. The Department of Trade and Industry issued an Order against Nat Mag to reduce the rates; Marcus refused and retaliated with a writ against the Minister on the grounds that the Order was *ultra vires* (that the Minister was not legally entitled to interpret the Counter Inflation Act in the way he had done).

Nat Mag was the only company to do battle on this issue. Some publishers had put up advertising rates and been ignored by the DTI; others had given way to them. The case hinged on legal technicalities and Nat Mag lost, due in part, Marcus thought, to the intransigence of the company's lawyer, George Coleman, and Bill Jackson, both of whom insisted that there was no case to answer. When the case came to appeal Marcus brought in Herbert Bart Smith as consultant; in the end, the Attorney General dropped the action and didn't ask for costs. Marcus told John Miller, 'The other side asked whether, if they dropped the case against us, we would publicise our victory. I have assured them that we would keep as quiet as possible, but the question does seem to indicate a) that government departments don't like to be seen publicly to have lost a case and b) that they are much less sure of the strength of their case than they were before.'

The court case, and the launch of *Cosmo*, took place during the miners' strike and the three-day week. Uta Canning, Marcus's PA at the time, had to assemble all the papers for the lawyers by gas lamp. Staff were kept fit walking up eight to eleven flights of stairs and the Good Housekeeping Institute ran a soup and sandwich kitchen – in the way of the British, the spirit of Dunkirk won through.

The 1970s saw the birth of one of the greatest successes in the world of magazines, a new distribution company. Between 1970 and 1975, Marcus had talks about forming a joint distribution company with Vere Sherren of City Magazines, with Argus Press and with Condé Nast, none of which bore fruit.

But in 1976 Bernard Leser, who had been running Condé Nast in Australia, became Managing Director of the company in the UK, and the following year he and Marcus explored the merging of their distribution operations. Bernard says, 'We examined whether we could run efficiently a jointly owned company in which we co-operated and worked as a team, and continue to be completely independent competitors. We found that, provided we had strong management and ran the company at arm's length, theoretically it should be possible. It wasn't as easy or quick as we thought it would be; negotiations were made more complicated by Bill Jackson and the fact that Marcus and Bill didn't speak to each other. To this day I can't fathom how a managing director and a financial director could run a company when the two were so totally antagonistic. This doesn't mean that we didn't have respect for Bill Jackson – he brought a very fine financial mind to our endeavours, but Marcus brought vision – he could see beyond Nat Mag and Condé Nast to the day when this would be a success. He would be so proud today – the new company makes more money before tax than Nat Mag and Condé Nast (UK) combined.

'Marcus was better with women than men – it's a chemical thing, I'm the same. We used to joke about it. We had some gloriously frank and confidential talks, considering we were competitors. We enjoyed each other – so much so that we invited each other to client parties, which puzzled the clients. We had philosophical discussions at dinner parties, not about how many pages of advertising. We had much more fun – it doesn't happen now.'

For the first year or so the two divisions which formed the new company, christened Comag by Marcus, operated in tandem. The Managing Director was Allan Boddy, MD of National Magazine Distributors, who was close to retirement, with Roy Britten from Condé Nast as his deputy. There were problems with the unions, with lack of investment and the operation of two different systems; by the end of the first year the company was losing money at an alarming rate. The first independent Managing Director, Phil Harris, paid off the union members, closed the old warehouse, persuaded

Nat Mag and Condé Nast to invest in new computer hardware and new premises and put the company on its feet. Brian Bouchier, the next MD, said, 'It scared the daylights out of the Americans. A posse descended on us, staying at the Dorchester at great expense. We made them understand that money had to be spent. . . . Marcus didn't question our assessment of what was needed. There was great trust between him, Bernie Leser and Comag. Without their support we'd have chucked it in, beaten by the Nat Mag Publishers and Bill Jackson, who did his best to make life difficult. The Nat Mag Publishers, apart from Jack Blanche, didn't like us at all, there was tremendous antagonism towards us until Marcus brought them to heel.'

When Comag was formed the company distributed fewer than one hundred titles; it now handles over 500 and is the biggest third party magazine distributor in the country, the third biggest distributor overall and contributes more to Hearst's coffers than does the National Magazine Company.

Phil Harris and Brian Bouchier had to contend, as had Allan Boddy before them, with Marcus's brother. Marcus was at his wits' end with Teddy, who had become very unstable. He had suffered for many years from Von Recklinhausen's Disease, which gave him disfiguring lumps all over his skin – it wasn't infectious at all, but it looked as though it might be. This naturally made poor Teddy even more unsure of himself, although he was highly intelligent and could be very good company. His failed relationships with women were partly due to the arrogant and opinionated manner he developed to compensate for his insecurity and he was inclined to blame his brother for all his misfortunes. Marcus had been supporting him financially for years. Teddy seems to have been happy only in Ceylon and Malaya where he had been a successful tea and rubber planter. When the Morris children were young he was their rich and exotic uncle with large cars and gifts of silver and ivory. He left the Far East after falling out with his superiors and throughout the late fifties and 1960s hankered to get back there; but the world had changed, the days of the Raj and the British planter had gone. He drifted from job to job, from lodging to hostel and from psychiatrist to psychoanalyst; as Walter said, 'It is all very sad. But for this – my last days might be happy.'

Peter Cooper employed him for a couple of years but even his patience ran out. In desperation, Marcus asked Allan Boddy if he could give Teddy a job. For two or three years Teddy worked at Comag, checking returns of magazines, occasionally knocking on Allan's door and asking 'When am I going to get a decent job? I could run this place.' He was given a reasonable salary and Marcus gave him an extra £10 a week, but he thought he was worth more. Allan called him 'a pain in the backside', but Phil Harris thought Teddy was 'a nice old soul. I just let him do what he wanted to do. It didn't cost us much. You can afford to carry one or two people of that nature.'

Sadly, Teddy began to drink heavily, as well as smoking eighty cigarettes a day and was at times unsure what day of the week it was. After a while Comag could no longer cope with him and he went downhill fast. He was thrown out of his bedsit, paralytic, and landed in hospital, where he refused to stay; before long, the hospital was refusing to keep him. Beverlie Flower eventually found him a place in a nursing home, which Marcus paid for. Teddy died there in 1983, aged sixty-six.

After the closure of *Eagle* Marcus got together with James Hemming to discuss a magazine for young teenagers which had been in Marcus's mind ever since he had heard, in the 1960s, of the dissatisfaction with *Eagle*, *Girl*, *Swift* and *Robin* expressed by the Incorporated Association of Preparatory Schools. The IAPS had complained to Cecil King of the Mirror Group about the lowered standards; they got no response and *Eagle* was banned from a number of schools in the Association. Marcus and James got no further than producing a dummy, partly due to the number of what Marcus described as 'so-called educational magazines like *Knowledge*, *Understanding Science* and *Look and Learn*' that were now on the market.

But, in the autumn of 1975, Marcus was approached by Michael Joseph with the suggestion that he edit an anthology of *Eagle*. At about the same time he was asked for an interview by comic buff Denis Gifford, who said he was researching a book on the history of British comics and preparing a feature on *Eagle* for one of the colour supplements.

At the beginning of November Frank Hampson went to Italy, at the instigation of Denis Gifford, as a guest of the Lucca Comics Convention, a bi-annual gathering of artists, animators, illustrators and scriptwriters from all over the world. Gifford persuaded Frank to take along samples of his artwork to be exhibited; with the result that Frank was presented with a specially created Yellow Kid Award for being the best strip cartoon illustrator since the end of the Second World War.

On 10 November Marcus wrote to Frank: 'I am absolutely delighted to read of the award that has been given to you. . . . It is very well deserved – and too long delayed – recognition of your genius in this field. I hope that because of this, and the excellent publicity you have received, you will find some financial and other rewards as a result. . . . '

Frank replied: 'It was good to hear from you. As you may guess I have been snowed under with reporters, old "fans", and even the TV team from *Nationwide*. It all seemed very incoherent to me, but no doubt they'll get it to say what they want!

'I *did* pick up some ideas in Italy. They were all very friendly and flattering. The main difference of approach was that they DON'T think of "Comics" in the context of children. And I'm not too sure that they're wrong.

'I certainly feel like coming up to London to have lunch with you, provided (a) it's a reasonably bombproof lush restaurant, and (b) you can make it a Saturday. There's a certain amount of green getting into certain people's eyes at the College where I work for my pittance – and I've used up all my leave going to Lucca.' They didn't manage a Saturday, but lunched together on Thursday, 11 December.

Marcus also wrote to Denis Gifford, 'I was very glad to read about the part you have played in getting Frank Hampson's genius recognised. I only hope this will lead to better things for him. . . . I hope that the interview you taped here will prove of some interest to you. When do you expect your book to appear?'

A month later, having had a number of telephone conversations with Marcus's assistant, Gifford wrote to him, expressing concern that Marcus was intending to publish a book on *Eagle*, since he, Gifford, had been working on a book on *Eagle* for some time: 'My book, *Eagle: Comic of the Century*, takes the form of a compilation of "best" pages from the entire run of *Eagle*. . . . I should say "was", for your recent interest in producing a virtually identical volume has caused IPC . . . to refuse the granting of rights to Souvenir [Press].

'I consider, of course, that my book has prior claim to yours, and that you would not have considered publishing yours had I not achieved a good deal of publicity recently for Frank, Dan Dare, and *Eagle*, and my own book.

'May I hope that you will withdraw from the project, or come up with a solution that will please us both?'

Marcus discussed the problem with Roger Barrett of Ebury Press, who were to be joint publishers of his own book; Roger also hadn't known that Gifford was writing a book on *Eagle* and doubted if there would be room for two, but 'Obviously your name would sell more than [Gifford's]'. Alan Brooke, Editorial Director of Michael Joseph, said that 'I didn't, of course, know anything about this gentleman or his proposal when we approached you to do what seems virtually the same book.'

Marcus wrote again to Gifford, explaining that he thought Gifford was producing a history of British comics. The Managing Directors of IPC hadn't mentioned that anyone else wanted to use copyright material from *Eagle*, although they had thought of producing such a book themselves, 'but [they] now felt it right to let me do so – which I think was generous of them'. Probably less generous than pragmatic; they would have known that Marcus's name would be the selling point. Marcus continued, 'But I hate the idea of messing up your plans. . . . Maybe we can work on the project jointly. Since you clearly have already done some work on choosing the material for the book, why don't you carry on as compiler of the contents, subject only to my approval of your choice of material and your presentation. I could be called Editor and write an appropriate introduction (and I think quite frankly that I am the best person to do this).'

The contract they signed in March split the advance and all royalties on the first printing 50/50; Michael Joseph did not want Gifford's name on the cover, but 'you would be featured on the preliminary pages as collaborating with me'.

The collaboration was a non-starter. Uta Thompson (née Canning) told us, 'Gifford had set himself up to be an authority on comics, and Marcus felt that rather than lose time he would go along with him. But I don't think he ever took to him as a kindred spirit – none of us did. Gifford was arrogant, and wouldn't listen to other people. I think that he was flushed with success and started to talk as if the book was his own creation. He was looking for a commercial way of exploiting the privilege that Marcus was giving him and Marcus began to resist.'

Marcus said later: 'Unfortunately what Gifford produced wasn't what was wanted. He approached it from the technical angle of the comic buff, lists of detailed analysis of the development of the strip cartoon. In the end I couldn't use his material.'

Before long Marcus had recruited Clifford Makins to help and to draft an introduction to *The Best of Eagle*. He dropped Marcus a note: 'The Ruari material is first class. It's a bit dotty and euphoric and hero-worshipping but has the true feeling of those early days. Equally dotty, but with a harder mind, is Chad. There is an overlap situation concerning the *Best of Eagle* and your autobiog; do you wish to call it *Metaphysics*, or, *A Funny Thing Happened on my way to the National Magazine Company*?'

In August Gifford wrote to Alan Brooke at Michael Joseph: 'I have been helping Clifford Makins assemble the *Eagle* book for Marcus. . . . I wish to put on record my disagreement on certain points: a) the selection by Marcus of 'Riders of the Range' by Frank Humphris in preference to my choice of Jack Daniel's original strips . . . b) Marcus's abridgement of Dan Dare is considerably different to the one I selected and arranged. c) And, of course, I am naturally disappointed that my name will not be featured on the cover. I would have thought that as organiser of the first British Comic Convention COMICS 101, publisher and editor of the first British comic magazine *Ally Sloper*, owner of the largest comic collection and author of *The British Comic Catalogue* . . . plus my other books, *Happy Days, A Century of Comics, Discovering Comics*, and *The History of the British Newspaper Strip*, and *Victorian Comics*, I would have rated as a selling point. . . .'

Alan Brooke apparently agreed with him, but nobody else did. Uta Thompson: 'Gifford became awkward. He would telephone and he felt he was the only person worth speaking to – he became too big for his boots. Marcus was so close to *Eagle*, that to see another man wanting to take hold of it in a commercial way upset him.'

The balloon went up at the beginning of 1977, when Gifford saw from the proofs that his name was not on the title page. He wrote to Marcus, 'I agreed, somewhat reluctantly, to your demand that only your name should appear on the cover of the book. But at the same time I specified that my name must appear alongside yours on the title page. . . . There has never been any suggestion from you that my name should be excluded, or that the work should be passed off as solely by yourself. May I have your comments, please, and will you contact Michael Joseph to have the "billing" put right. I also require the right for my name to be included in publicity. . . .'

Marcus replied: 'I cannot imagine what it is that makes you think you have any *rights* in this matter at all. . . . It was only because you told me that you yourself had been planning a similar book that, purely as a gesture

*Marcus with three of the country's best cartoonists – Norman Thelwell, David Langdon and Frank Hampson, 1977.*

of goodwill, I agreed that you should be associated with the book in some way and that you should receive some of the royalties. . . . You were never at any time in a position to "specify" that your name should appear any-where at all. . . . I agreed that your name should appear on the prelims as collaborating with me. This will happen, and I have no intention of altering the arrangements which have been made between us.'

The launch party for *The Best of Eagle* was held at the Savoy on 18 August. It was a very happy gathering of many of the people who worked on the magazine in its heyday; among them Jack Daniel, who wrote: 'Do you think we'll all be able to recognise each other? I have a long grey beard now and walk bent double, with a stick. People have to shout at me to make themselves heard. John Ryan and I meet at times over a glass of beer to talk of old times, peering with unbelieving eyes at all the goings-on in the world, and noting each other's grey hairs.'

Macdonald Hastings said: 'What a charming nostalgic notion. . . . I must go back to my own boyhood and collect all your autographs in my own copy of the book. My grandson will probably be able to flog it for a large price in due course at Sotheby's.' Ellen Vincent was ill, but Joan Porter, Ruari McLean, James Hemming, David Langdon, John Worsley, Derek Lord, Chad Varah, Charles Chilton, Stephen Williams, John Ryan, Clifford Makins, Martin Aitchison and Norman Thelwell all came and, of course, Frank Hampson, for whom Marcus arranged a car to travel from York, where he was attending an Open University Summer School.'

Denis Gifford was not invited. Marcus wrote to Frank Hampson: 'As for

*The Best of Eagle*, it is too early to say what I shall get from it. It will not be very much because of sheer stupidity on my part, which I will tell you about some day.'

Dorothy Hampson wrote to Marcus: 'Ever since Frank won the award at Lucca there have been many interviews etc. and now Dan Dare originals are being sold by dealers in London quite openly – although Mr Sanders of IPC can't imagine how they got hold of them – he said they were all lost or something!! makes me very cross! But that's life I suppose.'

Marcus agreed, 'It's disgraceful that Dan Dare originals should be on sale as they are. IPC assured me that they had no original artwork left. . . . I hope Frank was able to come to a proper arrangement with IPC about royalties – and also that the proposed Dan Dare film is going ahead.'

In March 1977 John Sanders, IPC's Publishing Director, was quoted in the *Observer*, in an article by Jerome Burne about artists' rights: ' "In 95 per cent of cases we buy all rights, and that means that we keep the original art work. We go in for syndication in a big way, and it would be impossible for us to contact an artist every time we need the boards.

' "Also, they might well get lost or not be kept in the right conditions. Keeping a photographic record of them would prove too expensive and would result in poorer quality reproductions.

' "I am aware that this distinction has been made between ownership and copyright, but a lot of creative work by other people goes into the strips. I don't see why the artist should get sole possession."

'I asked Mr Sanders about the Dan Dare boards. "Most of them were dumped in the sixties when nobody had any idea that they had any value," he said.

'How was it that several people had reported seeing them in IPC's archives at Fleetway House? "I'm not going to comment on that," he said. "Those people were trespassing. That is a private place." Original Dan Dare boards now fetch a considerable sum on the open market.'

And what happened to Frank Bellamy's artwork? Martin Aitchison told us, 'I heard a scandal about Bellamy's work being sold by people in IPC to collectors, they were doing Bellamy's widow out of it.' Nancy Bellamy says that 'I have a good idea who took the art work, someone at IPC, but I'm not saying who. I had to sell all I had to make ends meet.'

In 1980 Marcus tried, through Edward Court at IPC, to buy the Dan Dare artwork that IPC held and present it to Frank. John Sanders wrote: 'There are two problems involved in such a transaction. The first is that we have just signed an agreement with a [TV] film company to produce a 13-week Dan Dare series. . . . This venture has excited considerable interest in the comic and the TV worlds. . . . I have insisted . . . that we should retain all rights in all print and publishing merchandising.

'If the ATV series is a very great success, it follows that one useful one-shot publication that might emerge from it would be one based on the original Dan Dare, using the same artwork you propose to buy in for Frank Hampson, which would then be lost to us.

'Of course, it might be said that we could get back the artwork from Hampson at any time we wanted. I believe, however, that that may pose difficulties which give rise to the second problem.

'In my view, Mr Hampson has not been entirely gracious in the thoughts he has expressed about IPC in recent years, in particular the area which I head [the juvenile group]. I do not think that is entirely his fault; there is some evidence that he is being persuaded by a group of ex-contributors who are endeavouring to get IPC to change their traditional terms to contributors. I have no doubt that that group will see any situation in which Frank Hampson becomes the owner of the artwork he produced for us as a victory for their cause and a precedent for the future, even if Mr Hampson actually acquired the artwork through a third party.

'I am sorry that this may sound negative. . . . Certain people may well construct from the proposal you suggest, a situation which would not cast IPC in a good light.

'I will give some more thought to it, but I have in mind at this time proposing to offer all the Dan Dare artwork to Frank Hampson with IPC's compliments – this offer to take place in two years' time. By then we would know whether we had any further commercial use for the material.'

Marcus replied the following week: 'My only purpose in asking whether I could acquire some of the original art work was to give Frank Hampson a present. . . .

'He has had a series of illnesses over the last several years and I feel rather sorry for him, though he is of course somewhat embittered (against me too, I believe). He has been frequently quoted as saying that other

*The Best of Eaglers, 1984*

people have "made fortunes" out of Dan Dare. I can't think who he means.

'I had no idea that Frank was involved with a group of ex-contributors aiming to put pressure on you. All I know is that he has, so to speak, been "adopted" by the group of comic buffs who organised the *Eagle* Convention. I wouldn't have thought that my buying some of the art work and making a present of it to Frank Hampson would have had any effect on their cause or set a precedent. You are, of course, far more in the picture than I am. . . . '

Frank thanked Marcus, 'for endeavouring to get the release of the Dan Dare art work from IPC. As you say, maybe you will succeed eventually – I hope.' *Eagle* storyboards are still finding their way on to the open market, with prices at auction reaching many hundreds of pounds.

In 1980 a group of fans staged Eaglecon '80 in London; two days of discussions of all aspects of *Eagle*, with guest speakers including Frank Hampson, Macdonald Hastings, Charles Chilton, Frank Humphris, George Cansdale, Richard Jennings and Marcus. The now thriving fan club, the Eagle Society, produces a quarterly glossy magazine, *Eagle Times*, which interviews any and everyone who worked on the children's papers, minutely analysing features and characters. The members hold seminars and dinners all over the country in places with even the most tenuous link and have video taped interviews with many of the main *Eagle* contributors, including Marcus. Mentions of the Club on Radio Four and in the *Telegraph* brought in floods of applications to join.

Not long after Frank Hampson's early death in 1986, a biography of him was published. Ruari McLean, writing in *The Times Literary Supplement*, said, 'Frank . . . deserved a biography, but a better one than this. . . . [It] is neither an accurate biography nor a true account of the machinations of Fleet Street that ended in the sad and unnecessary demise of *Eagle*. . . . Marcus Morris . . . is subjected throughout the book to a series of misrepresentations. . . .'

The book was certainly full of wild inaccuracies and gratuitously snide remarks about Marcus; he thought of suing for libel but, as Ellen Vincent said to him, why bother? Marcus had no desire to drag Frank's memory and reputation through the mire, or to boost the sales of the book.

Keith Watson told us, 'When I was working in Epsom there was a TV programme on Dan Dare. Alan Stranks went down with Marcus, who walked round the studio where Gerry Palmer and I were working and walked out without saying a word. Gerry had heard rumours in Hulton House that there was a desire to cut the Dan Dare studio because it was too expensive, though nobody dared to tell Frank. Marcus gave the impression of looking round to see what could be given the chop. I said at the time, "He's coming round like a predatory beast" – a phrase I picked up from a TV thriller and thought it sounded impressive. I didn't really think he was a beast, predatory or otherwise. It slipped out again when I was being interviewed for that book about Frank Hampson. If I'd seen the first drafts of the book I'd have told the author to cut it out, it didn't represent my feelings towards Marcus. I wish I'd written to Marcus to apologise, I feel riddled with guilt about that.'

The resurrections of *Eagle* continue; through the seventies, eighties and nineties *Eagle* and Dan Dare have flown again, garbled, bastardised, crude, violent. Television and film versions seem to be always on the horizon; James Fox and Rodney Bewes were rumoured to be about to star as Dan and Digby in an ITV series; there was talk of a major film in 1985 and in 1991 the makers of *Inspector Morse* planned a 12-part series – Ladbrokes quoted odds of 4-1 on Nigel Havers in the role of Dan Dare.

Tom Tully, who scripted 'Heros the Spartan', was involved with one of the *Eagle* re-launches. He was asked to update Dan Dare 'which I did with some trepidation. My fears were justified. . . . I was bitterly attacked by Dan Dare afficionados. . . . Matters almost came to blows. . . . The fervour of these vintage Dan Dare fanatics can be somewhat intimidating.'

In 1990 a Dan Dare exhibition was staged at the Atkinson Art Gallery in Southport. There was talk in 1992 of a Space City to be built in Manchester's Trafford Park, based on Dan Dare and the Mekon.

Other people continue to profit from *Eagle* and *Girl*: anthologies and facsimile editions are regularly produced. Dan Dare made an appearance in the short-lived Sunday newspaper, *The Planet* in 1996. *Eagle* has been featured in advertisements, used by political cartoonists (we particularly like Peter Brookes' *Dan Blair* in *The Times*, and *Private Eye*'s *Dan Dire*), recalled by pundits who bemoan the lack of standards in today's youth. Students use it as a basis for theses and sociologists for papers on youth unemployment or leisure activities. In 1986 Marcus wrote to the author of *Eaglets in Action*, a 12-page analysis of youth culture: 'I am very pleased to know that you feel that *Eagle* made some contribution towards setting out some standards and values for young people to emulate, and may have had some effect. It was nostalgic to read the quotations you have included. I agree with you that on reading some of them now they do seem rather priggish, and I would not now, in hindsight, have put it in quite the same way.'

Many people over the years begged Marcus to start up another children's magazine but he said: 'Although I have often thought of producing another *Eagle* I have come to the conclusion that this is something which someone else ought to do because I do not think I should try to repeat myself.'

Professor Stephen Hawking, when asked what influence Dan Dare had on him, replied: 'Why am I in cosmology?' His second favourite strip was 'Harris Tweed'.

Kenny Everett told Sally: 'Marcus made my childhood a lot easier to bear. . . . Every week this divine colour magazine came through the letter box with lots of fab colour adventures; it was glossy and other worldly. . . . You don't know what this magazine meant to me. It saved me. . . .'

He chose an *Eagle Annual* as his book on *Desert Island Discs*.

# Chapter Twenty

By the early seventies, Marcus's personal life was happy enough. He and Jess were back together and, on the whole, content. The house in Ebury Mews was sold, but they lost the baby grand piano. It had been lowered down to the basement room before a spiral staircase was installed; the piano couldn't be moved and the old upright returned to its rightful place.

They both loved Narrow Street. In those days the Thames was still a working river and Marcus and Jess could sit on their terrace watching the barges bringing in coal to the power station next door, the occasional Royal Navy ship visiting the Pool of London, the ferries carrying commuters from Greenwich and, best of all, the Tall Ships Races. There was a great community spirit in Limehouse, in spite of (or because of?) the Kray Brothers who were still active in the area when Marcus first went there; he was warned not to pick up anything from the shoreline of the Thames – that was the Krays' territory. In return, Marcus's car was protected from vandals: 'Any trouble, Marcus, we'll get someone to lean on 'em'.

They enjoyed the Chinese restaurants and the local pubs, especially The Grapes, which was used by Charles Dickens as the model for the Six Jolly Fellowship Porters in *Our Mutual Friend*. Dickens likened it to 'A handle of a flat iron set upright on its broadest end' and in the 1970s its bar was still 'not much larger than a hackney coach'. For a time the artist Francis Bacon lived next door; and he would disconcert Jess by glowering out of the window for hours on end; he disconcerted the neighbourhood by the number of young men, frequently sailors, who would turn up at his door at all hours.

Other neighbours were much more congenial; Dr Dick and Lady Rozelle Raynes, Janet Street-Porter, the Royal Academician Edward Woolfe, George Rainbird's protégé Edmund Fisher and Dr David Owen, who created much amusement (and rather a lot of traffic jams) at the time of the Gang of Four's Limehouse Declaration.

The New Year's Eve parties took on a new lease of life at Narrow Street: parachute flares were fired from the roof at midnight when boats on the river let off their sirens. If the tide was right the river police would park their boats alongside and join in the fun. Friends such as John Betjeman made the journey east for leisurely Sunday lunches and a new Morris party was launched – the breakfast party, which assembled at dawn to watch the London Marathon, whose runners went right past the front door.

In 1970 Jess, who had developed asthma and emphysema, was advised to spend the winter abroad. She went to Kenya to work at the Donovan Maule Theatre in Nairobi, where she was a smash hit in *East Lynne*. Marcus joined her for Christmas but, in January, Jess developed pneumonia and ended up in an oxygen tent in hospital. Marcus flew out again and they spent some time on the coast, before Jess returned to the theatre having, at last, given up smoking.

They were both pleased to meet up with Nairobi resident Barbara Fleming, an old friend from Southport and Little Theatre days (and a parishioner of Walter's when a child), proving again the smallness of the world.

In 1972 Jess acted in what proved to be her last professional theatrical engagement, a play starring Jean Kent. The oddly named *Home on a Pig's Back* started at Richmond Rep before going on tour; it was not a good play and Jess hated every minute of it – she decided never to act again.

She didn't completely lose contact with that side of her life. Throughout the 1970s and 1980s she was closely involved with charity fund-raiser Iris Banham-Lee and, with Nat Mag as sponsor and the Good Housekeeping Institute providing magnificent buffet suppers, Jess chaired committees, attended elegant soirées and performed in recitals with actors such as Michael Hordern, James Villiers, Robin Bailey, Brian Cox, Rowland Davies and Anna Calder-Marshall. *People and Places* events were lovely, sophisticated affairs at prestigious venues: Lincoln's Inn, Syon House, Greenwich Palace, Osterley Park and Apsley House; a great deal of money was raised for Action Research for the Crippled Child.

Jan produced two more grandsons, Joe and Ben; Kate married Christopher Ulysses Williams (at St Bride's, of course) and gave them two granddaughters, Charlotte and Harriet (not that either Marcus or Jess were good grandparents. Marcus refused to be called Grandad and insisted on Marcus; Jess was known as Grandan or Ganna. They were seldom known to babysit or do grand-parently things and their grandchildren found them rather remote.)

Marcus had declined to marry Kate or to christen his younger granddaughter. He was by now thoroughly disillusioned with the Church, if not actually agnostic. Simon's death had confirmed the doubts that had been building up over the years; although Marcus remained Honorary Chaplain of St Bride's until 1983, he no longer officiated at services. He once said to Sheila Black, 'I've lived a life of being at odds with God, always at cross purposes with Him, because I wanted to love Him more than I ever could and now, yes, I'm bitter with Him.'

Sally went off on her travels and remained happily single, returning to Limehouse in between journeys. One of these trips was to work in the Seychelles, where Marcus and Jess flew to join her for a holiday. The night before they left the islands, one of the family's usual late-night discussions came close to a row. In answer to an apologetic note from Sally, Marcus sent an unusually revealing (and, unusually, handwritten) letter: 'As you say, late at night and after a good deal of drink, is not the best time to have a calm philosophical discussion – and I too wish we had had a chance to talk more together in a calmer, quieter situation. Except that, I'm afraid, I'm not very forthcoming and am rather "closed up" and don't find it easy to talk. You must forgive me for this – it certainly isn't lack of interest or concern (Business-wise, it's quite an advantage because it means people can't make me out – just as well?).

'I think I know just what you mean about introspection and depression –

because it's my problem too. (I always describe myself to any doctor I talk to as a "manic-depressive without the manic" which is meant as a joke but is near the truth.) These things are largely hereditary and one has to *accept* what one is. All one can do is to attempt to guide and control and develop what one is. That takes a lot of time and patience – but so long as one is aware of oneself and knows what one is trying to do (and tries to keep an inward sense of humour about oneself) it's not too bad.

'After all, why should we try to change our personalities? In the hope that if we were different we would suffer less? Everyone I have ever met in my life, suffers the same things – insecurity, self-doubt, depression. They differ in the way they react and put on a different "front". But underneath they differ only in degree.

'People can, I think, be divided broadly into the introverts and the extroverts – and we can't change what we are (though we can to some extent pretend if you want to give a particular social image). No one is completely one or the other – but of the two, I'd choose the introvert. He's likely to be more sensitive, more intelligent, more aware of other people's needs, more understanding and kinder. He may be taken for a ride sometimes but it's worth it. The extroverts, on the other hand, are likely to be amusing, entertaining, talkative – but also only concerned with the impression they are making on the world – a bit crude and insensitive. But one mustn't judge.

'So what is wrong with being introspective? It may be painful but surely this is what life is all about? To look into oneself and try to find out what one is, what one's purpose in life is, where one fits in, what (if anything) life means. You don't get the answer all at once – though you may suddenly get glimpses of part of the answer. . . .

'Try to *reason* your way out of depression – but even if you can't, remember to say to yourself: "This depression will only last so long, and then I shall feel cheerful, and that will bring a different set of problems!" But through all this, we have to try to achieve and maintain an honest estimate of oneself – without pretending. An inferiority "complex" – from which I have suffered all my life, for a variety of reasons, some of which I understand – really means a kind of emotional self-indulgence which we use as an excuse – instead of really facing the facts about oneself. . . .

'I'm afraid this letter has gone on an awful long time and is practically unreadable. But in answering your letter, I'm also in a way answering myself – or perhaps asking myself. It's not meant to be a lecture.'

Marcus was quite relieved when Jess gave up the theatre – it had interfered with his entertainment plans for the Americans. Thereafter she was given an allowance by Hearst to assist in looking after the executives from New York who regularly visited Britain with their wives. The Millers, particularly, were very welcome and frequent visitors, who spent many happy weeks being driven around the country by Jim Lucas.

John Miller was a great fisherman, so Marcus introduced him to Brian

Begg, a very keen and knowledgeable fisherman himself. On one of their fishing trips together, John suggested to Brian that he should persuade Marcus to buy a stretch of river and make a fishing camp for entertaining clients, such as Hearst had in Canada. Marcus and Jess had visited Murray Bay a number of times with the Berlins and the Millers and Marcus had rather half-heartedly attempted fishing. The idea for a Nat Mag fishing camp came originally from Bill Hearst (second son of William Randolph Hearst), who saw an ad in *Country Life* for a mile of the River Tweed with an average annual catch of 220 salmon. 'Bill knew it would capture my imagination, but he was not suggesting that we investigate it for my pleasure – rather as something that could be of use to you in entertaining customers,' said John.

John also thought that Marcus needed a hobby: 'When you go out to grass you've got to have something to keep you occupied.' He told Brian that if Marcus was too parsimonious to spend the money on a fishery he, John, would buy it himself. Brian and his friend Ken Fox, uncle of the actor brothers, after much arduous work sampling different rivers, found a stretch of the River Wye, near Hereford. The farmer who owned the land, David Lifeley, had two cottages to let and Marcus, entering into the spirit of the thing, engaged builders who stripped the cottages and rebuilt them to make a fishing lodge. Brian, Jess and Sally (now working on *SHE*) spent many happy hours buying furnishings while Ken equipped the camp with a caravan, Land Rover, dinghy and every aid to fishing known to man. He even taught Marcus how to charm worms out of the earth (sprinkle the lawn with a solution of washing up liquid!).

Marcus now took learning to fish very seriously, even to the extent of practising tying knots with pieces of string at his desk, though he never learnt to tie a fly (his hands were too shaky). Ken Fox managed to teach him to throw quite a pretty line and, for a few years, the Millers, the Morrises, the Foxes, Begg and sundry editors, publishers, advertisers and guests appreciated the peace and quiet of this glorious part of Herefordshire. Marcus was happiest fishing where he could cast from the bank; wading was difficult because of a lack of balance (he had developed an inner ear problem a few years earlier). And someone always had to take the wriggling fish off the hook for him – usually trout; in the early eighties the River Wye wasn't producing many salmon, although the Nat Mag fishers managed to get rid of quite a lot of pike. Perhaps Marcus's favourite parts of weekends at Eaton Bishop were the long picnic lunches by the riverside. The fishery was a marvellous place to discuss business and Marcus, John and Brian Begg spent many valuable hours deliberating on the past and future of the company.

Sadly the dream turned sour when Bill Jackson, horrified by the amount of money that had been spent on what came to be called the John Miller Centre, reported the company to the Inland Revenue, although Bill says, 'Marcus didn't spend as much of the company's money on himself as Kay and Ben had done. One thing you can say for Marcus, he wasn't interested in himself.'

But from then on, everyone who stayed at the fishery had to pay tax on the visit; Marcus was furious and, although Hearst agreed that he be reimbursed the tax he paid, the atmosphere was changed and his visits gradually tapered off. Eventually, the company started charging – even company employees on business had to pay. Not many did; Stephen Quinn said that it was cheaper to use the Dorchester for meetings. For a while it became a commercial venture, run by Ken Fox and Jack Blanche, but Marcus's successor wasn't a fisherman and John Miller's successor likened fishing to watching paint dry, so the cottages reverted to the farm and the one and a quarter miles of the River Wye lie almost unused.

Stephen Hemsted, Bill Jackson's successor, perhaps unsurprisingly, supported Bill's stand. During Stephen's job interview, Marcus said to him, ' "Tell me, Mr Hemsted, how does somebody become an accountant?".

'I thought it must be a trick question, a managing director must know, but explained to him anyway. When I recounted this story at Marcus's retirement party, Marcus said, 'Stephen, you've got to understand that I couldn't believe that anyone who was intelligent could ever possibly want to become an accountant!'

'I found that when Marcus had correct figures, he could manage, with a bit of guidance and wasn't uncomfortable with them. It wasn't in Bill's interest to make it easy for Marcus to understand. The way Bill presented figures was so obscure, unless you were an expert with numbers you wouldn't want to find your way through it.'

It was John Miller who insisted that Marcus should have a car more suited to his status than the elderly Bentley he'd had for some years. John had a hard time persuading Marcus to get a Rolls Royce – he thought them rather ostentatious. When Marcus said that he'd get Jim Lucas to look for a second hand Rolls, John contacted Jack Barclay for a new one. Marcus had, over the years, developed the American habit of taking a large amount of ice in his drinks; he was therefore delighted when he saw on the dashboard of the new car a light which said 'ice'. Jim Lucas had to explain gently that it was a sensor warning of ice on the road.

In the late seventies Brian Begg was asked to assist in finding a successor to take over the Managing Directorship; Marcus was due to retire in 1980. Brian talked to head hunters with enthusiasm, but was not helped much by Marcus himself, who viewed his retirement with dismay. John Miller, a year older, had always said that he intended to retire on his sixty-fifth birthday and had already chosen, and was grooming, his successor, Frank Bennack.

But John had more to look forward to in retirement, not only fishing but golf, another pastime that Marcus enjoyed without much dedication. Bernard Audley, a regular golf partner, said, 'Marcus had the sense of rhythm and athleticism to be a good golfer, but not the temperament. He was erratic, because he got very impatient if the ball didn't behave as he ordered that it should. He was the least boring golf partner because he didn't take it seriously. It was a constant surprise to me that he played as badly as he often did. It never mattered – the games we played were intervals between large gins.'

Bernard, Marcus, Paddy Dewar Watson (Marcus's friend and insurance adviser) and Ben McPeake played as a foursome for many years and Marcus played occasionally in the National Magazine Golf Tournament. During one match, on the police golf course at Hendon, Marcus hit the ball on to the edge of a pond; as he took a stance to play it his feet slid away from him and he fell backwards into the water. Paddy, a small, elderly man, went to help and was pulled in himself. With the aid of Jim Lucas, who was caddying, they managed to clamber out and retreated to the 19th hole, soaked and covered with weed. Jim was handed a walletful of very wet £10 notes to dry on the back shelf of the Rolls, while the Club Secretary produced Life Saving Certificates.

Jack Blanche remembered an occasion at Walton Heath when Marcus took Simon along as caddy. Just before Jack took an important shot, Simon said, 'You know, Mr Blanche, golf is not for intelligent people.' The shot was hooked. Jack complained vociferously to Marcus that not only was he giving him too many brandies, but that his caddy was trying to sabotage him.

In spite of a lack of interests to occupy his retirement, Marcus knew he couldn't go on working forever; he gave way under John's nagging and agreed to look for a successor.

One person who had assumed he was in line for the job was Brian Braithwaite, who insists that Marcus promised him the succession. Marcus always denied this; he said that Brian was the wrong age – he was only eleven years younger than Marcus. But it is also likely that something went wrong with their relationship; Brian's empathy with Dick Deems might have alienated Marcus. Jack Blanche also said that Marcus told him that he would take over as MD: 'He usually said it after we'd had a disagreement, or after a good lunch at the Mirabelle.'

One day in 1978, John Miller telephoned Marcus to report his decision to retire a year early. This was a great blow to Marcus: 'Your decision naturally came as a considerable shock to me and I can't help feeling very sad – as do others here. I had hoped that your miraculous transformation of the Hearst Corporation would have led you to continue for a little longer. . . . I have a great admiration for Frank Bennack, whom I think is very likeable and very clever. I am sure he will do an excellent job.'

Frank first met Marcus in 1976 and had heard tales of how good Marcus was to visiting Americans, of 'how to spend a week in London, have nice dinners, see everyone and have wonderful conversations and never get around to business before Marcus put you back on the plane. I really expected to be stiffed when I got to London, but we became friends.'

John carried on as Vice Chairman of Hearst and remained Chairman of the National Magazine Company, to Marcus's pleasure.

The same year Marcus appointed as Marketing Director forty-four-year-old Michael Bird, who had worked for Nat Mag previously on the sales promotion and research side. Michael was a statistician *par excellence* and Marcus was always impressed by anyone who understood figures. In 1979 he appointed Michael Deputy Managing Director and heir apparent. But by that summer, Marcus was becoming uneasy and was beginning to think that Michael might not be strong enough on the creative side. Frank Bennack commented: 'I think Marcus decided that Michael's propensity to look at the theoretical and numeric side of business, which had impressed him initially, was not the characteristic which would give the company the best overall leadership for editorial product.'

The crunch came in 1980 after Michael had what he describes as 'an extremely unpleasant interview' with John Miller, with whom he didn't get on at the best of times. John reported to Marcus that Michael had demanded that Marcus be told to retire so that he could take over straight away. John thought that Michael's services could be dispensed with; Marcus naturally agreed.

Michael says: 'I certainly did *not* ask John Miller to remove Marcus. What I did do was tell Marcus that I wished to hear from John certain assurances about the future. It would have been both immoral and stupid to have asked to displace someone who had done so much for me and from whom I still had such a lot to learn, and who was so respected by Hearst. I suppose what was in my mind was that Brian Braithwaite and Jack Blanche had got the mistaken idea into their heads that they were the anointed heir and I did not wish to make the same sad error. Hence the very direct approach. At least it cleared the air quickly!'

While Marcus was deciding that he'd made the wrong appointment he was putting out feelers to another Nat Mag executive, Terry Mansfield, the forty-one-year-old Publisher of *Harpers & Queen*. Terry and Marcus had got on well ever since Terry was brought into the company as a fresh-faced, bow-legged young fellow (his own words) by Brian Braithwaite. 'Brian talked Marcus into taking me as well, rather like Laurel and Hardy.' Jack Blanche, Marcus's oldest ally, thought Terry would make a good MD and he was strongly supported and recommended by Frank Bennack: 'I think I get most of the credit for having decided Terry was the right next choice. Terry was very bright and handled his relationship with Marcus in the right way, unthreateningly. It looked as if I was going to be living with the consequences of it so I decided on Terry.'

In 1979 the company decided to move away from Victoria and bring all departments, which had again become scattered around London with the growth of the company, under one roof. Marcus had been thinking about it for some time; he was spurred into action by receiving a very attractive offer from the other tenant of Chestergate House to vacate the building within three months. The idea of converting a warehouse in the East End was abandoned in case it caused a mass walkout of staff. They found a newly built office block overlooking Carnaby Street (built on the site of a plague burial ground) and Marcus gave Beverlie Flower the job of fitting out the building and organising the move. A number of major problems had to be overcome, not least of which was the reaction of the staff to the sudden uprooting. The very bright colour scheme upset many people, especially

Mrs C and Mr G, and Charlotte Lessing, who described the red and yellow of the *Good Housekeeping* floor as 'plums and custard'. Willie Landels hated the air conditioning and said, 'If I can't open a window I shall play a violin and the windows will break.' (He opened the windows anyway.) The move was successfully accomplished over the Christmas break, and people gradually got used to the colours, the open-plan design – and the fact that Liberty's, Regent Street and Soho were all on the doorstep.

That year Marcus was honoured by a 'Resolution of the Board' of the Hearst Corporation, a rare acknowledgement by the Directors of the contribution made by an individual to the Corporation. Signed by Randolph Hearst, Chairman; John Miller, Vice Chairman; Frank Bennack, President and William R. Hearst Jr, Chairman of the Executive Committee, the resolution stated: 'The members of the Board of Directors of The Hearst Corporation, meeting in New York on the 19th of September, 1979, unanimously requested that the following expression of their sentiments be conveyed to you.

'Whereas the National Magazine Company, Ltd., under your brilliant direction, attained this year the greatest record of achievement in its history;

'Whereas your inspiring leadership has encouraged many of the most outstanding magazine editors in the United Kingdom to join the National Magazine Company;

'Whereas your superior editorial talents and administrative ability have served in a significant manner to make the Hearst Magazines among the most popular and respected periodicals in the United Kingdom;

'Whereas the presentation to you of the Presidential Award by the Periodical Publishers Association in recognition of your distinguished achievements over thirty years of magazine publishing, and

'Whereas your integrity, dignity and modesty have enhanced the prestige of the Hearst organization in the United Kingdom,

'Now, therefore, the Board of Directors of The Hearst Corporation expresses to you deep appreciation for the services you have rendered.'

Touched and delighted as he was to receive such a tribute, Marcus was even more pleased by its being presented to him personally by John Miller, who read out the resolution in the presence of Jess and Sally.

Marcus would have been just as delighted by the award set up in his memory by the Periodical Publishers Association and the National Magazine Company. The Marcus Morris Award, described as the highest accolade in magazine publishing in the United Kingdom, 'recognises and commemorates the exceptional career and outstanding contribution to the UK magazine industry of the Reverend Marcus Morris. It honours an individual who has gained distinction through significant and long standing contribution to the publishing business; one who has demonstrated extraordinary leadership, skill, and understanding in unifying the editorial, advertising, circulation, and business aspects of magazine publishing into a successful enterprise; or one who is presently making notable contributions to the magazine industry.'

As well as a citation and a cheque for £1,000, the winner receives a silver trophy, a replica of the emblem of *Eagle*: the winners to date have been Nick Logan [*The Face*], Felix Dennis [microcomputer publishing], Chris Anderson [Future Publishing], David Arculus and Robin Miller [EMAP], John Mellon [IPC], Joan Barrell [National Magazines], Graham Sherren and Anthony Nares [Centaur Communications] and, in 1997, John Brown [John Brown Contract Publishing].

Although Marcus had been due to retire in April 1980, he was asked to stay on as Managing Director for an extra two years, to give his successor time to acclimatise. Terry went to New York 'to learn to become an executive' and returned to work in harness with Marcus, as Deputy MD. An article in the media magazine *Marketing Week* underlined the problems faced by the heir apparent: '[Marcus's] individual, editorial director style of management is clearly one reason why the question of Morris's succession has been a vexed one. He still personally approves the covers and cover lines of all his titles and, one suspects, does a fair bit of backdoor editing besides.

'This is hardly the role for the kind of factory-farmed publishers, generally a product of the advertising department, who tend to dominate the upper reaches of the larger publishing companies these days. Such a gentleman or lady is not likely to want to run the company the Morris way and one wonders how much this concerns him or his American masters.'

By the end of the 1970s, with retirement in sight, Marcus and Jess had somewhat reluctantly decided that they would have to leave Narrow Street; it had a lot of steep stairs, which they were both finding increasingly difficult and the East London air wasn't doing Jess's emphysema any good. While they were vaguely thinking about a move to the country, there came a knock at the door of No 82 and on the threshold stood a young man with a vaguely familiar face, who offered to buy the house, should they be thinking of selling. The young man didn't want to move in until the following summer – he was playing in *Amadeus* on Broadway until then. Ian McKellan bought the house with a completion date that gave Marcus and Jess plenty of time to look for somewhere else. In 1986 Sir Ian dropped Marcus a line to let him know how things were developing in Narrow Street. The house 'is all much as you left it. I can't ever imagine leaving but then I expect you thought the same and, who knows, someone may knock on the door (as we did). . . .'

Jess happily embarked on house-hunting, aided and abetted by Jim Lucas, who drove her all over Oxfordshire and environs: Jan and Kate and the grandchildren lived in Oxford. They had no luck until one day, returning from a visit to Mary Cook in Chard, they decided they might as well have a quick look at a house near Bath of which they'd been sent details, even though Bath was much too far from London for Marcus.

It was love at first sight. A seventeenth-century mill house, with mill attached (and with some of the machinery still intact). An acre of garden with a brook running through it, surrounded by glorious countryside; the village was only five miles south-east of Bath and had a pub. There would be room in the four-storey mill for all Marcus's books; the garden was big enough for vegetables and an asparagus bed and Marcus could fish for trout from outside the kitchen door. There was a large cellar, so he would at long last be able to catalogue and store the many bottles of wine he'd been acquiring over the years. It had a waggon house big enough to take the Rolls and was within reasonable reach of the M4 and M3; the train service to Paddington was reputed to be good.

They left Narrow Street in June 1981; the household was moved to Bath and Nat Mag rented a flat near the office for Marcus and Jess to stay in during the week. That summer the entire Board of the Hearst Corporation, and their wives, descended on London for their annual board meeting, the first time it had been held outside the United States. In October, in recognition of all Marcus had done for the company, Hearst paid for Marcus and Jess to make a grand tour of the American Mid-West, a journey planned by that most efficient travel agent, Bunny Miller. With Sally to act as chauffeur, they flew to New Orleans (jazz of course), San Antonio (The Alamo) and to Las Vegas, where they stayed at the splendidly vulgar Caesar's Palace and actually won $200 at roulette. Then they had a long, leisurely drive through Nevada, Utah and Arizona, visiting the canyons that litter the foothills of the Rocky Mountains. There was a moment of panic on reaching one hotel when they realised that Utah was a 'dry' state; the car was swiftly turned round for a quick hop over the border to load up the 'trunk' with supplies. They met up in Phoenix with Frank Bennack and his wife Luella; John and Bunny Miller were supposed to join the party, but John was ill.

He died the following January at the age of sixty-eight. At the funeral in New York Marcus was able to pay tribute to his friend by being one of the pall bearers. He felt a sense of grievous loss for a good, kind, clever, lovely man.

On 1 May 1982 Marcus handed over the Managing Directorship to Terry Mansfield, remaining as Deputy Chairman, a post to which he had been appointed in the spring of 1979 (the Chairmanship had passed from John Miller to Frank Bennack). Terry Mansfield was a fast learner, but it was a slightly troubled coalition since Marcus found it difficult to relinquish day to day authority. Terry describes their new relationship as 'a bit like Batman and Robin. It wasn't easy, as Marcus had never worked with anyone else; we had one or two skirmishes, but no major bust-ups.' Frank Bennack asked Marcus to accompany Terry to the regular meetings in New York, but Marcus felt it would be better for Terry to go alone, no doubt to Terry's relief. Frank wrote: 'I don't think I can state too often our gratitude for the job you've done during your tenure as Managing Director. . . . Terry [now] has the focal position . . . but your firm hand and good counsel will be indispensable.'

Terry was to say later that Marcus was a hard act to follow: 'To succeed a man who can christen you, marry you, bury you, and fire you is not normal. He told me that he never told secrets to anyone as he always got let down. I thought that he was exaggerating, but I've found he was right – everybody tells somebody.'

Marcus and Jess spent long weekends at Midford and put in hand various alterations to the house and garden. They enjoyed being in London during the week and Marcus still had occasional lunches with his pretty ladies.

On 1 January 1983, it was announced that he had been awarded the OBE in the New Year's Honours List, for services to publishing. Chad thought it should have been a knighthood, but Marcus was quite content with his O. On 29 March, accompanied by Jess and the two daughters allowed (Jan lost the toss), Marcus collected his gong at Buckingham Palace; a smile, a handshake, a few words, then an inclination of the head and a few steps backwards, the family holding their collective breath in case he fell over his legs. He never knew what the Queen said to him; being rather deaf, he couldn't hear her and didn't feel he could say 'I beg your pardon, Ma'am?' The occasion was celebrated in suitable style with lunch at the Mirabelle with all the family and his closest friends.

In spite of Marcus's fear of flying, over the years he and Jess took holidays in some fairly exotic places. They visited much of the Caribbean and West Indies; two holidays were spent on the British Virgin Islands at a hotel run by Jorgen and Libby Thonning. Jorgen is Danish, with a very dry, keen sense of humour, which marched well with Marcus's own. They had many lively discussions; politics was a favourite topic for argument, since Jorgen stands somewhere to the right of Attila the Hun: 'We couldn't have been further apart. Gradually, however, it appeared that he came to accept some of my views as valid and his final remark before he left Biras Creek the last time, I have never forgotten. He said "I came a convinced socialist and leave an enlightened democrat." A splendid turn of phrase and I do think he meant it.'

There was certainly a change in Marcus's political affiliations as he got older. He flirted with the Social Democrats while at Narrow Street, no doubt due to the proximity of David Owen, and he continued to become more right wing until, to the amazement of his daughters, in retirement he actually joined the Conservative Party. He was disappointed by the low calibre of the politicians running the Labour Party in the 1980s and was, theoretically anyway, all in favour of a woman Prime Minister.

In April 1984 Marcus finally retired. He said that he was as proud of having run the National Magazine Company as he was of launching *Eagle*. 'I felt I'd got somewhere running adult publications.' In his twenty-four years the company's turnover rose from £1.5 million to £50 million.

The occasion was marked by a series of parties; the one given by the Admin Department was the favourite – the choir of St Bride's Church was engaged to sing and Marcus and Jess were presented with a sundial. The dissipations culminated in a magnificent thrash at Claridge's. It was attended by 400 guests, colleagues past and present, associates from all over the publishing world, Hearst executives (and Bunny Miller), family, friends and ex-Hultonians. Pillars of daffodils decorated the ballroom; there was an oyster and seafood bar (Marcus's favourite foods) plus the usual hot and cold buffet; a pianist played in one room while a ragtime jazz band entertained in another and champagne (and everything else) flowed all night.

Frank Bennack said in his speech: 'When I first met Marcus I was curious about how a clergyman had been able to move so easily and successfully into the keenly competitive publishing world. Actually I was more than "curious"; I was incredulous! But early on in our relationship I learned that this modest, unassuming gentleman had what one of his former editors once referred to as a "core of steel". Marcus can be implacably immovable on those matters about which he has strong feelings, a characteristic many in this room well understand.'

Marcus, very nervous, made an excellent speech in reply, thanking Frank for the gift of a striking Steuben crystal eagle, which had been brought over from New York, perched very uncomfortably (for Frank) on Frank's knee. Eagles featured strongly that evening; many ex-*Eagle* staff were among the guests and a large ice-sculpture of the original brass ink well had pride of place in the lobby. The party was voted the best ever by everyone who attended. Carol Macartney, former Director of the Good Housekeeping Institute, reported for *NatMagNews*: 'It was a great evening for remembering times past as well as catching up on today's news in the magazine world. The Morris family have always been excellent party givers, they have a knack of making their guests happy and at home. This was clearly no exception. . . . Speeches were short, few and lively. . . . Marcus spoke with affection of John Miller and his widow Bunny and added his

*Grandfather shows off his gong to the boys.*

thanks to Hearst for having let him get on with the job in his own way. . . . To all the Nat Mag people there, past and present, he paid this tribute: "What a wealth of talent you represent – thank you all for your help". . . . When we left, the band was playing, an elderly elegant gentleman was jiving and MM's little granddaughters were bopping with their mother. And was that a tear of nostalgia rolling down the ice-eagle's beak?'

After the party, Marcus received a letter from Liz Rees-Jones, Promotions Editor of *Harpers & Queen*: 'I really wanted to say thank you for being such a wonderful mentor and friend over all these years. I can hardly believe that my eighteenth year of working for National Magazine Co is now upon me and a large proportion of the satisfaction and enjoyment of doing that has been inspired by you.'

From New York, W. R. Hearst Jr wrote: 'You know of the great personal feeling and regard that I and my brothers and family have for you. To be sure, a good deal of that admiration stems from the fact that anyone who could woo and wed someone as lovely and gracious as Jessica in less than a month must be a spectacular fellow.

'I have always felt that you really were predestined to wind up leading a Hearst company. After all your first great success was EAGLE, a children's magazine that had two elements long associated with Hearst – the comic strip and the Eagle itself, the symbol of Hearst Newspapers and our company . . . while I know that you may have thought that some American comic

*Guests at Marcus's retirement party, Brian Begg, Sheila Black, Jack Blanche and Sheila Scott*

strips were too violent for children you saw the power they contained to transmit ideas. . . .

'Your colleagues at Hearst will always be appreciative of the leadership you provided National Magazine in a period of phenomenal growth. During that time the company increased about 15-fold in size. Profitability increased even more. That is only one way to measure your performance. Another, perhaps even more meaningful, is the kind of people you assembled to run our magazines.'

Gillian Birbeck was Marcus's personal assistant in his final years at Nat Mag; she wrote to Sally: 'He was a man I greatly admired and loved. Working for Marcus was always interesting and rewarding. He gave me trust and support which brought out the best in me.

'In my years at Nat Mag, I always felt as if I was looking at the "glamorous world" of magazines from the sidelines. I saw so much shallowness there, so much creeping and crawling, so many people trying to impress and gain favour and, thankfully, Marcus always saw through all that. I would never have stayed except that I was working for Marcus, who was the total opposite of all I disliked there. Although he was at the top of the tree in that superficial world, he had never been seduced by it.

'For some reason I could never understand, Marcus never seemed to be sure of his own worth. Do you remember the night of his speech to the Hearsts at Claridge's when they all descended on London? He was so nervous, but really shouldn't have worried, he didn't have anything to prove. He'd already done that by the excellent profit figures he'd achieved and by the tremendous respect shown to both him and National Magazines whilst he was in charge.

'That, whilst holding down a demanding position, he should find time to be so very helpful to me, was typical of him. I am happy and proud to have known him.'

The London flat was given up and Marcus and Jess moved permanently down to Midford, where they cultivated the garden with the help of a local gardening company and the ride-on lawnmower which was a farewell present from the directors of Comag (and which Marcus later sold after he nearly drove it into the stream). Nat Mag made him a gift of the Rolls Royce and the nineteenth-century osteopath's chair from his office, on which Marcus had been wont to kip in the afternoons.

He put down an asparagus bed, at last, created a wild flower garden and orchard on the island and built a bridge to it over the stream. He indulged in a little fly-fishing and a lot of reading, until his eyesight began to fail due to cataracts, which were used as an excuse to delay the writing of his autobiography, even though he'd received an advance from publishers Michael Joseph. Three versions of an autobiography had been attempted in the fifties, ghosted severally by Peter Grey, Clifford Makins and, in 1958, by Bagenal Harvey's brother Don – with, of course, a ten per cent commission going to Bagenal. Perhaps Marcus had too much else on his mind to give them the assistance they needed, but all were so badly written that the manuscripts were pushed away into cupboards and forgotten. One version, which was sent to publishers William Heinemann, solicited the comment 'The writing tends to be slipshod. . . . The pages about Lady Hulton are very entertaining though I imagine they may well be defamatory'. But in 1976, Marcus had asked Clifford Makins to make a start on a fourth version.

After leaving Hulton Press Clifford spent twelve years on *The Observer* as Sports Editor. Although highly successful in terms of journalism, those years did Clifford no good at all physically; he was reputed to be the original of the *Private Eye* character 'Lunchtime O'Booze' and he emerged from Fleet Street an alcoholic. His third wife, the distinguished journalist Nora Beloff, tried hard to keep him off the drink, but the years of abuse took their toll, resulting in cirrhosis and diabetes.

Marcus retained his affection for Clifford throughout, helping him financially occasionally (Marcus was the only one who replied when Clifford's secretary, Ann Melsom, wrote to old friends for help) and passing work his way when he could. Clifford had two novels published, written with Ted Dexter, but never managed to get very far with Marcus's autobiography. In 1983 Nora wrote: 'It seems to me quite inconceivable that Clifford will ever have the stamina and self discipline to complete your biography. . . . You may find someone else to help you.' He never did.

In addition to bad eyesight, Marcus in later life became increasingly deaf, although, like his father before him, he could always hear when someone said 'What's yours?'. The pace of life in retirement was gentle: mornings pottering in his library of some 7,000 books, a couple of vodkas before lunch, wine with it, a sleep in the afternoon, some light work in the garden until time for the pre-prandial, then reading or watching TV with the sound turned up so loud that everyone else had to leave the room.

Marcus seemed to take to retirement surprisingly well; it was Jess who found it difficult, echoing someone or other: 'It's all very well, but I married him for better or worse, not for lunch.' Marcus did a certain amount of consultancy work, which occasionally took him up to London, but most of his time was spent happily in Midford.

There were lunches and parties; friends – Brian Begg, Ken Fox and family doctor Robin Abel – came down to fish the stream. George Rainbird lived not far away in the Cotswolds and Marcus renewed his acquaintance with Bishop Mervyn Stockwood, who had retired to Bath, and with Joy McWatters, who had worked for George Rainbird and Ruari McLean. He became somewhat reconciled to the Church and through Joy's husband George and Mervyn Stockwood, together with *Eagle* fan John Prescott-Thomas, then running BBC Bristol, the wheel turned full circle; Marcus became involved in the Bath and Wells Diocesan magazine, *The Grapevine*. He persuaded Ruari and Nat Mag to produce new layouts and dummies, but didn't stay on the diocesan committee for long, as he didn't enjoy driving over to Bristol for meetings.

In June 1985 the girls organised a party for Marcus and Jess's joint seventieth birthdays (there was less than a month between them); they did the catering and arranged for a marquee on the lawn, which was fortunate, as it poured with rain all day. Their closest and oldest friends braved the weather, including the Listers from Southport. Marcus and Jess saw the Listers for the last time when Sally drove her parents up to Southport to stay at the grandest hotel in town, something Marcus had wanted to do ever since his impecunious days as a vicar. They also saw Dargie Corelli, who was thrilled when the Rolls Royce drew up outside her retirement home.

Although Jess's bronchitis and emphysema were somewhat improved by the clean air of Midford and winter months spent in Menton near Nice, her health was deteriorating in other ways. After one particularly difficult day when she fell into the rose bed while dead-heading and Marcus fell on top of her trying to help her up, she was diagnosed as having Parkinson's Disease. This meant she could no longer drive and she began to feel rather housebound and isolated.

In the autumn of 1988 Jess fell awkwardly in the kitchen and broke her hip. Sally, who was now living in a village close by, arrived to find Jess in agony on the floor and Marcus rather ineffectually trying to make her comfortable with pillows and blankets. The hip was pinned but she had another fall, which impounded the pin and cracked a couple of ribs.

The girls tried to persuade Marcus to move to sheltered housing in Oxford, where Jan and Kate could look after them, but Marcus adamantly refused. He also refused to have living-in help, apart from nursing assistance, so most of the task of looking after Jess fell on Sally, who moved back to the Mill House from her bolthole.

In January 1989 they made their usual trip to the South of France, in spite of the pain in Jess's hip; Sally went down in February to bring her back for a hip replacement at the Edward VII Hospital in London. There were complications; Jess became gradually weaker and her life was feared for. At the end of the month, Sally returned to Menton to bring Marcus home; he had complained over the phone of having a bit of a cold. What she saw shocked her: he could hardly walk from one side of the room to the other without gasping for breath. She brought him back in a wheelchair and was frightened, as was he, that he was going to peg out on the aeroplane.

Marcus was put into a room near to Jess's and from then on, Jess seemed to improve; so did Marcus after they drained five litres of fluid from his lungs – a small tumour had been found a couple of years previously. The fridge provided for patients' use was filled with white wine, champagne, smoked salmon, chocolate mousse, pate and ice cubes for the Morrises. Visitors galore brought them flowers, books, whisky. Marcus seemed almost to enjoy the enforced rest and the attention and having the burden of looking after Jess lifted from his shoulders.

Towards the middle of March his condition worsened. Jan read him a card from Ruari McLean and he smiled wanly. Marcus had written to Ruari from Menton: 'You know I have, through you, learnt the important benefits of good typography. But just recently I came across an example of the damage which bad typography can do. I had occasion to visit a doctor here and handed him my card. . . . I noticed that he had put the prescription in the name of Mr M. Obema. [M. Morris, OBE, MA] And so I became known at the chemist. I had to go back and explain my real name with some difficulty. . . . I should never make a move without you – typographically I mean!'

On 16 March the doctors said they had found a thrombosis in Marcus's leg. He died at 3.30 p.m. with Jess at his side. 'I don't believe it,' she said. 'I don't believe it. I had my hair done especially for him. I always thought I'd be the first to go.' There were no tears. When Chad came it was she who comforted him.

A few days later, on doctor's advice and accompanied by a nurse, Jess was moved into the Park Lane Hotel, where she and Marcus had often stayed together. The porter was delighted to see her and enquired after Mr Morris; he nearly burst into tears when he was told.

Marcus and Chad had a long standing arrangement that, whoever died first, the other would take the funeral. Chad, being the elder, had not expected to arrange and conduct the service at St Stephen, Walbrook, on 22 March. Probably for the first time in his life, he lost his way in the Lord's Prayer.

There was a party at the hotel in the evening, of course. Bunny Miller, her son Mark and Chrissie Berlin had flown over from New York. When Jess was settled for the night, about twenty people had dinner together – the family and close friends, including Ruari, who was poured into a taxi just in time to catch the train back to Edinburgh. It was a party Marcus would have enjoyed.

On 4 May, Ascension Day, there was a Thanksgiving Service at St Bride's. In honour of his twenty four year connection with Hearst and of the Americans who flew over for the service, the organist played part of Aaron Copeland's 'Appalachian Spring' and the congregation joined in 'The Battle Hymn of the Republic'. Jan, Kate and Sal read the first *Eagle* Editor's Letter, a Bible extract and part of Marcus's unpublished autobiography and addresses were given by Sir Bernard Audley and Frank Bennack. The choir sang 'Any Dream Will Do', from *Joseph and His Amazing Technicolour Dreamcoat*, Marcus being a big fan of Tim Rice and Andrew Lloyd Webber; the choir's rendition of *Spread Your Wings*, the Eagle Club song, delightfully arranged by Robert Jones, the Musical Director, brought smiles to the faces of the 300 or so people crowded into the church.

A friend wrote afterwards: 'What a wonderful service of thanksgiving! It was most inspiring and carried out with such an overwhelming feeling of love and gratitude, in such a lovely setting and with the beautiful soaring music – I shall remember it always.'

And there was another party, at the Central London flat Jess had moved into the previous month; it was then that Chad told the girls they must write Marcus's biography.

After a year of increasing frailty, and a winter of bronchitis, Jess died quietly in a London nursing home – her rock was no longer there.

# Index

James Beetham

Beetham

THE STRIP
DELIVERED

"Marcus took le[...]
fish very serious[...]

Martin Aitchison

M.A. '98

". . . a proposal to drop Marcus by parachute into Hyde Park"

Bill Todd